Jihad in Saudi Arabia

Saudi Arabia, homeland of Usama bin Ladin and many 9/11 hijackers, is widely considered to be the heartland of radical Islamism. For decades, the conservative and oil-rich kingdom contributed recruits, ideologues and money to jihadi groups worldwide. Yet Islamism within Saudi Arabia itself remains poorly understood. Why has Saudi Arabia produced so many militants? Has the Saudi government supported violent groups? How strong is al-Qaida's foothold in the kingdom and does it threaten the regime? Why did Bin Ladin not launch a campaign there until 2003? This book presents the first ever history of Saudi jihadism based on extensive fieldwork in the kingdom and primary sources in Arabic. It offers a powerful explanation for the rise of Islamist militancy in Saudi Arabia and sheds crucial new light on the history of the global jihadist movement.

THOMAS HEGGHAMMER is a Senior Fellow at the Norwegian Defence Research Establishment (FFI).

Cambridge Middle East Studies 33

Cambridge Middle East Studies has been established to publish books on the nineteenth- to twenty-first-century Middle East and North Africa. The aim of the series is to provide new and original interpretations of aspects of Middle Eastern societies and their histories. To achieve disciplinary diversity, books will be solicited from authors writing in a wide range of fields including history, sociology, anthropology, political science and political economy. The emphasis will be on producing books offering an original approach along theoretical and empirical lines. The series is intended for students and academics, but the more accessible and wide-ranging studies will also appeal to the interested general reader.

A list of books in the series can be found after the index.

Jihad in Saudi Arabia

Violence and Pan-Islamism since 1979

Thomas Hegghammer

Norwegian Defence Research Establishment (FFI)

CAMBRIDGE UNIVERSITY PRESS
Cambridge, New York, Melbourne, Madrid, Cape Town, Singapore,
São Paulo, Delhi, Dubai, Tokyo

Cambridge University Press
The Edinburgh Building, Cambridge CB2 8RU, UK

Published in the United States of America by
Cambridge University Press, New York

www.cambridge.org
Information on this title: www.cambridge.org/9780521732369

First published 2010

Printed in the United Kingdom at the University Press, Cambridge

A catalogue record for this publication is available from the British Library

Library of Congress Cataloguing in Publication data
Hegghammer, Thomas.
Jihad in Saudi Arabia : violence and pan-Islamism since 1979 / Thomas Hegghammer.
p. cm. – (Cambridge Middle East studies ; 33)
Includes bibliographical references and index.
ISBN 978-0-521-51858-1 – ISBN 978-0-521-73236-9 (pbk.)
1. Islam–Saudi Arabia–History–20th century. 2. Islam–Saudi Arabia–History–21st century. 3. Islam and state–Saudi Arabia. 4. Jihad–History. I. Title. II. Series.
BP63.S33H44 2010
322.4'209538–dc22
2009052531

ISBN 978-0-521-51858-1 Hardback
ISBN 978-0-521-73236-9 Paperback

Contents

Figures and Tables

Acknowledgements

This book would never have seen the light of day without the remarkable generosity of many people around the world. First of all I thank Gilles Kepel, who expertly supervised the doctoral thesis on which this book is based. I am also grateful to my other academic mentor and long-time colleague Brynjar Lia, whose advice and support have been invaluable and whose talent and integrity remain a great inspiration.

My doctoral project was made possible by a three-year scholarship from the Norwegian Ministry of Defence. My employer, the Norwegian Defence Research Establishment (FFI), kindly offered me the supplementary resources and the time to carry it out. I am also indebted to Bernard Haykel at Princeton University and to Monica Toft and Steven Miller at Harvard University for awarding me postdoctoral fellowships in 2007–8 and 2008–9 that enabled me to turn my Ph.D. thesis into a book.

I cannot overstate my gratitude to the King Faisal Foundation and the King Faisal Centre for Research and Islamic Studies in Riyadh for hosting me as a visiting student on my five trips to Saudi Arabia. I thank Prince Turki al-Faisal, Yahya Ibn Junayd and their colleagues for their unconditional support and practical assistance during my fieldwork. I will repay in the currency I know they value the most: academic objectivity and sincerity.

I am also grateful to the many people I met during my fieldwork in Saudi Arabia, Pakistan, Jordan and elsewhere. I am forever indebted to Saud al-Sarhan, Mansur al-Nuqaydan and Yusuf al-Dayni who unselfishly shared their vast knowledge of Saudi Islamism and helped me in innumerable ways since I first arrived in the kingdom in April 2004. I am very thankful to Fahd al-Shafi, Nasir al-Huzaymi, Nasir al-Barrak, Hudhayfa Azzam, Abdallah Anas and certain anonymous friends, whose willingness to share knowledge seemed limitless. I thank Nawaf Obaid for his invaluable insights into the QAP's history, and Abd al-Rahman al-Hadlaq, Lt.-General Mansur al-Turki and Major Umar al-Zalal at the Saudi Ministry of Interior for their openness. I interviewed many other generous people who are unfortunately too numerous to be listed here.

In preparing this book, I have benefited from the fruitful interaction with colleagues in the field who have generously shared documents, contacts, information and ideas with me. My closest companion in this process has been Stéphane Lacroix, with whom I have enjoyed an exceptionally fruitful and trustful working relationship since we first enrolled in Sciences-Po together in 2003. I also thank Steffen Hertog, William McCants, Marc Lynch, Robert Lacey, Lawrence Wright and Peter Bergen, all of whom, along with Brynjar Lia, kindly commented on parts of the manuscript. I also thank my other colleagues at FFI's terrorism research project for their help and inspiration over the years. I have also benefited from discussions with, and the travel companionship of, fellow doctoral students at Sciences-Po in Paris, notably Carine Abou Lahoud, Abd al-Asiem al-Difraoui, Amelie Le Renard, Nabil Mouline, Thomas Pierret, Omar Saghi and Abdallah Tourabi. Many other brilliant scholars and reporters have helped me in various ways on this project, including Mariam Abou Zahab, Awadh al-Badi, Faiza Ambah, Faris Bin Huzzam, Christopher Boucek, James Buchan, Frank Gardner, Roger Hardy, Andrew Higgins, Gregory Johnsen, Sean Keeling, Michael Knights, Roel Meijer, Rolf Mowatt-Larsen, Tim Niblock, Reuven Paz, Bernard Rougier, Kjetil Selvik, Guido Steinberg, Camille Tawil and Christoph Wilcke.

I am also grateful to all the people who offered practical assistance during my field research. I especially thank Bishoy Salah, Ashraf Ibrahim and Nicholas Stivang for helping me around Cairo in 2003; I thank Ambassador Jan Bugge-Mahrt and Trond Rudi at the Norwegian Embassy in Riyadh; I thank the librarians at the Arab World Documentation Unit in Exeter University; and I thank Wyn Bowen, Michael Clarke and Peter Neumann for facilitating my research visit at King's College London in 2005–6.

Finally I am thankful for the support and patience of my editor Marigold Acland, the extremely useful and detailed comments by manuscript reviewer David Commins and the invaluable helping hand of copy-editor Monica Kendall. They have greatly improved the original text. All remaining errors and inaccuracies are mine alone.

Last but not least I thank my family and close friends for their unrelenting support and patience throughout this laborious process. Above all, I thank my wife Målfrid, who put up with my long absences, commented on several chapters and, in the midst of it all, gave me two wonderful children.

A note on conventions

Transliteration

Words and titles in Arabic are transcribed using a simplified version of the *Encyclopaedia of Islam* system. Ayn is not included at the beginning of names (e.g. Abdallah not 'Abdallah). Transcribed Arabic words are never capitalised. Arabic words in unabridged English dictionaries (Qur'an, hadith etc.) are not italicised.

Names

Arabic names are transcribed according to the above-mentioned system (though capitalised) unless a different transcription is dominant in English-language texts (e.g. Khobar not Khubar). Where different usages occur, I use the one closest to the above-mentioned system (e.g. Usama bin Ladin not Osama bin Laden). The article is dropped before common place-names (e.g. Riyadh not al-Riyadh).

Footnotes and references

Footnotes pertain to the entire preceding paragraph, not only the preceding sentence. Full URL and consultation date of Internet sources have been omitted, but all cited documents have been stored electronically by the author. Some interviewees have been anonymised.

Introduction

It was a quiet Monday evening in Riyadh when car bombs ripped through the housing compounds. The triple suicide attack on 12 May 2003 killed thirty-five people and marked the beginning of a protracted wave of violence in Saudi Arabia. Over the next few years, the campaign waged by 'al-Qaida on the Arabian Peninsula' (QAP) would take the lives of around 300 people and maim thousands. Never before in its modern history had Saudi Arabia experienced internal violence of this scale and duration.

The 2003 violence is intriguing because it put an end to the paradox which marked Saudi Islamism in the 1980s and 1990s, namely the curious discrepancy between the large number of Saudis involved in militancy abroad and the near-absence of Islamist violence at home. Apart from a few isolated incidents, the kingdom had largely been spared the unrest which haunted Egypt and Algeria in previous decades. Why, then, did the QAP campaign break out in 2003 and not before?

The reason, this book argues, is that the jihadist movement in Saudi Arabia differs from its counterparts in the Arab republics in being driven primarily by extreme pan-Islamism and not socio-revolutionary ideology. The outward-oriented character of Saudi Islamism is due to the relative lack of socio-economic grievances and to the development of a peculiar political culture in which support for suffering Muslims abroad became a major source of political legitimacy and social status. The 2003 violence was a historical anomaly, undertaken by an extreme offshoot of the Saudi jihadist movement which had radicalised in Afghan training camps. Unlike the Egyptian and Algerian insurgencies which lasted for years, the QAP campaign lost momentum after only eighteen months, because the militants represented an alien element on the Islamist scene and had almost no popular support.

Saudi Arabia occupies a central place in the modern history of militant Islamism. Since the oil boom in the 1970s, the kingdom has promoted its ultra-conservative Wahhabi interpretation of Islam across the world. Since the 1980s, Saudi Arabia has been a prominent supplier of fighters and funds to Muslim guerrillas in Afghanistan, Bosnia, Chechnya and elsewhere. More recently, it gained infamy as the homeland of al-Qaida leader Usama bin Ladin as well as fifteen of the nineteen hijackers on 9/11. To many in the West, Saudi Arabia is synonymous with, and partly responsible for, the rise of Muslim extremism in the late twentieth and early twenty-first centuries.

Yet the inner workings of Saudi Islamism remain notoriously underexplored. In much of the literature, Saudi Arabia features as a black box from which radicalism is steadily pumped into the international system. Until recently, very few studies treated Saudi Islamism as having internal dynamics and a variety of politically minded actors. The opaqueness of Saudi Islamism has been illustrated several times in recent decades by spectacular but isolated violent incidents, such as the 1979 Mecca mosque takeover, the 1995 Riyadh bombing or the 1996 Khobar bombing. Each event took observers by complete surprise, only to fade rapidly into a mist of secrecy and speculation. This book will use new primary sources to shed light on the history and dynamics of violent Islamism in the kingdom.

In a comparative political perspective, Saudi Islamism is highly interesting because of the many apparent idiosyncracies of Saudi politics and society. Most obvious is the central role and conservative interpretation of religion in the kingdom. The kingdom cultivates its identity as the heartland of Islam by conceding considerable power and funds to the Wahhabi religious establishment and making religion a central part of its own discourse. The political system is also uncommon: Saudi Arabia is an absolute monarchy ruled by an extensive royal family (the Al Sa'ud) in alliance with a family of clerics (the Al al-Shaykh). Moreover, the kingdom has one of the region's longest-ruling families and is one of few Middle Eastern countries untouched by Western colonialism or military coups. Economically, oil has made Saudi Arabia considerably wealthier than most of the other countries that have produced large jihadist communities, such as Egypt or Yemen. Socially, the kingdom is characterised by, among other things, the prominence of traditional social structures such as tribes and noble families. Perhaps even more striking is the speed and scale of socio-economic change in late twentieth-century Saudi Arabia. These and other factors raise intriguing questions whose significance extends beyond the narrow fields of Saudi studies or jihadism studies. For example, how can militant Islamism emerge in an Islamic state? How do the specificities of Saudi politics and society affect dynamics of contestation? How does individual radicalisation occur in ultra-conservative, tribal and wealthy societies?[1]

With these broader questions on the horizon, this book focuses on the evolution of jihadism in Saudi Arabia after 1980. Jihadism is used here as a synonym for 'militant Sunni Islamism', while Islamism is defined broadly as 'Islamic activism'. Non-violent Islamist actors will be considered where relevant, but this is neither a book about Saudi Islamism as such, nor about the Saudi political system as a whole. Shiite Islamist militancy, such as the 1979 riots in the Eastern Province, the 1987 Hajj riots and the 1996 Khobar bombing, will also be left out because it represents a largely separate political phenomenon. Earlier Sunni violence such as the 1920s Ikhwan revolt is not included either, because it has been treated by other scholars and has few direct implications for militancy after 1980.[2]

The analysis downplays two of the most well-known parts of Saudi Islamist history for reasons that are less intuitive. The first is the famous Mecca mosque siege in November 1979. This spectacular event, which caused the death of hundreds of people, was the work of an apocalyptic sect led by the charismatic Juhayman al-Utaybi. The rebels, who called themselves the *Ikhwan*, represented a radicalised clique of an extreme pietist organisation known as *al-Jama'a al-Salafiyya al-Muhtasiba* (JSM) that had been established in Medina in the late 1960s. The clique, radicalised by arguments with scholars in Medina, the fiery personality of Juhayman and finally by a two-year desert existence, had come to believe that the end of the world was nigh. They believed that the Mahdi, an Islamic messianic figure, had manifested himself in one of the group's members, and that the latter needed to be consecrated in the Great Mosque at the end of the fourteenth century of the Islamic calendar. The Juhayman group is not treated in detail here because as an organisation it died out in 1979 and because it represented a pietist current of Saudi Islamism that is distinct from the pan-Islamist

[1] For general works on Saudi Arabia, see Alexei Vassiliev, *The History of Saudi Arabia* (London: Saqi Books, 2000); Madawi al-Rasheed, *A History of Saudi Arabia* (Cambridge University Press, 2002); and Robert Lacey, *The Kingdom: Arabia and the House of Saud* (New York: Avon, 1981).

[2] For more on Shiite militancy, see Fouad Ibrahim, *The Shi'is of Saudi Arabia* (London: Saqi, 2007); Toby Jones, 'Rebellion on the Saudi Periphery: Modernity, Marginalization, and the Shi'a Uprising of 1979', *International Journal of Middle East Studies* 38, no. 2 (2006); and Thomas Hegghammer, 'Deconstructing the Myth about al-Qa'ida and Khobar', *The Sentinel* 1, no. 3 (2008). For more on the 1920s Ikhwan, see John Habib, *Ibn Saud's Warriors of Islam: The Ikhwan of Najd and Their Role in the Creation of the Sa'udi Kingdom, 1910–1930* (Leiden: Brill, 1978); and Joseph Kostiner, *The Making of Saudi Arabia: From Chieftaincy to Monarchical State* (Oxford University Press, 1993).

movement that produced the QAP. The Mecca event had an important indirect effect on Saudi Islamism by prompting the regime to give the ulama more power and Islamic activists more political space in the early 1980s. However, there are practically no substantial links, neither organisational nor ideological, between Juhayman and al-Qaida.[3]

Similarly, the rise of the so-called Sahwa (Awakening) movement in the 1980s and early 1990s is treated only peripherally in this book, because the Sahwa was a non-violent reformist movement whose aims, means and social base were different from that of the extreme pan-Islamists on the foreign jihad fronts. The Sahwa, whose ideology represented an amalgam of Wahhabi conservatism and Muslim Brotherhood pragmatism, grew on Saudi University campuses from the early 1970s onward under the influence of exiled teachers from the Egyptian and Syrian Muslim Brotherhood. Sahwists began engaging in open polemics in the mid-1980s against the modernist literary current known as the *hadatha*. After the Gulf crisis and the deployment of US troops to Saudi Arabia, the Sahwa, led by the charismatic preachers Safar al-Hawali and Salman al-Awda, presented formal political demands to the Saudi government, most famously through the petitions known as the *Letter of Demands* in 1991 and the *Memorandum of Advice* in 1992. At this point part of the Sahwa movement also produced a formal organisation, the 'Committee for the Defence of Legitimate Rights', the founders of which were soon forced into exile in London. After a crackdown in September 1994, the movement was silenced until it re-emerged severely weakened in the late 1990s. The Sahwa will necessarily feature in our analysis, because it was such an important part of the political landscape in which the jihadist movement operated, but the Sahwa's history and internal dynamics will not be a major line of inquiry.[4]

The choice of terms and concepts used in this book to differentiate between various actors and ideological currents is based on two fundamental assumptions. The first is that Islamism is politically heterogeneous. Islamists work towards different short- and mid-term aims and

[3] Yaroslav Trofimov pushes the Juhayman–al-Qaida link a little too far in his otherwise brilliant account of the Mecca siege; Yaroslav Trofimov, *The Siege of Mecca: The Forgotten Uprising in Islam's Holiest Shrine and the Birth of al Qaeda* (New York: Doubleday, 2007); for more on the origin of Juhayman's group, see Thomas Hegghammer and Stéphane Lacroix, 'Rejectionist Islamism in Saudi Arabia: The Story of Juhayman al-Utaybi Revisited', *International Journal of Middle East Studies* 39, no. 1 (2007).

[4] For more on the Sahwa, see Mamoun Fandy, *Saudi Arabia and the Politics of Dissent* (New York: Palgrave Macmillan, 2001); and Stéphane Lacroix, 'Les champs de la discorde: Une sociologie politique de l'islamisme en Arabie Saoudite (1954–2005)' (Ph.D. thesis, Institut d'Etudes Politiques de Paris, 2007).

display systematic differences in political behaviour. The second is that many of the theological descriptors commonly used in the literature on Islamism, such as *salafi*, *wahhabi*, *jihadi salafi* and *takfiri*, do not correspond to discrete and observable patterns of political behaviour among Islamists. I therefore rely instead on terms that signal the political content of the ideology at hand or the immediate political priorities of a given actor, such as 'revolutionary' or 'pietist'. This approach, I argue, is a prerequisite for analysing social movements, because a social movement is by definition united by a shared set of political preferences. It makes no sense to speak of a 'salafi social movement', for the simple reason that actors labelled salafi have wildly different, often diametrically opposing, political agendas. This is not to say that the terms Salafism or Wahhabism should be discarded, only that they are more useful for analysing theological discourse than political behaviour.[5]

For the same reason, it is not fruitful to look at the relationship between Wahhabism and contemporary militancy as a causal one. Wahhabism, although named after a historical figure, the eighteenth-century scholar Muhammad ibn Abd al-Wahhab, is not a political doctrine, but a living theological tradition, interpreted and contested by successive generations of scholars. In the modern era, both the regime and its violent opponents anchor their discourse in the Wahhabi tradition, but they draw vastly different conclusions about politics, as Madawi al-Rasheed has shown in *Contesting the Saudi State*. Wahhabism shapes the way in which activists and their opponents articulate and legitimise their agenda; it does not, however, dictate the core content of their activism.[6]

The actor labels used in this book derive from a broader conceptual framework for distinguishing between ideal types of Islamist activism (see Table 1). The framework is based on the idea that five main rationales for action underlie most forms of Islamist activism. Under the term rationale, I subsume observed mid-term political aims and strategy. These rationales, which may have both a violent and a nonviolent manifestation, represent the five principal purposes for which

[5] John D. McCarthy and Mayer N. Zald, 'Resource Mobilization and Social Movements: A Partial Theory', *American Journal of Sociology* 82, no. 6 (1977): 1218; Thomas Hegghammer, 'Jihadi Salafis or Revolutionaries? On Theology and Politics in the Study of Militant Islamism', in *Global Salafism*, ed. Roel Meijer (London and New York: Hurst and Columbia University Press, 2009).

[6] For more on Wahhabism, see David Commins, *The Wahhabi Mission and Saudi Arabia* (London: I.B. Tauris, 2006); Guido Steinberg, *Religion und Staat in Saudi-Arabien* (Würzburg: Egon, 2002); Madawi al-Rasheed, *Contesting the Saudi State: Islamic Voices from a New Generation* (Cambridge University Press, 2007); and Mohammed Ayoob and Hasan Kosebalaban, eds., *Religion and Politics in Saudi Arabia: Wahhabism and the State* (Boulder, CO: Lynne Rienner, 2008).

Table 1. *A rationale-based typology of Islamist activism with examples from Saudi Arabia*

<table>
<tr><th rowspan="2">RATIONALE</th><th colspan="2">NON-VIOLENT FORM</th><th colspan="4">VIOLENT FORM</th></tr>
<tr><th>Manifestation</th><th>Examples</th><th colspan="2">Manifestation</th><th colspan="2">Examples</th></tr>
<tr><td>State-oriented</td><td>Reformism</td><td>Sahwa</td><td colspan="2">Socio-revolutionary Islamism</td><td colspan="2">n/a</td></tr>
<tr><td>Nation-oriented</td><td>Irredentism</td><td>n/a</td><td colspan="2">Violent irredentism</td><td colspan="2">n/a</td></tr>
<tr><td rowspan="2">Umma-oriented</td><td rowspan="2">Soft pan-Islamism</td><td rowspan="2">World Muslim League</td><td colspan="2">Violent pan-Islamism</td><td rowspan="2">Saudis in Afghanistan, Chechnya, Bosnia, Iraq</td><td rowspan="2">al-Qaida, QAP</td></tr>
<tr><td>Classical jihadism</td><td>Global jihadism</td></tr>
<tr><td>Morality-oriented</td><td>Pietism</td><td>JSM</td><td colspan="2">Vigilantism</td><td colspan="2">Juhayman's Ikhwan, Unorganised hisba</td></tr>
<tr><td>Sectarian</td><td>Sectarianism</td><td>n/a</td><td colspan="2">Violent sectarianism</td><td colspan="2">n/a</td></tr>
</table>

Islamists act. For violent groups, they represent the most important mid-term objectives for the armed struggle:

- *Socio-revolutionaries* fight for state power against a Muslim regime perceived as illegitimate.
- *Violent irredentists* struggle for a specific territory against a local non-Muslim occupier.
- *Violent pan-Islamists* fight to defend the entire Muslim nation and its territories from non-Muslim aggression. Among these, classical jihadists will fight conventionally in local conflict zones, while global jihadists fight the West with all means in all places.
- *Vigilantists* use violence to correct the moral behaviour of fellow Muslims.
- *Violent sectarians* kill to intimidate and marginalise the competing sect (Sunni or Shiite).

These are not mutually exclusive categories, but ideal-type motivations that partially overlap. Most Islamists act to promote several or even all of these objectives, but all actors will, at any given time, have one dominant rationale which determines the principal modalities of the actor's violent behaviour.

Three terms feature prominently in the following analysis and require further elaboration, namely 'socio-revolutionary Islamism', 'classical jihadism' and 'global jihadism'. The first term is associated with the ideas of Sayyid Qutb and refers to activism intended to topple a Muslim government through a military coup. This was the principal form of militant Islamist activism in 1970s Egypt and Syria, as well as in 1990s Algeria. The violence of these groups struck primarily targets associated with the government, and the dominant discursive theme or frame in their texts was the corruption, repression and malgovernance of the Muslim ruler.

The two latter terms refer to extreme forms of pan-Islamist activism. Classical jihadism is so termed by this author because the underlying doctrine is closer than other militant ideologies to orthodox conceptions of jihad, though not identical to them. The classical jihadist doctrine is a modern invention, first articulated by Abdallah Azzam in the context of the 1980s jihad in Afghanistan. Azzam argued that non-Muslim infringement of Muslim territory demanded the immediate military involvement of all able Muslim men in defence of the said territory, wherever its location. He thus redefined the political content of contemporary jihad from a struggle against Muslim regimes over state power to a defensive struggle against non-Muslims over territory. This conception of jihad was closer to orthodox views on legitimate jihad – hence its popularity – but Azzam differed from mainstream ulama in arguing that all Muslims, not just the population immediately concerned, had a duty to fight.[7]

Classical jihadism has long been confused with its more radical ideological sibling, the doctrine of global jihadism, which was developed by Usama bin Ladin in the mid-1990s. Both considered the fight against non-Muslim powers involved in the oppression of Muslims as more important than the fight against corrupt Muslim governments. Both framed their struggle similarly, using a rhetoric whose discursive theme was the humiliation of Muslims at the hands of non-Muslims, usually illustrated by long lists of symbols of Muslim suffering. However, while Azzam advocated guerrilla warfare within defined conflict zones against enemies in uniform, Bin Ladin called for indiscriminate mass-casualty out-of-area attacks. This is why Arabs in 1980s Afghanistan or 1990s Bosnia and Chechnya, all of whom were classical jihadists, practically never undertook international terrorist operations, while

[7] For overviews of the concept of jihad in the classical tradition, see David Cook, *Understanding Jihad* (Berkeley: University of California Press, 2005); and Michael Bonner, *Jihad in Islamic History: Doctrines and Practice* (Princeton University Press, 2006).

al-Qaida militants have attacked a broad range of Western targets in a variety of locations. The difference between classical and global jihadists is important because in late 1990s and early 2000s Saudi Arabia, the two communities opposed each other, notably on the issue of whether to fight in Saudi Arabia or abroad.

Interestingly, extreme pan-Islamism shares a number of structural similarities with nationalist-type ideologies, notably the focus on the liberation of territory, the primacy placed on the fight against the external enemy and the emphasis on internal unity in the face of outside threats. It is indeed possible to view pan-Islamism as a macro-nationalism centred on the imagined community of the umma, which is defined by religion and to some extent by language (Arabic having a special status in Islam). Although the Muslim nation is by definition aterritorial – the umma is wherever Muslims are – pan-Islamists have a clear sense of what constitutes Muslim territory, namely all lands once ruled by Muslims, from Andalucia in the West to Indonesia in the East. Some scholars may object to the view of pan-Islamism as a macro-nationalism. However, the perspective makes better sense when linked to the ideal-type distinction between revolutionary-utopian and ethno-nationalist ideologies, which has proved heuristically very fruitful in the analysis of militancy outside the Middle East. Peter Waldmann documented generic differences in behaviour and recruitment patterns between ethno-nationalist and leftist extremist groups in 1970s and 1980s Europe. As we shall see later in the book, some of these same differences characterise the relationship between socio-revolutionary and pan-Islamist activists.[8]

If we examine the history of Sunni Islamist violence in the kingdom with the above-mentioned concepts in mind, a clear and interesting pattern emerges, namely that most of the violence has been of the extreme pan-Islamist kind. There has been some moral vigilantism, while socio-revolutionary violence is very rare. Seven episodes of Sunni Islamist violence have marked the kingdom's recent history. First was the 1979 Mecca incident, which was a sui generis phenomenon, although closest to vigilantist violence because it was intended as an act of collective moral purification. Second was a series of three small attacks on US targets during the 1991 Gulf war. Third was a little-known series of around ten non-lethal attacks on symbols of moral corruption (video shops, women's centres, etc.) in the Qasim

[8] Peter Waldmann, 'Ethnic and Sociorevolutionary Terrorism: A Comparison of Structures', in *Social Movements and Violence: Participation in Underground Organisations*, ed. Donatella Della Porta (Greenwich: JAI, 1992).

province and in Riyadh around 1991. The attacks were carried out by a small group of extreme pietists who viewed their deeds as *hisba*, or moral policing. Fourth was the 1995 Riyadh bombing, which targeted a US military facility. The fifth wave took place between 2000 and early 2003 in the form of a series of small-scale attacks (booby traps on cars, drive-by shootings, letter bombs etc.) on Western expatriates. Although none of the perpetrators were ever found, the violence was most likely the work of amateur militants driven by anti-Westernism. The sixth wave was a series of five assassination attempts on judges and policemen in the northern city of Sakaka in the Jawf province in late 2002 and early 2003. The Sakaka events represent arguably the only cases of violence against civilian representatives of the government in modern Saudi history.[9]

The seventh and by far the most important wave of violence was the QAP campaign. Through both acts and discourse, the QAP exhibited a primarily pan-Islamist agenda. Most premeditated attacks were on Western targets, and there was never a single successful attack on a Cabinet member, royal palace or civilian government building outside the security apparatus. There were attacks on security forces and the Interior Ministry, but only relatively late in the campaign when vengeance had become a factor. In its publications, the QAP consistently justified its violence as a defensive reaction to US aggression in the Muslim world. The top al-Qaida leadership may well have wanted regime change, but it is clear from the QAP literature, in particular the many interviews with and biographies of militants published in the magazine *Sawt al-Jihad* (Voice of Jihad), that most mid- and low-level operatives saw themselves as waging primarily a pan-Islamist struggle.

Extreme pan-Islamism thus seems to have been the dominant, though not the only, rationale behind Islamist militancy in the kingdom in recent decades. The history of Saudi jihadism is therefore largely the history of the extreme pan-Islamist subcurrent of Saudi Islamism. How, then, can we best go about explaining the rise of this current and the outbreak of the QAP campaign?

Broadly speaking, the existing literature offers three main paradigms for explaining the evolution of Saudi jihadism. First are

[9] For the 1991 attacks, see Elizabeth Rubin, 'The Jihadi Who Kept Asking Why', *New York Times*, 7 March 2004; author's interviews with Mansur al-Nuqaydan, Riyadh, April 2004 and Nasir al-Barrak, Dammam, December 2005. For the 1995 Riyadh bombing, see Joshua Teitelbaum, *Holier than Thou: Saudi Arabia's Islamic Opposition*, vol. LII (Washington, DC: Washington Institute for Near East Policy, 2000). For the 2000–3 attacks and the Sakaka assassinations, see J. E. Peterson, 'Saudi Arabia: Internal Security Incidents Since 1979', *Arabian Peninsula Background Note*, no. 3 (2005).

organisational-level analyses which attribute the QAP campaign to a decision by Usama bin Ladin and al-Qaida to open a battlefront in Saudi Arabia. Anthony Cordesman, Nawaf Obaid, Dominique Thomas and Bruce Riedel have each provided very valuable insights into al-Qaida's strategic thinking and the early history of the QAP organisation. However, these analyses do not adequately explain why Bin Ladin suddenly decided to launch the campaign in 2003 and not before. Moreover, organisational-level analyses tend to skirt the deeper causes of the violence.[10]

Some scholars have therefore presented structuralist explanations which see the violence as the natural result of deep socio-economic problems or fundamental dysfunctions in the Saudi state system. Some have emphasised the economic dimension and argued that Saudi Arabia experiences violence because it is in a terrorism-prone stage of economic development. Others, such as Joshua Teitelbaum, have acknowledged the importance of socio-economic factors, but suggested that the real problem is the 'ideology of religious extremism' which underlies the legitimacy of the Saudi state. A related, but more sophisticated analysis is that presented by Madawi al-Rasheed in her landmark work on Saudi Islamism, *Contesting the Saudi State*. Al-Rasheed explains Saudi jihadism as one of several permutations of Wahhabism after the authoritarian Saudi state lost the monopoly over Wahhabi discourse under the pressures of globalisation. Al-Rasheed does not articulate a clear explanation for the outbreak of the 2003 violence, presumably because this is not the focus of her book, but she does allude to the authoritarian nature of the state and its instrumentalisation of Wahhabism as root causes of Saudi jihadism. The key problem with these explanations, however, is that they rarely account for chronological variation in levels of violence, and they are particularly badly suited to explain small-scale violence of the kind that has taken place in the kingdom. Political violence is rarely the linear expression of structural strain, because violent contestation requires actors who can mobilise followers and operationalise intentions.[11]

[10] Nawaf Obaid and Anthony Cordesman, *Al-Qaeda in Saudi Arabia: Asymmetric Threats and Islamic Extremists* (Washington, DC: Center for Strategic and International Studies, 2005); Dominique Thomas, *Les hommes d'Al-Qaïda: Discours et stratégie* (Paris: Michalon, 2005), 39–58; and Bruce Riedel and Bilal Y. Saab, 'Al Qaeda's Third Front: Saudi Arabia', *The Washington Quarterly* 31, no. 2 (2008).

[11] Robert Looney, 'Combating Terrorism Through Reforms: Implications of the Bremer-Kasarda Model for Saudi Arabia', *Strategic Insights* 3, no. 4 (2004); Joshua Teitelbaum, 'Terrorist Challenges to Saudi Arabian Internal Security', *Middle East Review of International Affairs* 9, no. 3 (2005); al-Rasheed, *Contesting the Saudi State*, 134–74.

A third and related type of explanation has therefore drawn on social movement theory and presented the QAP campaign as the violent phase in a 'cycle of contention' of the Saudi Islamist movement. This is the approach used by Roel Meijer to argue that the violent phase was brought about by the 1995 repression of the non-violent Islamist opposition. However, this approach assumes the existence of a coherent Saudi Islamist movement, while there are important ideological differences and few organisational links between the QAP and the opposition of the early 1990s. Moreover, this approach does not adequately explain the specific timing of the QAP campaign.[12]

To overcome this triple methodological challenge – namely that organisational analyses omit root causes, that structural explanations cannot explain timing and that social movement theory does not work well on the Saudi Islamist movement as a whole – I propose to apply a multi-level social movement framework to the more narrowly defined Saudi jihadist movement. I draw here on the work of Donatella Della Porta, who studied leftist extremism in Italy and Germany by distinguishing between macro-level variables such as styles of protest policing, meso-level variables such as underground organisational dynamics, and micro-level variables such as recruitment and radicalisation processes. This powerful framework makes it easier to capture both root causes and tactical variations, and to assess the effect of synchronic changes at different levels of analysis.[13]

The following analysis will therefore identify the most crucial chronological periods and study each of them on the macro, meso and micro levels. At the macro level I will look primarily at international political developments, the domestic political space for jihadist activism and ideological developments in the wider Islamist community. At the meso level the focus will be on 'first movers' and entrepreneurs, and on the strategies they employed to mobilise followers. At the micro level, I will look at the socio-economic profiles, declared motivations and patterns of joining of individual recruits. All chapters at a given level of analysis are not entirely symmetrical, partly because they cover time periods of very different length. However, they do answer the same broad questions about context, agency and individual radicalisation respectively.

[12] Roel Meijer, 'The "Cycle of Contention" and the Limits of Terrorism in Saudi Arabia', in *Saudi Arabia in the Balance*, ed. Paul Aarts and Gerd Nonneman (London: Hurst, 2005).

[13] Donatella Della Porta, *Social Movements, Political Violence and the State: A Comparative Analysis of Italy and Germany* (Cambridge University Press, 1995), 9–14.

The central concern throughout the analysis is to understand and explain *mobilisation*, that is, why and how human, material and immaterial resources were marshalled and organised for political action. I will also pay some attention to the way in which actors frame their struggle to attract followers, and to the dynamics that affect the mobilising power of their frame. The broader notion of 'ideology' thus comes in at all three levels of analysis: as part of the environment in which agents operate, as part of their strategy to mobilise followers and as part of the individual recruitment process.[14]

The problem, of course, is that this type of analysis requires a considerable amount of detailed information about the actors, whereas the groups we are dealing with here are small, violent and secretive. Indeed, ten years ago it probably would not have been possible to write this book. However, three recent developments have made Saudi jihadism considerably more transparent. First and most important is the Internet, which has revolutionised the academic study of militant Islamism. Since the late 1990s, jihadists have used the Internet as a distribution platform, library and information exchange for texts, recordings and videos. The QAP in particular published an astonishing amount of documentation about itself in 2003 and 2004, making it arguably one of the best-documented terrorist groups in history. Documentation from jihadist websites must obviously be used with caution, but authenticity is less of an issue than sceptics think. Forgery is difficult because individual documents can always be checked against other sources for consistency of style and content. Inaccuracies, on the other hand, are a more serious concern, but this problem can be addressed by relying on accumulated evidence. This study is based on thousands of texts, recordings and videos systematically collected from the Internet over a period of six years.[15]

Another change which made this study possible was Saudi Arabia's opening up to Western social scientists from around 2002 onward.

[14] David A. Snow and Robert D. Benford, 'Ideology, Frame Resonance, and Participant Mobilization', in *International Social Movement Research: From Structure to Action*, ed. Bert Klandermans, Hans Peter Kriesi and Sidney Tarrow (Greenwich: JAI Press, 1988).

[15] The remarkable textual production of the QAP included five different publication series: *Sawt al-Jihad* (Voice of Jihad), published in thirty issues (30–50 pages each); *Mu'askar al-Battar* (Camp of the Sabre), twenty-two issues (30–50 pages); *al-Khansa'* (named after a seventh-century female poet), one issue; *al-Taqrir al-Ikhbari* (News Report), twenty-three issues; and *al-Bayan* (Statement), at least three issues. The QAP also produced several 40–90-minute films documenting their operations in remarkable detail, such as *Wills of the Martyrs*, *Martyrs of the Confrontations*, *Badr of Riyadh*, *The Quds Squadron* and *The Falluja Raid*.

This author was able to conduct extensive fieldwork in Saudi Arabia on five trips between 2004 and 2008. Although I was never able to access active QAP members, I interviewed their friends and families, veterans of foreign jihad fronts, former radicals, moderate Islamists, journalists and expert commentators across the country. Some of the informants have been anonymised in this book for obvious reasons.

The third development was the change of attitude among Saudi authorities towards information-sharing after the outbreak of the QAP violence. From May 2003 onward, the Interior Ministry was considerably more forthcoming with information about security incidents than it had been in the past. The change likely reflected a realisation that the Internet and satellite TV had broken the state's monopoly on information, and that the government needed to present its own version of events as an alternative to that of the militants. Local Saudi media, while state controlled, were also allowed to undertake a certain amount of investigative reporting.

For the micro-level analysis the book relies on a collection of 539 biographies of Saudi militants whose activities span a range of arenas from the 1980s Afghan jihad to the QAP campaign (but excluding Iraq). The biographies were collated from open sources by this author alone over a period of over four years. More detailed information about the sources and the socio-economic data is included in Appendix 1. The ambition of the micro-level analysis is not primarily comparative, so it does not engage systematically with the vast and growing corpus of profile-based studies of individual radicalisation. It does, however, provide a relatively detailed look at how some Saudis became militants.[16]

This book will inevitably contain factual errors and omissions, as do all empirically rich studies of clandestine phenomena. Nevertheless, I believe the data is sufficiently extensive and varied to provide relatively well-founded answers to some of the above-mentioned questions.

[16] For studies of individual radicalisation in other contexts, see e.g. Saad Eddin Ibrahim, 'Anatomy of Egypt's Militant Islamic Groups: Methodological Notes and Preliminary Findings', *International Journal of Middle East Studies* 12, no. 4 (1981); Ayla Hammond Schbley, 'Torn Between God, Family and Money: The Changing Profile of Lebanon's Religious Terrorists', *Studies in Conflict and Terrorism* 23 (2000); Ami Pedahzur, Leonard Weinberg and Arie Perliger, 'Altruism and Fatalism: The Characteristics of Palestinian Suicide Terrorists', *Deviant Behaviour* 24 (2003); Alan B. Krueger and Jitka Malečková, 'Education, Poverty and Terrorism: Is there a Causal Connection?', *Journal of Economic Perspectives* 17, no. 4 (2003); Marc Sageman, *Understanding Terror Networks* (Philadelphia: University of Pennsylvania Press, 2004); Edwin Bakker, 'Jihadi Terrorists in Europe', in *Clingendael Security Paper no. 2* (The Hague: Netherlands Institute of International Relations, 2006).

The central argument, put very simply, is that Saudi jihadism has been more pan-Islamist than revolutionary, in contrast to the Arab republics where the reverse has been true. I further argue that the QAP campaign represented the homecoming of a Saudi jihadist movement which had developed in three stages. The first stage lasted from the mid-1980s to the mid-1990s and saw the formation of a classical jihadist movement which engaged in local struggles of national liberation in places such as Afghanistan, Bosnia and Chechnya in the name of pan-Islamism. The classical jihadist movement emerged at this time for three reasons. First, the increase in the number and visibility of conflicts pitting Muslims versus non-Muslims made pan-Islamist rhetoric more empirically credible. Second, domestic political factors produced a beneficial political opportunity structure for extreme pan-Islamist activism. Third, Abdallah Azzam and his associates exercised excellent social movement entrepreneurship.

The second phase, from the mid-1990s to 2001, witnessed the emergence of the more radical 'global jihadist' branch of the Saudi jihadist movement. The global jihadists were also extreme pan-Islamists, but differed from the classical jihadists by their anti-Americanism and their willingness to use international terrorist tactics. The global jihadists, represented by the al-Qaida organisation, attracted many Saudis in the late 1990s because Bin Ladin succeeded in establishing a local recruitment infrastructure, winning the support of radical clerics and exploiting popular sympathy for the Chechen and Palestinian causes.

In the third phase, from 2002 to 2006, the global jihadist branch produced an organisation, the QAP, which waged war on the Western presence in Saudi Arabia. The immediate cause of the QAP campaign was a strategic decision by Usama bin Ladin, taken after the US-led invasion of Afghanistan, to open a battlefront in the kingdom. In the spring of 2002, several hundred Saudi fighters returned from Afghanistan to Saudi Arabia and began making military preparations under the supervision of Yusuf al-Uyayri. The mobilisation was facilitated by inconsistent policing, a polarisation of the Islamist field and new symbols of Muslim suffering.

The book is structured over a basic 3x3 grid with three chronological periods and three levels of analysis. The first part explains the rise of classical jihadism in Saudi Arabia between 1979 and 1995. Chapters 1, 2 and 3 analyse the emergence of a classical jihadist movement at the macro, meso and micro level respectively. The second part moves forward in time, narrows the focus to the global jihadists and examines the mobilisation of Saudis to al-Qaida between 1996 and 2001. Chapters 4, 5 and 6 are thus devoted to the context, the agents and the subjects of recruitment to al-Qaida in Afghanistan. The third and final part examines the formation of the QAP in 2002 and 2003, with chapters 7, 8 and 9 devoted to the macro-, meso- and micro-level aspects of the group's formation. Chapter 10 serves as an epilogue that explains how the campaign evolved and why it failed.

1 The politics of pan-Islamism

> In the past few years, a number of sister Islamic nations ... have experienced unusual crises and natural disasters ... The government has consistently come to the rescue of these ravaged countries in order to strengthen the ties of fraternity among Islamic countries, inspired by the precepts of Islam that call for cooperation and solidarity among mankind.
>
> Saudi Ministry of Finance, 1991[1]

From the mid-1980s to the mid-1990s, thousands of Saudis left quiet lives of material comfort to fight in Afghanistan, Tajikistan, Bosnia and Chechnya. They put their lives at risk for people they had never met and for territories they could barely place on a map. In a time of low oil prices, the Saudi state spent billions of dollars to liberate countries thousands of miles away. Its army was too weak to defend Saudi oil-fields against Iraq in 1990, yet it encouraged its young men to take part in other Muslims' wars in Europe and Central Asia.

The driving force behind this curious behaviour was *pan-Islamism*, an ideology based on the view that all Muslims were one people who had a responsibility to help each other in times of crisis. In the 1980s the Muslim world witnessed the rise of an increasingly militarised interpretation of pan-Islamism, which saw the umma as threatened from the outside and placed a special emphasis on helping Muslims involved in conflicts against non-Muslims. The most extreme proponents of this ideology sought to convince average citizens to get militarily involved in other Muslims' struggles of national liberation.

To understand why this endeavour succeeded when it did, and why it was more successful in Saudi Arabia than in most other Muslim countries, we need to examine the evolution of the political opportunities for extreme pan-Islamist activism in the kingdom from the mid-1970s to the mid-1990s. As we shall see, these opportunities were shaped by the

[1] *The Kingdom of Saudi Arabia's Economic and Social Development Aid to the Islamic World* (Riyadh: Ministry of Finance and National Economy, 1991), 24.

Saudi state's evolving concern for pan-Islamist legitimacy as well as the dynamics of Saudi domestic politics.

The rise of pan-Islamism

While the ideal of Muslim unity is encapsulated in the Qur'anic notion of the *umma* (the community of believers), the intellectual history of pan-Islamism goes back to the late nineteenth century and the rise of modern Islamism. In the course of the twentieth century, the idea of the umma gave rise to a variety of political phenomena. Broadly speaking, we can distinguish between three political manifestations of pan-Islamism: caliphism, foreign policy coordination and popular mobilisation.

For early Islamist thinkers such as Rashid Rida, who wrote around the time of the end of the Ottoman caliphate in 1924, pan-Islam connoted a concrete project of creating formal political unity in the Muslim world. The 1920s and the 1950s would see several attempts at uniting Muslim countries in a caliphate-like organisation. However, local nationalisms and realpolitik prevented the realisation of this project which was all but dead by the late 1950s.[2]

In the 1960s and early 1970s, pan-Islamism was revived in a less utopian form, namely Saudi King Faisal's call for coordination and mutual aid between Muslim countries. A foreign policy doctrine rather than political unification project, King Faisal's notion of 'Muslim solidarity' (*al-tadamun al-islami*), was articulated largely as a counterweight to Nasser's secular Arab nationalism. King Faisal's pan-Islamism was above all an alliance-building tool in the Arab cold war between Egypt and Saudi Arabia. However, it also served a domestic political purpose, namely to boost the Saudi regime's religious credentials. Containing the birthplace of Wahhabism and the cradle of Islam, Saudi Arabia had made religious integrity a key pillar of its legitimacy. Leading and helping the Muslim nation was King Faisal's way of laying claim to religious integrity.[3]

Of course, the promotion of pan-Islamism under King Faisal was somewhat ironic given the Wahhabi ulama's historical hostility towards non-Wahhabi Muslims. Up until the early twentieth century, Wahhabi scholars often did not consider non-Wahhabis Muslims at all. This changed with globalisation, which brought Saudis into contact

[2] J. M. Landau, *The Politics of Pan-Islam: Ideology and Organization* (Oxford University Press, 1990); James Piscatori, 'Imagining Pan-Islam', in *Islam and Political Violence*, ed. Shahram Akbarzadeh and Fethi Mansouri (London: I. B. Tauris, 2007).

[3] Abdullah M. Sindi, 'King Faisal and Pan-Islamism', in *King Faisal and the Modernisation of Saudi Arabia*, ed. Willard Beling (London: Croom Helm, 1980).

with 'original infidels' from the non-Muslim world. By the 1950s, the Saudi religious establishment had come to see other Muslims as believers who should be supported. The official recognition of non-Wahhabis as Muslims came in 1954 when the Saudi Great Mufti Muhammad Bin Ibrahim met for the first time formally with senior non-Wahhabi ulama such as the Egyptian Mufti Hasanayn Muhammad Makhluf and the Tunisian Maliki scholar Muhammad Tahir Ashur.[4]

To promote pan-Islamism, King Faisal established a number of institutions at the national and supranational level which worked to promote cooperation, mutual solidarity and religious awareness in the Muslim world. The two most important of these were the Muslim World League (MWL), founded in May 1962, and the Organisation of the Islamic Conference (OIC), established between 1969 and 1972. The MWL became involved in a vast range of cultural, educational and charitable activities and served as the umbrella organisation for a plethora of smaller organisations. Although formally a non-governmental organisation, it has remained influenced and generously funded by Saudi Arabia until today. The Mecca-based MWL was also influenced by the Muslim Brotherhood, whose members, having fled persecution in Egypt and Syria, were strongly represented in the organisation. Whereas the MWL operated on the societal level, the OIC was an inter-governmental organisation with greater influence in the diplomatic sphere. In addition to being a forum for foreign policy coordination between Muslim countries, the OIC had the power to set up financial institutions and charities. This became particularly significant after the 1973 oil crisis filled the treasuries of its member states.[5]

The international Islamic organisations set up by King Faisal helped foster a third manifestation of pan-Islamism, namely a movement promoting popular assistance to Muslims in need. This populist pan-Islamist movement, which emerged in the international atmosphere of 1970s Hijaz, developed a particularly alarmist discourse about external threats to the umma and the need for grassroots inter-Muslim assistance. Populist pan-Islamists benefited from Saudi funding through the MWL and worked with state actors when convenient, but they were essentially non-state actors unfettered by realpolitik. Instead they would pressure states into extending more support for Muslim causes around the world.

[4] Reinhard Schulze, *Islamischer Internationalismus im 20. Jahrhundert* (London: E. J. Brill, 1990), 123.

[5] For more on the OIC, see Naveed S. Sheikh, *The New Politics of Islam* (London: Routledge-Curzon, 2003); for the WML, see Schulze, *Islamischer Internationalismus*.

For the populist pan-Islamists, the notion of Muslim solidarity was intrinsically linked with Muslim suffering. Since their foundation, the international Islamic organisations therefore sought to spread awareness of the plight of Muslims around the world through publishing and the media. This concerted effort, combined with technological advances in printing and distribution, led to a proliferation in the late 1970s of Islamic publications reporting on the plight of Muslims around the world. In magazines such as *Akhbar al-Alam al-Islami* (News of the Muslim World) and *Majallat Rabitat al-Alam al-Islami* (Journal of the MWL), Muslims in Morocco could now read about the Muslim diaspora in the Balkans or the situation in Indonesia. The umma was becoming smaller.[6]

Pan-Islamism also took on a more political dimension in the course of the 1970s. With the exception of the support for Palestine, the early activities of the MWL and the OIC were apolitical and focused on humanitarian aid and disaster relief. This period therefore saw the establishment of numerous charities and development funds which worked to alleviate poverty and promote economic development in the Muslim world. From the late 1970s, however, apolitical issues gave way to politically grounded suffering such as war, oppression and discrimination. This is clear both from the agendas of OIC and MWL annual meetings and from the contents of MWL-sponsored magazines. Of course, in the pan-Islamist world-view, these predicaments were two sides of the same coin. Muslim solidarity therefore came to be used as justification for a range of different types of assistance, from development aid on the one hand to clandestine weapons shipments on the other.[7]

This process was helped by the precedent set by King Faisal's support for the Palestinian cause, which had been framed in pan-Islamist terms. In 1948, then Prince Faisal had supervised the setting up of a 'Committee for Aid to Palestine'. As King, he would generously fund the armed Palestinian struggle against Israel and direct most of Saudi Arabia's development aid to Israel's immediate neighbours and enemies. After the 1967 war, the Saudi government launched a number of domestic

[6] William Ochsenwald, 'Saudi Arabia and the Islamic Revival', *International Journal of Middle East Studies* 13, no. 3 (1981): 281.

[7] For the emergence of the Islamic charitable sector, see J. Millard Burr and Robert O. Collins, *Alms for Jihad* (Cambridge University Press, 2006); Jonathan Benthall, 'L'humanitarisme islamique', *Cultures et Conflits*, no. 60 (2005); Abdel-Rahman Ghandour, *Jihad humanitaire: Enquête sur les ONG islamiques* (Paris: Flammarion, 2002). For the politicisation of the MWL, see *qararat wa tawsiyat ahamm al-mu'tamarat allati 'aqadatha rabitat al-'alam al-islami* [Resolutions and Recommendations of the Most Important Conferences Organised by the Muslim World League] (Mecca: MWL, 1991).

initiatives to raise funds for the Palestinian cause. In December 1967, King Faisal notably established the 'Popular Committee for Aiding Martyrs' Families, Prisoners and Mujahidin of Palestine,' an organisation which exists to this day. The Committee, chaired then as it is today by Faisal's half-brother, Prince Salman, worked 'to offer all kinds of political, moral and material support to the Palestinian people'. In the 1970s and 1980s, the Committee would organise special fundraising campaigns and telethons, notably during regional crises such as the Israeli invasion of Lebanon in 1982 and the outbreak of the intifada in 1987. As we shall see below, many of the organisational structures and awareness-raising strategies pioneered in the late 1960s were reproduced in the 1980s and 1990s to muster support for other causes such as Afghanistan, Bosnia and Chechnya.[8]

The Saudi support for the Palestinian resistance was consistently justified and rationalised with reference to religion, and the government sought the approval of senior religious scholars for its policies. In late 1968, the Popular Committee asked Great Mufti Muhammad bin Ibrahim for a ruling on the issue of whether alms money collected in Saudi Arabia could be used to fund the Palestinian struggle. On 3 December 1968, the Mufti issued a fatwa authorising 'the use of part of the *zakah*, on the condition that it is the Government which supervises its expenditure, ... to purchase weapons for the *fida'in* who are fighting the Jewish enemies of God'. This ruling set an important precedent and contributed to a widening of the notion of charity to include private support for violent struggle.[9]

The late 1970s and early 1980s saw a securitisation of pan-Islamism. In February 1979 the newly established OIC-sponsored 'Islamic Institute of Defence Technology' (IIDT) in London organised the first 'Muslim security conference', which focused on 'ways and means to

[8] In 1968, the Committee launched a project called 'Riyal of Palestine' under the slogan 'Pay a Riyal, Save an Arab'. Another project was 'Record the Honour', a call for regular (subscribed) donations. The same year saw the launch of 'The Five Percent Palestinian Commitment Project', whereby Palestinians in Saudi Arabia committed to giving 5 per cent of their salary to the Popular Committee. This was followed in 1969 by 'The One Percent Project' which called on Saudis to donate 1 per cent of their salary to the Palestinian resistance. According to political economist Steffen Hertog, this 'jihad tax' represents the first and last government-proposed income taxation scheme in Saudi history. See Abd al-Rahim Mahmud Jamus, *al-lijan al-sha'biyya li-musa'adat mujahidiy filastin fi'l-mamlaka al-'arabiyya al-sa'udiyya* [The Popular Committees for the Support of Palestine's Mujahidin in the Kingdom of Saudi Arabia] (Riyadh: Darat al-Malik Abd al-Aziz, 2001), 26 and 34. For a bibliography of Saudi writings on the Palestinian issue, see *al-qadiyya al-filastiniyya bi-aqlam sa'udiyya* [The Palestinian Cause in Saudi Authors' Words] (Mecca: Umm al-Qura University, 2002).

[9] Jamus, *al-lijan al-sha'biyya*, 46 and 94.

strengthen the defence of the Islamic world'. The same year the IIDT began publishing a monthly magazine called *Islamic Defence Review*. In 1980, the OIC adopted a resolution entitled 'The Security of Muslim States and their Solidarity', which for the first time emphasised that 'the security of any Muslim state is a concern for all Muslim states', and the following year an 'Islamic security committee' was established within the OIC. Throughout the 1980s and 1990s the OIC expressed solidarity with a number of member states in conflict with non-Muslim states, most of which happened to be Christian: with Iran against the USA in 1980, with Lebanon against Israel in 1982, with the Comoros Islands against France throughout the 1980s, with Somalia against Ethiopia in 1984, with Azerbaijan against Armenia over Nagorno-Karabakh in 1988 and with Sudan against 'foreign designs' in 1991. In the cases of Afghanistan and Bosnia, of course, the OIC members would adopt measures that went far beyond verbal condemnation. Pan-Islamism was acquiring a military dimension.[10]

The securitisation of Islamic solidarity also manifested itself in Saudi Arabia. The late 1970s and 1980s were characterised by greater Saudi involvement in international political struggles pitting Muslims versus non-Muslims. For a start, the level of Saudi financial support for Muslims in conflict increased markedly from the late 1970s onward. In the late 1980s, spending on both Afghanistan and Palestine would increase considerably, despite a marked decrease in oil revenues in the same period (see Figures 1 and 2). Moreover, in the case of Afghanistan, Saudi support began to include military assistance (though support for Palestine remained purely financial). The Afghanistan war became the first foreign conflict since the 1948 and 1967 Arab–Israeli wars to see the personal military involvement of Saudi nationals (the Saudi military had dispatched small Army units to Jordan in 1948 and 1967). Finally, the geographical sphere of involvement expanded, from the Arab world in the early 1970s, via Central Asia in the 1980s, to Europe in the 1990s.[11]

The rise of populist pan-Islamism in the 1980s was above all a result of the accumulated propaganda effort of the international Islamic organisations, which had been working relentlessly since the 1970s to

[10] *Journal of the Muslim World League* 6, no. 4 (1979), 64 and 8, no. 4 (1981), 63; Mohammad El Sayed Selim, ed., *The Organisation of the Islamic Conference in a Changing World* (Cairo: Center for Political Research and Studies, 1994), 117 and 119.

[11] A military unit of 513 Saudis allegedly took part in the 1948 war for Palestine, 134 of whom 'fell as martyrs'; Jamus, *al-lijan al-sha'biyya*, 18. During the 1967 war, a Saudi brigade of 3,000 soldiers was sent to southern Jordan but did not fight; Vassiliev, *The History of Saudi Arabia*, 384.

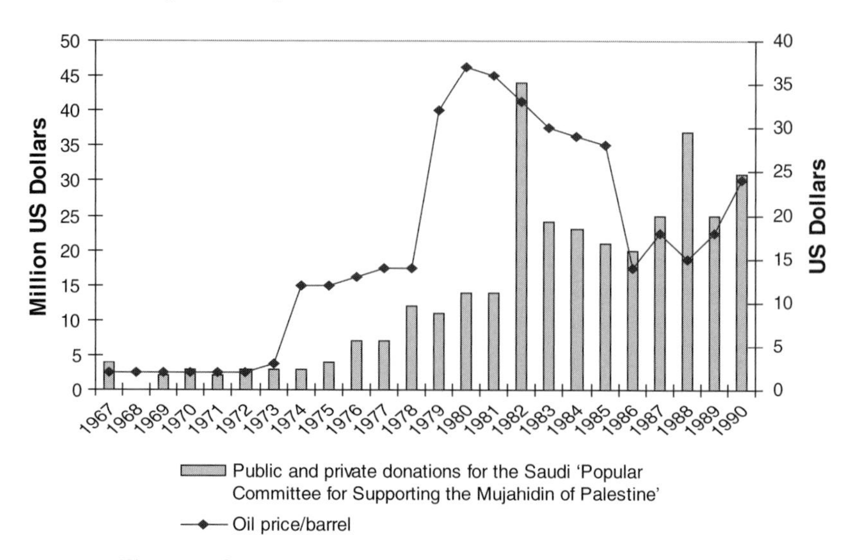

Figure 1: Saudi funding for Palestinian resistance compared with oil prices, 1967–90. Sources: Jamus, *al-lajan al-sha'biyya*, 56; BP Statistical Review of World Energy, June 2006

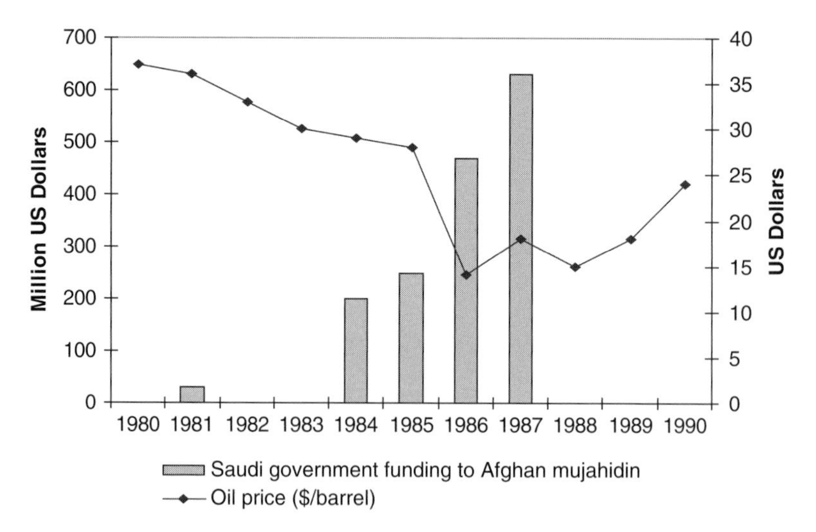

Figure 2: Saudi government funding of Afghan mujahidin compared with oil prices, 1980–90 (data lacking for 1982 and 1983). Sources: Steve Coll, *Ghost Wars* (New York: Penguin, 2004), 65, 102 and 151; BP Statistical Review of World Energy, June 2006

promote awareness of Muslim suffering around the world. A second factor was the de facto increase in the number of violent conflicts in the region, such as Afghanistan, the war in Lebanon and the Palestinian intifada. This gave the pan-Islamist frame more empirical credibility and thus more mobilising power. The spread of news media ensured that the same conflicts were visible to a larger number of people in Saudi Arabia. Yet another factor was the decline of the pan-Islamists' major ideological competitor, namely Arab nationalism. Pan-Arabism, having been discredited by the 1967 war, the Egyptian–Israeli peace treaty and the Lebanese civil war, left an ideological vacuum which could be filled by the pan-Islamists. This tendency was strengthened by the fact that many of the conflicts which preoccupied the Muslim world in the 1980s and early 1990s occurred in non-Arab countries such as Afghanistan, Bosnia and Chechnya.

Apart from factors specific to the Afghan jihad, which we shall examine below, two developments inspired a more active pan-Islamist policy on the part of the Saudi state in the 1980s. One was the rise of revolutionary Iran, which challenged Saudi Arabia for the leadership of the Muslim world and adopted a populist discourse deeply hostile to the United States, a key Saudi ally. The other factor was the decline in oil prices in the mid-1980s which triggered a serious economic crisis. The kingdom was notably forced to abandon the promise of guaranteed employment to university graduates, among other things.[12]

These developments challenged two key pillars of Saudi regime legitimacy, namely its religious integrity and the ability to provide economic welfare. Sensing these pressures, and noting the rise of the Sahwa movement in the late 1980s, the government came to see promotion of pan-Islamist causes as a useful way to deflect some of the internal domestic dissent. Diversionary politics is well known from other Muslim countries. In 1980s Algeria, for example, government spending on the religious sector increased markedly as GDP per capita went down. Populist pan-Islamism was thus to some extent Saudi Arabia's 'opium for the people'.[13]

[12] For the Saudi–Iranian cold war, see Jacob Goldberg, 'Saudi Arabia and the Iranian Revolution: The Religious Dimension', in *The Iranian Revolution and the Muslim World*, ed. David Menashri (Boulder, CO: Westview Press, 1990). For the economic decline, see e.g. Elaine Sciolino, 'In Saudi Oasis of Calm, Some See Seeds of Unrest', *New York Times*, 15 May 1985; and Robert Lacey, *Inside the Kingdom* (New York: Viking, 2009), chapter 10.

[13] For the rise of the Sahwa in the late 1980s, see Matrook Alfaleh, 'The Impact of the Processes of Modernization and Social Mobilization on the Social and Political Structures of the Arab Countries with Special Emphasis on Saudi Arabia' (Ph.D.

The rise of pan-Islamism in the 1980s coincided with the distinct process of social conservatisation of Saudi society. In the beginning of the decade, partly in response to the 1979 Juhayman incident, the regime decided to slow down the process of social liberalisation which had accompanied the 1970s oil boom. The state awarded the religious establishment significantly increased powers and budgets. The ulama, who had been pressuring for such a change for years, jumped at the opportunity to promote and reinforce the strict Wahhabi rules on ritual observance and moral behaviour more intensively than before. In the 1980s, therefore, Saudi Arabia was swept by a wave of social conservatism. Cinemas were closed, female news presenters were taken off the air and the religious police became more visible in cities across the country.[14]

However, the 'Wahhabisation' and the 'pan-Islamisation' of 1980 Saudi Arabia represented two distinct processes with different causes and results. While the first was a purely domestic process promoted by the Najdi Wahhabi ulama and resulting in social conservatism, the latter had international ramifications, was promoted by the Hijaz-based organisations such as the MWL and produced political radicalism. Nevertheless, both processes left more political space for Islamist activism of all kinds. The political opportunity structure for Islamist activists – especially those seeking to mobilise people for the jihad in Afghanistan – thus became highly beneficial.

The Afghan jihad and the Saudi state

The Soviet invasion of Afghanistan in 1979 led the transnational Islamic organisations to issue calls for jihad against the Soviet occupation. This gave the conflict a religious dimension which would mobilise colossal levels of state and non-state resources from the Muslim world in general and from Saudi Arabia in particular. With its involvement in Afghanistan, Saudi Arabia moved from a passive and financial to an active and military approach to pan-Islamism.[15]

The range and depth of Saudi support for the Afghan resistance was entirely unprecedented, and it exceeded even the assistance for

dissertation, University of Kansas, 1987), 176; and Lacroix, 'Les champs de la discorde', 327ff. For Algeria's diversionary policies, see Abdelaziz Testas, 'The Roots of Algeria's Ethnic and Religious Violence', *Studies in Conflict and Terrorism* 25 (2002).

[14] Gwenn Okruhlik, 'Networks of Dissent: Islamism and Reform in Saudi Arabia', *Current History* (2002); Michaela Prokop, 'Saudi Arabia: The Politics of Education', *International Affairs* 79, no. 1 (2003): 78; Tim Niblock, *Saudi Arabia: Power, Legitimacy and Survival* (London: Routledge, 2006), 83–5.

[15] Gilles Kepel, *Jihad: The Trail of Political Islam* (Cambridge, MA: Belknap, 2002), 136ff.

the Palestinians. The Saudi financial support to the Afghan mujahidin between 1984 and 1989 was larger than that provided to the PLO in any five-year period since the 1970s. The PLO received a total of SAR 3.72 billion (US$992 million) from the Saudi government in the fourteen-year period from 1978 to 1991, while the Afghan mujahidin received a total of at least SAR 6.75 billion (US$1.8 billion) in the three years from 1987 to 1989. The Saudi military support in Afghanistan was also more direct than it had been in Palestine. Saudi Arabia had funded many of PLO's weapons purchases, but the Palestinians never needed Saudi help for weapons procurement and they certainly did not need unfit Saudi volunteers. Saudi Arabia's alliance with the United States also made it politically difficult to send fighters to Palestine. Israel's borders were also notoriously difficult to penetrate for volunteer fighters, and after 1970, none of its neighbours provided a suitable base for infiltration. In Afghanistan, on the other hand, volunteerism was sanctioned by the USA, welcomed by the Afghans and facilitated by the presence of a transit territory, namely Pakistan. As a result, the Saudi state provided direct military and logistical support, and Saudi citizens took part in the fighting.[16]

In the early 1980s, the Saudi support was primarily diplomatic, political and humanitarian. Diplomatically, the Saudis worked through the OIC to ensure the isolation of the Kabul regime and to rally support behind the Afghan resistance. Politically, Riyadh exerted considerable pressure on the Afghan mujahidin factions to close ranks and insisted on unity as a condition for expanding aid. The Saudi government also provided a certain amount of financial aid, mainly to charities and to Abd (Rabb) al-Rasul Sayyaf's Ittihad party. The official Saudi aid in the first few years was channelled through two principal organisations: the Saudi Red Crescent and the 'Popular Committee for Fundraising'. The latter was set up in early 1980 under the chairmanship of Prince Salman on the model of the Popular Committee for Palestine. Later the same year the Popular Committee became the 'Saudi Relief Committee'. As early as May 1980, Foreign Minister Saud al-Faisal delivered a cheque of SAR 81.3 million (US$21.7 million) to the OIC to help Afghan refugees, and in July 1981 Prince Salman delivered an additional SAR 50 million (US$13.3 million) to Pakistan 'from the Saudi people'.[17]

However, the Saudi state support for the Afghan resistance did not reach significant proportions until the mid-1980s. Abdallah Azzam, the

[16] 'The Kingdom of Saudi Arabia's Economic and Social Development Aid.' These figures do not include private donations.

[17] William B. Quandt, *Saudi Arabia in the 1980s: Foreign Policy, Security and Oil* (Washington, DC: Brookings, 1981), 42; Steve Coll, *Ghost Wars: The Secret History of the*

main entrepreneur of the Arab mobilisation, later said that the Saudi government and its people were with the Afghan jihad only from 1983 onward. Why did support increase in the mid-1980s? An important part of the answer is to be found in American politics. In 1980 or 1981, the kingdom had pledged, at the request of the Americans, to match US congressional funding for the Afghan resistance. The two parties agreed to contribute equally to a CIA-administered fund destined for the Afghan mujahidin from 1982 onward. However, in 1984 and 1985 the amount of money allocated by the US Congress – and by extension also by Saudi Arabia – skyrocketed as the result of political developments in the domestic American arena. Without the American pressure and initiative, the Saudi involvement in Afghanistan would probably not have taken the proportions it did. The mid-1980s funding increase was not just a budget issue. It was also a clear political signal from Washington to use all means available to help the Afghan mujahidin.[18]

When discussing the Saudi support for the Afghan jihad, it is important not to view the sender and the recipient of this support as unitary actors. For a start, the Saudi government did not supervise and control the entire flow of money and volunteers emanating from Saudi Arabia. Much of the assistance came from semi-official organisations such as charities and religious organisations, as well as from private donors. In the mid- and late 1980s, a large number of Saudi charities were operating in Afghanistan and Pakistan. Many of them extended logistical and other services to combatants in addition to their humanitarian or missionary activities. For example, the MWL's representative in Peshawar from 1986 onward was none other than Wa'il Julaydan, a close friend of bin Ladin and early member of Abdallah Azzam's Services Bureau. The Saudi Red Crescent was part of the weapons pipeline – it maintained offices in the border regions partly to alleviate the cost of

CIA, Afghanistan and Bin Laden, from the Soviet Invasion to September 10, 2001 (New York: Penguin, 2004), 82–3; David Holden and Richard Johns, *The House of Saud* (London: Sidgwick & Jackson, 1981), 537; Barnett R. Rubin, *The Fragmentation of Afghanistan: State Formation and Collapse in the International System*, 2nd edn (New Haven, CT: Yale University Press, 2002), 193; Basil Muhammad, *al-ansar al-'arab fi afghanistan* [The Arab Supporters in Afghanistan], 2nd edn (Riyadh: Lajnat al-Birr al-Islamiyya, 1991), 37–8; 'Support for the Afghan Jihad Effort', *Journal of the Muslim World League* 7, no. 8 (1980), 60; 'Aid for Afghan Refugees', *Journal of the Muslim World League* 8, no. 10 (1981), 43.

[18] Bashir Abu Rumman and Abdallah Sa'id, *al-'alim wa'l-mujahid wa'l-shahid al-shaykh 'abdallah 'azzam* [The Scholar, Mujahid, Martyr and Sheikh Abdallah Azzam] (Amman: Dar al-Bashir, 1990), 84; Jonathan Randal, *Osama: The Making of a Terrorist* (New York: Vintage Books, 2004), 72; Coll, *Ghost Wars*, 81–2, 90–1, 102; George Crile, *Charlie Wilson's War* (New York: Grove, 2003), 238; Rubin, *The Fragmentation of Afghanistan*, 180, 196.

transporting weapons. On at least one occasion, ambulances were used to transport healthy fighters to and from the battlefront. This blurring of the lines between humanitarian and military assistance was an important corollary of the rise of militarised pan-Islamism in the 1980s and 1990s, and contributed to the view of participation in violent jihad as an act of charity. However, the degree of government control over the charitable sector was far from complete.[19]

A good example of the fluid nature of the early Saudi support is the role of Nasir al-Rashid, a senior official of the Saudi Red Crescent and one of the first Saudi aid workers in Afghanistan. In the autumn of 1981 or 1982, al-Rashid visited Afghan mujahidin camps and was appalled to find that thousands of fighters in the Warsak and Abu Bakr camps lacked blankets and tents for the winter. So he proceeded to buy the necessary equipment with his own private money. It is hard to categorise this kind of assistance as strictly official or non-official.[20]

The government of course had its own programmes and instruments for supporting the Afghan jihad. Saudi intelligence services cooperated closely with the CIA and allowed the latter to use Saudi territory as a transit point for weapons shipments to Pakistan. Saudi intelligence also operated independently from the Americans in Pakistan and Afghanistan. At the height of the Saudi involvement in Afghanistan, the Saudi intelligence director, Prince Turki al-Faisal, travelled to Pakistan up to five times a month. However, the vast majority of the official Saudi support for the Afghan jihad went to the Afghans, not the Arabs. There was of course a degree of contact and limited collaboration between Saudi officialdom and the Arab fighters. Prince Turki al-Faisal is known to have been in contact with Usama bin Ladin at the time, although the precise nature of their relationship remains unclear. Saudi diplomats and intelligence officials cooperated on an ad hoc basis with Abdallah Azzam's 'Services Bureau' (SB). Bin Ladin himself has described how the Saudi ambassador in Islamabad, Tawfiq al-Madar, helped him transport a bulldozer from Saudi Arabia to Pakistan in 1985. The bulldozer was later used for the construction of training camps in Afghanistan. Nevertheless, this support is negligible compared to the hundreds of millions of dollars provided by the Saudi government to the Afghan militias.[21]

19 Muhammad Amir Rana and Mubasher Bukhari, *Arabs in Afghan Jihad* (Lahore: Pak Institute for Peace Studies, 2007); Rubin, *The Fragmentation of Afghanistan*, 197 and 231; Muhammad, *al-ansar al-'arab*, 186; Coll, *Ghost Wars*, 86.

20 Abdallah Azzam, *ayat al-rahman fi jihad al-afghan* [Signs of the Merciful in the Afghan Jihad] (Amman: Maktabat al-Risala al-Haditha, 1986), 184; Jasir al-Jasir, '*qissat al-afghan al-sa'udiyyin*' [The Story of the Saudi Afghans]', *al-Majalla*, 11 May 1996: 20.

21 Mark Huband, *Warriors of the Prophet: The Struggle for Islam* (Boulder, CO: Westview, 1999), 10; Mohammad Yousaf and Mark Adkin, *Afghanistan: The Bear Trap*, 2nd edn

The precise division of labour between state, semi-state and non-state actors may not be crucial for our analysis. The key point is that the political opportunities for mobilisation were excellent. The state did not place any obstacles whatsoever in the way of those, like Abdallah Azzam and Usama bin Ladin, who sought to recruit Saudis for Afghanistan and raise funds for their activities. If anything, the state, or semi-governmental entities like the Muslim World League, actively encouraged the departure of Saudis to Afghanistan. Saudi Airlines famously gave a 75 per cent discount on flights to Peshawar in the late 1980s. The government-controlled media reported extensively from Afghanistan from the mid-1980s onward. State television would broadcast the Afghan mujahidin leader Sayyaf's lectures in Mina before the King during Hajj. Saudi newspapers reproduced statements and fatwas from religious scholars about Afghanistan, and some articles even reported the so-called *karamat* (miracles) of Arab martyrs fallen in battle in Afghanistan. The authorities also organised telethons to raise funds for Prince Salman's Committee for the Assistance of Afghan Mujahidin.[22]

Perhaps the only part of the Saudi state which was somewhat hesitant about encouraging young men to fight in Afghanistan was the religious establishment. A common misperception in the historiography of this period is to present the Wahhabi religious scholars as prime movers behind the mobilisation to Afghanistan. In fact, very few, if any, of the scholars in the religious establishment actively promoted the Afghan jihad as an individual duty (*fard 'ayn*) for Saudis. The majority of ulama viewed the jihad as a collective duty (*fard kifaya*) and were anxious to ensure that the resources and personnel devoted to the Afghan cause went to people and organisations with a sound doctrinal orientation. The Saudi government's insistence on funding the Saudi-trained but politically marginal Sayyaf, as opposed to other more politically legitimate parts of the Afghan resistance, was an implicit concession to the religious establishment. In the late 1980s, concerns over doctrine led to a divergence in the respective funding preferences of the scholars and

(Barnsley: Leo Cooper, 2001), 100; Coll, *Ghost Wars*, 82, 86–7; Jamal Khashoggi, 'Kingdom Has Big Role to Play in Afghanistan's Reconstruction: Prince Turki', *Arab News*, 9 November 2001; Jamal Khashoggi, 'Osama Offered to Form Army to Challenge Saddam's Forces: Turki', *Arab News*, 7 November 2001; Muhammad, *al-ansar al-'arab*, 87.

[22] Huband, *Warriors of the Prophet*, 3; *al-Quds al-Arabi*, 20 March 2005; Fathi al-Zubaydi, *al-jihad al-afghani fi'l-kitabat al-'arabiyya al-mu'asira* [The Afghan Jihad in Contemporary Arab Writings] (Damascus: Dar al-Ma'rifa, 1996); Muhammad, *al-ansar al-'arab*, 46; Salih al-Wardani, *fuqaha' al-naft: rayat al-islam am rayat al sa'ud?* [Oil Scholars: The Banner of Islam or the Banner of the Al Saud?] (Cairo: al-Madbuli al-Saghir), 87–94; Coll, *Ghost Wars*, 84.

the government. While Saudi intelligence favoured Sayyaf, the Wahhabi establishment endorsed the more socially conservative Jamil al-Rahman and his community in Kunar (see below).[23]

The broader Islamist community, notably the Sahwa, was also sceptical about Saudis going to Afghanistan to fight. The Sahwa's opposition was based on two arguments: first, that the Afghan resistance was not doctrinally pure, and second, that the struggle benefited American interests. Among the most prominent sceptics was Safar al-Hawali, who criticised Abdallah Azzam in a famous lecture entitled 'The Concept of Jihad'. Al-Hawali's position subsequently earned him the scorn of prominent jihadist ideologues such as the Egyptian Abd al-Qadir bin Abd al-Aziz (in the early 1990s) and Yusuf al-Uyayri (in 2003). The other Sahwist icon, Salman al-Awda, was less outspoken, but in 2004 he would point to his opposition to Saudi involvement in 1980s Afghanistan to dismiss accusations that he was inciting Saudis to fight in Iraq. Yet another public critic of the Arab Afghan involvement was Muhammad al-Munajjid, a prominent religious figure in the Eastern Province.[24]

Nevertheless, in the second half of the 1980s, as the Afghan cause gained popularity, very few mainstream scholars would publicly rule against going to Afghanistan. Most ulama in Saudi Arabia and elsewhere adopted a rather vague position. For example, the leading Saudi scholar Sheikh Abd al-Aziz bin Baz ruled that 'helping and aiding our fighting and exiled Afghan brothers is an individual duty on Muslims today, financially and physically or one of the two according to one's capability'. At first sight the fatwa looks clear – but on closer inspection it does not say that all Muslims should fight in Afghanistan. Most Saudi sources interviewed by this author agree that Bin Baz never declared the jihad in Afghanistan to be an individual duty for all Muslims.[25]

Looking back on the 1980s, Saudi officials have insisted that they only responded to popular demand for action in Afghanistan. In a 2001 interview, Prince Turki al-Faisal said the government had no

[23] Rubin, *The Fragmentation of Afghanistan*, 195 and 199; Coll, *Ghost Wars*, 83; Rubin, *The Fragmentation of Afghanistan*, 242 and 261.

[24] Author's interview with Nasir al-Barrak; author's interview with Yusuf al-Dayni, Jidda, April 2004; Safar al-Hawali, '*mafhum al-jihad* [The Concept of Jihad]' (www.alhawali.com, 1989); Abd al-Qadir bin Abd al-Aziz, '*radd kalam al-hawali fi kitab al-difa*' [Response to Hawali's Talk on the Book 'The Defence' (of Muslim Lands)]' (www.tawhed.ws, dated 1990); Yusuf al-Uyayri, '*al-hamla al-'alamiyya li-muqawamat al-'udwan* [The Global Campaign of Resistance to Aggression]' (www.tawhed.ws, 2003); Salman al-Awda, '*ya ibn (al-watan) la taftari 'ala ahlak* [Oh Son of the Nation, Do Not Bring Calumny on your People]' (www.islamtoday.net, 2004).

[25] *al-Jihad*, no. 22 (September 1986): 25; and Muhammad, *al-ansar al-'arab*, 74.

choice but to support the Saudi volunteers. He said it would have been a 'grave mistake' for any Arab state to have prevented volunteers from doing their 'sacred duty' in Afghanistan, because 'for the first time in many years, many Muslims were doing something against an invader and appearing to be succeeding'. Prince Turki's advisor Jamal Khashoggi has said that 'it was the right thing for Saudi Arabia to send Jihadis to Afghanistan. All Saudi Jihadis came back in 1992. They were nice people.'[26]

These statements gloss over the fact that the government instrumentalised pan-Islamism for domestic and foreign political gain. The Afghan jihad constituted a golden opportunity for Saudi Arabia to consolidate its image as the champion of Islamic causes and liberator of Muslim territory. The kingdom's pan-Islamic offensive thus gave the regime a momentary legitimacy boost. However, it also set in motion the powerful forces of extreme pan-Islamism, which would soon prove to be a potent tool in the hands of the domestic Saudi opposition.

Pan-Islamist bidding games

The fortunes of the Saudi government were reversed on 2 August 1990 by Saddam Hussain's invasion of Kuwait. The perceived Iraqi threat to Saudi oil fields led King Fahd to authorise the deployment of American troops on Saudi soil, a decision which seriously undermined the kingdom's pan-Islamist credentials, because the Arabian Peninsula enjoys a special and sacred status in Islam as the 'Land of the Two Sanctuaries', a reference to the holy cities of Mecca and Medina.[27]

In the autumn of 1990, as the crisis escalated and American soldiers poured into the kingdom, the government did its best to frame the conflict with Iraq in pan-Islamist terms, and to mobilise both domestic and foreign Muslim support 'in defence of Islam's Holy Places'. Saudi Arabia invited military forces from as many Muslim allies as possible to come and fight under Saudi command – a request met by twenty-four countries from West Africa to South Asia. The government also launched an entirely unprecedented civil defence mobilisation effort. Recruitment centres were set up across the country and volunteers were given uniforms and training – boot camps for men and nursing courses for women. To boost patriotism, the Saudi press wrote about the overwhelming popular response to the call for

[26] Khashoggi, 'Osama Offered to Form Army'; al-Rasheed, *Contesting the Saudi State*, 102.

[27] Bernard Lewis, 'License to Kill: Usama Bin Ladin's Declaration of Jihad', *Foreign Affairs* 77, no. 6 (1998).

homeland defence, while describing in detail the atrocities of the evil Iraqi forces to the north.[28]

But the authorities were fighting an uphill ideological battle. Most Saudis were sceptical about the arrival of the US troops and many believed Saddam's invasion had been staged by the Americans to provide an excuse to invade the region. In Islamist communities inside and outside the kingdom, the Saudi decision to call for US support was met with wild condemnation. This was not surprising, because there was already considerable resentment towards the Western presence in Saudi Arabia prior to the deployment. Most Islamists saw the arrival of American troops as a defilement of holy land and an affront to the Prophet's alleged deathbed wish that 'there should not be two religions on the Arabian Peninsula'. For many, the intrusion of 'Crusaders' was far more serious than the threat represented by Saddam Hussain. In Saudi Arabia, none reacted more strongly to the deployment of US forces than the Sahwa, the moderate Islamist opposition movement that had been gaining strength through the 1970s and 1980s and that was now ready to confront the regime politically.[29]

One of the most hard-hitting criticisms of the US military presence was articulated by Safar al-Hawali in his book *Revealing the Sorrow to the Scholars of the Nation* (also known as *Kissinger's Promise*). Al-Hawali's book, which was based on a compilation of lectures held in the autumn of 1990, and which was styled as an open letter to the country's most senior scholar Abd al-Aziz Bin Baz, became extremely popular inside and outside Saudi Arabia. *Revealing the Sorrow* was essentially a geopolitical analysis of the causes and implications of the Gulf war. Al-Hawali argued that America had orchestrated the Gulf war in order to secure a military presence on the Arabian Peninsula, humiliate Islam and crush the Islamic movement. In al-Hawali's view, the US policy was clearly intended to control Saudi territory:

> It is clear to you that the calumny which has befallen the umma will not be forgotten by history until the day of judgement. It began with the Iraqi Baathist army's invasion of Kuwait, then the invitation of the Christian Western nations and their followers to the whole region, and the deployment of tens of thousands of American troops in Riyadh, Jidda, Ta'if, Yanbu and Asir, rather

[28] Alan Munro, *An Embassy at War: Politics and Diplomacy behind the Gulf War* (London: Brassey's, 1996), 131–2.

[29] For Islamist reactions to the arrival of US forces, see James P. Piscatori, 'Religion and Realpolitik: Islamic Responses to the Gulf War', in *Islamic Fundamentalisms and the Gulf Crisis*, ed. J. P. Piscatori (University of Chicago Press, 1991); and Maha Azzam, 'The Gulf Crisis: Perceptions in the Muslim World', *International Affairs* 67, no. 3 (1991). For 1980s anti-Americanism, see Sciolino, 'In Saudi Oasis of Calm, Some See Seeds of Unrest'.

than the Eastern and Northern provinces, and the encirclement of all the seashores of the Arabian Peninsula under the pretext of the economic blockade on Iraq.[30]

Al-Hawali's analysis was articulated in explicit pan-Islamist discourse. It emphasised the territorial infringement committed by non-Muslim forces and stressed that the issue concerned the entire Muslim nation. He spoke of an 'occupation' of the Arabian Peninsula by 'Crusaders' who wanted to 'steal the resources' of the Muslim nation. The book was also very anti-American and reminded the reader that 'the West is our enemy from now till the day of judgement'.[31]

However, the Sahwists' use of pan-Islamist discourse was instrumentalist. The core of the Sahwa's agenda was internal political reform, as was made clear in the movement's two main petitions, namely the *Letter of Demands* and the *Memorandum of Advice*. By criticising the government's failure to protect the Arabian Peninsula and deploring the situation in Bosnia, the reformists tapped into the reservoir of popular pan-Islamism and used it in their confrontation with the government. For the Sahwa, the issue of the US troops was thus primarily a symbolic cause. The Sahwist critique nevertheless represented a severe challenge to the regime's credibility as a champion of Islamic causes. The political capital acquired through the support for the Afghan jihad had been swept away in a matter of months.[32]

What the Sahwa did was essentially to contest the very same source of legitimacy which had benefited the state in the late 1980s, namely pan-Islamism. The regime now found itself accused of betraying the umma: how could the King aspire to the role of the liberator of Muslim territory when his own country was flooded with American soldiers? The challenge from the Sahwa forced the government to look for ways to compensate for the credibility lost by emphasising other Islamic causes. In 1992, a new opportunity for displays of pan-Islamic solidarity would arise in the least likely of places: Eastern Europe.

The Bosnian war, which pitted Bosnian Muslims against Bosnian Serbs (and temporarily against Bosnian Croats) between March 1992 and November 1995, was a complex conflict in which religion was

[30] Safar al-Hawali, *kashf al-ghumma 'an 'ulama al-umma* [Revealing the Sorrow to the Scholars of the Nation] (Riyadh: Dar al-Hikma, 1991), 7. For more on the Sahwist criticism, see Fandy, *Saudi Arabia and the Politics of Dissent*, 67ff.

[31] al-Hawali, *kashf al-ghumma*, 21 and passim; al-Hawali, quoted in Khalid Bin Sayeed, *Western Dominance and Political Islam* (Albany: State University of New York Press, 1995), 86.

[32] For details of the Sahwa's programme of domestic reform, see Lacroix, 'Les champs de la discorde', 410ff.

arguably more important as an identity marker than a driving force. However, pan-Islamists in the Arab world saw the conflict in simplistic terms as a war of aggression by Christian Serbs against oppressed Muslims. Thus the 'Bosnian jihad' became the first major pan-Islamic battleground after the Afghan jihad and the new destination of choice for large numbers of Arab volunteer fighters. As such, it was also the first opportunity for the Saudi state to regain some of the pan-Islamist credibility lost in the Gulf crisis.

However, Bosnia was not an easy place to mount an international jihad effort. For a start, the international community no longer welcomed the participation of Arab Islamists, who had acquired a bad reputation in early 1990s Egypt and Algeria. Moreover, Bosnian Muslims were more secular and less connected with the Arab world than the Afghans and Pakistanis. In addition, there was no neighbouring country to provide strategic depth for the jihad effort, as Pakistan had done for Afghanistan. Finally, while Afghanistan had been a 'free zone' ungoverned by the minutiae of international law, the Bosnian conflict was handled from an early stage within a UN framework and eventually with NATO involvement. All these factors restricted the ability of foreign jihadists to establish a sizeable infrastructure in Bosnia, and limited the range of support that the Saudi government could extend to the Bosnians.

Inside Saudi Arabia, on the other hand, there was ample opportunity for private recruitment and fundraising for Bosnia. The regime was blowing the pan-Islamist trumpet more than perhaps ever before, because it was facing both international and domestic competition over the championship of pan-Islamic causes.

At home, the Sahwa was questioning the regime's pan-Islamic credentials and presenting itself as a more legitimate and sincere defender of the Land of the Two Sanctuaries. The Sahwa was a very vocal supporter of the Bosnian jihad. In the summer of 1993, Sahwist scholars signed a collective statement which implicitly denounced the government for not providing enough support for the Bosnian cause.[33]

Internationally, countries like Sudan and Iran were also trying to exploit the Bosnian crisis for regional political gain. In April 1991, following the Gulf war, the Sudanese Islamist Hasan al-Turabi created the Popular Arab and Islamic Conference (PAIC) as a countermovement to the OIC, which he accused of representing the 'Islam of the Wealthy'. The PAIC was quick to declare support for the Bosnian Muslims, and Sudan's open-door policy for Arabs allowed militant Islamist networks

[33] *al-Jazira al-Arabiya*, no. 31 (August 1993): 9, cited in Stéphane Lacroix, 'Les islamistes saoudiens', unpublished book manuscript.

to run operations in Bosnia from Sudan. Iran had long-standing links with Bosnian political leaders and was the first Muslim state to provide substantial material support for Bosnia. In the mid-1990s, a war of words erupted between Saudi Arabia and Iran over who provided the most aid to Bosnia. According to one Saudi official, Tehran had 'the loudest mouth' but did not contribute nearly as much money to the Muslim cause as Riyadh.[34]

The official Saudi support for the Bosnian cause followed a tried and tested pattern. Saudi Arabia used the OIC to rally support for the Bosnian cause, and to push for UN sanctions against Serbia and a lifting of the arms embargo on Bosnia. The kingdom also urged its American ally to get more directly involved in the defence of the Muslims in Bosnia. The next step was the establishment of a fundraising committee chaired by Prince Salman. On 5 June 1992, the government set up the 'High Committee for Fundraising to the Muslims of Bosnia-Herzegovina' which incorporated a number of local branches known as 'People's Committees'.[35]

The Saudi government also ran a sustained media campaign to raise funds and public awareness about Bosnia. The Saudi Ministry of Information organised trips for Saudi journalists to Sarajevo, as well as a series of extensively advertised telethons featuring senior religious figures and members of the royal family. Many of the symbolic displays of Islamic solidarity used during the Afghan jihad were repeated. The kingdom sponsored pilgrimage travel and organised Id celebrations for Bosnian Muslims, just as it had done for Afghan refugees during the 1980s. In 1993, the President of Bosnia-Herzegovina, Ali Izetbegovich, was awarded the King Faisal International Prize for service to Islam, just as Abd (Rabb) al-Rasul Sayyaf had been in 1985. Several Saudis and veteran expatriates interviewed by this author have insisted that

[34] For more on the PAIC, see Abdullahi A. Gallab, *The First Islamist Republic: Development and Disintegration of Islamism in the Sudan* (Burlington: Ashgate, 2008), 125–6. For Iranian and Saudi funding, see Evan F. Kohlmann, *Al-Qaida's Jihad in Europe: The Afghan–Bosnian Network* (London: Berg, 2004), 45; John Pomfret, 'How Bosnia's Muslims Dodged the Arms Embargo', *Washington Post*, 22 September 1996; Ann Devroy, 'Internal US Probe Faults Policy on Bosnian Arms', *Washington Post*, 16 April 1996; Michael Dobbs, 'Saudis Funded Weapons for Bosnia, Official Says', *Washington Post*, 2 February 1996.

[35] Selim, ed., *The Organisation of the Islamic Conference*, 121–3; Dobbs, 'Saudis Funded Weapons'; Ziyad Salih al-Hadhlul and Muhammad Abdallah al-Humaydhi, *al-qissa al-kamila li'l-dawr al-sa'udi fi'l-busna wa'l-harsak* [The Full Story of the Saudi Role in Bosnia-Herzegovina] (Riyadh: Al-Homaidhi Printing Press, 1998), 165–95; *ukhuwwat al-islam: al-mamlaka al-'arabiyya al-sa'udiyya wa muslimu al-busna wa'l-harsak* [Brotherhood of Islam: The Kingdom of Saudi Arabia and the Muslims of Bosnia-Herzegovina], (London: Al-Hani International Books, 1993), 29.

the Bosnian jihad was even more visible in the public sphere than the Afghan jihad had been in the 1980s.[36]

A good measure of the scope and impact of the media campaign is the amount of money raised for the Bosnian cause. By its own figures, the High Commission had collected an astonishing SAR 1.4 billion (US$373 million) from public and private donors between 1992 and 1997. No other international cause has ever solicited a similar level of popular Saudi donations in such a short space of time. By comparison, Saudi donations to the Popular Committee for Palestine during the entire fourteen-year period from 1978 to 1991 amounted to a 'mere' SAR 850 million (US$227 million). The bidding game between the state and the Sahwa had brought popular pan-Islamist fervour to unprecedented heights. As a former Arab fighter in Bosnia later said, 'all of Saudi Arabia, starting with the government, the religious scholars, and the ordinary people, was on the side of driving the youths towards jihad in Bosnia-Herzegovina.'[37]

The level and nature of the material government support for Bosnia are difficult to assess because, as in Afghanistan, there was not always a clear division between state and private actors. There is evidence that the Saudi state provided direct military assistance to the Bosnian authorities. In February 1996, the *Washington Post* cited high-level Saudi sources as saying that the Saudi government had funded a US$300 million covert operation to channel weapons to Bosnia with the knowledge and tacit cooperation of the United States.[38]

However, most of the Saudi military assistance went to the Bosnian army, not to the foreign fighters. Moreover, the Saudi government took a number of measures in 1993 to keep the financial support for the Bosnian jihad under state supervision. It imposed restrictions on overseas wire transfers and closed the Jidda office of the Islamic Benevolence Committee (IBC), a self-declared charity which operated as the 'Services Bureau' of the Arab fighters in Bosnia. As a result, the Saudi state found itself under frequent criticism from the jihadist community for

[36] al-Hadhlul and al-Humaydhi, *al-qissa al-kamila*, 391; author's interviews with various Saudis and Western expatriates, Riyadh, January 2007.

[37] al-Hadhlul and al-Humaydhi, *al-qissa al-kamila*, 185; 'The Kingdom of Saudi Arabia's Economic and Social Development Aid'; *al-Quds al-Arabi*, 2 April 2005. The Saudi figures are credible because a 2003 German Police Investigation documented that Prince Salman transferred a total of over US$120 million to the Austrian bank account of the Third World Relief Agency between July 1992 and November 1995; see Federal Office of Criminal Investigation, *Expert Report Concerning the Area Financial Investigation*, 28 August 2003 (available at www.nytimes.com).

[38] Dobbs, 'Saudis Funded Weapons'; Irwin Molotsky, 'US Linked to Saudi Aid for Bosnians', *New York Times*, 2 February 1996; Stephen Engelberg, 'US Denies Aiding Saudis in Arming the Bosnians', *New York Times*, 3 February 1996.

not doing enough for Bosnia. The Arabs in Bosnia themselves lambasted the kingdom for not supporting the Arab mujahidin and for channelling funds to international agencies or shared reconstruction projects instead. Usama bin Ladin issued a special statement in August 1995 complaining about government restrictions on private support for the Bosnian jihad.[39]

In order to fend off criticism from the Islamist community, the government did its best to publicise its contributions to the Bosnian cause. In 1998, for example, it sponsored the publication of a 740-page book entitled *The Full Story of the Saudi Role in Bosnia-Herzegovina*. This expensively bound work listed the contributions of the Saudi government, particularly the royal family, to the Bosnian jihad. However, the Saudi government's public displays of pan-Islamic solidarity did not impress the jihadists. In his 1995 statement, Usama bin Ladin quite accurately observed that 'the King is attempting to escape from the internal facts by drawing attention away from his problems to those going on outside the country. He is creating a diversion, tickling the nation's emotions by raising the slogan of the support for Bosnia Herzegovina.'[40]

The increasing restrictions on private support for the Arab mujahidin in Bosnia were part of a gradual re-evaluation of government policy towards the jihadist community which would culminate in a clean break in late 1995. In the early 1990s, the regime had begun to realise that jihadists were uncontrollable and represented a threat to international and domestic stability. Atrocities in Algeria, Egypt and Bosnia as well as the 1993 attack on the World Trade Center in New York had illustrated the threat posed by the so-called Arab Afghans. Moreover, the Saudi government strongly resented the fact that many of the biggest recipients of Saudi financial support over the years, such as Palestinian and Afghan Islamists, publicly criticised the kingdom for its handling of the Gulf crisis in 1990.

The Saudi government's strategy was to promote pan-Islamism for political purposes while trying to keep the Saudi assistance to Bosnia under state control. The problem was that the state's hands were tied by the arms embargo and the reluctance of the international community to intervene. With no official military option on the table, the state

[39] Steve Coll and Steve LeVine, 'Global Network Provides Money, Haven', *Washington Post*, 3 August 1993; Sam Roe, Laurie Cohen and Stephen Franklin, 'How Saudi Wealth Fuelled Holy War', *Chicago Tribune*, 22 February 2004; 'Interview with Sheikh al-Mujahideen Abu Abdel Aziz', *al-Sirat al-Mustaqeem*, no. 33 (1994); Usama bin Ladin, '*ma'sat al-busna wa khida' khadim al-haramayn* [The Bosnia Tragedy and the Treason of the Custodian of the Two Holy Mosques]' (Statement no. 18 from the Advice and Reform Committee, 1995).

[40] al-Hadhlul and al-Humaydhi, *al-qissa al-kamila*; Bin Ladin, '*ma'sat al-busna*'.

found itself caught between its own lofty promises and the demands of the Islamist community.

The rise of pan-Islamism in the 1980s and early 1990s created a very beneficial political opportunity structure for actors seeking to mobilise Saudis to jihadist activism abroad. Classical jihadism became socially accepted in the kingdom, not as a result of Wahhabism or an inherent Saudi radicalism, but rather of historically specific political processes. State populism and bidding games led to growing popular support for militarised pan-Islamism, which in turn produced a political climate where participation in resistance struggles abroad came to be considered as altruism. Herein lies the key to understanding Saudi Arabia's historically ambiguous relationship with Islamist violence, a relationship which at times produced what Daniel Byman and others would call 'passive sponsorship of terrorism'.[41]

Despite the end of direct official support for jihadist causes in the mid-1990s, private support for such causes continued. Pan-Islamism could not be ruled out by decree – it would remain a very strong force in Saudi politics for years to come. As a result, the state's ability to crack down on jihadist support networks in the kingdom would remain restricted. For example, authorities could not easily arrest people involved in fundraising for Chechnya in the late 1990s, because most Saudis viewed this sort of activity as charity, not terrorism. After 9/11 this reluctance would become a major source of friction between the United States and Saudi Arabia. It was not until after the outbreak of the QAP campaign in 2003 that the Saudi regime dared take measures that ran counter to pan-Islamist sentiment. However, by that time, the Saudi jihadist movement had exploited the beneficial opportunity structure to grow remarkably strong.[42]

[41] Daniel Byman, *Deadly Connections: States that Sponsor Terrorism* (Cambridge University Press, 2005), 223–8.

[42] Gawdat Bahgat, 'Saudi Arabia and the War on Terrorism', *Arab Studies Quarterly* 26, no. 1 (2004): 51–63; F. Gregory Gause, 'Saudi Arabia and the War on Terrorism', in *A Practical Guide to Winning the War on Terrorism*, ed. Adam Garfinkel (Stanford: Hoover Press, 2004), 94–100; Roger Hardy, 'Ambivalent Ally: Saudi Arabia and the "War on Terror"', in *Kingdom without Borders: Saudi Arabia's Political, Religious and Media Frontiers*, ed. Madawi Al-Rasheed (New York: Columbia University Press, 2008), 99–112.

2 The classical jihadists

> When I wrote this text, it did not cross my mind that it might bring about such a great revolution, so that our numbers would increase close to tenfold.
>
> Abdallah Azzam, preface to the 2nd edition of *Join the Caravan*, 1988

One of the most remarkable aspects about the Saudi jihadist movement was the speed at which it formed. In the early 1980s, there was no sizeable community of militant Sunni Islamists in the kingdom. Juhayman and his rebels had represented a small and exceptional phenomenon in the Saudi political landscape. By the mid-1990s, there were thousands of Saudi veterans of the Afghan, Bosnian and Chechen battlefronts. How did this mobilisation come about?

Afghanistan, cradle of the jihadist movement

The Saudi jihadist movement was born in Afghanistan in the 1980s. It was here that the personal connections, organisational structures and internal culture that would later shape its evolution were created. But why and how exactly did Arabs get involved? Clearly it was not an automatic response to the Soviet invasion, because Arabs had not volunteered for other conflict zones in the past and did not go to Afghanistan in significant numbers until the mid- to late 1980s.

Interestingly, many Islamists and officials today contend that the Arab mobilisation for Afghanistan was massive and immediate; that thousands of volunteer fighters travelled for Afghanistan within months of the invasion. This is in stark contrast to the historical evidence from the early 1980s, which strongly suggests only a few tens of fighters made it to Afghanistan before 1984. It would seem that the collective Muslim memory of the Afghan jihad has been retroactively constructed to fit the idealised notion of a spontaneous rise of the Muslim nation. For state officials, this myth has the additional benefit of exonerating governments from responsibility for the Arab Afghan phenomenon. In reality, Arabs did not rise at once to liberate Afghanistan; their involvement came about in a much less romantic fashion.[1]

The story of the Arab mobilisation for Afghanistan began in November 1980, when the Supreme Guide of the Egyptian Muslim Brotherhood (MB) dispatched an envoy named Kamal al-Sananiri, a brother-in-law of Sayyid Qutb, on a forty-day trip to Pakistan to assess the state of the Afghan jihad and consider the scope for involvement. In this period, part of the Muslim Brotherhood was promoting a pan-Islamist agenda, and the Egyptian branch had long-standing connections with Afghan Islamists who had studied in Cairo's famous al-Azhar University. Around September 1981, on the way home to Egypt to bring his family to Pakistan, al-Sananiri stopped over in Saudi Arabia for the pilgrimage. In Mecca, he stumbled upon a Jordanian-Palestinian friend and fellow Muslim Brother named Abdallah Azzam. Al-Sananiri told Azzam about the situation in Afghanistan and convinced the latter to travel with him to Islamabad once he had picked up his family in Egypt. However, September 1981 was not a good time to be an Islamist in Egypt. Al-Sananiri was caught in the massive police crackdown which struck the Islamist community that month and allegedly died from torture in prison. However, Azzam kept his part of the deal and travelled to Islamabad on his own in late 1981. Abdallah Azzam would become the single most important individual behind the mobilisation of Arab volunteers for Afghanistan.[2]

[1] In an October 1983 interview, the Afghan commander Abd Rabb al-Rasul Sayyaf said of the Arab presence: 'If we consider the participation of two or three [Arabs] a year, then maybe they are participating; and if we do not take this number into consideration, then they are not participating', see *Majallat al-Da'wa*, 19 October 1983. In 1984, Abdallah Azzam wrote: 'no more than a tiny negligible number of non-Afghans have entered the battlefield. As for those who have continued into battle, they are fewer than the fingers of two hands.' See Azzam, *ayat al-rahman*, 185. Saudi officials have claimed, based on an alleged count of exit visas, that around 1,000 Saudis travelled to Pakistan in 1980 (see Lacey, *Inside the Kingdom*, chapter 13). However, this figure means little until we know how many Saudis used to go to Pakistan before the invasion, and how many of the 1,000 were fighters, as opposed to humanitarian workers and preachers. In researching this book I collected all the names of Saudi volunteer fighters from the 1980s I could find – 113 in total – and only a tiny fraction of these went before 1984. There is no reason why the earliest fighters should simply disappear from the historical record – if anything they should be more visible because they were pioneers.

[2] Muhammad, *al-ansar al-'arab*, 39; Ayman al-Zawahiri, '*fursan taht rayat al-nabi* [Knights under the Prophet's Banner]', *al-Sharq al-Awsat*, 2–12 December 2001; author's interview with Hudhayfa Azzam, Amman, September 2006. Kamal al-Sananiri was married to Sayyid Qutb's sister Amina. He had been arrested in Nasser's crackdown on the Muslim Brotherhood in 1954 and spent the following twenty years in prison; see John Calvert, *Sayyid Qutb and the Origins of Radical Islamism* (London: Hurst, forthcoming), conclusion.

The chance encounter between Azzam and al-Sananiri may constitute one of history's great accidents, but it also illustrates the crucial role of Muslim Brotherhood networks in the Arab mobilisation for Afghanistan. Muslim Brothers served as the main interface between the Arab world and the Afghan mujahidin in the early 1980s. For example, in 1983, when Afghan mujahidin leaders, having failed to agree on the leadership of a political union, delegated the appointment of a leader to a committee of seventeen Arab scholars, the majority of the committee members were MB figures. The Brotherhood also exercised influence through the international Islamic organisations such as the Muslim World League, where they were well represented owing to the influx to the Hijaz of Egyptian and Syrian Muslim Brothers fleeing persecution in the 1950s and 1960s. The MWL was present in Pakistan from 1981 onward and would come to play an important role in the mobilisation. Perhaps most telling of all is the fact that the MWL paid Abdallah Azzam's salary at the International Islamic University in Islamabad from his arrival in 1981 until he left the position in 1986.[3]

The first Saudi involvement in Afghanistan came through the MWL and the MB. Because the Muslim Brotherhood influence in Saudi Arabia was greatest in the Hijaz, and especially in Medina, the mobilisation for Afghanistan started here. The first 'Saudi Afghans' were aid workers from the Saudi Red Crescent and the Saudi Relief Committee who went in 1980. Then, in 1981, began the arrival of envoys of the Muslim World League in Jidda and students and staff from the University of Medina. Afghan mujahidin leaders – especially Abd (Rabb) al-Rasul Sayyaf – would stay in the region and socialise there during their visits to the kingdom. However, the Saudis who went between 1981 and 1984 were mostly aid workers and administrators. The military involvement came later and was above all the result of the entrepreneurship of Abdallah Azzam.[4]

The Palestinian-born and al-Azhar-trained sheikh Abdallah Azzam had risen to prominence in the Jordanian Muslim Brotherhood in the 1970s, acquiring the nickname of 'the Sayyid Qutb of Jordan'. After losing his university post for political reasons in early 1981, he emigrated to Saudi Arabia, where he took up a position at King Abd al-Aziz University in Jidda the same spring. However, only half a year later he met

[3] Muhammad, *al-ansar al-'arab*; Muhammad al-Majdhub, *ma' al-mujahidin wa'l-muhajirin fi bakistan* [With the Mujahidin and the Emigrants in Pakistan], 1st edn (Medina: Nadi al-Madina al-Munawwara al-Adabi, 1984); author's interview with Jamal Isma'il, Islamabad, March 2008; Gilles Kepel, *The War for Muslim Minds: Islam and the West* (Cambridge, MA: Belknap, 2004), 174–6.

[4] Author's interview with Yusuf al-Dayni; al-Jasir, '*qissat al-afghan al-sa'udiyyin*', 20.

al-Sananiri and towards the end of the year he was on a plane to Islamabad, where he would take up a job at the newly founded International Islamic University with a salary from the Muslim World League. Over the following three years, Azzam divided his time between his teaching duties, inter-Afghan diplomacy in Peshawar and international awareness-raising for the Afghan jihad. Azzam paid particular attention to Saudi Arabia and held numerous talks in the Hijaz in the early 1980s.[5]

In May 1982, Azzam published his first article about the Afghan jihad in the MB journal *al-Mujtama'*. He later collected his journal articles in a book, *Signs of the Merciful in the Afghan Jihad*, which presented stories on the so-called *karamat* – the miracles which occur when the *mujahid* falls a martyr. *Signs of the Merciful* became so popular and influential in the Arab world that it would be printed in more than ten editions over the next decade. In 1984, Azzam wrote *The Defence of Muslim Lands*, in which he famously argued that the jihad in Afghanistan is an individual duty (*fard 'ayn*) for all Muslims. These two books had an enormous influence on the mobilisation of Arabs for Afghanistan. As Basil Muhammad, the main historiographer of the Arab Afghans, later noted: 'Two things mobilised Muslim public opinion for Afghanistan: the *karamat* and the fatwas on jihad in Afghanistan.'[6]

Azzam's fatwa on jihad in Afghanistan was far from uncontroversial. The mainstream position of religious scholars at the time was that jihad was only an individual duty for the Afghans, not for all Muslims. In addition to the Saudi scholars mentioned in the previous chapter, prominent international figures remained sceptical. Sheikh Yusuf al-Qaradawi argued that it was enough to support the Afghans materially. Hasan al-Turabi practically ridiculed Azzam, saying the latter's fatwa implied that all Islamic movements should assemble in Afghanistan, which would make them vulnerable and weaken struggles against infidels elsewhere in the world. As Azzam himself later said, 'I distributed it, and some were angry, some were pleased, some reproved. Our brothers scolded us and sent a storm in our face, saying "you are urging

[5] Muhammad, *al-ansar al-'arab*, 45; Abu Mujahid, *al-shahid 'abdallah 'azzam bayna al-milad wa'l-istishhad* [The Martyr Abdallah Azzam from Birth to Martyrdom] (Peshawar: Markaz al-Shahid Azzam al-Ilami, 1991); author's interview with Hudhayfa Azzam and Jamal Isma'il.

[6] Abdallah Azzam, '*ayat wa basha'ir wa karamat fi'l-jihad al-afghani* [Signs and Tidings and Miracles in the Afghan Jihad]', *Al-Mujtama'*, no. 569 (1982); Azzam, *ayat al-rahman*; Abdallah Azzam, *al-difa' 'an aradi al-muslimin* [The Defence of Muslim Lands] (Amman: Maktabat al-Risala al-Haditha, 1987); Muhammad, *al-ansar al-'arab*, 73. The earliest physical copies of *Signs of the Merciful* and *Defence of Muslim Lands* located by this author are dated 1985 and 1987 respectively. It is Basil Muhammad who credibly argues (in *al-ansar al-'arab*) that the works were first written in 1983 and 1984 respectively.

the youth to rebel against us".' However, as the mobilisation gained momentum and the tide of the war turned in favour of the mujahidin, more scholars adopted Azzam's position.[7]

Abdallah Azzam's doctrine was controversial because it broke with the predominant conceptions of jihad of both mainstream clerics and most extremist groups at the time. Azzam essentially advocated universal private military participation in any territorial struggle pitting Muslims versus non-Muslims. All Muslims, Azzam argued, had a duty to fight for all occupied Muslim territories. This unsettled mainstream clerics, who argued that only the populations most concerned had a duty to fight in territorial struggles such as the Afghan jihad. More importantly, Azzam's agenda differed from that of most militant Islamists at the time, who were either involved in revolutionary struggles against local regimes, such as in Egypt and Syria, or in territorial struggles against a local occupier, such as in Palestine. The territorial focus of Azzam's doctrine set it apart from the socio-revolutionaries, while his pan-Islamist vision differed from that of the irredentists. As such, Azzam's classical jihadist doctrine represented no less than a paradigmatic shift in the history of radical Islamist thought.

The combined effect of the increased involvement of the Islamic organisations, Sayyaf's frequent visits to Saudi Arabia and Azzam's advocacy was increased Arab interest in Afghanistan. From late 1983 onwards, the flow of Arab volunteer fighters increased, albeit still only at a rate of a handful of people a month. In early 1984, a group of about ten to twenty young Arabs resided in Peshawar, and the first steps towards coordinating a specific Arab effort were taken. In February 1984, a group of Arabs were allowed to train in the Sayyaf-controlled Badr camp near the village of Babi on the Afghan–Pakistani border. The Badr camp had allegedly been paid for by a Saudi businessman who had wanted 'a Badr brigade of 313 men educated about Islam'. This was the beginning of the development of a training infrastructure specifically for Arab volunteers.[8]

Among the people who arrived in 1984 was Usama bin Ladin, the 27-year old son of the Saudi–Yemeni construction mogul Muhammad bin Ladin. Usama had politicised in late 1970s Jidda under the influence of a high-school teacher who was also a Syrian Muslim Brother. Despite the considerable literature on Bin Ladin, we do not yet know

[7] *al-Jihad*, no. 5 (21 April 1985): 21; *al-Jihad*, no. 37 (December 1987): 12; Muhammad, *al-ansar al-'arab*, 74, 76, 89. For post-1986 scholarly endorsements of Azzam's view, see for e.g. *al-Jihad*, no. 22 (September 1986): 32 and al-Jihad, no. 40 (March 1988): 18.

[8] Abdallah Anas said there were twelve Arabs in Peshawar when he arrived in late 1983; Abdallah Anas, *wiladat al-afghan al-'arab* [The Birth of the Afghan Arabs] (London: Saqi, 2002), 19.

exactly what made him invest himself so much in the Afghan cause. Abdallah Azzam is likely to have exercised considerable influence, either in 1981 when their paths crossed at the university in Jidda or at some of Azzam's Afghanistan rallies in Jidda in 1982 and 1983. Whatever the precise reasons, Bin Ladin would come to play a crucial role in the early mobilisation for Afghanistan as the main sponsor of Azzam's Services Bureau (*maktab al-khidmat*), established in October 1984.[9]

Azzam had a triple motivation for setting up the Services Bureau at this particular point in time. First, he had grown tired of mediating between bickering Afghan mujahidin leaders; second, he had grown frustrated and eventually broke with the Muslim Brotherhood in Jordan, which focused on relief work and refused to recruit fighters for Afghanistan; and finally, he felt a responsibility to accommodate the growing numbers of Arabs who were showing up in Peshawar.[10]

The foundation of the Services Bureau was a turning point in the Arab involvement in the Afghan jihad because it provided a basis for a much more systematic approach to mobilisation. It streamlined the entire chain from international fundraising and recruitment, via the accommodation of volunteers arriving in Pakistan, to the personnel deployment and weapons distribution inside Afghanistan. The SB placed great emphasis on media activities, such as the publication of the magazine *al-Jihad* and the production of propaganda videos, all of which greatly improved the awareness of the Afghan jihad in the Muslim world from 1985 onward. The Services Bureau was not simply a paramilitary logistics office, it also had a humanitarian mission. In fact, much if not most of its activities in Peshawar consisted of providing healthcare, food and education to Afghan refugees, especially orphans. The Bureau's fundamentally ambiguous portfolio was less an attempt at concealing military work than a reflection of the fact that classical jihadists saw no distinction between humanitarian and military assistance to oppressed Muslims.[11]

[9] For more on Usama's pre-Afghanistan politicisation and his presumed 1981 contacts with Azzam, see Steve Coll, *The Bin Ladens: An Arabian Family in the American Century* (New York: Penguin, 2008), 198–212 and 245–60 and Randal, *Osama*, 57–67; Muhammad, *al-ansar al-'arab*, 88. New evidence suggests Bin Ladin may have met Azzam in the United States in 1979; Najwa bin Laden *et al.*, *Growing Up bin Laden* (New York: St Martin's, 2009), 25.

[10] Bernard Rougier, *Everyday Jihad: The Rise of Militant Islam among Palestinians in Lebanon* (Cambridge, MA: Harvard University Press, 2007), 83–4.

[11] Author's interview with Abu Abdallah al-Balkhi, Amman, May 2008, and with Hudhayfa Azzam and Jamal Isma'il. The first issue of *al-Jihad* came out in December 1984. The magazine was published in over sixty issues. The SB's film producer Abu Umran produced three videos called *Tushawni* 1, *Tushawni* 2 and *Reflection of Jihad* (*mira'at al-jihad*); Muhammad, *al-ansar al-'arab*, 194. For more on the *al-Jihad* magazine and the other Arab media in Peshawar, see Ahmad Muaffaq Zaidan, *The 'Afghan Arabs' Media at Jihad* (Islamabad: ABC Printers, 1999).

The Services Bureau also helped draw real Islamic charities into the military effort. One strategy consisted of having key SB-affiliated individuals appointed as representatives of the Islamic organisations in Peshawar. Thus in 1985, Jamal Khalifa and Wa'il Julaydan, both close friends of Bin Ladin and active SB members, were appointed Peshawar representatives of the MWL and the Saudi Red Crescent respectively. Another strategy consisted of cajoling Arab charities and organisations in Peshawar to extend logistical support to the SB, thus drawing the former into the war effort. Usama bin Ladin also used his family connections to muster resources for the Services Bureau. In addition to spending his own yearly allowance, which amounted to around US$300,000 a year, he convinced his less religious brothers to help him procure weapons and transport-construction equipment from Saudi Arabia for Afghanistan.[12]

Early Saudi recruitment was slow. In late 1984, there were only a handful of Saudis in the Jordanian-dominated Arab community in Peshawar, and none of them were based there permanently. Basil Muhammad's history of the Afghan jihad only mentions some sixteen Saudi fighters who had been to Afghanistan prior to 1985. It was only in 1985 that the recruitment of Saudi volunteer fighters slowly began to pick up, but the permanent Saudi contingent would not exceed fifty people until early 1987. In 1985 and 1986, the Saudi recruitment effort was led by Usama bin Ladin personally. He would give talks in Jidda and Medina, distribute the writings of Abdallah Azzam and advertise the latter's visits to the kingdom. He urged his friends and acquaintances to go to Afghanistan, and offered to pay their expenses. Partly as a result of Bin Ladin's efforts, the majority of the Saudis who went to Afghanistan in this period were from Medina and Jidda. Many of them, such as Wa'il Julaydan and Musa al-Qarni, came from Muslim Brotherhood-leaning circles.[13]

After Bin Ladin finally settled in Pakistan in March 1986, he began seeking a degree of independence from Abdallah Azzam and the Services Bureau. In October 1986, after a battle at Jaji had convinced him of the Arabs' desperate need for training, he founded a separate camp in Afghanistan which would later become known as the Lion's Den (*al-ma'sada*). This inspired him to step up his recruitment efforts in Saudi Arabia considerably. From November 1986 to May 1987, Bin Ladin went on at least five trips to the kingdom, each time bringing back

[12] Muhammad, *al-ansar al-'arab*, 140, 165–6, 193, 198; Coll, *The Bin Ladens*, 284–96.

[13] Muhammad, *al-ansar al-'arab*, 85–6, 119; al-Jasir, '*qissat al-afghan al-sa'udiyyin*', 20; Lacroix, 'Les champs de la discorde', 312–14.

between ten and thirty new volunteers, primarily from Medina. He also dispatched his friends on recruitment missions to different parts of the kingdom: for example, Abd al-Rahman al-Surayhi was sent to Jidda, Tamim al-Adnani to the Eastern Province and a certain Abu Hanifa to Ta'if.[14]

In mid-1987, the flow of volunteers from Saudi Arabia began to pick up significantly, and more volunteers came from other parts of the kingdom than the Hijaz. This increase was above all the result of more publicity. The Arab media industry in Peshawar was growing, and an increasing number of jihadist magazines were sold in Saudi Arabia. Abdallah Azzam also continued to write influential treatises such as the very popular *Join the Caravan* (1987). Moreover, the mainstream Saudi press began to write more about the Afghan Arabs from 1986 onward. Bin Ladin and Azzam actively encouraged and facilitated the visit of Saudi journalists such as Jamal Khashoggi to Afghanistan. From 1986 onward the MWL-sponsored magazines such as *al-Rabita* and *Akhbar al-Alam al-Islami* began highlighting the Saudi participation, implicitly encouraging others to follow suit. In April 1987, for example, *al-Rabita* proudly declared on its front page that 'Most of the Martyrs are Saudis', and in May 1988 it republished biographies of Arab martyrs from *al-Jihad* magazine.[15]

Another factor was the natural network effect of the arrival of Saudi volunteer fighters from 1984 onward. Each new person could potentially inspire many more people in his family, social circle, school or neighbourhood to go. Mid-1987 seems to have represented the tipping point of the mobilisation, after which recruitment transcended personal social networks and reached most parts of the country. At this point, Bin Ladin scaled down his recruitment efforts in Saudi Arabia, as they were no longer needed. Saudi jihadism had effectively become a social movement.

The best indication that the jihadist movement had acquired a momentum of its own in the late 1980s was that it continued to drive

[14] Muhammad, *al-ansar al-'arab*, 184, 214, 216, 243, 305; *al-Jihad*, no. 50 (December 1988): 33; *al-Jihad*, no. 53 (April 1989): 36.

[15] Hasin al-Binayyan, '*aqdam al-afghan al-'arab al-sa'udiyyin: shahadtu milad al-qa'ida, fikrat al-tanzim misriyya* [The Oldest of the Saudi Afghan Arabs: I Witnessed the Birth of al-Qaida; it was an Egyptian Idea]', *al-Sharq al-Awsat*, 21 November 2001; Zaidan, *The 'Afghan Arabs' Media at Jihad*; *al-Jihad*, no. 53; Peter Bergen, *The Osama bin Laden I Know* (New York: Free Press, 2006), 50ff; Huband, *Warriors of the Prophet*, 3; Jamal Khashoggi, 'Arab Youths Fight Shoulder to Shoulder with Mujahideen', *Arab News*, 4 May 1988; Jamal Khashoggi, 'Arab Mujahideen in Afghanistan-II: Masada Exemplifies the Unity of Islamic Ummah', *Arab News*, 14 May 1988; *al-Rabita*, no. 265 (April 1987) and *al-Rabita*, no. 278 (May 1988), 49–53.

people to Afghanistan long after the Soviet withdrawal in February 1989. There was a significant Arab presence in Peshawar and Afghanistan throughout the so-called Afghan civil war between the mujahidin and the communist regime of Najibullah. Only in April 1992, when the capture of Kabul by the mujahidin made the Arab presence in the area unnecessary and unwanted – particularly by the Pakistani authorities – did the era of the first Afghan jihad really come to a close.

Although many Arab volunteers, including Usama bin Ladin himself, returned to their home countries in 1989, guest houses and training camps remained open and continued to receive thousands of new volunteers in the period from 1989 to 1992. Most, though not all, of the Saudis who went in the 1989–92 period joined Jamil al-Rahman's 'Society for Da'wa to the Qur'an and the Ahl al-Hadith' in the remote north-eastern Afghan region of Kunar.[16]

Jamil al-Rahman was the pseudonym of an Afghan mujahidin leader named Maulavi Hussain who had broken with Gulbuddin Hekmatyar's Hizb-e-Islami on ideological grounds in 1985. Around 1986 he set up an independent organisation in Kunar with the encouragement and financial support of conservative Saudi and Kuwaiti businessmen. This organisation drew many Saudis because it was rigidly salafi and thus enjoyed the backing of the official Saudi ulama. Saudi sheikhs considered Jamil al-Rahman's group more doctrinally pure than the Muslim Brotherhood-dominated Services Bureau or the revolutionary Egyptian and Jordanian factions in Peshawar. Jamil al-Rahman had studied with Ahl-e-Hadith in Pakistan, and his 'Society for Da'wa' had a stronger focus on social and ritual issues than other factions. They engaged in violent enforcement of the Wahhabi ban on grave worship and other local practices considered religious innovations (*bid'a*). Al-Rahman's group had extensive contacts in Saudi Arabia and published a magazine in Peshawar called *al-Mujahid*, which was even more widely available in the kingdom than Azzam's *al-Jihad* magazine. The flow of Saudis slowed down after the assassination of Jamil al-Rahman in 1991 and all but ceased after the fall of Kabul in 1992.[17]

[16] The Society for Da'wa had very close links with the Pakistani Islamist organisation Markaz al-Da'wa wa'l-Irshad and its armed wing Lashkar-e Tayyiba. Some Arab fighters were involved in the training of Lashkar-e Tayyiba militias in Kunar in the early 1990s. See Mawlana Amir Hamza, *qafilat dawat jihad* (in Urdu) (Dar al-Andalus, 2004).

[17] Barnett R. Rubin, 'Arab Islamists in Afghanistan', in *Political Islam: Revolution, Radicalism, or Reform?*, ed. John Esposito (Boulder, CO: Lynne Rienner, 1997), 196–7; Olivier Roy, *Islam and Resistance in Afghanistan*, 2nd edn (Cambridge University Press, 1990), 118; Lacroix, 'Les champs de la discorde', 318–22. When this author consulted the King Sa'ud University Library in Riyadh in November 2005, the 1980s

There are no good figures for the total number of Saudis who went to Afghanistan in the 1980s and early 1990s. Some writers have suggested numbers as high as 20,000. Estimates by former Afghan Arabs vary from a few thousand to 15,000. The Saudi Interior Ministry allegedly compiled a report in 1995 which estimated that 12,000 Saudis had gone to Afghanistan.[18] Whatever the total number, only a fraction had significant exposure to military training and combat. The majority of Saudis only went for a month or two during their summer holidays, and anecdotal evidence suggests that most of them were never involved in fighting. The jihadi literature indicates that only between 50 and 300 Saudis were killed during the Afghan war. However, even if the number of 'real' Saudi jihadists was in the low thousands – probably between 1,000 and 5,000 – it was still a remarkable figure, given the near-absence of a militant Islamist community in Saudi Arabia in the early 1980s. An entire movement had been created in the space of five years.[19]

The Afghan experience politicised the Saudi volunteers and exposed them to the heated debates in the ideological melting pot of Peshawar. The Pakistani border city was home to some of the most important socio-revolutionary groups and ideologues in the Muslim world at the time. By contrast, the Saudis who came to Peshawar in the 1980s had virtually no concept of violent anti-regime activism. Some Saudis were no doubt influenced by the revolutionary atmosphere and by the publication in 1989 of the book entitled *The Obvious Proofs of the Saudi State's Impiety* by the Peshawar-based and Saudi-trained Jordanian ideologue Abu Muhammad al-Maqdisi. *The Obvious Proofs* represented the first socio-revolutionary treatise articulated in Wahhabi religious discourse and was thus particularly flammable in the kingdom. For this reason, the Saudi government has long considered al-Maqdisi as one of its arch-enemies. However, the 'takfiri influence' of Peshawar on Saudi Islamism should not be exaggerated. The vast majority of Saudis returned from Afghanistan as classical jihadists with no intentions of fighting the Saudi regime.[20]

jihadist magazines were still on the shelf. Issues of *al-Jihad* were available in one copy, while issues of *al-Mujahid* were available in ten copies each.

[18] al-Jasir, '*qissat al-afghan al-sa'udiyyin*'; Akram Hijazi, '*rihla fi samim 'aql al-salafiyya al-jihadiyya* [A Journey Through the Mind of Salafi Jihadism]', *al-Quds al-Arabi*, 29 August 2006; Bergen, *The Osama bin Laden I Know*, 41–2; Huband, *Warriors of the Prophet*, 2–3; James Bruce, 'Arab Veterans of the Afghan War', *Jane's Intelligence Review* 7, no. 4 (1995); Anthony Cordesman, *Islamic Extremism in Saudi Arabia and the Attack on al-Khobar* (Washington, DC: CSIS, 2001), 4.

[19] al-Jasir, '*qissat al-afghan al-sa'udiyyin*', 23; Randal, *Osama*, 76. This author has collected the names and basic biographies of forty-three Saudis who died in Afghanistan before 1992.

[20] Mishari al-Dhaidi, '*matbakh bishawar wa tabkhat gharnata* [The Peshawar Kitchen and the Grenada Cooking]', *al-Sharq al-Awsat*, 15 May 2003; Abu Muhammad

On the other hand, the overall importance of the Afghan experience on the evolution of the jihadist movement cannot be overestimated. The Afghan jihad produced a discourse, mythology and symbolic universe which shaped militant Islamist activism in the 1990s and continue to do so today. Moreover, key elements of the mobilisation structures and recruitment mechanisms from the Afghan jihad were reproduced in subsequent contexts, as we shall see below. Most importantly, Afghanistan created reputations and forged social bonds which generated a cadre of professional jihadists. These individuals would become key entrepreneurs in the jihad zones of the 1990s, starting with Bosnia.[21]

Jihad in Bosnia, the anticlimax

Few would have guessed, much less the Arab Afghans themselves, that the next major jihad after Afghanistan would take place in a province of Yugoslavia. When the first Arab fighters arrived, they knew virtually nothing about the area. As one Saudi jihadist in Bosnia explained: 'we were unable to understand where Bosnia was, was it in America or in the southern hemisphere or in Asia? We had no idea where it was. When we found out that it is a part of Yugoslavia in Eastern Europe, we still had no idea of how many Muslims there were and we had no idea as to how and when Islam reached there.' Within six months of the first arrivals, hundreds of volunteer fighters from all over the Arab world were roaming the Bosnian hills in combat gear, and many were to follow.[22]

The Bosnian conflict erupted at a time when the rug was being pulled from under the Arab Afghans in Pakistan, and many militants needed a new place to go. The jihadist involvement in Bosnia began in late April or early May 1992, when a delegation of four prominent Afghan Arabs from Peshawar led by the Saudi Abd al-Rahman al-Dawsary (aka Abu Abd al-Aziz, aka 'Barbaros' after the sixteenth-century Ottoman admiral) linked up with the Italy-based Egyptian Sheikh Anwar Sha'ban and went on a joint expedition to Bosnia to check out the conditions for Arab involvement. The parties knew each other from Afghanistan and saw the excursion as mutually beneficial: Barbaros was seeking an alternative base to Peshawar, and Sha'ban aspired to the

al-Maqdisi, *al-kawashif al-jaliyya fi kufr al-dawla al-sa'udiyya* [The Obvious Proofs of the Saudi State's Impiety] (1989).

[21] See e.g. Anthony Davis, 'Foreign Combatants in Afghanistan', *Jane's Intelligence Review* 5, no. 7 (1993); Gilles Kepel, 'Les stratégies islamistes de légitimation de la violence', *Raisons Politiques*, no. 9 (2003): 88; and Gilles Kepel, 'Terrorisme islamiste: De l'anticommunisme au jihad anti-américain', *Ramses* (2003): 45–6.

[22] Kohlmann, *Al-Qaida's Jihad in Europe*, 19.

role of the Abdallah Azzam of the Bosnian jihad. They liked what they saw, set up camp near Zenica and began mobilising their multinational Arab Afghan network. They spread the word of the need for mujahidin, and within weeks more Arab Afghans were on their way, and recruiters and fundraisers were at work across the Middle East.[23]

Sha'ban and Barbaros, probably with the Services Bureau model in mind, also moved quickly to get two crucial organisational components in place, namely a logistics unit and a cadre of elite instructors. At some point in the early summer of 1992, the charity known as the 'Islamic Benevolence Committee' (IBC) set up an office headed by a certain Enaam Arnaout in Zagreb in neighbouring Croatia. The IBC, also known as 'Benevolence International Foundation', effectively became the Services Bureau of the Bosnian jihad. According to Arnaout himself, the IBC sponsored volunteer fighters, met them at the airport, brought them into Bosnia and provided accommodation in IBC facilities. It also shipped weapons and military equipment into Bosnia, all under the cover of humanitarian work. The IBC also produced publications and videos aimed at raising funds from wealthy donors in the Gulf. Several other Islamic charities, such as the International Islamic Relief Organisation and Third World Relief Agency, would also extend services such as visas and fake ID cards to Arab combatants, but the IBC was the most significant actor. In 2005, a Bahraini former fighter detained in Bosnia named Ali Ahmad Ali Hamad revealed numerous details about the Saudi charities in Bosnia during the war. He notably said that the Haramayn Foundation and the Saudi High Commission for Refugee Affairs were largely staffed by Saudi veterans from Afghanistan. He also said the Saudi High Commission had supplied money, vehicles and healthcare to Arab fighters, and had used vehicles with diplomatic licence plates to transport wounded fighters. The United Nations High Commissioner for Refugees later noted that 'although the majority of these agencies were experienced and highly professional, others were not. Some had dubious links with the warring parties, fundamentalist groups, mercenaries, secret intelligence agencies, arms smugglers and black-marketeers.'[24]

The second key component, namely a military cadre, fell into place in the autumn of 1992 after a visit to Zagreb by Usama bin Ladin's envoy from Sudan, Jamal al-Fadl. Al-Fadl met with Barbaros, Enaam

[23] See 'Interview with Sheikh al-Mujahideen Abu Abdel Aziz' and Kohlmann, *Al-Qaida's Jihad in Europe*, 23.

[24] Evan F. Kohlmann, 'The Role of Islamic Charities in International Terrorist Recruitment and Financing', in *DIIS Working Paper* (Copenhagen: Danish Institute for International Studies, 2006), 6–10; *USA* v. *Enaam Arnaout – Government's Evidentiary*

Arnaout and Abu Zubayr al-Madani (a cousin of Bin Ladin) in Zagreb and agreed to send a joint recommendation that nine elite instructors from the Sada camp in Afghanistan be sent to Bosnia. This step was important, because it signalled to the Arab Afghan community that leading figures such as Usama bin Ladin were backing the Bosnian jihad effort.[25]

The first reports of Arab deaths in combat came in June 1992, and by September 1992 units of up to fifty Arabs were operational. By the end of 1992, some 500 foreign (mostly Arab) volunteers had gone to Bosnia. The flow of recruits continued, at least until mid-1993, when it seems to have slowed down somewhat. When the conflict ended in December 1995, at least 1,000 Arabs had fought in Bosnia.[26]

The mujahidin seem to have been divided, at least in the first half of the war, into two separate structures. On the one hand there was a well-organised and conventional unit known as the 'mujahidin battalion' which was incorporated into the Bosnian army, and on the other hand a smaller, looser constellation of groups involved in more improvised and controversial operations. The first group, which was considered the main unit for foreign volunteers, consisted of Egyptians, Algerians and a mixture of other nationalities. It seems to have counted around 500 men at the most. Its first amir was Barbaros, who was succeeded in 1993 by a certain Abu Mu'ali. The political and spiritual leader of the mujahidin brigade was Anwar Sha'ban. The second structure, which was commanded by the Saudi Abu al-Zubayr al-Ha'ili, was smaller and consisted of more experienced fighters. This structure was made up of small groups distributed in many areas, which would join forces when hot battles erupted. Some of the Arab units, particularly in al-Ha'ili's camp, evolved into incontrollable thuggish gangs who alienated most people in their path and tarnished the Arabs' reputation.[27]

Proffer (Northern District of Illinois, 2003); *al-Sharq al-Awsat*, 25 February 2005 and 8 August 2006; Eric Lichtblau, 'Documents Back Saudi Link to Extremists', *New York Times*, 24 June 2009 (see also related source documents on www.nytimes.com); Mark Cutts, 'The Humanitarian Operation in Bosnia, 1992–95: Dilemmas of Negotiating Humanitarian Access', in *New Issues in Refugee Research* (Geneva: UNHCR, 1999), 24.

[25] *USA* v. *Usama bin Ladin et al* (District Court of Southern New York, 2001), 315–16.

[26] Milan Vego, 'The Army of Bosnia and Hercegovina', *Jane's Intelligence Review* 5, no. 2 (1993). Estimates of the total number of Arab fighters vary from 'between 500 and 1,000' (Bruce, 'Arab Veterans of the Afghan War') to as many as 6,000 (Stephen Schwartz, 'Wahhabism and al Qaeda in Bosnia Herzegovina', *Terrorism Monitor* 2, no. 20 (2004)).

[27] *al-Quds al-Arabi*, 24 March and 2 April 2005; 'Interview with Sheikh al-Mujahideen Abu Abdel Aziz'; 'Bin Laden and the Balkans' (Brussels: International Crisis Group, 2001), 11–12; Bruce, 'Arab Veterans of the Afghan War'.

Saudis were present in Bosnia from a very early stage. Some, like the pioneer Barbaros, came straight from Peshawar, while most came directly from the kingdom. In the battles involving Arabs in the autumn of 1992, the Saudis were clearly the majority group. Later in the war, the flow of Saudis seems to have abated somewhat. Saudis seem to have predominated in al-Ha'ili's ranks.

Barbaros played a key role in promoting the Bosnian cause in Saudi Arabia. In December 1992 he went on a major fundraising trip to the Middle East, touring Turkey, Jordan, Kuwait, Bahrain, Saudi Arabia and Pakistan. He was particularly active in his native country, giving lengthy interviews with the Saudi press and lecturing extensively. Recordings of his speeches circulated in the kingdom and elsewhere. A particularly popular audio cassette featured a discussion between Barbaros and the leading salafi sheikh Sheikh Nasir al-Din al-Albani recorded during a meeting in Amman.[28]

One of Barbaros' most important missions was to convince religious clerics that the situation in Bosnia was a legitimate jihad worthy of financial and military support. Barbaros and his fellow activists found many scholars willing to listen, given the pan-Islamist atmosphere in the kingdom at the time. As former jihadist Nasir al-Bahri later noted, 'there was no religious sheikh or preacher who did not talk about jihad in Bosnia-Herzegovina and about the suffering of Muslims everywhere'. The scholars played a crucial role, not only because they established the religious legitimacy of the cause, but also because they constituted the main intermediary between the donors and the volunteers. When volunteers inquired about how to get to Bosnia, the same scholars could put them in touch with a donor or give them money from available funds. As the former militant Nasir al-Bahri explained:

> I was equipped for my first jihad by a woman. She worked as a schoolteacher. She had heard about the tragedies that had befallen the Muslims in Bosnia-Herzegovina and wanted to contribute to their defence. She asked: What is the best thing I can contribute? The answer was: Equip a mujahid. She said: I will donate a full month's salary to equip a mujahid. It was equivalent to approximately $2,000. That sum was to equip me for my first jihad in Bosnia-Herzegovina.[29]

Another important Saudi recruiter was a friend of Barbaros called Khalid al-Harbi (aka Abu Sulayman al-Makki), who had worked as a religious teacher in Mecca before becoming a renowned mujahid in Afghanistan. After visiting Bosnia in the early summer of 1992, al-Harbi

[28] Kohlmann, *Al-Qaida's Jihad in Europe*, 75; *al-Quds al-Arabi*, 20 March 2005.
[29] *al-Quds al-Arabi*, 20 March 2005.

returned to Saudi Arabia to bring more volunteers. As a former teacher and Arab Afghan, he had a vast network of contacts from which to draw recruits, particularly in his native Mecca and the rest of the Hijaz. Many of the first Saudis who went to Bosnia were therefore from Mecca and Jidda.[30]

The mobilisation of Saudis started well, but gradually slowed down. By 1995 it was clear that the Bosnian jihad had flopped. The international community was working against the Arabs, the Saudi government would not help them as much as they wanted, and the Bosnians seemed ungrateful and unobservant. By the time the Dayton accord was signed in December 1995, most of the Saudis had left Bosnia and returned to the kingdom. Some considered their mission completed and wanted to go back to their normal lives. Others simply stopped to 'refuel' on the way to new adventures. When asked where the Arab mujahidin went after the Bosnian jihad, Nasir al-Bahri said 'a group of them decided to head for the Philippines, while another group headed for Chechnya. I was with a third group that headed for Somalia. That is why they turned from one "meteor" into several "shooting stars".'[31]

Tajikistan, Chechnya and the minor jihad fronts

The Bosnian war was not the only conflict to attract Saudi jihadists in the first half of the 1990s. A number of armed conflicts evolved more or less in parallel, notably in Algeria, Somalia, the Philippines, Kashmir, Eritrea, Tajikistan and Chechnya. Saudi militants would get involved in all of these conflicts at one point or another, although to very varying degrees.

When the Afghan jihad came to an end in the spring of 1992, jihadists were looking for new arenas where they could fight in defence of the umma. Many of the activists were young and not very knowledgeable about international politics or foreign cultures, so the search for new battlefields often had an improvised element to it. In Peshawar rumours of many different jihad opportunities circulated, each of which enticed small delegations of adventurous individuals. After the fall of Kabul, some Saudis tried to make it to Kashmir. However, the Pakistani government did not want them there for fear of damaging relations with India. Others travelled to places like the Philippines or Eritrea in the mid-1990s, although the details of this involvement are not very well known.[32]

[30] *al-Quds al-Arabi*, 2 April 2005. [31] *al-Quds al-Arabi*, 2 April 2005.

[32] 'Interview with Sheikh al-Mujahideen Abu Abdel Aziz', and al-Jasir, '*qissat al-afghan al-sa'udiyyin*', 22. Bin Ladin's Saudi brother-in-law Jamal Khalifa allegedly served as a liaison between Bin Ladin and Philippine militant groups in the 1990s; Anonymous,

Algeria featured prominently in Saudi public debates, not least because Sahwist preachers such as Safar al-Hawali took a great interest in the Algerian war and criticised the Saudi regime for not supporting the Front Islamique du Salut (FIS). The entire Saudi Islamist field was sympathetic to the Algerian Islamists, but for most Saudi jihadists, getting militarily involved in Algeria was out of the question because it was an internal conflict, not a classical jihad pitting Muslims versus non-Muslims. Usama bin Ladin had sporadic contacts with Algerian militants from his base in Sudan, but it seems that he did not send people to Algeria. One of the very few Saudi jihadists to have gone to Algeria was Abd al-Aziz al-Muqrin, who went there for about a month in 1994 or 1995 after coming into contact with Algerians in Bosnia. He was allegedly involved in weapons smuggling between Spain and Algeria, but had to flee when his cell was dismantled by Algerian authorities.[33]

Somalia would also witness an influx of small numbers of Saudi jihadists. This involvement came in two different stages. First was Bin Ladin's 1993 attempt to support the Somali resistance against the UN forces deployed in 'Operation Restore Hope'. To Bin Ladin, this intervention represented yet another infringement on Muslim territory and an attempt by the US to gain a foothold in Africa in order to invade countries in the Middle East. Bin Ladin thus dispatched a small team of military instructors from Sudan to Somalia. The mission was led by experienced Egyptian militants such as Abu Hafs al-Masri, but it included a few Saudis, such as Yusuf al-Uyayri (the future founder of the QAP), and Muhammad Awda, one of the co-conspirators in the 1998 East Africa bombings. The precise role of the Arabs in the 1993 events remains unclear, but recent evidence suggests Bin Ladin's involvement was greater than has thus far been assumed.[34]

Through our Enemies' Eyes (Washington, DC: Brassey's, 2002), 180–2. In late December 1995, two Saudis – Salih al-Quway'i and Zayid al-Amir – were arrested in Manila on terrorism charges; Robert McFadden, 'Nine Suspected of Terrorism are Arrested in Manila', *New York Times*, 31 December 1995. Jamal al-Fadl described meetings in Khartoum in the early 1990s between al-Qaida and an Eritrean group called 'Jamaat e Jihad Eritrea'; *USA* v. *Usama bin Ladin et al*, 328–9. We know of at least two named Saudis who fought in Eritrea: Abd al-Aziz al-Muqrin and a certain Abu Hisan al-Makki; see Hamad al-Qatari and Majid al-Madani, *min qisas al-shuhada' al-'arab fi'l-busna wa'l-harsak* [From the Stories of the Arab Martyrs in Bosnia and Herzegovina], 2nd edn (www.saaid.net, 2002), 168–9.

33 Fandy, *Saudi Arabia and the Politics of Dissent*, 83–4; *'liqa' ma' ahad al-matlubin al-tisa' 'ashar* (1)' [Interview with One of the Nineteen Wanted Men]', *Sawt al-Jihad*, no. 1 (2003).

34 Muhammad al-Salim, *'yusuf al-'uyayri: shumukh fi zaman al-hawan* [Yusuf al-Uyayri: Standing Tall in an Age of Lowliness]', *Sawt al-Jihad*, no. 1 (2003); *Al-Qaida's*

The second round of Arab involvement in Somalia came in the context of the conflict between Somalia and Ethiopia in Ogaden. In 1994 or 1995, small groups of Arabs who had fought in Bosnia travelled via Saudi Arabia or Yemen to Ogaden to fight with the 'Islamic Union' against the Christian Ethiopians. Among the people who went was subsequent QAP lieutenant Abd al-Aziz al-Muqrin, who ended up being captured and imprisoned in Ethiopia for two and a half years before being extradited to Saudi Arabia.[35]

A more significant arena for Arab Afghan involvement in the early 1990s was Tajikistan, where a five-year civil war broke out in 1992, a year after independence. A series of massacres in January and February 1993 forced the Tajik Islamist opposition and thousands of civilians into exile in Afghanistan. The Tajik Islamist al-Nahda party sent a request for help to the Arabs in Peshawar. This happened at a time when Arabs had begun to leave Pakistan and Afghanistan, and when many of them had become disillusioned with the infighting between the Afghan warlords. As in Algeria, the Islamist struggle in Tajikistan was not a clear-cut classical jihad, because the incumbent regime was nominally Muslim. However, the strong Russian support for the Tajik government made some foreign fighters see the conflict as a case of de facto Russian occupation and an extension of the jihad in Afghanistan. Thus in the spring and summer of 1993, three successive groups of Arab fighters, numbering about 100, ventured to Tajikistan to take part in the jihad against the Russian-backed regime in Dushanbe. A majority of the fighters were Saudis and included subsequently famous figures such as Samir al-Suwaylim (Khattab). These fighters would stay in south Tajikistan until they were forced out in 1995.[36]

In 1996 the conflict escalated again and prompted the intervention of Russian troops, which gave the jihad a more 'classical' character. This inspired a new attempt by Arabs to join the Tajik jihad in mid-

(Mis)adventures in the Horn of Africa, Harmony Project (West Point: Combating Terrorism Center, 2007).

[35] *'liqa' ma' ahad al-matlubin al-tisa' 'ashar* (1)'.

[36] The three groups were led by Ya'qub al-Bahr, (Ibn) Khattab (Samir al-Suwaylim) and Usama Azmaray (Wali Khan) respectively. One of the groups allegedly received funding through Sheikh Salman al-Awda. While the latter group disbanded early, the former groups fought for about two years. Ya'qub al-Bahr's group went deep into Tajikistan while Khattab operated in the border areas. In Khattab's company were a number of people who later become prominent QAP members, such as Khalid al-Subayt and Salih al-Awfi. *Al-Sharq al-Awsat*, 27 December 2004; *al-Quds al-Arabi*, 20 March 2005; *USA* v. *Usama bin Ladin et al*, 355; al-Qatari and al-Madani, *min qisas al-shuhada' al-'arab*, 119–20; Huband, *Warriors of the Prophet*, 14; Isa bin Sa'd Al Awshan, '*khalid bin abdallah al-subayt: fida' wa tadhiyya*', *Sawt al-Jihad*, no. 15 (2004); Raid Qusti, 'Background of the Most Wanted Terrorists – Part 2', *Arab News*, 12 December 2003.

1996. This contingent, which became known as the 'Northern group', included some of those expelled in 1995 as well as a number of new volunteers. The group was led by a certain Hamza al-Ghamidi and numbered thirty-six people, most of whom were Saudis. They made it to north Afghanistan, but were unable to enter Tajikistan and headed south to Jalalabad, where they met another Saudi who had recently settled in Afghanistan, namely Usama bin Ladin. Several members of the Northern group, including subsequently well-known figures such as Abd al-Rahim al-Nashiri, Umar al-Faruq and Nasir al-Bahri, would eventually join al-Qaida.[37]

As the Tajik jihad came to an end, new opportunities arose in the Caucasian republic of Chechnya, where a war between secessionist rebels and Russia erupted in late 1995 and a second war would break out in 1999. The Chechen conflict could easily be framed as a classical jihad because it pitted a local Muslim population against a non-Muslim occupier, and a very brutal one at that. For the Saudi jihadist movement in particular, Chechnya would become an extremely important cause which attracted volunteers well into the 2000s. In fact, in the late 1990s and early 2000s, Chechnya was a more attractive destination than Afghanistan for Saudi volunteer fighters, because as a classical jihad it was considered a less controversial struggle than Bin Ladin's global jihad against America.

The initial Arab involvement in Chechnya was facilitated by a Jordanian-born Chechen Islamist called Fathi Muhammad Habib (aka Abu Sayyaf). Raised in Amman, Habib studied engineering in Germany and America before going to Afghanistan in the 1980s, where he worked closely with Sayyaf. In early 1992 he settled in Chechnya where he set up an Islamic school and began using his Arab connections to solicit funds for *da'wa* (missionary) work in Chechnya. When the first war broke out in late 1994, he used his contacts to draw Arab Afghans to Chechnya. In early 1995, news of the Russian invasion reached Khattab just as the opportunities in Tajikistan were narrowing. Khattab received a letter from Sheikh Fathi urging him to come to Chechnya, which he did some time in the spring of 1995. Khattab's closest comrades in arms from Afghanistan then followed suit. Several of Khattab's early companions would become legendary jihadist figures, such as Muhammad al-Tamimi (aka Abu Umar al-Sayf), the chief ideologue of the Chechen Arabs; Abd al-Aziz al-Ghamidi (aka Abu Walid al-Ghamidi), one of Khattab's successors as commander of the foreign mujahidin in Chechnya, and Suhayl al-Sahli (aka Yasin

[37] *al-Quds al-Arabi*, 20 March 2005.

al-Bahr), who would lead the first battalions of foreign fighters in northern Iraq in early 2003.[38]

Shortly after his arrival in Chechnya, Khattab began building a training infrastructure which he would run in partnership with the legendary Chechen commander Shamil Basayev. By mid-1995 a logistics chain had been set up to facilitate the arrival of foreign volunteers. The main stations on this chain were Istanbul (Turkey) and Baku (Azerbaijan). The Baku safe house was run by Arabs operating under the cover of the Islamic Benevolence Committee. Khattab enjoyed a certain amount of logistical and financial support from Saudi Arabia. Saudi sheikhs declared the Chechen resistance a legitimate jihad, and private Saudi donors sent money to Khattab and his Chechen colleagues. As late as 1996, mujahidin wounded in Chechnya were sent to Saudi Arabia for medical treatment, a practice paid for by charities and tolerated by the state. After the end of the first Chechen war, Khattab expanded his activities in Chechnya, built more camps and set up an institute in which old Saudi friends of Khattab taught religion and military science to Chechen rebel leaders. The second Chechen war which broke out in late 1999 led the Russians to practically seal off the country, so, after 2000, very few foreign volunteers made it to Chechnya. Funds continued to flow, but they decreased significantly after the crackdown on Islamic charities after 2001.[39]

It is not clear exactly how many Arabs joined Khattab between 1995 and 1999, but the number seems to have stayed in the low hundreds, perhaps not even exceeding 100. The Jordanian journalist and researcher Murad al-Shishani compiled 51 biographies of Arabs in Chechnya, 30

[38] Murad al-Shishani, *The Rise and Fall of Arab Fighters in Chechnya* (Washington, DC: Jamestown Foundation, 2006), 7; Mowaffaq al-Nowaiser, 'Khattab, the Man who Died for the Cause of Chechnya', *Arab News*, 4 May 2002; al-Qatari and al-Madani, *min qisas al-shuhada' al-'arab*, 127; author's interview with Faris bin Huzzam, Dubai, November 2005; 'World Exclusive Interview with Field Commander Shamil Basayev' (Azzam Publications (posted on www.islamicawakening.com), 2000); Julie Wilhelmsen, *When Separatists Become Islamists: The Case of Chechnya* (Kjeller: Norwegian Defence Research Establishment (FFI/Rapport), 2004), 33; Khattab was not the first Arab in Chechnya. A Saudi named Fayhan al-Utaybi (aka Abu Turab al-Najdi) had allegedly gone before him, but he had left because he was the only Arab and could not communicate with the locals; see al-Qatari and al-Madani, *min qisas al-shuhada' al-'arab*, 121.

[39] Aukai Collins, *My Jihad: The True Story of an American Mujahid's Amazing Journey* (Guilford, CT: Lyons Press, 2002), 123; *USA* v. *Usama bin Ladin et al*, 300–2; Isa bin Sa'd Al Awshan, '*khalid bin 'abdallah al-subayt: fida' wa tadhiyya* [Khalid bin Abdallah al-Subayt: Courage and Sacrifice]', *Sawt al-Jihad*, no. 15 (2004); al-Shishani, *The Rise and Fall of Arab Fighters in Chechnya*, 13–14; Miriam Lanskoy, 'Daghestan and Chechnya: The Wahhabi Challenge to the State', *SAIS Review* 22, no. 2 (2002): 177ff. For more on the Arabs in Chechnya, see Yossef Bodansky, *Chechen Jihad: al Qaeda's Training Ground and the Next Wave of Terror* (New York: Harper, 2007).

of whom were from Saudi Arabia. Most of the Saudis in Chechnya arrived in the inter-war period, that is, between 1996 and 1999. The outbreak of the second war in the autumn of 1999 made a new generation of Saudis want to join the jihad, but at this point Chechnya was extremely difficult to reach. As a result, many of the recruits who headed out for Chechnya between 1999 and 2001 ended up in Afghanistan, were they were drawn into Bin Ladin's al-Qaida organisation.[40]

The relationship between Khattab and Bin Ladin is said to have been lukewarm. In Afghanistan in the late 1980s, Khattab had sought a degree of independence from both Bin Ladin and Azzam. Around 1997–8, Bin Ladin allegedly invited Khattab to cooperate more closely with him, an offer which was rejected by Khattab after a polite written correspondence. The Khattab–Bin Ladin enmity was not just about personal chemistry or rivalry; it also reflected a significant ideological division, namely between the 'classical' and the 'global' branches of the Saudi jihadist movement. Khattab did not subscribe to Bin Ladin's doctrine of attacking the United States and did not approve of the targeting of civilians. Saudi sources have described the jihadist community in the kingdom as being divided between the 'Khattabists' and the 'Bin Ladinists', the former being more numerous.[41]

There was a continuous Saudi presence in Chechnya up until at least the mid-2000s. Khattab was active as a guerrilla leader until his assassination by a poisoned letter from Russian intelligence on 20 March 2002. His old companion Abu Umar al-Sayf would rise to become one of the most prominent ideologues in the international jihadist community until he too was killed in early December 2005.

In the Islamist historical narrative, the emergence of the Saudi jihadist movement represents a spontaneous 'rise of the people' in the face of outside aggression in Afghanistan, Bosnia and Chechnya. The reality was far more complex. 'The people' never rose to any of these causes, and the mobilisation was far from spontaneous. A few thousand men were mobilised, and only as the result of the systematic and sustained effort of entrepreneurial groups of devoted individuals.

The most crucial factor behind the success of the mobilisation was the articulation, in the early 1980s, of Abdallah Azzam's doctrine of classical jihad, which offered a new and very powerful ideological justification for private involvement in other Muslims' struggles of national liberation. Azzam's doctrine had great mobilising power because it

[40] Wilhelmsen, *When Separatists Become Islamists*, 29; al-Shishani, *The Rise and Fall of Arab Fighters in Chechnya*.

[41] '*Almrei* v. *Canada* (2005 FC 1645)' (Federal Court of Canada, Ottawa, 2005), paragraph 366; author's interviews with Nasir al-Barrak and Faris bin Huzzam.

appealed to pan-Islamist sentiment and stayed close to orthodox jihad theology. At the same time, his insistence that jihad participation is an individual duty for all sidelined the ulama and left the jihadists free to fight where they wanted.

At the organisational level, the mobilisation relied on a formula which was developed in 1980s Afghanistan by the Services Bureau. It consisted of creating a separate infrastructure for Arab fighters, working systematically with the media and exploiting charities for military purposes. The same principles were applied in the mobilisation of Saudis for Bosnia and Chechnya, and to some extent also in the recruitment to al-Qaida's Afghan camps in the late 1990s. However, some of these same factors would contribute to the weakening of the jihadist movement in the mid-1990s. Insularity became a liability: in Bosnia the Arabs appeared as foreign intruders, while their presence in Chechnya was used by the Russians to delegitimise the Chechen resistance. Formal organisation was a weakness if state actors worked against them. Exploitation of charities was eventually uncovered and undermined the credibility of the movement.

With weakness came radicalisation. The Saudi classical jihadist movement arguably reached its peak, in terms of numbers and popular support, around 1989. From then on, the number of people able and willing to travel abroad for jihad seems to have decreased, for a number of different reasons. The people left in the movement were the most committed individuals, who were willing to sacrifice more than just their holidays for the Muslim nation. As the movement grew smaller, it became more radical and more controversial, eventually giving birth to global jihadism. It is easy to understand how the experience of training camps and war contributed to the radicalisation of Saudi jihadists over time. The more intriguing question is why people sought out these experiences in the first place.

3 Recruitment to the early jihad fronts

> We realised we were a nation [umma] that had a distinguished place among nations. Otherwise, what would make me leave Saudi Arabia – and I am of Yemeni origin – to go and fight in Bosnia?
>
> Nasir al-Bahri[1]

In most historical accounts of the 1980s jihad in Afghanistan, the storyteller is so keen to emphasise the size of the Arab mobilisation that the reader is left with the impression that the Arab Afghans was a mainstream movement. However, this was clearly not the case. Even if we accept the highest estimates of the number of Saudi mujahidin, that is, 20,000, this is still just a fraction of a population which numbered between 6 and 12 million at the time. If one believes, like this author, that the number of Saudis who underwent substantial weapons training in this period is more likely to have been somewhere between 1,000 and 5,000, then we are certainly talking about a marginal phenomenon. This prompts the question: exactly who went for jihad and why? In this chapter I shall analyse the biographies of 161 Saudis who went for jihad in Afghanistan, Bosnia, Tajikistan and Chechnya prior to 1996, by looking in turn at their backgrounds, motivations and recruitment patterns.[2]

Hijazi domination

Socio-economically speaking, the early Saudi jihadists were an unremarkable group (see specific data in Appendix 1). Most were men in their early twenties from urban middle-class backgrounds, but the range of individual backgrounds was considerable and included both delinquents and notables. The early jihadists represent a more heterogeneous group than both the late 1990s al-Qaida recruits and the 2003 QAP fighters, which probably reflects the fact that jihad volunteerism

[1] *al-Quds al-Arabi*, 20 March 2005.

[2] For 1980s Saudi population figures, see Vassiliev, *The History of Saudi Arabia*, 457.

in the 1980s and early 1990s was a relatively uncontroversial and low-risk activity.

As a group, early jihadists were neither underprivileged nor fanatically religious before their departure. Several fighters are described as having led 'sinful lives', and only a small number of people worked in the religious sector. This is not to say that they were criminals or drug addicts either: while there are signs of delinquency in a minority of biographies, few if any had run-ins with police prior to their first departure. Overall, alienation and deprivation seem not to have been very important factors. Some recruits had in fact very promising futures. Usama bin Ladin could have lived a life in opulence and the young Samir al-Suwaylim (Ibn Khattab) was a brilliant pupil who had interned at Aramco and planned to study in the United States.[3]

One of the few distinguishing features of the early jihadists as a population is their geographical origin. The Hijaz region is strongly overrepresented, especially among pre-1987 recruits. This is most likely because the first movers were Hijazis and because the crucial international Islamist networks were particularly strong in the relatively cosmopolitan Mecca–Medina–Jidda triangle. As the Afghan jihad proceeded, the mass of recruits became more geographically heterogeneous. From the late 1980s onward most regions are represented, although not nearly to the same extent. Worth noting is the strong presence of recruits from the Eastern Province in the Chechen sub-sample, which probably reflects the network effect from the early involvement of Khattab and his companions. On the whole, however, the socio-economic profiles do not tell us much about why people went to Afghanistan.

For the umma and the afterlife

To judge motivations from the jihadists' own statements is no doubt a perilous exercise. Biographies from the jihadi literature are usually hagiographic and provide post-facto rationalisations of a person's decision to join the jihad. Moreover, motivations are complex and composite, while any overview like the one provided here will necessarily be reductive. However, for all their imperfections, these sources remain our only, and a hitherto underexploited, window into the minds of the early Saudi jihadists.

The principal type of declared motivation found in biographies of Saudis in the early jihad fronts is the desire to help oppressed Muslims

[3] See 'The Martyrs of Afghanistan' (www.alfirdaws.org), 64–7; and al-Nowaiser, 'Khattab, the Man who Died for the Cause of Chechnya'.

in need. Most biographies highlight the obvious: that Muslim populations in Afghanistan, Bosnia or Chechnya were being occupied and oppressed by non-Muslims.

One of the best explanations for the role of pan-Islamism in driving Saudis abroad for jihad in the 1980s and early 1990s was provided by Nasir al-Bahri, a former Bin Ladin bodyguard who gave an extensive interview to *al-Quds al-Arabi* in 2005. With surprising analytical clarity, he described his increasing political awareness about the situation in other parts of the Muslim world, and a sense of victimhood and pan-Islamic solidarity:

> Our basic motive in jihad was to defend Muslim lands. We were greatly affected by the tragedies we were witnessing and the events we were seeing: children crying, women widowed and the high number of incidents of rape. We were greatly affected by all that. When we went forward for jihad, we experienced a bitter reality. We saw things that were more awful than anything we had expected or had heard or seen in the media. It was as though we were like 'a cat with closed eyes' that opened its eyes at those woes. We began to have real contact with the other trends, the enemies of the umma, and the ideology of the umma began to evolve in our minds. We realised we were a nation [*umma*] that had a distinguished place among nations. Otherwise, what would make me leave Saudi Arabia – and I am of Yemeni origin – to go and fight in Bosnia? The issue of nationalism was put out of our minds, and we acquired a wider view than that, namely the issue of the umma. The issue was very simple at the start, yet it was a motive and an incentive for jihad.[4]

There are many other examples of people who seem to have been motivated by a desire to defend or redress the honour of the Muslim nation. One Saudi Afghan wrote in his will that 'Jihad is the only way to restore to the umma its full honour.' In interviews with this author, several Saudi Islamists have argued that the Arab military participation in Afghanistan in the 1980s reflected the accumulated frustration and sense of impotency over the humiliation of Muslims, particularly in Palestine. 'After all these years of humiliation', one source said, 'they could finally do something to help their Muslim brothers.' Pan-Islamist motivations are particularly prominent in the biographies of Saudis who fought in Bosnia, presumably because the pan-Islamist atmosphere was particularly heated in the early 1990s. For example, one biography of a Saudi martyred in Bosnia noted that 'he would follow the news of his brothers with the deepest empathy and he wanted to do something, anything, to help them'. The friend of another Bosnia volunteer recalled: 'we would often sit and talk about the slaughtering to which Muslims are

[4] *al-Quds al-Arabi*, 20 March 2005.

subjected, and his eyes would fill with tears. When he heard about the events in Bosnia, he did not hesitate.'[5]

Pan-Islamist sentiment also affected recruitment indirectly through the families of the jihadists. In the case of one fighter, we are told how 'one day his mother was sitting at home and she saw the news on the television reporting the genocide of the Muslims in Bosnia. When she saw this she said to Abu Sayf, "My son, get up and go! Look what they are doing, they are raping our sisters and killing our brothers. My son, get up and go – I don't want to see you again!"'[6]

The pan-Islamist discourse emphasised solidarity and altruism towards the victims of oppression more than expressions of hatred of the oppressor. In the biographies, descriptions of the suffering of the Bosnians are much more frequent than deliberations on the wickedness of the Serbs. The Russians and the Serbs are often simply referred to as 'the enemy' without further ado. This is in line with Marc Sageman's observation that jihadi activism is more about in-group love than out-group hatred. In one telling account we read about a young Saudi who 'grew up hearing about the exploits of his brothers in Tajikistan'. So he decided to join them there and flew over in 1992, 'all for the love of his brothers'.[7]

At the same time, there is little doubt that recruits believed they were doing something divinely ordained. They may have had different levels of religious conviction and piety, but they all saw their jihad as a religious duty. As one Saudi martyr in Afghanistan wrote in his will, 'I am fighting with my money and my soul in the complete conviction that jihad is an individual duty; this is why I went for jihad.' The biography of another Saudi Afghan noted that 'when he heard the fatwa saying that jihad is an individual obligation, he went to Afghanistan'. There was undoubtedly a ritual dimension to jihad participation; being a mujahid, the recruits believed, was the ultimate display of devotion and the best way to be a Muslim.[8]

Even better was being a mujahid during Ramadan, because of the special benefits that allegedly befall those who are martyred during the month of fasting. There are strong indications, in the biographies and elsewhere, that many, if not the majority of the militants, were driven partly by a desire for martyrdom. A Saudi journalist who interviewed

[5] 'The Martyrs of Afghanistan', 23–6; Muhammad, *al-ansar al-'arab*, 33; author's interview with unidentified Saudi Islamist.

[6] al-Qatari and al-Madani, *min qisas al-shuhada' al-'arab*, 40, 122–5; 'In the Hearts of Green Birds', Azzam Publications, cited in Kohlmann, *Al-Qaida's Jihad in Europe*, 89.

[7] al-Qatari and al-Madani, *min qisas al-shuhada' al-'arab*, 119–21.

[8] *al-Jihad*, no. 16: 12; *al-Mujahid*, no. 5: 22.

Saudi Afghans noted that 'many of them said they came to be martyred' and that more Saudis than others died in Afghanistan. Biographies of Saudi volunteers convey what appears to be a genuine belief in the benefits of martyrdom. One fighter, killed in Afghanistan in 1985, wrote in his will, 'some people see life as a road to death; I see it as a road to life'. However, while everyone probably believed in the miracles (*karamat*) of martyrdom, not everyone was hoping or expecting to die in battle. One fighter allegedly used to say '[I'll go to] university after the jihad.' Ironically, he was killed in Afghanistan.[9]

For some, jihad participation seems to have represented a religious purification process. There are several accounts of individuals who led 'sinful lives' until they were 'guided by God' and went to Afghanistan as if to compensate for their previous transgressions. One volunteer 'had begun looking for a place that could wash away his sins and accept his repentance'. Another recruit led a completely unobservant life until being 'guided by God' and heading off for jihad. When he came to Afghanistan, Ramadan was approaching, but the problem was that he had never fasted in his entire life, despite being in his late twenties and living in Mecca. He had to be taught how to fast by the camp instructor, and 'when he managed to fast a whole day, the mujahidin threw a small party'.[10]

A similar dynamic seems to have driven a small number of people who left for jihad after a traumatic experience such as the loss of a parent, a divorce or an accident. We find a good account of trauma-induced religious conversion and jihad participation in the biography of Fahd al-Qahtani, a Saudi martyr in Bosnia. Al-Qahtani was a truck driver who led a less than pious existence until mid-1993, when he had an accident while drink-driving on the King Fahd causeway on the way back from Bahrain (where alcohol and other sinful things are widely available). He was helped out of the car and treated by a couple of religious young men who befriended him and inspired him to change his lifestyle. Shortly afterwards, his two saviours went off to Bosnia, but when they came back, the now deeply religious al-Qahtani begged them to take him to the jihad. In early 1994 he went, only to be killed a year later.[11]

[9] al-Jasir, '*qissat al-afghan al-sa'udiyyin*', 21 and 23; Jasir al-Jasir, '*mu'azzam al-afghan al-sa'udiyyin yumarisun hayatihim bi-sura tabi'iyya ba'd 'awdatihim* [Most Saudi Afghanis Lead Normal Lives after their Return]', *al-Majalla*, no. 847 (1996); *al-Jihad*, no. 54/5: 40.

[10] al-Qatari and al-Madani, *min qisas al-shuhada' al-'arab*, 54–7, 108–9; *al-Jihad*, no. 53: 27; *al-Jihad*, no. 54/5: 43.

[11] *al-Jihad*, no. 56: 25; Untitled collection of martyrdom biographies; al-Qatari and al-Madani, *min qisas al-shuhada' al-'arab*, 31–2.

While politics and religion were important motivations for early Saudi mujahidin, many recruits also seem to have been attracted to the adventurous and militaristic dimension of the jihad experience. For many, the excitement of travel, weapons training and companionship seems to have been more important than ideological factors. One young Saudi, named Sawad al-Madani, travelled to America in the early 1990s intending to settle down, and allegedly 'lived like any other lost youth there, far from his Lord'. In 1994, he went back to Saudi Arabia to visit his parents, right at the time when his cousin, who was fighting in Bosnia, was gravely wounded and sent back to the kingdom for medical treatment. When Sawad went to see his cousin, he met all of the latter's mujahidin friends who were constantly talking about jihad, battles and martyrs. Sawad was deeply impressed by the stories of heroism and companionship and decided to go to Bosnia to experience the same adventure.[12]

The stories of hardship and heroism added an element of chivalry to the jihad experience which imbued the returnees from jihad with a certain status in many youth communities. As Nasir al-Bahri explained,

> the youth used to envy those who went to Afghanistan and were greatly influenced by them ... When we used to look at the Afghan suits that the mujahidin who returned from Afghanistan wore as they walked the streets of Jidda, Mecca or Medina, we used to feel we were living with the generation of the triumphant companions of the Prophet, and hence we looked up to them as an example and an authority ... I recall that one of our colleagues went to Afghanistan and spent two weeks there during the month of Ramadan. When he returned, we gave him a hero's welcome. He influenced us greatly.[13]

This social dimension may help explain why so many Saudi teenagers travelled to Pakistan and Afghanistan for very short periods, often during their summer holidays. For many, obtaining the social status of a mujahid was clearly a driving force.[14]

Very interestingly, anti-Americanism is practically absent from these biographies. In a rare mention of America, one recruit says he regretted 'the hamburger and Coca-Cola life' that he had lived as a student in the United States. Such remarks seem harmless when compared to the ferocious anti-Westernism of the global jihadists of the 2000s. Nasir al-Bahri confirmed this general disinterest in America, saying 'we did not go because of the Americans, but because there was a conflict between Muslims and others'. Equally interesting is the fact that these texts

[12] al-Qatari and al-Madani, *min qisas al-shuhada' al-'arab*, 196–9.
[13] *al-Quds al-Arabi*, 20 March 2005.
[14] Author's interview with Abdallah Anas, London, January 2006; al-Jasir, '*mu'azzam al-afghan al-sa'udiyyin*'.

contain practically no indications of disaffection with the Saudi regime. Some fighters in Afghanistan even bore *noms de guerre*, or *kunyas*, that ended in 'al-Saudi' (such as Abu Ubayda al-Saudi), which was unheard of in jihadist circles in the 1990s and 2000s because of the implicit recognition of the ruling Al Sa'ud family.[15]

Recruitment in the open

The question of how people join militant activism is one of the most fascinating and complex issues in the study of political violence. As Marc Sageman has pointed out, the notion of 'recruitment' is problematic because it connotes a formalised act of agent acquisition, while the reality of individual mobilisation is considerably more complex and informal. The term 'joining' is vaguer and thus better suited to capture the multiplicity of possible trajectories from normalcy to militant activism. It notably facilitates the basic distinction between top-down and bottom-up joining processes. Yet the term does not solve the other major conceptual problem, namely that involvement in militant activism is often a long and multi-staged process where it is difficult to tell exactly at which point a person actually joins. For this reason, recent scholarship has tended to prefer the term 'radicalisation', which is indeed flexible and useful, but also vague. In the following I focus specifically on the social circumstances immediately preceding and facilitating the person's departure, not on the broader ideological process which may have underpinned the decision to depart.[16]

There was no organised large-scale recruitment apparatus for jihad in the 1980s and early 1990s Saudi Arabia, for the simple reason that the Arabs in Afghanistan or Bosnia were never organised in a coherent and hierarchical entity. However, as we saw in the previous chapter, some key entrepreneurs undertook ad hoc recruitment missions to the kingdom, especially in the early stage of the mobilisation to Afghanistan and Bosnia. Usama bin Ladin, for example, travelled extensively between Saudi Arabia and Peshawar to 'bring more people' and would even pay the travel expenses of some volunteers. He also dispatched representatives to Saudi Arabia charged with recruiting new mujahidin. Several jihadi biographies speak of recruitment at the hands of Bin Ladin, Abdallah Azzam or their envoys.[17]

[15] *al-Quds al-Arabi*, 24 March 2005; *al-Jihad*, no. 53: 27.

[16] Sageman, *Understanding Terror Networks*, 121–5.

[17] Muhammad, *al-ansar al-'arab*, 145; *al-Jihad*, no. 47: 36; *al-Jihad*, no. 59: 39; *al-Jihad*, no. 54/5: 37; Untitled collection of martyr biographies; Chris Hedges, 'Saudi Fighter in Afghanistan Becomes "Martyr" in Bosnia', *New York Times*, 5 December 1992.

There are several cases of Saudi teachers and scholars encouraging or in some cases accompanying pupils to Afghanistan. For example, the biography of Muhammad al-Zahrani explained how he and a group of other pupils from a school in Dammam went to Afghanistan in a delegation led by their teacher. Other accounts tell of students allegedly being dispatched by religious scholars to the jihad in Afghanistan. In the early 1980s, a certain Nur al-Din al-Jaza'iri, a religious student in Medina, was allegedly 'sent by Sheikh Abu Bakr al-Jaza'iri every year to join the mujahidin'.[18]

Others were inspired at rallies or public lectures. For example, one of the first Saudis in Afghanistan, a certain Nur al-Din, decided to go to Afghanistan after attending a lecture by the Afghan leader Abd Rabb al-Rasul Sayyaf in Medina in 1982. The most influential public speaker in the 1980s was undoubtedly Abdallah Azzam himself. Barbaros, the entrepreneur of the Arabs in Bosnia, described his involvement in the Afghan jihad:

> Now, concerning the beginning of Jihad in my case, I was one of those who heard about Jihad in Afghanistan when it started. I used to hear about it, but was hesitant about this Jihad. This is most probably because we forgot the concept of Jihad in Islam. One of those who came to our land was Sheikh Dr Abdallah Azzam. I heard him rallying the youth to come forth and go to Afghanistan. This was in 1984, I think. I decided to go and check the matter for myself. This was, and all praise be to God, the beginning of my Jihad.[19]

Another example of Azzam's personal influence as well as the role of family members is the following passage from a biography of a Saudi in Afghanistan:

> When Azzam came to give a sermon in the al-Shu'aybi mosque [in Riyadh], Khalid and his father were there. After the lecture, his father went up to Azzam, took him by the hand and said 'my son wants to leave his wife and two children to go to Afghanistan. What is the ruling on this?' Azzam said jihad was an individual duty, whereupon the father said 'so be it'.[20]

Some early jihadists joined the battlefront on their own initiative, without the mediation of a personal recruiter or a preacher. For example, one of the people interviewed by this author, a former Saudi Islamist

[18] Untitled collection of martyr biographies; Muhammad, *al-ansar al-'arab*, 80–1.

[19] *al-Bunyan al-Marsus*, no. 16/17 (November/December 1986): 30; Bergen, *The Osama bin Laden I Know*, 27–8; Sam Roe, Laurie Cohen and Stephen Franklin, 'How Saudi Wealth Fueled Holy War', *Chicago Tribune*, 22 February 2004; 'Interview with Sheikh al-Mujahideen Abu Abdel Aziz'.

[20] *al-Jihad*, no. 54/5: 39.

called Muhammad, offered an illustrative account of his departure to Afghanistan in 1986:

> I was a first-year student in the college of Sharia in Dammam. Everyone was talking about Afghanistan so I just decided to go and see for myself. I was not recruited by anybody, and I travelled on my own. My father was not very happy about it. I went to an office in the Rawda district of Riyadh where they helped me with the practicalities, and then I went from Riyadh to Pakistan. I had sold my car before going, and when I came to Peshawar I gave the money to Bayt al-Ansar. Then I trained near Jaji, and I remember meeting Abd al-Rahman [Hasan] al-Surayhi. Then I went to Ma'sadat al-Ansar. Most of the people there were from Jidda. I didn't stay long because I didn't like it.[21]

However, the biographies suggest that such solo acts were relatively rare. In a majority of cases, the decision-making process and the journey were carried out in the company of others. The process of joining the jihad was fundamentally a social experience, and the main vehicles of mobilisation were networks of kinship and friendship. The idea of going to Afghanistan or Bosnia often came from a friend or relative who had already visited. The examples are numerous. Sayyid Ahmad Khalifa went to Peshawar after his son-in-law Wa'il Julaydan settled there. Many in Bin Ladin's extended family, like his brother-in-law Jamal Khalifa and his cousin Muhammad al-Habashi, went for jihad. Abd al-Aziz al-Muqrin, who went to Afghanistan in 1991, followed in the footsteps of several of his relatives and neighbours.[22]

Group adherence emboldened individuals and reduced the psychological barrier to departure. There are several examples of groups or pairs of old friends who travelled together to Afghanistan. Others went to Afghanistan with an older brother. Many decisions to go for jihad were no doubt partly driven by group processes of one-upmanship. For example, the biography of Abu Hammam al-Janubi explained how 'he would often sit with one of his friends exchanging complaints about the situation in Bosnia and expressing their desire to go there. Then they began to ask around and follow up on information on how to get there. Then they found a way and they travelled to Croatia.' Another example is the aforementioned story of Sawad al-Madani, who decided to go to Bosnia after meeting his injured cousin's jihadist friends who were trying to outdo each other with heroic battle stories.[23]

[21] Author's interview with unidentified Saudi Islamist.
[22] *al-Jihad*, no. 47: 37.
[23] al-Qatari and al-Madani, *min qisas al-shuhada' al-'arab*, 27–30, 40.

An often overlooked dimension of political mobilisation in conservative societies is the role of parents. In these biographies there are several examples of parents encouraging their children to go to Afghanistan. We already mentioned the mother who practically chased her son off to Bosnia. Another fighter's biography said 'his father sent him to Afghanistan when he was only 15 years old'. Khalid al-Qablan's mother encouraged him to go to Afghanistan, and 'would write him letters to keep his spirits up'. However, other parents, probably the majority, prevented their sons from going. The biography of Mish'al al-Qahtani explained that his mother refused to let him go abroad for jihad, but as soon as she was dead, he went straight to Bosnia. There are accounts of fathers and elder brothers travelling to Afghanistan to bring their sons and brothers back. Sometimes, however, the parents ended up joining the mujahidin themselves.[24]

The role of friendship and kinship in these processes of joining helps to shed light on the geographical pattern of mobilisation to the early jihad fronts. Practically all Saudis who went to Afghanistan prior to 1986 were from the Mecca–Medina–Jidda triangle. This Hijazi domination reflects the fact that recruitment began with entrepreneurs from this area and subsequently followed their social networks. Similarly, the overrepresentation of Saudis from the Eastern Province in Chechnya is explained by the fact that prominent Arab leaders in Chechnya, as Khattab and Abu Umar al-Sayf, were from the East.

When asked why some people went to Afghanistan while others did not, most Saudi Islamists interviewed by this author did not initially understand the question. 'That's like trying to find out why two brothers in the same family chose to study different subjects at university', said a Saudi who was in Islamabad for most of the 1980s. His perception was that the Saudi contingent was a cross-section of the Saudi youth population, drawn from all locations and all social strata. In contrast, Saudi liberals often said that the Saudi Afghans represented a disadvantaged stratum of Saudi society. 'They were mainly criminals and delinquents, people with problems, some were even drug addicts', said one source.[25]

This review has shown that the puzzle of selective recruitment to classical jihadism is difficult to explain with socio-economic indicators, and that social networks and the contingency of ideological exposure

[24] 'Battle of Tishin, North Bosnia, October 1992: 25 Mujahideen Defeat 200 Serb Special Forces' (www.azzam.com); *al-Jihad*, 46, 25; al-Qatari and al-Madani, *min qisas al-shuhada' al-'arab*, 27–30; 'The Martyrs of Afghanistan', 33–7.

[25] Author's interviews with unidentified Saudi Islamist and Mansur al-Nuqaydan.

were more significant factors. The most counterintuitive finding was that anti-Americanism and hostility to the Saudi regime were not major motivations, probably because the ideology driving most people was Abdallah Azzam's classical jihadism. This would change in the mid-1990s with the rise of the global jihadist movement.

4 Opportunities for global jihad

In the mid-1990s, the environment for Islamist activism in Saudi Arabia changed considerably. The government came to view the Sahwa as a political threat and jihad veterans as a security threat. By the late 1990s, most forms of Islamist activism, including classical jihadism, represented clandestine and relatively perilous endeavours. How, then, was Usama bin Ladin able to recruit so many Saudis to his Afghan camps in the late 1990s? A crucial part of the answer lies in the evolution of the political opportunity structure for global jihadism in the kingdom between 1996 and 2001. Of particular importance were developments in three areas: policing, international conflicts involving Muslims, and the Saudi Islamist arena. However, before we examine these developments more closely, it is useful to recall the events between 1994 and 1996 which forever changed the relationship between the state and the Islamist community.

From the Burayda intifada to the 1995 Riyadh bombing

The rise of the reformist opposition in the early 1990s represented the most serious challenge to the Saudi state's legitimacy in the kingdom's modern history. While it never turned violent, the Sahwa articulated a more explicit and biting critique of the Saudi system than the regime was willing to tolerate. Tensions escalated throughout 1992, arrests began in May 1993 and by the autumn of 1994 the time had come for a final showdown. In mid-September 1994, after a series of rallies in Burayda and Riyadh that became known as the 'Burayda intifada', the authorities imprisoned all the main leaders and top activists of the Sahwa, some 110 people in total. Arrests continued until the late summer of 1995, by which time the domestic opposition, with the exception of its London-based branch, had effectively been silenced and over a hundred Sahwists lingered in prison.[1]

[1] Lacroix, 'Les champs de la discorde', 453–6.

The repression of the Sahwa affected the jihadist movement in three important ways. For a start, it convinced some jihadists that non-violent protest against the US military presence was futile. Usama bin Ladin and others concluded that the mujahidin had no choice but to resort to violence. Second, there were now no influential clerics to rein in renegade elements in the jihadist community. Despite their sometimes fiery rhetoric, the Sahwist leaders had been a moderating influence on the radicals, because they discouraged violence inside the kingdom. Third, the September 1994 developments triggered a chain of specific events that would lead to the 1995 Riyadh bombing.[2]

This chain of events began on 11 November 1994, when a young Islamist named Abdallah al-Hudhayf walked up to a police officer in central Riyadh and threw sulphuric acid in his face. The victim was Saud al-Shibrin, a police interrogator in the Ha'ir prison where the Sahwists were being held. Al-Hudhayf allegedly believed that police were torturing the detained Islamists, who included al-Hudhayf's father, brother and several personal friends.

For people who knew al-Hudhayf, the attack did not come as a surprise. He had radicalised as a student in the United States in the early 1980s and fought in Afghanistan in the late 1980s. In 1991, he became part of a circle of moral vigilantes who carried out non-lethal attacks on symbols of moral corruption such as video stores in the Qasim and Riyadh. However, he was more politicised than his comrades and held very anti-American views already in 1991. According to Nasir al-Barrak, the leader of the vigilante group, al-Hudhayf was consistently pushing for more violent tactics. On several occasions in 1991 and 1992, he allegedly suggested bombing compounds for Westerners in Riyadh.[3]

Partly for these reasons, al-Barrak and al-Hudhayf went their separate ways in about 1992. Al-Barrak drew closer to the Sahwa, to the point of becoming a close aide to Salman al-Awda, a relationship that would earn him his arrest in 1994. Al-Hudhayf became part of a new network of very radical Islamists in Riyadh that included extreme vigilantes (such as Sa'ud al-Utaybi, Ibrahim al-Rayis and Abd al-Aziz al-Mi'thim) and jihad veterans (such as Khalid al-Sa'id, Riyadh al-Hajiri, Muslih al-Shamrani and Abd al-Aziz al-Muqrin). Although these new radicals had only peripheral links with the Sahwa, they respected the Sahwist scholars and saw the government's repression of them as further evidence of the regime's un-Islamic character and submission to the

[2] *al-Quds al-Arabi*, 20 March 2005.

[3] '*al-sulta taftah bab al-damm: awwal shahid fi masirat al-islah* [The Authorities Open the Gates of Blood: The First Martyr on the Road to Reform]', *Bayan (CDLR)*, no. 38 (1995); author's interview with Nasir al-Barrak.

Americans. For al-Hudhayf, the September 1994 arrests and the (most likely unfounded) rumours that the Sahwist sheikhs (and his old friend Nasir al-Barrak) were being tortured constituted the final straw.[4]

Al-Hudhayf was arrested shortly after the acid attack and allegedly executed in prison on 12 August 1995. The news of his death was received with outrage in the Islamist community, because the prevailing interpretation was that he had been tortured to death by vengeful security officers, a suspicion that is probably not unfounded, for his body was never returned to his family. Al-Hudhayf immediately gained the status of a martyr and became a legend in the jihadist community. Islamists accused the Saudi government of having 'opened the gates of blood'. For al-Hudhayf's old comrades, the gloves were off.[5]

Shortly before midday on 13 November 1995, a 100 kg car bomb detonated in downtown Riyadh outside a building used by the Vinnell Corporation, a US military contractor involved in the training of the Saudi National Guard. Five Americans and two Indians were killed and some sixty people were wounded. The attack was carried out by four people in the network frequented by Abdallah al-Hudhayf in 1993 and 1994. Riyadh al-Hajiri, Muslih al-Shamrani and Khalid al-Sa'id were all veterans of Afghanistan and avid readers of Usama bin Ladin, while the fourth perpetrator, Abd al-Aziz al-Mi'thim, was a personal friend of the radical Jordanian ideologue Abu Muhammad al-Maqdisi. The four had entertained the idea of an attack since late 1994, but they decided to go ahead with their plan after they learned of al-Hudhayf's execution. According to Nasir al-Bahri, many of those who were close to Muslih al-Shamrani reported that he would often say 'By God, we are not men if we do not avenge sheikh Abdallah.'[6]

Contrary to widespread assumptions, there is no concrete evidence that the Riyadh bombing was orchestrated by al-Qaida. The militants were operating independently, although they were no doubt ideologically influenced by Usama bin Ladin. The cell obtained explosives in Yemen and rigged the device thanks to Khalid al-Sa'id's bombmaking skills acquired in Afghanistan. The attack served a triple purpose: it was a signal to the

[4] Author's interview with unidentified Saudi Islamist.

[5] '*kayfa mat al-hudhayf* [How Did al-Hudhayf Die?]', *Bayan (CDLR)*, no. 39 (1995); 'Urgent Action 200/95' (London: Amnesty International, 1995); '*al-sulta taftah bab al-damm*'.

[6] 'Four Saudis Held for Riyadh Blasts', *Arab News*, 23 April 1996; Ethan Bronner, 'In Bomber's Life, Glimpse of Saudi Dissent', *Boston Globe*, 7 July 1996; Mishari al-Dhaidi, '*'abd al-'aziz al-muqrin: kayfa tahawwala min haris marma ila haris mawt?* [Abd al-Aziz al-Muqrin: How Did he Change from a Goalkeeper to a Deathkeeper?]', *al-Sharq al-Awsat*, 18 June 2005; *al-Quds al-Arabi*, 31 March 2005; author's interview with Nasir al-Barrak.

USA for its troops to leave; a punishing blow to the Saudi government for repressing the Sahwa; and a gesture to al-Hudhayf, who had long advocated attacks against Western targets. The fact that the four gave televised confessions, no doubt under duress, before being executed in May 1996, has led some to doubt the responsibility of these four individuals. However, in the jihadist literature, the four are consistently hailed as heroes and presented matter-of-factly as the perpetrators, including by people, such as Abd al-Aziz al-Muqrin, who knew them personally.[7]

The 1995 Riyadh bombing shook the Saudi state to the core. It was the first large-scale bombing in the kingdom's history and it took both Saudi and US authorities by complete surprise. The shock was compounded by the occurrence, just half a year later, on 25 June 1996, of an even bigger bomb attack in Khobar on the east coast. An explosives-filled tanker truck ripped through a US Air Force barracks, killing 19 American servicemen and wounding nearly 400 people, in what was the largest terrorist attack on a US target since the 1983 Marine barracks bombing in Lebanon. For a long time, many suspected al-Qaida involvement, primarily because Bin Ladin praised the attack in several of his speeches. However, Bin Ladin never explicitly claimed the attack, and no concrete evidence of direct al-Qaida involvement has ever surfaced. Instead, there is considerable evidence that the attack was carried out by a militant Shiite group known as the Saudi Hizbollah. However, Khobar would indirectly affect the jihadist community through the response of the Saudi state.[8]

[7] 'Four Saudis Held for Riyadh Blasts'. For verbatim transcripts of two of the confessions, see '*i'tirafat al-mu'taqal al-awwal* [Confessions of the First Detainee]', (http://alquma.net, undated), and '*i'tirafat al-mu'taqal al-thani* [Confessions of the Second Detainee]', (http://alquma.net, undated). Several authoritative sources have dismissed the idea of a direct al-Qaida connection, including the 9/11 Commission (*The 9/11 Commission Report* (New York: W. W. Norton, 2004), 60), Saudi Interior Minister Prince Nayif (*al-Siyasa*, 4 November 1998), Saudi-raised jihadist Nasir al-Bahri (*al-Quds al-Arabi*, 31 March 2005) and not least Bin Ladin himself (Scott McCleod, 'The Paladin of Jihad', *TIME*, 6 May 1996). For evidence from the jihadi literature of the responsibility of the four accused, see e.g. Abu Jandal al-Azdi, *usama bin ladin: mujaddid al-zaman wa qahir al-amrikan* [Usama bin Ladin: Renewer of the Century and Victor over the Americans] (www.qa3edoon.com, 2003), 182; Sulayman al-Dawsary, '*al-iftitahiyya* [Opening Word]', *Sawt al-Jihad* (2003): 4; Abd al-Aziz al-Muqrin, *dawrat al-tanfidh wa harb al-'isabat* [A Course in Operational Execution and Guerrilla Warfare] (www.qa3edoon.com, 2004), 39.

[8] Hegghammer, 'Deconstructing the Myth'. Investigative journalist Gareth Porter has argued that the Saudi authorities deliberately covered up evidence of al-Qaida involvement and concocted charges against the Shiite suspects; see *Inter Press Service* (www.ips.org), 22–26 June 2009. Porter bases his argument mainly on testimonies from US analysts who say the investigation of the al-Qaida track was diverted by senior American officials wanting to implicate Iran. Still, Porter presents no concrete operational evidence of al-Qaida involvement.

Between police oppression and complacency

The Riyadh bombing prompted the government to crack down with an iron fist on veterans of the Afghan and Bosnian jihad, the very people who only a few years previously had gone out to fight with the state's blessing. The crackdown ushered in a new and confrontational phase in the relationship between the state and the jihadist movement. The Saudi response to the Riyadh bombing was a classic case of government overreaction to terrorism. Lacking a clear trail of investigation, the authorities proceeded to mass arrests and harsh interrogations in the hope of identifying the culprits. Around 200 people were arrested, about 30 of whom were members of the Libyan Islamic Fighting Group that had been living in exile in the kingdom.[9]

The next three years saw another three major waves of arrests. After the June 1996 Khobar bombing, an estimated 2,000 people were arrested as part of the police attempt to find the perpetrators. While the vast majority of detainees were Shiites, a number of Sunni jihadists were also detained and interrogated, including future QAP leader Yusuf al-Uyayri. A third wave of arrests came in February and March 1998 after the discovery of the so-called 'missile plot' against the US consulate in Jidda (see next chapter). This time over 800 people – mostly Saudi jihad veterans, including the famous Barbaros – were arrested. The fourth and last major wave of arrest of jihadists prior to 9/11 occurred in late 1998 or early 1999, when authorities allegedly arrested around 300 people after the discovery of a second missile-smuggling attempt.[10]

The crackdowns had a traumatising effect on the jihadist community because the police made widespread use of torture. The evidence of torture in prisons such as al-Ruways in Jidda between 1995 and 1998 is overwhelming and unquestionable. For a start, the Saudi jihadist literature is full of detailed and mutually corroborating torture accounts from this period. Former al-Ruways detainees interviewed by this author have confirmed that torture was used. Amnesty International and Human Rights Watch have also documented the use of torture in

[9] Author's interviews with unidentified Saudi Islamists; '*al-shaykh abu layth al-qasimi ahad qiyaday al-jama'a al-muqatila ba'd fararihi min sijn al-ruways* [Abu Layth al-Qasimi, One of the Leaders of the Fighting Group, after his Escape from Ruways Prison] (www.almuqatila.com, undated); Abu Jandal al-Azdi, *wujub istinqadh al-mustad'afin fi sujun al-tawaghit* [The Obligation to Rescue the Oppressed in the Tyrants' Prisons] (www.tawhed.ws, 2004); *al-Islah*, no. 88.

[10] Author's interview with Faris bin Huzzam; 'World Report 1997' (New York: Human Rights Watch, 1998), 297; '820 Mujahideen Imprisoned in Saudi Arabia, March 1998' (www.azzam.com, 1998); 'Saudi Torturers Rape Mujahideen During Interrogation' (www.azzam.com, undated); 'Over 300 Bin Laden Companions Arrested in Saudi Arabia', *Ausaf*, 26 March 1999.

Saudi prisons in this period. Needless to say, many detainees were also held for long periods without trial.[11]

The shock of the maltreatment was amplified by the fact that the detainees had perceived their activities abroad as entirely legitimate and even encouraged by the state. A common theme in the Saudi jihadist literature is the profound bitterness about the state's ingratitude towards the sacrifice of the jihadists. As QAP militant Ali al-Harbi explained in 2003:

> we went out to Bosnia to defend our brothers with the encouragement of [Saudi] television and its ulama. So we went there and came back, only to find prison and torture. I personally stayed in a cell for a year and three months for no reason whatsoever, except that I had gone to Bosnia. Many of the brothers were imprisoned ... and they were tortured systematically.[12]

The 1996 and 1998 crackdowns traumatised a generation of jihadists and contributed strongly to the radicalisation of the Saudi jihadist movement. Many accounts describe how the interrogators accused the detainees of being *takfiris* (Islamists who consider other Muslims infidels), something which the detainees vehemently denied. They were then tortured into confessing that they considered the King and the regime as infidels. There is strong evidence to suggest that many of the detainees genuinely did not consider the regime as infidel, but were rather classical jihadists supportive of pan-Islamic struggles outside Saudi Arabia. By the time they left prison they were naturally more critical – although even then not always *takfiri* – of the regime. The authorities thus created the very phenomenon they were trying to counter. As Nasir al-Bahri noted:

> These youths were 'against' and have now become 'for'. They were against operations inside Saudi Arabia, and now they themselves carry them out in Saudi Arabia. Why did many of them join al-Qaida? This is because they now find in al-Qaida a means through which to avenge what happened to them. All this must be taken into consideration.[13]

The torture in al-Ruways would also lead some militants to seek vengeance on the security establishment in general and on specific

[11] See e.g. 'Torture in the Saudi Prisons', *Nida'ul Islam*, no. 21 (1997); 'Saudi Torturers Rape'; al-Azdi, *wujub istinqadh al-mustad'afin*. See also Ali al-Harbi's testimony in the QAP film *badr al-riyadh*; author's interviews with three unidentified Saudi Islamists; 'Behind Closed Doors: Unfair Trials in Saudi Arabia' (Amnesty International, 1997); 'Saudi Arabia: A Secret State of Suffering' (Amnesty International, 2000); 'Saudi Arabia Remains a Fertile Ground for Torture with Impunity' (Amnesty International, 2002).

[12] '*badr al-riyadh* [Badr of Riyadh]' (Al-Sahhab Foundation for Media Production, 2004).

[13] 'Saudi Torturers Rape'; *al-Quds al-Arabi*, 3 August 2004.

interrogators in particular. The QAP allegedly had a 'wanted list' of the top ten security officers it wanted liquidated. In June 2005, militants killed a well-known interrogator called Mubarak al-Sawat outside his home in Riyadh. Known simply as 'Mubarak', al-Sawat was infamous in the jihadist community for his alleged mistreatment of prisoners in al-Ruways in the 1990s. In April 2007, a high-ranking police officer in the Qasim was decapitated by militants in a similarly motivated attack. Another symbolic revenge attack came in December 2006 when gunmen attacked security guards at the gate of the al-Ruways prison.[14]

Around 1999, however, the policing of the Islamist community softened as the result of a broader process of limited political liberalisation in Saudi Arabia. This liberalisation manifested itself primarily in the media, which was allowed a somewhat greater degree of freedom of expression from 1998 onward. This notably allowed a small group of progressive Islamist intellectuals to assert themselves in the public arena. These writers, whom Stéphane Lacroix has termed 'Islamo-liberals', notably found an outlet in the recently established and politically more daring *al-Watan* newspaper based in the southern city of Abha. Another development was the release, in trickles, of the imprisoned Sahwists, which began in 1997. Salman al-Awda, Safar al-Hawali and Nasir al-Umar, the icons of the Sahwa, were released last, on 25 June 1999. With a few exceptions (such as the hardliner Sa'd bin Zu'ayr), all Sahwists had been released by mid-1999.[15]

Three main factors account for this limited liberalisation process. First was the political ascent of Crown Prince Abdallah, who had assumed gradually more power since King Fahd's stroke in 1996. By 1998, the slightly more reform-oriented Abdallah may have felt confident enough in his own position to allow for more public debate. The 100-year anniversary (in Islamic calendar years) of the Saudi state in 1999 may have been exploited by Abdallah as a suitable occasion for symbolic acts and a slight change of political course. Second was the 'al-Jazeera effect'. The Qatar-based satellite TV network had been launched in 1996 and

[14] Saad al-Matrafi, 'Terrorists Wanted to Film Killing of al-Sawat', *Arab News*, 30 June 2005; Samir al-Sa'di, 'Officer Killed in Drive-By Shooting', *Arab News*, 20 June 2005; Biography of Suhayl al-Sahli (aka Yasin al-Bahr) in Muhibb al-Jihad, '*shuhada' ard al-rafidayn* [Martyrs of the Land of the Two Rivers]' (www.al-hikma.net, 2005); Samir al-Sa'di, 'Terrorists Likely Killed Officer', *Arab News*, 16 April 2007; Ebtihaj Nakshbandy, 'Gunmen Kill Two in Attack outside Saudi Prison', *Reuters*, 7 December 2006.

[15] Author's interview with Sa'ud al-Sarhan, Riyadh, April 2004; author's interview with Abdallah Bijad al-Utaybi, Riyadh, April 2004; 'Saudi Arabia Releases Three Activists', *ArabicNews.com*, 28 June 1999.

was being watched extensively in Saudi Arabia despite an official ban on satellite dishes. The openness of the debates on al-Jazeera exposed the staleness of the Saudi media and brought with it a certain demand for media reform in the kingdom. Third was the decline in the oil price in the late 1990s, which rentier state theorists would argue may have led the government to pay more attention to public demands as a way of compensating for its reduced ability to provide social and economic services.

As part of this limited political opening, the government ordered reforms in the prison system and the end to the use of torture of security detainees. Torture victims were recognised and allegedly even awarded financial compensation by the state. By all accounts, the use of torture in Saudi prisons decreased significantly at this point. Subsequent security suspects were probably not given VIP treatment, but the most vicious practices seem to have been scrapped for good.[16]

With the 1999 prison reform, the Saudi security establishment reverted to its 'normal' mode of relatively soft and non-intrusive policing of Islamists. There are few available reports of violent police raids between early 1999 and late 2002. The Saudi police seem to have treated their jihadist community relatively gently, at least as long as their militant activities took place abroad and were not too conspicuously linked to Bin Ladin.

The reluctance to break up jihadist fundraising and recruitment networks between 1999 and 2002 was not simply a question of police culture, it was also about politics. The state still relied on its image as a defender of Islamic causes for political legitimacy, and large parts of the Saudi population still viewed support for Muslim resistance groups as synonymous with solidarity and altruism. There are good reasons to believe that parts of the Saudi security establishment had personal sympathies for the resistance struggles in Chechnya and Palestine or for the Taliban regime, and were happy to let classical jihadist fundraisers and recruiters operate relatively freely. Like the Pakistani ISI, the Saudi police and security services are known to include many pious officers. While many of the Western post-9/11 speculations about 'al-Qaida sympathies' in the Saudi security establishment are no doubt exaggerated, it would be naïve to think that the Saudi police force was entirely free of pan-Islamist sympathies. There exists concrete evidence of jihadi penetration of Saudi security services in the

[16] Author's interviews with unidentified Saudi Islamist and Sa'ud al-Sarhan; author's interview with Human Rights Watch researcher Christoph Wilcke, New York, March 2007.

late 1990s. Among documents retrieved from al-Qaida safe houses in Afghanistan by allied forces in late 2001 were classified Saudi intelligence reports.[17]

The fundamental problem about the Saudi police approach to Islamist activism from the mid-1990s onward was neither its harshness nor its complacency, but its *inconsistency*. The Saudi security establishment was in fact hard and soft at the same time. Or to be more precise, it was at first oppressive and finally complacent, which proved to be a very bad formula, reminiscent of Egyptian president Anwar Sadat's sudden release of Islamists in 1970–1 following years of draconian policing under Nasser. The torture of the mid-1990s radicalised a generation of militants who were subsequently given considerable room for manoeuvre. This opening in the political opportunity structure was reinforced by a number of near-simultaneous international political developments.

New pan-Islamist causes

After half a decade of relative quiet on the battlefronts of the umma, a series of events between 1999 and 2001 caused a resurgence of pan-Islamist sentiment in the Saudi population in general and in Islamist circles in particular. The real increase in violent and visible conflicts involving Muslims on the losing side gave the pan-Islamist discourse greater resonance.

The first conflict to touch the pan-Islamist nerve was Kosovo, where Slobodan Milosevic's Serb forces escalated their campaign of ethnic cleansing against the Muslim Kosovo–Albanian population in early 1999. As in previous conflicts involving Muslim populations, the Organisation of the Islamic Conference rapidly convened to issue a declaration in support of the Muslims in Kosovo. The Saudi government issued vocal condemnations of the Serb actions and made efforts to bring the Kosovo issue onto the domestic and international agendas. Soon after the conflict hit the news, the kingdom established a Joint Committee for Kosovo (headed by Prince Nayif), which by August 1999 had delivered US$45 million in aid. Saudi media, now accompanied by

[17] In late 2001, journalists from the *Wall Street Journal* purchased a computer in Kabul from an Afghan who had obtained it from a house used by al-Qaida in the Afghan capital. The Afghan entered the property after it was bombed by US planes and its Arab occupants had fled. The computer had been used by Ayman al-Zawahiri and other Arab militants, many of them members of Egyptian Islamic Jihad. Among the many interesting documents discovered were classified documents from the Saudi security services; author's interview with Andrew Higgins, Paris, March 2005.

al-Jazeera, covered the developments extensively. There is also evidence of limited military participation by Saudi jihadists in Kosovo.[18]

By far the most important development was the second Chechen war, which broke out in late August 1999, when Russia invaded Chechnya in response to the raids by the rebel leader Shamil Basayev into Dagestan. The massive Russian air campaign and ground offensive killed thousands of civilians and flattened the capital Grozny. These events received extensive media coverage in Saudi Arabia and the Arab world. The situation prompted official Saudi expressions of sympathy with the Chechens, although the official condemnations were somewhat measured, probably in consideration of the power of Putin's Russia. Saudi authorities also provided considerable economic and humanitarian, though not military, assistance to Chechnya. More significantly, clerics from the Saudi religious establishment such as Muhammad bin Uthaymin, as well as influential Islamist clerics such as Abdallah bin Jibrin, also issued fatwas in late 1999 declaring the Chechen resistance a legitimate jihad.[19]

The Chechen conflict was crucial for the growth of the global jihadist movement in the kingdom. Outrage at the war in Chechnya was one of the most oft-cited motivations of Saudis who went to Afghanistan from 1999 onward. Several factors explain why the Chechen cause sparked such strong reactions in Saudi Arabia. First was the sheer scale of the bloodshed. The scope and brutality of the Russian genocide in Chechnya arguably exceeded that of all previous conflicts involving Muslim populations. Second was the role of al-Jazeera. Chechnya was the first major pan-Islamist cause outside Palestine and Lebanon to be covered by Arab satellite TV. Third was the presence in Chechnya of Khattab, the Saudi leader of the Arab fighters in Chechnya. Khattab installed a

[18] 'OIC Denounces Serbs' Aggression on Kosovo', *ArabicNews.com*, 22 March 1999. The official Saudi aid to Kosovo was described in detail in a magazine published by the Saudi embassy in Washington in late 1999; see 'Extending a Helping Hand to Those in Need Throughout the World', *Saudi Arabia* 16, no. 3 (1999) (available at www.saudiembassy.net). At least one Saudi, a certain Samir al-Thubayti, is known to have fought in Kosovo; see al-Qatari and al-Madani, *min qisas al-shuhada' al-'arab*, 45–57. The American convert and jihadist Aukai Collins, who wrote about his adventures in Kosovo, mentioned the presence of Arab fighters and foreign Islamic organisations in Kosovo in the spring of 1999; see Collins, *My Jihad*, 177–212.

[19] 'Saudi Arabia Renews its Sorrow towards the Attacks against Chechnya', *ArabicNews.com*, 30 December 1999; 'Saudi Monarch Donates 5 Million Dollars for Chechens', *ArabicNews.com*, 28 December 1999; 'Saudi Denies Supporting Chechen Rebels', *ArabicNews.com*, 21 September 1999; Muhammad bin Uthaymin, '*Untitled Fatwa on Chechnya*' (www.qoqaz.com, 1999); and Abdallah bin Jibrin, '*hal al-mujahidin wa-wajib al-muslimin nahwhum* [The State of the Mujahidin and the Duty of Muslims towards them] (Decree no. 1528)' (www.qoqaz.com, 1999).

sense of national pride in young Saudi Islamists, and many of Khattab's personal friends in the kingdom such as Khalid al-Subayt worked hard on raising awareness about the Chechen cause.

A third international political development which also helped the growth of global jihadism in the kingdom was the tensions between the Taliban regime and the West, which peaked in early 2001. Disagreement over the Bin Ladin extradition issue from 1998 onward, the destruction of the Buddhist statues in Bamiyan in March 2001 and general concerns about the human rights situation fuelled a continuous war of words and made the Taliban an international pariah. The Afghanistan issue did not fuel Saudi pan-Islamism to the same extent as Chechnya and Palestine in this period, but it affected recruitment to al-Qaida because the Taliban caught the interest of radical clerics in the al-Shu'aybi school (see below).

The fourth factor which contributed to the rise of pan-Islamism in the kingdom was the second Palestinian intifada. In October 2000 a visit to the Temple Mount by Ariel Sharon sparked a revolt which had been brewing in a Palestinian community disillusioned with the 1993 Oslo agreement. The Saudi government was very vocal in its condemnation of Israel's heavy-handed suppression of the revolt, and the kingdom contributed vast sums of money to humanitarian relief in Palestine. In October 2000, the Saudi government established a pan-Arab 'al-Aqsa fund' to finance projects destined for 'safeguarding the Arab and Islamic identity of the Al-Quds' as well as an 'Intifada fund' for the 'families of martyrs'. Saudi Arabia contributed a quarter of the funds' total capital of US$1 billion. A 'Support Committee for the al-Aqsa Intifada' was set up under the auspices of Prince Nayif. Saudi TV organised several fundraising campaigns which brought in massive private donations. The authorities also implemented a widely publicised boycott of foreign companies dealing with Israel.[20]

Not surprisingly, the intifada enflamed Saudi popular opinion and caused a dramatic increase in the level of anti-Americanism in the kingdom. According to diplomatic cables from the US embassy in Saudi Arabia in 2000 and 2001, American officials in Saudi Arabia detected

[20] 'Saudi Cabinet Denounces Israeli Attacks against the Palestinians', *ArabicNews.com*, 3 October 2000; 'More Saudi Arabian Aid to the Palestinian Government', *ArabicNews.com*, 7 November 2000; 'Saudi Aid to the Palestinians', *ArabicNews.com*, 4 July 2001; 'Saudi Arabia Completes Contribution to Arab Funds for Palestinians', *ArabicNews.com*, 10 December 2001; 'SR600 Million Raised for Palestinians in Three-Day Telethon', *Arab News*, 15 April 2002; 'New Saudi Donation Campaign for the Intifada', *ArabicNews.com*, 7 June 2001; 'One Saudi Donates $6 Million to the Palestinian Intifada', *ArabicNews.com*, 3 September 2001; 'Saudi Defense Minister Calls for Boycotting Companies Dealing with Israel', *ArabicNews.com*, 18 June 2001.

a 'radical shift' in local attitudes towards Americans in late 2000. The cables reported a dramatic increase in the number of threatening phone calls, rock throwings and acts of vandalism on cars. The rise in anti-Westernism also inspired a series of much more serious attacks on Westerners in the kingdom. In fact, from late 2000 to early 2003 as many as six Westerners were killed and thirteen were wounded in a series of bombings and assassinations. This 'quiet insurgency' went largely unnoticed in the West.[21]

In late 2000 and early 2001, four small bombs went off under the cars of British and Irish expatriates in Riyadh, killing one and wounding two. While most outside observers assumed the involvement of radical Islamists, Saudi police blamed the attacks on infighting between illegal Western alcohol traders. A number of expatriates were arrested and paraded on television in 2001 appearing to confess. Today, few outside Saudi Arabia believe that alcohol traders carried out the bombings. Authorities never publicised the nature of the forensic evidence against the accused. The suspects, who were well-paid professionals with no prior record of violent crime, have all denied any involvement in the bombings and said they were beaten into confessing. Finally and most importantly, attacks of a very similar type continued after the initial suspects had been imprisoned. In mid-2002 four new car bombings struck Western expatriates, taking two lives. The Saudi Interior Ministry continued to insist that the car bombings were linked to turf wars between illegal alcohol traders in Riyadh and arrested more people.[22]

[21] 'Intifada Stirs up Gulf Arab Resentment against Israel and the USA', *Jane's Intelligence Review* 13, no. 5 (2001); Susan Taylor Martin, 'Americans Feared Attacks in Arabia', *St Petersburg Times*, 3 August 2003; 'Bin Laden/Ibn Khattab Threat Reporting' (Defendant's exhibit 792 – *US* v. *Moussaoui* (www.rcfp.org, 2001)).

[22] 'Briton Killed in Saudi Blast', *BBC News Online*, 17 November 2000; 'New Saudi Car Blast', *BBC News Online*, 23 November 2000; 'Another Briton Hurt by Bomb in Saudi Arabia', *Reuters*, 17 December 2000; Saeed Haider, 'Briton Hurt in Car Bombing Loses a Hand', *Arab News*, 18 December 2000; 'Saudis Investigate Fourth Bomb', *BBC News Online*, 17 January 2001; Neil MacFarquhar, 'Car Bomb Kills a British Banker in Saudi Arabia', *New York Times*, 21 June 2002; Brian Whitaker, 'Saudi Car Bomb Find Fuels Fears of Terror Campaign', *Guardian*, 1 July 2002; 'Man Killed by Saudi Car Bomb', *BBC News Online*, 29 September 2002. For the 'confessions' of the alcohol traders see 'Westerners Confess to Saudi Bombs', *BBC News Online*, 4 February 2001; and 'Britons Confess to Saudi Bombings', *BBC News Online*, 13 August 2001. For the torture claims, see Mark Hollingsworth and Sandy Mitchell, *Saudi Babylon: Torture, Corruption and Cover-Up Inside the House of Saud* (Edinburgh: Mainstream, 2005); 'Saudi Justice?', *CBS News Online*, 9 May 2004; and 'Belgian Sues Saudi Interior Minister', *Reuters*, 29 October 2005. For Saudi denials, see e.g. 'Kingdom not Targeted by Al-Qaeda, Sultan Says', *Arab News*, 23 June 2002; 'Saudis Deny Blasts Link to Terror', *BBC News Online*, 30 September 2002; and 'Saudi Prince: No Political Motives Behind Riyadh Explosion', *ArabicNews.com*, 1 October 2002.

The year 2001 saw several other incidents in Saudi Arabia that went unexplained. On 15 March, a bomb exploded in front of the al-Jarir bookstore on al-Ulaya street in central Riyadh, slightly injuring a Briton and an Egyptian. On 2 May, an American doctor was injured by a letter bomb sent to his office in Khobar. On 6 October 2001, a bomb blast on a busy shopping street killed an American and wounded at least four others. On 15 November, an acid-filled bottle was thrown at the car of a German family in Riyadh.[23]

The quiet insurgency would continue into 2002 and early 2003, with intermittent Molotov cocktails at McDonald's restaurants and drive-by shootings at random Westerners. On 5 June 2002 an Australian was shot at by a sniper in Tabuk. In early February 2003, a gunman fired at an Australian expatriate in Khamis Mushayt. On 6 February, a British engineer was wounded by unidentified gunmen firing at his car as he entered a residential compound. On 20 February, another Briton was shot and killed in Riyadh by a gunman at a traffic light. In Jubayl on 1 May 2003, a Saudi militant dressed in Saudi naval uniform penetrated the base and killed an American before getting away unhurt.[24]

We do not know who was behind these attacks, because Saudi police never investigated any of the incidents seriously. Aside from the alleged alcohol traders, nobody was ever brought to justice, at least publicly, for any of the attacks on Westerners between November 2000 and May 2003. At the same time it was obvious to informed observers that most attacks were the work of amateur militant Islamists driven by anti-Western sentiment. The high level of activity on jihadist websites in the 2000–3 period indicated that there were thousands of grassroots activists with extremely anti-Western views in Saudi Arabia. A strong indication of Islamist involvement in the quiet insurgency was the appearance on jihadist Internet forums in 2004 of a book entitled *Encouraging the Heroic Mujahidin to Revive the Practice of Assassinations*. The 114-page manual described a variety of suggested assassination methods against

[23] 'Saudi Blast Injures Briton and Egyptian', *BBC News Online*, 16 March 2001; 'An Explosion in Front of a Library in al-Riyadh', *ArabicNews.com*, 16 March 2001; 'US Doctor Wounded by Parcel Bomb', *BBC News Online*, 3 May 2001; 'Target: Westerners', *St Petersburg Times*, 22 July 2002; Neil MacFarquhar, 'Package Bomb Kills American in Saudi Arabia', *New York Times*, 7 October 2001; John R. Bradley, 'Saudi-Sniper in camouflage fires on Australian at BAE compound', *Arab News*, 18 June 2002; Peterson, 'Saudi Arabia: Internal Security Incidents since 1979', 8.

[24] 'Gunman Ignites fire at McDonald's', *Arab News*, 21 November 2002; 'Saudis Arrest McDonald's Bomb Suspect', *BBC News Online*, 27 February 2003; Donna Abu Nasr, 'String of Crimes Leaves Sense of Insecurity', *Associated Press*, 27 February 2003; 'Shooting: Brits Rethink Saudi Work', *BBC News Online*, 21 February 2003; 'Briton Killed in Saudi Arabia', *BBC News Online*, 21 February 2003; Andrew Hammond, 'Gunman Wounds US Defense Worker in Saudi Arabia', *Reuters*, 1 May 2003.

Westerners in a Saudi context. All of the methods which had been used in the 2000–3 period – parcel bombs, car bombs and drive-by shootings – were described in detail in this book.[25]

The violent anti-Westernism that would produce the QAP campaign thus had antecedents going back to 2000, when the crises in Palestine and Chechnya sparked a pan-Islamist renaissance. However, this renaissance was not simply a response to international events; it was also fuelled by the writings of a group of radical scholars that rose to prominence in late 1990s Burayda and Riyadh.

The rise of the al-Shu'aybi school

In the mid-1990s, the idea of a global war with America was something very few Saudi religious scholars were prepared to support. In the aftermath of 9/11, however, it became clear that there was an entire community of religious scholars in the kingdom who were happy to endorse mass-casualty terrorism against the West. These scholars were not linked to al-Qaida, but operated as independent ideological actors in the domestic Islamist arena. They shaped the political opportunities for jihadism by offering Wahhabi religious legitimacy to increasingly radical pan-Islamist positions. But where did these people come from and how did they become so prominent?

The rise of the 'al-Shu'aybi school' of clerics constitutes only one of several changes that occurred in the Saudi Islamist field in the late 1990s. The changes were brought about by two main factors: first was the theological power vacuum left by the disappearance, in rapid succession, of the three grand old men of salafi Islam: Abd al-Aziz bin Baz (d. 13 May 1999), Nasir al-Din al-Albani (d. 1 October 1999) and Muhammad bin Uthaymin (d. 10 January 2001). Unlike their docile successors, these figures had enjoyed credibility in radical circles because they were charismatic, very learned and dared say no to the royal family. Second was the absence (due to imprisonment) and subsequent co-optation of the Islamist mainstream, represented by the leading figures of the Sahwa, notably Salman al-Awda and Safar al-Hawali. The al-Shu'aybi school was thus a product of the power struggles on the radical side of the Saudi Islamist field in the absence of strong religious authorities and charismatic figures.

The al-Shu'aybi school developed as a loose network of Burayda- and Riyadh-based scholars who shared a certain number of political views,

[25] Abu Jandal al-Azdi, *tahrid al-mujahidin al-abtal 'ala ihya sunnat al-ightiyal* [Encouraging the Heroic Mujahidin to Revive the Practice of Assassinations] (www.tawhed.ws, 2004).

remained in personal contact with each other and taught an interconnected community of religious students. The three-tiered network consisted of the central, albeit mainly symbolic, figure of Hamud al-Uqla al-Shu'aybi, the middle-aged and very articulate scholars Nasir al-Fahd and Ali al-Khudayr, and younger sheikhs like Sulayman al-Ulwan and Abd al-Aziz al-Jarbu'. Many more actors were included in this network but these five individuals were the most influential.[26]

The central figure was the blind septuagenarian Hamud bin Uqla al-Shu'aybi, a stern and serious man who commanded considerable authority in conservative religious communities by virtue of his age and his background from the Wahhabi scholarly establishment. In fact, al-Shu'aybi's biography reads like a history of the Najdi religious education system. He was born in 1927 in the village of Shaqra near Burayda, into the tribe of Banu Khalid, well known for its many Wahhabi ulama. Al-Shu'aybi had lost his eyesight from smallpox at the age of 7, and had devoted himself to religious studies as did many blind children for lack of other avenues. In 1948 he moved to Riyadh to study informally with prominent Wahhabi scholars such as Abd al-Latif Al al-Shaykh. In 1952, al-Shu'aybi enrolled in the newly opened 'Scientific Institute' (*al-ma'had al-'ilmi*) in Riyadh, where he was taught by other famous scholars, including Abd al-Aziz bin Baz and Muhammad al-Amin al-Shanqiti. In 1955, at age 28, he became one of the first students of Imam Muhammad bin Sa'ud University, where he would obtain a teaching position three years later. In the course of the next three decades he taught generations of aspiring Wahhabi scholars and established himself as one of the kingdom's most respected clerics.[27]

In 1986, the 59-year-old al-Shu'aybi moved back to his native Burayda to teach in the Qasim branch of Imam University. At this time, the Sahwa movement was on the rise, and al-Shu'aybi would become drawn into the Islamist activism of 1990s Burayda. In 1994, al-Shu'aybi

[26] Others included Ahmad al-Khalidi and Abdallah al-Sa'd, and to a lesser extent Muhammad bin Fahd al-Rashudi, Abd al-Karim al-Humayd, Abd al-Aziz al-Julayyil and Abd al-Aziz Abd al-Latif. Apart from the Hofuf-based al-Khalidi, all of the above lived in Burayda. For more on these figures, see Lacroix, 'Les champs de la discorde', 601–9.

[27] Abd al-Rahman al-Harfi, '*al-sira al-dhatiyya li-samahat al-shaykh hamud bin 'uqla al-shu'aybi* [The Biography of Sheikh Hamud bin Uqla al-Shu'aybi]' (www.saaid.net, 2001); Abd al-Rahman al-Jafn, '*inas al-nubala' fi sirat shaykhina al-'uqla* [Noble People in the Life of our Sheikh al-Uqla]' (www.saaid.net, 2002); Abu Anas al-Libi, '*al-shaykh al-'uqla 'alam shamikh fi zaman al-inhitat* [Sheikh al-Uqla – Eminent Personality in an Era of Decline] (www.almuqatila.com, 2002). Al-Shu'aybi's former students include many prominent religious and judicial figures in Saudi Arabia, such as the present Great Mufti of Saudi Arabia Sheikh Abd al-Aziz Al al-Shaykh, Minister of Justice Abdullah bin Muhammad bin Ibrahim Al al-Shaykh, former Minister for Islamic Affairs Abdullah bin Abd al-Muhsin al-Turki and many others.

was dismissed from his teaching position. There may have been some personal issues involved – he was known to be on very bad terms with the great star of his faculty, Muhammad bin Uthaymin, whose small teaching load and positive stance on the sale of Zamzam water had long annoyed al-Shu'aybi. The main reason for his dismissal, however, was his involvement in the Sahwa. In 1992, al-Shu'aybi was one of the senior scholars called upon by the Sahwist activists to provide legitimacy and political backing to the *Memorandum of Advice*. Al-Shu'aybi was not among the most active Sahwists and therefore escaped the late 1994 crackdown, but in June 1995 he was imprisoned for a few weeks allegedly for distributing the writings of the exiled CDLR (Committee for the Defence of Legitimate Rights) leader Muhammad al-Mas'ari among his students.[28]

Shu'aybi's expulsion from Imam University is important for understanding his subsequent role. After a lifelong university career, al-Shu'aybi suddenly found himself outside the structure and control of the religious establishment. Al-Shu'aybi continued teaching at home, but after his release from prison he attracted more radical students than he had in the past. From 1998 onward, he would draw considerable attention within Saudi Arabia for his extreme positions on a number of issues.[29]

Al-Shu'aybi's politicisation and rise to infamy in the late 1990s had less to do with his own intellectual trajectory than with the people around him. Old and blind, al-Shu'aybi himself was not the driving force behind the radicalisation of the al-Shu'aybi school – he was being led and incited by younger and more politically minded scholars and students. Al-Shu'aybi was a classic example of what some Saudis refer to as a 'fatwa udder', that is, a scholar who will provide any fatwa the seeker wants if the question is asked in the right way. Austere and extremely socially conservative, al-Shu'aybi's instinct was to denounce all things new and non-Muslim. By framing an issue in a certain way, a follower could obtain al-Shu'aybi's approval or a denouncement and then distribute it on the Internet.[30]

It has also been suggested that people in al-Shu'aybi's entourage exploited his blindness to publish texts in his name. From 1999 onward, the scale and reaction speed of al-Shu'aybi's fatwa production increased dramatically. Between 1999 and 2001, his production also followed

[28] Author's interview with unidentified Saudi Islamist, who was studying with al-Shu'aybi at the time of the arrest.

[29] Author's interview with unidentified Saudi Islamist.

[30] Author's interview with Fahd al-Shafi, Riyadh, April 2004; author's interviews with Abdallah Bijad al-Utaybi and Sa'ud al-Sarhan.

political developments very closely – fatwas would be posted online literally within days of a particular event. According to sceptics, this publication pattern was very unlike that of aging Wahhabi sheikhs. While it is difficult to verify the hypothesis of fake authorship, it seems clear that al-Shu'aybi was being incited and exploited by other actors in his later years. Al-Shu'aybi was a very useful figurehead because he was old and highly respected. Behind the cover of al-Shu'aybi's reputation, the real movers in the al-Shu'aybi school could go much further than they otherwise could have done. These real leaders were Ali al-Khudayr and Nasir al-Fahd.[31]

Ali bin Khudayr al-Khudayr was born in Riyadh in 1954. He studied at Imam University under al-Shu'aybi and others before moving to the university's Qasim branch to study for a Master's degree under Sheikh Muhammad bin Uthaymin, a diploma he obtained in 1983. He then worked for several years as a religious teacher in a school for teenage delinquents in Burayda. This modest career path suggests that he was probably not exceptionally bright, despite al-Shu'aybi's later endorsement of him as his 'best student ever'. Al-Khudayr also taught in his home, like most scholars in Burayda, but al-Khudayr's students up until the mid-1990s were madkhalis, that is, apolitical mainstream Wahhabis, which suggests that he himself was not initially very politicised. For the same reason, most of al-Khudayr's publications from before the late 1990s were apolitical theological commentaries of the classics of Wahhabi literature.[32]

Nevertheless al-Khudayr, like al-Shu'aybi, appeared on the fringes of the Sahwa in the early 1990s as a signatory to the *Memorandum of Advice*. A former student also recalls that al-Khudayr wrote a letter to the prince of Qasim in 1992 or 1993 protesting against the organisation of a large sports event in Burayda. After Salman al-Awda was arrested in September 1994, al-Khudayr allegedly worked to establish a pressure group under the name 'Society for the Defence of the Muslim Scholars' which was to work for the release of the Sahwist leaders. He also began distributing tapes and leaflets from al-Mas'ari. Not surprisingly, this earned him arrest and imprisonment in late September or early October 1994.[33]

[31] al-Shu'aybi's unique status explains why the general secretary of the Council of Senior Scholars came out in defence of al-Shu'aybi on 17 October 2001, days after the *Ukaz* newspaper had questioned al-Shu'aybi's judgement in an editorial; see Dore Gold, *Hatred's Kingdom: How Saudi Arabia Supports the New Global Terrorism* (Washington, DC: Regnery, 2004), 258–9; author's interview with Abdallah Bijad al-Utaybi.

[32] Author's interview with Sa'ud al-Sarhan; '*nubdha 'an al-shaykh* [Biographic Note on the Shaykh]' (www.alkhoder.com, 2003); Ali al-Khudayr, '*al-wijaza fi sharh al-usul al-thalatha* [An Abridged Explanation of the Three Foundations]' (www.tawhed.ws, 1994).

[33] Author's interview with Sa'ud al-Sarhan.

Al-Khudayr came out of prison in 1998 considerably more politicised and sceptical towards the regime than when he entered. A former student who met him at this time said he was 'still a very humble and nice man' but 'much more political and more resolute'. Over the next few years he would emerge as one of the most prominent radical sheikhs in Burayda. He became very close to his former teacher Hamud al-Shuʿaybi and no doubt pushed the latter in a more radical direction. Exactly what drove Ali al-Khudayr's radicalisation is not quite clear. Most likely it was the disillusionment and trauma of imprisonment, combined with the ideological influence of another inmate who would become a close friend, namely Nasir al-Fahd.[34]

Nasir bin Hamad al-Fahd al-Humayyin (aka Abu Musʿab) was born in Riyadh in late 1968 or early 1969 to a family originally from the village of al-Thuʿayr near Zulfi. Like many Zulfawis, al-Fahd's family was quite conservative, and many of his relatives worked in the religious sector. His father was a close aide to Sheikh Abd al-Latif Al al-Shaykh, the brother of the former Great Mufti Muhammad bin Ibrahim. One of Nasir's uncles, Fahd al-Humayyin, was a hardline preacher in the al-Suwaydi area of Riyadh. The young Nasir proved an exceptionally bright pupil. He first studied engineering at King Saʿud University in Riyadh, which suggests that he left high school with excellent grades. After two years of study he changed vocation and entered the Department of Sharia. In January 1992 he obtained a Master's degree with distinction, and he allegedly impressed the faculty so much that he was offered a position as assistant professor.[35]

In his early days, Nasir al-Fahd held ideological positions very close to the pietist rejectionist school, and he was a hardliner already in the early 1990s. In 1992 and 1993 he published texts in which he declared the Ottoman state infidel and denounced the poet Ahmad Shawqi. Al-Fahd was critical of the Sahwa, whom he labelled the *ghafwa* (slumber). In 1991 or 1992, Nasir al-Fahd and his friend Abd al-Aziz al-Jarbuʿ had gone to visit Salman al-Awda to find out why the latter supported Hasan al-Turabi, a figure al-Fahd disliked intensely. In the heated discussion that ensued, al-Awda allegedly offended the young al-Fahd and planted the seeds of what would become a long enmity.[36]

[34] Author's interview with unidentified Saudi Islamist.

[35] '*tarjama* [Biography]' (www.al-fhd.com, 2002); author's interview with Muhammad al-Sayf, Riyadh, April 2005; author's interview with Saʿud al-Sarhan.

[36] See Nasir al-Fahd, '*al-dawla al-uthmaniyya wa mawqif daʿwat al-shaykh muhammad bin ʿabd al-wahhab minha* [The Ottoman State and the Position of the Call of Sheikh Muhammad ibn Abd al-Wahhab on it]' (manuscript, 1993), and Nasir al-Fahd, '*shiʿr ahmad shawqi fi'l-mizan* [The Poetry of Ahmad Shawqi in the Balance]' (manuscript,

In August 1994, Nasir al-Fahd was arrested and imprisoned together with his older friend and mentor Muhammad al-Farraj for allegedly writing a poem attacking the loose morals of Prince Nayif's wife Maha al-Sudayri, a long-time target of gossip in the radical Islamist community. The fact that he was arrested before the Sahwists and on a different count would negatively affect al-Fahd's subsequent status in the Islamist community. Because he did not take part in the most critical phase of the Sahwist confrontation with the government he did not benefit to the same extent from the credibility boost of imprisonment, and he was not counted among the 'imprisoned leaders'. He thus got the worst of two worlds: as an Islamist imprisoned at the time of the Sahwa he received a long sentence, but as a non-Sahwist, he did not get the credibility that came with it.[37]

Partly for this reason, the prison experience radicalised al-Fahd considerably. In prison he came into contact with radical figures such as Walid al-Sinani (aka Abu Subay'i), a charismatic young ideologue famous for his extreme hostility to the Saudi regime (who remains in prison to this day as a result). However, it was above all the interaction with the Sahwa which changed Nasir al-Fahd. He found himself in Ha'ir prison together with the main leaders of the Sahwa, who ignored and brushed aside the bright and ambitious young scholar in their debates. Angry and humiliated, al-Fahd challenged Salman al-Awda and clashed verbally with him on a number of occasions. The bad personal chemistry was reinforced by politics, because al-Fahd was radicalising at a time when al-Awda was moderating his positions. One of the few people who supported al-Fahd in prison was Ali al-Khudayr, and the two developed a close relationship.[38]

After his release from prison in November 1997, Nasir al-Fahd devoted himself to writing and research while allegedly making money from working in a perfume factory in Riyadh. His first works after the release were historical: he wrote an acclaimed biography of Sheikh Muhammad bin Ibrahim as well as a large genealogical work on a Najdi branch of the Utayba tribe. However, he rapidly turned to politics, and in 1998 the newly released Ali al-Khudayr introduced him to Hamud

1994). Another early work is Nasir al-Fahd, '*haqiqat al-hadara al-islamiyya* [The Truth of Muslim Civilisation]' (manuscript, 1993?). Author's interview with Abdallah Bijad al-Utaybi.

37 Author's interview with Abdallah Bijad al-Utaybi.

38 Author's interview with Muhsin al-Awaji, Riyadh, January 2007; Mansur al-Nuqaydan, '*al-kharita al-islamiyya fi'l-sa'udiyya wa mas'alat al-takfir* [The Islamist Map in Saudi Arabia and the Question of Takfir]', *al-Wasat*, 28 February 2003; Lacroix, 'Les champs de la discorde', 594.

al-Shu'aybi. They all shared a disillusionment with the Sahwa, a deep antipathy towards the modernists and a desire to assert themselves in the Islamist field. From then on, Ali al-Khudayr and Nasir al-Fahd would collaborate from their respective bases in Burayda and Riyadh.[39]

Nasir al-Fahd soon became the dynamic leader of a rapidly growing radical Islamist community in the capital. In his network were his old friends Abd al-Aziz al-Jarbu' and Muhammad al-Farraj, new allies like Sulayman al-Kharrashi, as well as an increasing number of students and hangers-on. Al-Fahd was one of the first radical Saudi Islamists to make systematic use of the Internet. Extremely bright, charismatic and a very prolific writer, Nasir al-Fahd was the leading ideologue of the al-Shu'aybi school. Although he was in the same generation as the younger sheikhs described below, his phenomenal intellectual abilities earned him the level of recognition and influence of someone much older.[40]

The third component of the al-Shu'aybi network was a group of younger scholars who remained below al-Shu'aybi, al-Khudayr and al-Fahd in the informal scholarly hierarchy. First among these was Sulayman al-Ulwan, who was born in 1970 in Burayda to a relatively poor family. As a young boy, he proved to be an exceptionally gifted student, so from an early age private benefactors in the area funded his religious education. In the 1980s, al-Ulwan studied with Abdallah al-Duwaysh, Muhammad al-Rashudi and Abdallah al-Qar'awi, the main sheikhs of the community known as 'Ikhwan Burayda'. This was a pietist community characterised by an extreme social conservatism and a refusal to engage with the state and its institutions. Unlike the Sahwists, who emerged in universities and used modern technology to distribute their message, the Ikhwan Burayda, including al-Ulwan himself, viewed radio and cassette tapes as sinful and shunned state education. Some of the members of the community would break radio antennas and not speak to people with radios in their cars. They also viewed Qur'an memorisation classes and summer camps for youth – the backbone of Sahwist mobilisation in the 1980s – as sinful. He had

[39] Author's interview with Abdallah Bijad al-Utaybi; Nasir al-Fahd, '*ma'jam al-ansab al-usar al-mutahaddira min 'ashirat al-asa'ida* [Genealogy of the Sedentary Families of the Asa'ida Branch]' (www.al-fhd.com, 1999); Nasir al-Fahd, '*sirat samahat al-shaykh muhammad bin ibrahim al al-shaykh* [Biography of His Excellency Sheikh Muhammad bin Ibrahim Al al-Shaykh]' (www.al-fhd.com, 1999).

[40] Author's interview with Abdallah Bijad al-Utaybi. Muhammad al-Farraj, born in the 1950s in Zulfi, was a respected figure on the radical Islamist scene in Riyadh. Considered by some as al-Fahd's mentor, he was arrested in 1994 with al-Fahd and arrested again in 2000 for writing poetry very hostile to the Sahwa leaders. A former associate of al-Fahd said he first ever saw the Internet at al-Fahd's house in 1999. Author's interview with unidentified Saudi Islamist.

been arrested in the late 1980s for distributing leaflets saying Qur'an memorisation classes were sinful. Before 1993, al-Ulwan was hostile to the Sahwists and allegedly refused to meet Salman al-Awda. In the early 1990s, al-Ulwan taught students both from inside and outside the Ikhwan Burayda community. A source who studied with al-Ulwan in 1992 said the Ikhwan members would not speak to what they called the 'people of the schools' (*ahl al-madaris*), and al-Ulwan would purposely make his morning class last so long that the university students missed their first class.[41]

However, in mid- or late 1993, al-Ulwan changed his ideological orientation and drew closer to the Sahwa. This was partly the result of the efforts of Salman al-Awda, who had seen the potential in al-Ulwan's abilities and went to great lengths to cajole and befriend him. According to one account, al-Awda organised for the printing of one of al-Ulwan's books and had the famous scholar Abdallah bin Jibrin write the foreword. The same source said the wealthy al-Awda also bought a house for al-Ulwan. By the time of the events of September 1994, al-Ulwan had become relatively close to al-Awda and the Sahwists. Another former student has said he saw leaflets by Usama bin Ladin in al-Ulwan's house in late 1994. However, he did not assume a prominent role as an activist, which is why he was 'only' banned from teaching, and not arrested, towards the end of 1994.[42]

Former students have described the small-built and fragile-looking al-Ulwan as a powerful and loudmouth speaker. However, he was also timid and afraid of government sanction. After the crackdown on the Sahwa, al-Ulwan kept a low profile until about 1998, when al-Fahd and al-Khudayr began rocking the Islamist boat again. From 1999 onward, al-Ulwan became a prominent member of the al-Shu'aybi network. Ali al-Khudayr would find his right-hand man in al-Ulwan, just as, down in Riyadh, Nasir al-Fahd found a deputy in Abd al-Aziz al-Jarbu'.

Abd al-Aziz bin Salih bin Sulayman al-Jarbu' was born in 1967 in al-Bada'i' in Qasim, though he grew up in Riyadh, where he became religious in the early 1980s. He studied with Sheikh Abdallah al-Tuwayjiri and worked as a mosque imam before entering the College of Sharia in Imam University in Riyadh in the late 1980s, where he met Nasir al-Fahd. After graduating from Imam University in 1992, he worked as a religious teacher in technical and vocational schools. It is not clear how politicised he was in the early 1990s or whether he was imprisoned with al-Fahd and the Sahwists. However, in the late 1990s and early

[41] Author's interviews with Sa'ud al-Sarhan and Mansur al-Nuqaydan.
[42] Author's interview with Sa'ud al-Sarhan.

2000s, he emerged as one of the most extreme of all the ideologues in the al-Shu'aybi network. He was known for his sharp tongue, but as one former Islamist put it, he was 'only a talker'. The violent tone and content of his writings – such as his famous statement endorsing the 9/11 attack – make one wonder if he was trying to compensate for his young age and limited religious authority with very explicit rhetoric. The fact that his website in 2003 included prominently placed written recommendations from al-Shu'aybi and al-Khudayr suggests that he felt the need to prove his credentials.[43]

Many figures appeared within and on the periphery of the al-Shu'aybi network from 1998 onward, but space does not allow for a comprehensive biographical review. Our main concern is the two processes which led these scholars to escalate their rhetoric from 1998 onward, namely the polemic with the progressive Islamists on social issues and with the Sahwists on international issues.

The second half of the 1990s saw the emergence of an interesting intellectual phenomenon in Saudi Arabia, namely the gradual transformation of some formerly conservative Islamists into relatively progressive Islamist intellectuals. From about 1998 onward, writers such as Hasan al-Maliki and Mansur al-Nuqaydan started articulating a critique of the role of religion in Saudi society and eventually of Wahhabi doctrine as such. These intellectuals, often referred to as 'modernists' (*'asraniyyun*), represented an important precursor to the so-called 'Islamo-liberal' trend which gained prominence in the early 2000s.[44]

[43] Author's interview with Abdallah Bijad al-Utaybi; '*nubdha 'an al-shaykh 'abd al-'aziz al-jarbu'* [Biographic Note on Shaykh Abd al-Aziz al-Jarbu']' (www.geocities.com/aljarbo, 2003); Abd al-Aziz al-Jarbu', '*al-mukhtar fi hukm al-intihar khawf ifsha al-asrar* [Selected Sayings on the Ruling on Suicide for Fear of Divulging Secrets]' (www.tawhed.ws, 2001); Abd al-Aziz al-Jarbu', '*al-i'lam bi-wujub al-hijra min dar al-kufr ila dar al-islam* [Declaration on the Need to Emigrate from the Abode of Infidelity for the Abode of Islam]' (www.tawhed.ws, 2001); Abd al-Aziz al-Jarbu', '*al-ta'sil li-mashru'iyyat ma hasal fi amrika min al-tadmir* [The Foundation of the Legitimacy of the Destruction that Happened in America]' (www.tawhed.ws, 2001).

[44] These intellectuals are also sometimes referred to as 'rationalists' (*'aqlaniyyun*), 'centrists' (*wasatiyyun*), 'enlighteners' (*tanwiriyyun*) or 'reformists' (*islahiyyun*). Other prominent modernists who became active during this time include Abdallah al-Hamid, Abd al-Aziz al-Qasim, Ibrahim al-Sakran, Sulayman al-Duhayyan, Mishari al-Dhayidi, Abdallah Bijad al-Utaybi, Yusuf al-Dayni, Sa'ud al-Sarhan and others. For examples of al-Nuqaydan's writings in this period, see Mansur al-Nuqaydan, '*hal kan ibn abi dawud mazluman?* [Was Ibn Abu Dawud Unjustly Treated?]', *al-Hayat*, 23 February 1999; Mansur al-Nuqaydan, '*da'wa ila taqnin wazifat rijal al-hisba* [A Call for the Regulation of the Work of Religious Policemen]', *al-Majalla*, 30 April 2000; Mansur al-Nuqaydan, '*al-hijra ila al-mustahil: maqati' min sira ruhiyya* [Emigrating to the Impossible: Excerpts from a Spriritual Life]', *al-Majalla*, 2 May 2000. For al-Maliki, see Hasan al-Maliki, *nahwa inqadh al-tarikh al-islami* [Towards

The modernists may have been few in number and politically marginal, but their ideas made big waves in the Islamist community because they touched upon important taboos, and because the people articulating them were not Westernised liberals, but religious students like the radicals themselves. Many of them also knew each other personally. The modernists and the radicals had been on the same side in the early 1990s, but prison had changed them in completely different ways. While Nasir al-Fahd came out of prison as an angry and bitter man, Mansur al-Nuqaydan emerged as a critical thinker.

From 1998 onward, a bitter enmity and fierce polemic developed between the modernists and the al-Shu'aybi school. The latter launched scathing personal attacks – later escalating to declarations of *takfir* – on the progressives. Between 1999 and 2001, the sheikhs of the al-Shu'aybi school issued numerous statements on the Internet lambasting the modernist intellectuals. Hasan al-Maliki was denounced by both Nasir al-Fahd and Ali al-Khudayr in August 2001. Mansur al-Nuqaydan was the target of numerous attacks in this period. The sheikhs of the al-Shu'aybi school also wrote extensive treatises on the dangers of modernist thought in general. Hamud al-Shu'aybi used his contacts in the religious establishment to have the modernists sacked from their jobs; hence al-Nuqaydan lost his position as mosque imam in 1999 and al-Maliki was removed from the Ministry of Education in 2001. Another person who attracted the ire of al-Shu'aybi and his like was the author Turki al-Hamad, who was publicly declared an infidel by several of the scholars in August 2001. Leftists or progressives from other Arab countries, such as Palestinian Mahmud Darwish and the Druze Samih al-Qasim, were not spared either.[45]

Saving Islamic History]; Hasan al-Maliki, *manahij al-ta'lim* [Education Curricula] and Hasan al-Maliki, '*naqs kashf al-shubuhat* [The Imperfection of "Unveiling the Deceptions"]'. For biographies of al-Maliki and al-Nuqaydan see Stéphane Lacroix, 'Between Islamists and Liberals: Saudi Arabia's Islamo-Liberal Reformists', *Middle East Journal* 58, no. 3 (2004).

[45] Author's interview with Hasan al-Maliki, Riyadh, April 2004; author's interview with Mansur al-Nuqaydan; Lacroix, 'Between Islamists and Liberals', 353; Nasir al-Fahd, '*kashf shubhat hasan al-maliki* [Exposing Hasan al-Maliki's Deception]' (www.al-fhd.com, 2001); Ali al-Khudayr, '*bayan fi hasan bin farhan al-maliki* [Statement on Hasan bin Farhan al-Maliki]' (www.tawhed.ws, 2001); Hamud al-Shu'aybi, '*risala ila ahl al-hisba* [Letter to those who Carry out Hisba]' (www.aloqla.com, 2000); Ali al-Khudayr and Ahmad al-Khalidi, '*bayan fi riddat mansur al-nuqaydan* [Statement on the Apostasy of Mansur al-Nuqaydan]' (www.alkhoder.com, 2003); Nasir al-Fahd, '*manhaj al-mutaqaddimin fi'l-tadlis* [The Modernists' Method of Deceit]' (www.al-fhd.com, 2000); Nasir al-Fahd, '*risala ila 'asrani* [Letter to a Modernist]' (www.al-fhd.com, undated); Ali al-Khudayr, '*risala fi bayan hal ta'ifat al-'asraniyyin al-dalla* [Letter regarding the Statement on the Status of the Misled Faction of Modernists]' (www.tawhed.ws); Ali al-Khudayr, '*al-qawa'id al-arba' allati tufarriq bayna din al-muslimin wa din al-'almaniyyin* [The Four Rules which Separate the Religion of Muslims and

The obsession with the modernist intellectuals was indicative of a deep concern among the radical sheikhs about the social liberalisation and Westernisation of Saudi society. The radicalisation of the al-Shu'aybi school was to some extent a reaction to what they perceived as moral and doctrinal corruption inside Saudi Arabia. Al-Shu'aybi and his colleagues wrote extensively on social and moral issues in this period, always taking conservative positions. They issued statements denouncing everything from clapping and the millennium celebrations to the Pokémon toy. Like all social conservatives, they were particularly concerned about women; in the course of a few months in 2000 al-Shu'aybi denounced the participation of women in the Janadiriyya festival, ruled against the introduction of identity cards for women and declared social clubs for women sinful. In March 2001 he attracted international attention by declaring the Kuwaiti singer Abdallah al-Ruwayshid an infidel for singing the opening verse of the Qur'an.[46]

From 1999 onward, the clerics in the al-Shu'aybi school would take a greater interest in issues of international politics and gradually adopt a more pronounced pan-Islamist rhetoric. Two main factors account for this ideological change. First was the de facto increase in the number of pan-Islamist causes, which led to a rise in demand from young religious students and jihadist activists for opinions on the international issues of the day. Second was the political vacuum left by the Sahwist sheikhs, who came out of prison in 1999 much less keen to take controversial political stances.

the Religion of the Secularists]' (www.tawhed.ws, date unknown). See Hamud al-Shu'aybi, '*fatwa fi'l-katib turki al-hamad* [Fatwa on the Writer Turki al-Hamad]' (www.aloqla.com, 1999); Ali al-Khudayr, '*fi turki al-hamad* [On Turki al-Hamad]' (www.alkhoder.com, 2001); Nasir al-Fahd, '*al-qasimi: min al-tawhid ila al-ilhad* [Al-Qasimi: From Tawhid to Unbelief]' (www.al-fhd.com, undated); Hamud al-Shu'aybi, '*taqrib al-muharifin wa takrimihim* [Approaching and Honouring Deviants]' (www.aloqla.com, 2000).

[46] Nasir al-Fahd, '*mas'alat al-tasfiq* [The Issue of Clapping]' (www.al-fhd.com, 1999); Hamud al-Shu'aybi, '*al-musharaka fi ihtifalat al-alafiyya* [Taking Part in Millennium Celebrations]' (www.aloqla.com, 1999); Hamud al-Shu'aybi, '*lu'bat bukimun* [The Pokémon Toy]' (www.aloqla.com, 2001); Nasir al-Fahd, '*hukm al-'uturat al-kuhuliyya* [Ruling on Perfumes with Alcohol]' (www.al-fhd.com, 1999); Hamud al-Shu'aybi, '*musharakat al-nisa' fi'l-janadiriyya* [The Participation of Women in Janadiriyya]' (www.aloqla.com, 2000); Hamud al-Shu'aybi, '*hukm bitaqat al-mar'a* [Ruling on Identity Cards for Women]' (www.saaid.net, 2000); Hamud al-Shu'aybi, '*al-nawadi al-nisa'iyya* [Women's Clubs]' (www.aloqla.com, 2000); Nasir al-Fahd, '*libas al-mar'a amam al-nisa'* [Women's Dressing before Women]' (www.tawhed.ws, 2000); Hamud al-Shu'aybi, '*fatwa fi kufr al-mughanni 'abdallah al-ruwayshid* [Fatwa on the Infidelity of the Singer Abdallah al-Ruwayshid]' (www.saaid.net, 2001); 'Fatwa Against Kuwaiti Singer', *BBC News Online*, 2 April 2001; Nasir al-Fahd, '*risala fi hukm al-ghana' bi'l-qur'an* [Letter on the Ruling of Singing the Qur'an]' (www.tawhed.ws, 2001).

From a relatively early stage, the sheikhs of the al-Shu'aybi school raised the issue of the US military presence in Saudi Arabia and emphasised their hostility towards it. Already in early 1999, al-Shu'aybi himself explicitly stated, in language echoing Bin Ladin, that the presence of non-Muslims in Saudi Arabia was strictly prohibited, that it was sinful to call upon infidels for any kind of assistance, and that it was incumbent upon Muslims to evict the Jews and the Christians from the Peninsula.[47]

From late 1999 onward, they turned their focus to conflicts in other parts of the Muslim world. In November 1999, al-Shu'aybi ruled on the need for Muslims to assist the jihad against the Russians in Chechnya. In October 2000, he did the same for the 'jihad in the Philippines', using classical jihadist arguments reminiscent of Abdallah Azzam. In November 2000, he issued two statements in support of the Palestinian intifada, as did many scholars at the time. The Palestinian issue sparked two important debates in Saudi religious circles in the spring of 2001: the first concerning a general economic boycott of Western companies, and the other about the issue of suicide bombings. In both debates, government-affiliated clerics held the more moderate positions, to the loud protests of al-Shu'aybi and his followers.[48]

The main foreign policy issue to preoccupy the al-Shu'aybi school before 9/11 was the Taliban. From late 2000 onward they would take a great interest in the Taliban regime and defend it vigorously against outside criticisms. Their focus on the Taliban was the result of three factors. One was the media focus on Afghanistan that accompanied the

[47] Hamud al-Shu'aybi, '*al-qawl al-mukhtar fi hukm al-isti'ana bi'l-kuffar* [Selected Sayings on the Ruling of Seeking Help from the Infidels]' (www.aloqla.com, 2001). See also Hamud al-Shu'aybi, '*hukm iqamat al-yahud wa'l-nasara fi'l-jazirat al-'arab wa tamallukhum al-'aqarat wa istithmarha* [Ruling on Jews and Christians Residing on the Arabian Peninsula and their Owning and Development of Property]' (www.saaid.net, 2000).

[48] Hamud al-Shu'aybi, '*hukm al-jihad fi shishan wa wajib al-muslimin tijahhum* [Ruling on the Jihad in Chechnya and the Duty of Muslims towards them]' (www.qoqaz.com, 1999); Hamud al-Shu'aybi, '*al-jihad fi'l-filibin* [The Jihad in the Philippines]' (www.aloqla.com, 2000); Hamud al-Shu'aybi, '*al-bayan al-awal 'an ahwal ikhwanina al-muslimin fi filastin* [The First Statement on the Situation of our Muslim Brothers in Palestine]' (www.aloqla.com, 2000); Hamud al-Shu'aybi, '*al-bayan al-thani ila 'umum al-muslimin 'amma yadur fi filastin* [Second Statement to All Muslims regarding what is Going on in Palestine' (www.aloqla.com, 2000); Hamud al-Shu'aybi, '*bayan fi haththh 'ala al-muqata'a al-iqtisadiyya didd a'da' al-muslimin* [Statement on Encouraging Economic Boycott of the Muslims' Enemies]' (www.saaid.net, 2001); Hamud al-Shu'aybi, '*al-radd 'ala man afta bi-'adam jawaz muqata'a al-yahud wa'l-nasara* [Answer to those who Ruled against Boycotting Jews and Christians]' (www.aloqla.com, 2001); Hamud al-Shu'aybi, '*mashru'iyyat al-'amaliyyat al-istishhadiyya* [The Legitimacy of Martyrdom Operations]' (www.aloqla.com, 2001).

rising tensions between the Taliban and the international community. Another factor was the mounting criticism from ultra-conservative Wahhabi scholars (the so-called Madkhali school), who viewed the Taliban as doctrinally impure. A third factor was the prodding by al-Qaida-linked activists such as Yusuf al-Uyayri, who wanted scholars to dispel doubts among potential recruits over the religious legitimacy of the Afghan government.[49]

The Shu'aybi school emerged as particularly vocal supporters of the Taliban in March 2001 at the height of the controversy over the destruction of the Buddhist statues at Bamiyan. Both al-Shu'aybi and al-Fahd published several statements defending Mulla Umar's decision. In the spring and summer of 2001, the clerics began actively encouraging their students to go to Afghanistan and help the Taliban regime against the threat from the Northern Alliance (NA).[50]

The strong support for Muslim fighters abroad and for the Taliban was part of an attempt to win domestic political terrain from the Sahwa. In 1999, Salman al-Awda was not particularly concerned with the Chechen cause, and he refused to vouch for the Chechen mujahidin vis-à-vis Saudi donors. Similarly, in 2001, the Sahwist leaders allegedly opposed the destruction of the Buddhist statues (albeit not very vocally). The Sahwist moderation reflected their gradual co-optation by the regime. The Sahwists were becoming more like the official ulama, who only spoke about politics when forced to by popular demand. The religious establishment tried to stay clear of politics and focused most of their energy on promoting social conservatism. For them, the US presence in the kingdom was of course a non-issue. They viewed Palestine and Chechnya as legitimate jihads, but considered that only the locals should fight. Saudis should support the locals materially, but they

[49] Hamud al-Shu'aybi, '*hawla shar'iyyat hukumat taliban* [On the Legitimacy of the Taliban Government]' (www.aloqla.com, 2000); Lacroix, 'Les champs de la discorde', 619.

[50] Hamud al-Shu'aybi, '*nusrat taliban li-hadmihim al-awthan* [Supporting the Taliban in their Destruction of the Idols]' (www.aloqla.com, 2001); Hamud al-Shu'aybi, '*bayan li-a'da' munazzamat al-mu'tamar al-islami bi-sha'n tahtim hukumat taliban al-islamiyya li'l-asnam* [Statement to the Members of the Organisation of the Islamic Conference Concerning the Destruction of the Idols by the Islamic Taliban Government]' (www.saaid.net, 2001); Nasir al-Fahd, '*iqamat al-burhan 'ala wujub kasr al-awthan* [Establishing the Proof for the Obligation to Break the Statues]' (www.tawhed.ws, 2001); Nasir al-Fahd, '*al-radd 'ala maqal hadm al-tamthil min manzur islami li-katibihi sulayman bin 'abdallah al-turki* [Answer to the Article "Destruction of Statues from an Islamic Viewpoint" by Sulayman bin Abdallah al-Turki' (www.tawhed.ws, 2001); Ali al-Khudayr, '*fatwa fi ta'yid hadm al-asnam* [Fatwa on Supporting the Destruction of the Statues]' (www.tawhed.ws, 2001); Hamud al-Shu'aybi, '*hukm al-jihad wa isti'dhan al-walidayn fihi* [Ruling on Jihad and Parental Permission]' (www.aloqla.com, 2001).

should not participate because the Saudi political leadership (*wali al-amr*) had not given permission. However, they rarely pressed this point publicly, because it carried political cost. Their position on the Taliban was sympathetic, because of the latter's social conservatism, but the ulama were divided on controversial issues such as the destruction of the Bamiyan statues.[51]

The enthusiastic support for the Taliban amounted to an implicit criticism of the Saudi regime. By describing Afghanistan as the world's only Islamic state, al-Shu'aybi was essentially saying that he did not grant Saudi Arabia the same status. Before 9/11 and the US-led invasion of Afghanistan, the sheikhs of the al-Shu'aybi school were very careful not to voice any public criticism of the Saudi regime. They would write general treatises on the need to implement Sharia or the need to support Muslim struggles abroad and how to judge regimes that fail to do so, but they never explicitly declared the Saudi government as infidel. In private, on the other hand, their tone was allegedly much harsher. Former Islamists have said that al-Shu'aybi and some of the other sheikhs issued fatwas in private which straightforwardly accused the regime of apostasy and which authorised the use of force by Islamist activists against the Saudi police for self-defence reasons. However, if such controversial fatwas were given, they were not put down in writing.[52]

The al-Shu'aybi school cannot easily be classified as classical jihadist, global jihadist or revolutionary. As religious scholars they did not need to articulate clear operational priorities in the way activists would. As Stéphane Lacroix has shown, the scholars of the al-Shu'aybi school were fundamentally local ideological actors concerned with power and influence in the Saudi Islamist field. Their principal concern was to take a more hardline position than the Sahwa on whatever issue preoccupied the Islamist community at any given time. As exogenous factors made the 'topics of the day' more international after 1999, the al-Shu'aybi school turned more pan-Islamist. Theologically speaking, they were more strictly Wahhabi than other extreme pan-Islamist ideologues such as Abdallah Azzam or Usama bin Ladin. At the same time

[51] al-Salim, '*yusuf al-'uyayri (2)*'; Yusuf al-Uyayri, '*hamsa fi udhn fadilat al-shaykh salman al-'awda* [A Whisper in Sheikh Salman al-Awda's Ear]' (2001); author's interview with Ali al-Umaym, Riyadh, April 2004; author's interview with Fahd al-Shafi.

[52] Author's interview with Mansur al-Nuqaydan; Hamud al-Shu'aybi, '*fatwa fi takfir al-hukkam wa'l-musharri'in li'l-qawanin al-wada'iyya* [Fatwa on Takfir of Rulers and Legislators of Man-Made Laws]' (www.saaid.net, 2001); Hamud al-Shu'aybi, '*nida' ila hukkam al-'arab wa'l-muslimin* [A Call to the Rulers of Arabs and Muslims]' (www.aloqla.com, 2001).

the al-Shu'aybi school was more politicised than mainstream Wahhabi scholars were. What the al-Shu'aybi did was to articulate a Wahhabi justification for global jihad in much the same way that Abu Muhammad al-Maqdisi had articulated a Wahhabi socio-revolutionary discourse in the late 1980s.

With their increasingly loud rhetoric and their skilful use of the Internet, the sheikhs of the al-Shu'aybi school became very visible on the Saudi Islamist scene. With increased visibility and notoriety came more students. Young conservative religious students, hungry for more political rhetoric than they got at university, travelled from all over the country to study with these charismatic scholars. In Riyadh, a considerable entourage of young Saudis clustered around Nasir al-Fahd and Abd al-Aziz al-Jarbu', while al-Shu'aybi, al-Khudayr and al-Ulwan entertained a comparable following in Burayda.[53]

The al-Shu'aybi school was thus quite successful in filling the vacuum left by the co-opted Sahwists. Like Salman al-Awda and Safar al-Hawali had done in the early 1990s, al-Shu'aybi, al-Fahd and al-Khudayr skilfully capitalised on the growing pan-Islamist sentiment in the youth population for their own domestic political advantage. The new hardliners sought to cast themselves as the 'real' continuation of the Sahwa, as scholars that would not yield in the face of the many outside threats against the Muslim nation.

The writings of the al-Shu'aybi school fuelled recruitment to jihadist activism in Saudi Arabia in this period because they provided Wahhabi religious legitimacy for activities that would otherwise have been viewed as very controversial, such as volunteerism for the Taliban's fight against the Northern Alliance. Although Bin Ladin's political rhetoric resonated strongly among young Saudi Islamists, al-Qaida's leaders and recruiters lacked the religious legitimacy to authorise recruits to go abroad for jihad or for donors to support the Taliban. For some recruits, politics trumped theology, but there was a large 'grey area' of recruits and donors for whom religious sanction by trained scholars was extremely important.

The political opportunity structure for global jihadist activism thus improved considerably from around 1999 onward, as the result of a number of near-simultaneous changes. The policing of the jihadist community, which had been quite brutal between 1996 and 1998, became less heavy-handed, and political liberalisation left more political space for both Islamists and progressives. Images of hostilities

[53] Author's interview with Abdallah Bijad al-Utaybi; Qusti, 'Background of the Most Wanted Terrorists – Part 2'.

in Kosovo, Chechnya and Palestine, projected by satellite TV and the Internet, sparked a pan-Islamist renaissance in the kingdom. The vacuum of authority in the Islamist community allowed a group of vocal and radical scholars in Burayda and Riyadh to gain prominence and spark a polarisation of the Islamist field. The fact that all these changes occurred around 1999 is very significant, because, as we shall see, they coincided with important developments within the al-Qaida organisation.

5 Al-Qaida and Saudi Arabia

For most Saudis who went to Afghanistan in the 1980s, jihad was about repelling infidels in blatant cases of territorial invasion and occupation. In the mid-1990s emerged a new community of activists for whom jihad meant something much more drastic: confronting America with terrorist operations anywhere in the world, including in Saudi Arabia. The doctrine of global jihad was articulated by Usama bin Ladin and implemented by the al-Qaida organisation through a series of spectacular attacks on US targets, culminating with 9/11. But why did the global jihadist doctrine emerge at this particular point in time, and what exactly did it say about Saudi Arabia? What accounts for al-Qaida's growth and how did its infrastructure evolve in the kingdom?

The global jihadists

The global jihadi doctrine took shape in the first half of the 1990s within an increasingly uprooted and embattled Arab Afghan community. The Afghan jihad had produced transnational networks of militants, many of whom could not return to their home countries for fear of persecution. Over time, life in exile isolated these activists from their original political environment and imbued them with a more transnational political vision. Moreover, most of the Islamist struggles of the early 1990s failed. The revolutionary experiments in Algeria and Egypt ended in bloodbath and failure for the Islamists. In the irredentist struggles in Bosnia, Chechnya and Kashmir, the foreign activists were unwanted and unable to 'liberate' the local population. In Saudi Arabia, the non-violent political opposition to the US military presence did not budge the authorities, who responded with the imprisonment of the Sahwist opposition leaders. All this made it easier for certain jihadist thinkers to argue that localised struggle had proved futile and that non-violent options had been exhausted. A global jihad against the far enemy, on the other hand, was an untried approach.

The new strategy would be spearheaded by a particular part of the Arab Afghan community known as the al-Qaida organisation. Al-Qaida had been founded in Peshawar in August 1988 by a group of prominent Arab fighters who wanted a military organisation that could outlive the war in Afghanistan. The group, led by Usama bin Ladin, consisted primarily of disgruntled members of Abdallah Azzam's Services Bureau and recently arrived veteran Egyptian Islamists. The new organisation was vague in purpose – the original minutes of the founding meetings reveal no specific political aims or areas of operation. However, al-Qaida was the first truly transnational jihadi organisation.[1]

In the first few years of its existence, al-Qaida seems to have been more of an alumni society than an active military organisation. It did not possess significant buildings, training camps or financial resources of its own. Moreover, after the Soviet withdrawal from Afghanistan, al-Qaida's founding members dispersed and pursued different political projects. Usama bin Ladin returned to Saudi Arabia in October 1989 and became preoccupied at first with the situation in Yemen and later, from August 1990, with the Gulf crisis. In 1990, the Egyptian wing of al-Qaida headed to Khartoum where the new pro-Islamist junta offered a useful base for the fight against the Mubarak regime. Yet other al-Qaida members stayed in Peshawar where Bin Ladin would also return, for unclear reasons, in April 1991.

In the spring of 1992, Usama bin Ladin relocated from Peshawar to Khartoum, bringing leadership, money and commitment to the organisation. In Sudan, al-Qaida became a relatively structured enterprise with a central leadership, functionally differentiated committees and a salary system. It was a small organisation with members in the low hundreds, but its access to a safe haven and Bin Ladin's fortune enabled it to grow and consolidate. However, despite this bureaucratisation, al-Qaida still did not have a clear political or military agenda in the Sudan phase. Its various factions continued to pursue their respective pet projects. The Egyptians plotted against the Mubarak regime, while Bin Ladin issued statements urging the Saudi regime to expel the American soldiers. Al-Qaida's principal joint operation in this period was a series of moderately successful deployments in the Horn of Africa, including to Somalia in 1993. Al-Qaida was also implicated in, and perhaps responsible for, a handful of international terrorist attacks in this period, such as the two hotel bombings in the Yemeni port of Aden in

[1] Lawrence Wright, *The Looming Tower: Al Qaeda and the Road to 9/11* (New York: Knopf, 2006), 131–4. For more on al-Qaida's early history, see Bergen, *The Osama bin Laden I Know*, and R Kim Cragin, 'Early History of al-Qa'ida', *The Historical Journal* 51, no. 4 (2008).

1992 and the assassination attempt on the exiled Afghan King in Rome in 1991. However, Bin Ladin was not behind the first global jihadi operation against America, namely the attack on the World Trade Center in New York in February 1993. This attack was orchestrated by Ramzi Yousef, an independent Arab Afghan, with the help of a radicalised community of New York-based Egyptian Islamists.[2]

The main reason why al-Qaida did not have a clear strategic agenda in the early 1990s is that it was ideologically divided. Al-Qaida had been founded by people who, although united in the Afghan jihad, had slightly different mid-term objectives. Some, especially the Egyptians, had a socio-revolutionary outlook and wanted to use al-Qaida to topple Arab governments. Others, like Usama bin Ladin, were closer to the classical jihadist position and saw al-Qaida's role primarily as an elite reaction force to be used against infidel invaders. While this schism never produced outright confrontations, it did prevent the organisation from developing a consistent military strategy.

However, from 1992 onward, the al-Qaida leadership converged on an increasingly anti-American world-view, motivated mainly by the continued US military presence in Saudi Arabia, but also by the US deployment to Somalia and the arrest of the prominent radical Egyptian sheikh Omar Abd al-Rahman in New York. The jihadi movement had always been hostile to America, but for the first time Sunni Islamists began to seriously contemplate all-out war against the United States. The idea of an anti-American jihad had the benefit of appealing to both the socio-revolutionaries and the classical jihadists in al-Qaida. The former saw it as a way to undermine local regimes, while the latter saw it as the logical extension of Abdallah Azzam's struggle to liberate the umma from infidel oppression.

For Bin Ladin, the principal ideologue behind the new doctrine, the turning point was the Saudi regime's crackdown on the Sahwist opposition in September 1994, which convinced him that non-violent protest against the US military presence was futile. Bin Ladin was not a Sahwist, because he was not very interested in the minutiae of the Sahwa's domestic reform programme, but he respected and supported the Sahwa because of its clear stance on the issue of US troops. By 1995, Bin Ladin had concluded that war with America was inevitable, but he refrained from publicly declaring jihad for fear of straining relations with the Khartoum regime. When the Sudanese government bowed

[2] *USA* v. *Usama bin Ladin et al*; Anonymous, *Through our Enemies' Eyes*; *Al-Qaida's (Mis)adventures in the Horn of Africa*; Simon Reeve, *The New Jackals: Ramzi Yousef, Osama bin Laden and the Future of Terrorism* (London: André Deutsch, 1999).

to international pressure and evicted the al-Qaida leader in May 1996, Bin Ladin was free to speak his mind.

In the second half of the 1990s, Bin Ladin took pan-Islamism to its most radical conclusion and articulated the doctrine of global jihadism which advocated global warfare against the United States. In August 1996, his groundbreaking *Declaration of War* called for a guerrilla campaign on US forces in the kingdom, while his February 1998 statement of the *World Islamic Front for Jihad against the Jews and the Crusaders* declared all-out war on the USA and the West in the name of defending the umma.[3]

The global jihadist doctrine and Saudi Arabia

Bin Ladin's global jihadist doctrine contained three core elements which set it apart from other Islamist currents. First was the singling out of America and its allies as the main target of armed struggle, frequently referred to as the shift from the 'near enemy' to the 'far enemy'. This set the global jihadists apart from socio-revolutionary Islamists who declared their respective regimes as the main focus of their struggle. The anti-American approach also differed from that of irredentist Islamists and classical jihadists who focused on attacking the immediate occupier in their respective battlefields, such as the Israelis in Palestine, the Serbs in Bosnia or the Russians in Chechnya. The global jihadists did not disagree on the importance of toppling local regimes or fighting provincial occupations, but they argued that fighting the United States was a notch more urgent at this point in time.

Second, global jihadism was articulated in pan-Islamist discourse. Al-Qaida's violence was rationalised primarily as a struggle to defend the entire umma from non-Muslim aggression. In this respect, the global jihadists were close to the classical jihadists, but it set them apart from socio-revolutionaries, who framed their jihad as a struggle against internal oppression and corruption. The global jihadists, like the classical jihadists, called for ecumenism and Muslim unity in the face of the outside enemy, and played down internally divisive issues such as the debate over *takfir* (excommunication).

The third distinctive feature was the *global view on warfare*. While most Sunni militants had previously confined their activity to a particular country or region, Bin Ladin declared all US targets worldwide as legitimate and even encouraged attacks inside the United States. Equally

[3] Bruce Lawrence, ed., *Messages to the World: The Statements of Osama Bin Laden* (London: Verso, 2005).

significantly, Bin Ladin argued that no infidel occupation of Muslim land should be tolerated, whatever the local Muslim administrators said. Hence no exception should be made for Saudi Arabia, where the continued American military presence, Bin Ladin argued, amounted to an occupation of the heartland of Islam. The global jihadists thus differed from the classical jihadists in that they did not recognise the right of the local Muslim governments to decide whether non-Muslim presence on their territory should be tolerated or not. With their global view of warfare, the global jihadists also distinguished themselves from the socio-revolutionary or irredentist Islamists who tended to avoid out-of-area operations for fear of losing international political support and compromising their logistical support structures abroad.

Was global jihadism simply a new tactic to fulfil the existing ideological vision of regime change in Arab countries? The question presents itself not least because, in his 2001 book *Knights under the Prophet's Banner*, al-Qaida's second in command Ayman al-Zawahiri explicitly described the anti-American approach as a means to capture the states of the Middle East. If the USA could be coerced into ending its support for the Arab regimes and Israel, al-Zawahiri argued, then both Cairo and Jerusalem would easily be conquered by the mujahidin. This has led many observers to assume that al-Qaida were simply revolutionaries in disguise.[4]

However, the instrumentalist interpretation of global jihadism is reductive, because it ignores the crucial role of discursive frames in mobilisation processes. By presenting their struggle as a defensive war against outside invaders and playing down talk about regime change, the global jihadists tapped into a set of frustrations that differed from those targeted by old-school socio-revolutionaries. The appeal of this message among constituencies that felt more strongly about pan-Islamist causes than socio-economic problems thus broadened. Bin Ladin probably sensed that in the 1990s, the pan-Islamist frame would have more mobilising power than the socio-revolutionary frame, especially in Saudi Arabia. It is no coincidence that the most explicit socio-revolutionary statements by al-Qaida members appear in internal memos and strategy documents. Al-Qaida in fact went to great lengths to conceal their revolutionary aims from prospective recruits. As we shall see in the next chapter, the majority of Saudi recruits to al-Qaida were motivated by pan-Islamist sentiment, not regime discontent, and recruiters systematically tricked recruits into going to Afghanistan, telling them

[4] al-Zawahiri, '*fursan*'.

the Afghan camps were merely a station on the way to the Palestinian or Chechen battlefronts.

This point has important implications for how we view the root causes of global jihadist violence. The instrumentalist view of global jihadist ideology, which dismisses framing as tactics and focuses solely on the end objectives of al-Qaida's top leadership, leads to the argument that al-Qaida's violence ultimately derives from a problem of governance in the Muslim world. By including framing in the equation, we are brought to consider also the factors that made al-Qaida's pan-Islamist and anti-American rhetoric resonate so strongly among recruits, factors that are more likely to lie in the realm of international politics and new media. Global jihadism should thus be considered an ideological doctrine in its own right.

Saudi Arabia occupies a central place in the intellectual history of global jihadism, because it was the original cause for which the doctrine was formulated. The American 'occupation of the land of the two holy places' was a central theme in most of Usama bin Ladin's statements in the second half of the 1990s. Bin Ladin considered the US military presence in Saudi Arabia totally unacceptable, for several reasons. First, the US presence ran counter to religious imperatives regarding the purity of the Arabian Peninsula and the sanctity of Mecca and Medina. Second, the foreign military presence was politically unacceptable because it amounted to an occupation of sovereign Muslim territory and the domination of the Saudi population by a non-Muslim power. Third, the occupation had deep economic consequences because it facilitated the exploitation of the oil resources and enforced expensive arms deals on the Saudi state. Indeed, in Bin Ladin's view all the problems and evils in Saudi society were the result of the American occupation.[5]

Moreover, Bin Ladin argued in the late 1990s, the occupation of the Arabian Peninsula was not like the occupation of any other Muslim territory, because Saudi Arabia holds a unique position in the Islamic world. For a start, it represents the cradle of Islam and includes the holy sanctuaries to which all Muslims turn during prayer and travel during pilgrimage. Second, it is a symbol of the political unity and strength of the Muslim nation. Indeed the only comparable territory in terms of religious and symbolic value is Palestine. Third, it is strategically located, so the Crusader occupation facilitates Jewish domination

[5] *1996 Declaration of War*; *ABC News Interview, December 1998*; *16 February 2003 Statement*; all in Thomas Hegghammer, *Dokumentasjon om al-Qaida: Intervjuer, kommunikéer og andre primærkilder, 1990–2002* [Documentation on al-Qaida: Interviews, Communiqués and Other Primary Sources, 1990–2002] (Kjeller: Norwegian Defence Research Establishment (FFI/Rapport), 2002), 19, 60, 65, 68, 126 and 131.

in the region and enables the US military to bomb Muslims in Iraq, Afghanistan and elsewhere.[6]

By emphasising Saudi Arabia's special status in the Muslim nation, Bin Ladin no doubt displayed a certain Saudi nationalism and ethnocentrism. He proudly stated that, unlike the rest of the Middle East, Saudi Arabia had remained untarnished by foreign occupation for fourteen centuries. He also insinuated that the inhabitants of the Arabian Peninsula enjoyed a special status as the direct descendants of the first Muslims. Moreover, he said, Saudis had been exceptional in responding to the call for jihad abroad, so they could be expected to fight even harder on their home territory.[7]

According to Bin Ladin, the urgency of liberating the Arabian Peninsula was amplified by the fact that the rest of the Muslim world was in such a dire state. The occupation of the Arabian Peninsula was all the more humiliating because other territories and sanctuaries were already under occupation. He reminded his readers that the Muslims lost the 'first qibla' (Jerusalem) in 1948, and now they were about to lose the 'second qibla' (Mecca). In Bin Ladin's view, the deployment of US troops represented an act of aggression against the entire umma, and all Muslims must therefore fight the United States.[8]

In the eyes of the al-Qaida leader, the continued US military presence on Saudi territory was not only a *casus belli* against America, but also the final nail in the coffin for the legitimacy of the Saudi regime. By inviting US troops and allowing them to stay indefinitely, while at the same time stifling domestic opposition, the regime had become an accomplice to the crusader occupation. Bin Ladin rarely, if ever, literally said that the regime or any of its individual members were infidel, but he went a very long way in denying the political and religious legitimacy of the Al Sa'ud. There was in other words an important revolutionary dimension to the global jihadist doctrine, although in the final analysis, the fight against the far enemy was deemed to have priority.[9]

Bin Ladin suggested that, in the past, the regime had at least made some effort to try to appear Islamic, but the arrival of the American

[6] *John Miller Interview, May 1998*; *Statement no. 20 by the Advice and Reform Committee*; *1996 Declaration of War*; *John Miller Interview 1997*; all in Hegghammer, *Dokumentasjon*, 44, 48 and 131.

[7] *Abd al-Bari Atwan Interview, 1996*; *1996 Declaration of War*; *John Miller Interview, 1997*; all in Hegghammer, *Dokumentasjon*, 23, 131 and 135.

[8] *1996 Declaration of War*; *Statement no. 20 by the Advice and Reform Committee*; *CNN Interview, 1997*; *Abd al-Bari Atwan Interview, 1996*; *Robert Fisk Interview, 1996*; Hegghammer, *Dokumentasjon*, 20, 23, 32, 131 and 135.

[9] *CNN Interview, 1997*; *John Miller Interview, 1998*; *Hamid Mir Interview, 2001*; Hegghammer, *Dokumentasjon*, 31, 35 and 103.

troops had exposed the un-Islamic nature of the government and sparked a process of serious societal decay. The turning point, according to Bin Ladin, was the imprisonment of the leaders of the Sahwa, after which the Saudi regime completely 'stopped ruling in accordance with God's revelation'.[10]

However, Bin Ladin explained that although corruption increased after the arrival of the Crusaders, the Saudi regime had a long history of treason towards the Islamic nation. (Bin Ladin did not, of course, mention that up until 1990, he himself had been a loyal supporter of the Saudi regime.) Throughout its existence, he now argued, the modern Saudi state had served foreign imperial interests, first the British and then the Americans. Moreover, Bin Ladin held King Abd al-Aziz, the founding father of the modern Saudi state, responsible for the loss of Palestine. Bin Ladin said that Abd al-Aziz, on the orders of the British, sent two of his sons to calm down the Palestinian revolt in 1936, thus paving the way for the creation of the state of Israel. Bin Ladin thus retroactively constructed a historical continuity: like Abd al-Aziz had caused the loss of the first qibla, so his son Fahd caused the loss of the second. King Fahd had also betrayed the Muslim nation by supporting the Socialists in Yemen and the secular PLO in Palestine. The only exception to this history of treason, Bin Ladin argued, was King Faisal in his late days, because he 'genuinely helped the Palestinian cause'.[11]

Although Bin Ladin was very hostile to the Saudi regime and displayed clear socio-revolutionary tendencies, his main focus was still on the United States. If he viewed the regime as illegitimate, it was primarily because of its collusion with the Crusaders. As he noted in 1997:

> Regarding the criticisms of the ruling regime in Saudi Arabia and the Arabian Peninsula, the first one is their subordination to the US. So, our main problem is the US government while the Saudi regime is but a branch or an agent of the US ... The people and the young men are concentrating their efforts on the sponsor and not on the sponsored. The concentration at this point of jihad is against the American occupiers.[12]

In 1998 he put it in even clearer terms:

> our work targets world infidels in the first place. Our enemy is the crusader alliance led by America, Britain and Israel. It is a Crusader–Jewish alliance. However, some regimes in the Arab and Muslim worlds have joined that alliance, preventing us Muslims from defending the holy Ka'ba. Our hostility is in

[10] *CNN Interview, 1997*; in Hegghammer, *Dokumentasjon*, 19 and 31.

[11] *Nida al-Islam Interview, 1996*; *1996 Declaration of War*; *Robert Fisk Interview, 1996*; all in Hegghammer, *Dokumentasjon*, 19, 26 and 132.

[12] *CNN Interview, 1997*; in Hegghammer, *Dokumentasjon*, 31.

the first place, and to the greatest extent, levelled against these world infidels, and by necessity the regimes which have turned themselves into tools for this occupation.[13]

Bin Ladin's intention to focus the military struggle on the Americans first, and the Saudi regime second, was not just a slogan. There is strong evidence that Bin Ladin also promoted this strategy internally in al-Qaida in the late 1990s. Nasir al-Bahri, who worked as Bin Ladin's bodyguard in Afghanistan in this period, said the following in an interview with *al-Quds al-Arabi* in 2005:

Some of the brothers used to say: 'Sheikh Usama, we want to carry out an operation against this or that Arab leader because the Egyptian, Iraqi, and other governments are apostate governments.' They were very zealous. He used to answer them: 'Leave them alone and do not preoccupy yourselves with them. They are scum ... When they witness the defeat of the United States, they will be in their worst situation.' ...

(*Journalist*) Did Bin Ladin consider the United States his only target?

(*Al-Bahri*) Yes, he considered it his only target. Therefore, he restricted the activities of his organisation to the United States.[14]

As al-Bahri's account suggests, the top al-Qaida leadership saw the war against the US presence in the kingdom both as an important cause in its own right and as a means to topple the Saudi government. This is further corroborated by an internal al-Qaida strategy document uncovered by the US military in Afghanistan in late 2001 and declassified in 2006. The fifty-two-page letter, written by a Saudi-based figure with the pseudonym Abu Hudhayfa, was addressed to Bin Ladin and contained the following interesting passage:

The brothers are completely in agreement with the goal presented by (Abu Abdallah) and that is fighting the Americans ... Based on the situation of our brothers and their capabilities, they believe that they ought to start with the Crusader enemy by a strategy that can achieve the sought goals, some of which are:

1) Reinstituting confidence in the hearts of Muslim masses
2) Preparing the environment for fighting the Saudi system ...
3) Acquiring the political, military and Administrative experiences through field battles ... War builds combatants.
4) Discrediting the awesome image of the Saudi system
5) Breaking the barrier of fear and hesitation from the minds of the mujahidin
6) Expanding the circle of jihad horizontally and vertically via assassinating some of the leaders of disbelief in the system

[13] *ABC News Interview, December 1998*; in Hegghammer, *Dokumentasjon*, 60.

[14] *al-Quds al-Arabi*, 31 March 2005.

7) After the escalation of operations against the crusader enemy in a compounding rate and at the critical point, the mujahidin command declares war against the Saudi system at the appropriate circumstance and after a long practice in carrying out item 7 while taking into consideration the principles and techniques of guerrilla war.[15]

It seems, then, that Bin Ladin envisaged a two-step process in which, first, the United States would be confronted and evicted, whereupon the regime would fall almost automatically. On the horizon of his worldview was thus a socio-revolutionary aim. However, the most urgent and most challenging task facing the umma was the jihad against America. The vanguard of this jihad was the al-Qaida organisation.

Al-Qaida central

Bin Ladin's move from Sudan to Afghanistan in May 1996 marked the beginning of al-Qaida's golden age. Over the next five years, the size of al-Qaida's infrastructure, operations and membership would witness a spectacular increase. By the time the US-led coalition invaded Afghanistan in October 2001, al-Qaida had trained several thousand Arab volunteers and orchestrated the most spectacular terrorist attack in history. Without getting deep into the details of al-Qaida's history in this period, which has been covered well by writers such as Peter Bergen, Lawrence Wright and Michael Scheuer, it is worth reflecting on why al-Qaida grew so strong in this period.

The first and most significant reason was al-Qaida's safe haven in Afghanistan. The arguably most important lesson from the history of al-Qaida is that unhampered access to territory can dramatically increase a terrorist group's military capability. For a start, the safe haven allowed al-Qaida to quietly plan operations on its own schedule with virtually no outside interference. Moreover, it allowed Bin Ladin to build a core organisation with a relatively high degree of bureaucratisation and functional task division, which in turn improved organisational efficiency. Most important of all, territorial access enabled Bin Ladin to set up an elaborate military educational system, the like of which has never been seen in the hands of a transnational terrorist organisation with such a radical agenda. This infrastructure – or 'University of Global Jihadism' – greatly improved al-Qaida's ability to operationalise recruits. The training camps are also key to understanding the characteristic organisational duality of al-Qaida, namely the simultaneous existence

[15] 'Letter from Abu Hudhayfa to Abu Abdallah', *HARMONY Database (AFGP-2002-003251)*, 20 June 2000.

of a hierarchical and bureaucratic core and a much larger and looser network of camp alumni.

Beyond increasing the recruits' paramilitary expertise, the camps constituted an arena for social processes that improved al-Qaida's operational capability. Many of these processes imitated those cultivated by professional military organisations. Instructors first of all sought to desensitise the recruits through intensive weapons practice and through the promotion of an ultra-masculine and weapons-fixated camp culture. Moreover, the hardship of camp life made recruits forge strong personal relationships, thus building the deep internal loyalty and trust needed for long-winded operations such as the 9/11 attacks. Finally the 'graduates' of these camps were imbued with self-confidence and a sense of being part of a vanguard, which turned many into leading or entrepreneurial figures in the militant communities in their home countries. In addition to these social processes came the ideological indoctrination into global jihadism. Recruits were exposed to lectures and writings of global jihadi ideologues. Instructors also encouraged anti-American statements within the camps, leading recruits to try to rhetorically outdo one another. On the whole, the alumni from these training camps were more brutal, more bound together and more anti-Western than most of their peers.[16]

Al-Qaida's training infrastructure evolved over time and made a quantum leap in 1999 when Bin Ladin was allowed by the Taliban to set up the famous al-Faruq camp (for new recruits) and the Airport camp (for advanced courses) near Qandahar. Until then, al-Qaida did not have camps under its direct and sole control. Older camps such as Khalden or Derunta near Jalalabad were in fact not controlled by Bin Ladin, but run jointly by several Arab factions, many of which did not share Bin Ladin's global jihadist agenda. After 1999, more camps fell under the direct control of al-Qaida. This facilitated the circulation of recruits and consolidated al-Qaida's control over the new generation of Saudi jihadists who began arriving in large numbers precisely at this time.[17]

[16] Rohan Gunaratna, 'The Terrorist Training Camps of al Qaida', in *The Making of a Terrorist: Recruitment, Training and Root Causes*, ed. James J. F. Forest (Westport, CT: Praeger, 2006); Anthony Davis, 'The Afghan Files: Al-Qaeda Documents from Kabul', *Jane's Intelligence Review* 14, no. 2 (2002); 'Substitution for the Testimony of Muhammad Manea Ahmad al-Qahtani (Phase 2)', *Defendant's exhibit ST001 – US* v. *Moussaoui* (www.rcfp.org).

[17] *The 9/11 Commission Report*, 157. '*qissat al-afghan al-'arab min al-dukhul ila afghanistan ila al-khuruj ma' taliban* [The Story of the Afghan Arabs from the Entry into Afghanistan to their Departure with the Taliban] (part 4)', *al-Sharq al-Awsat*, 11 December 2004; Brynjar Lia, *Architect of Global Jihad: The Life of Al-Qaeda Strategist Abu Mus'ab Al-Suri* (London: Hurst, 2007); Abu Mus'ab al-Suri, *da'wat al-muqawama al-islamiyya al-'alamiyya* [The Global Islamic Resistance Call] (2004), 727–9; available at www.tawhed.ws.

The second major factor behind al-Qaida's growth in the late 1990s was Bin Ladin's formidable ability to create alliances with other key players in the world of radical Islamism. Most important of these actors was of course the Taliban regime, the guarantor of al-Qaida's safe haven. That Bin Ladin should forge such a strong relationship with Mulla Umar, the Taliban leader, was by no means inevitable. When Bin Ladin arrived in Afghanistan in 1996, he had more friends among the Taliban's Afghan enemies than among the Taliban themselves. Up until mid-1998, the relationship was uneasy, with the Taliban disapproving of Bin Ladin's international media offensives and even considering extraditing the al-Qaida leader to Saudi Arabia. However, the US missile strikes on Afghanistan following the East Africa bombings in August 1998 brought al-Qaida and the Taliban much closer together.[18]

Bin Ladin was also able to reduce some of the factionalism that had crippled the broader community of Arab Afghans since the 1980s. There were many Arab jihadi factions in Afghanistan in the late 1990s – fourteen, according to the jihadi writer Abu Mus'ab al-Suri – most of which were working for regime change in their respective home countries. Bin Ladin succeeded in convincing some of these to join him in his global jihad against America, most famously Ayman al-Zawahiri's Egyptian Islamic Jihad, which formally merged with al-Qaida in 2000 after several years of de facto collaboration. Another important type of actor courted by Bin Ladin were irredentist Islamist groups in places such as Kashmir, Chechnya, the Philippines and East Turkestan. Al-Qaida sought to help these groups in various ways, partly out of conviction – helping irredentist Muslims was after all a crucial element of pan-Islamism – and partly because it boosted al-Qaida's image as the champion of the oppressed umma. Moreover, it extended the operational reach of the al-Qaida network, as many of these relationships could be exploited on an ad hoc basis for military or logistical purposes.

Al-Qaida's relative diplomatic successes were partly due to what he had to offer, namely training, refuge and money. However, another source of success was Bin Ladin's personal attributes – notably his charisma, his reputation and his rhetorical skills. He consciously cultivated the image of a grandfatherly, humble and inclusive figure that appealed to fellow jihadi leaders as well as to new recruits. He also knew how to exploit political windows of opportunities – such as the aftermath of the August 1998 missile strikes – to his own political advantage. Bin

[18] Alan Cullison and Andrew Higgins, 'A Once-Stormy Terror Alliance Was Solidified by Cruise Missiles', *Wall Street Journal*, 2 August 2002; Ahmed Rashid, *Descent into Chaos* (New York: Viking, 2008), 15–16.

Ladin's success in building alliances is all the more remarkable given that the agenda he was pursuing – war against America – was actually shared by very few of his allies. In the post-9/11 world there has been a tendency to forget how marginal the global jihadist doctrine really was in the broader landscape of militant Islamism.[19]

For these and other reasons, al-Qaida developed a formidable operational capability in the late 1990s. The number of al-Qaida operations in this period is difficult to count because the nature of the involvement of the core organisation varied greatly. While some operations were coordinated from the top down, others were initiated from below. Bin Ladin continuously received suggestions for international operations from entrepreneurs in the periphery of the al-Qaida network, and he extended partial support for a number of these, such as the plot to bomb Los Angeles airport and the plan to attack multiple tourist targets in Jordan around the millennium. However, the al-Qaida leadership clearly emphasised quality over quantity, because they were deeply invested in only three major operations during the Afghanistan period, namely the 1998 East Africa bombings, the 2000 USS *Sullivans*/USS *Cole* operations and the 9/11 attack. This series of increasingly ambitious attacks – from a soft target on land to a hard target by sea to a strategic target by air – reflected the spectacular growth in al-Qaida's capabilities.[20]

The impact of the attacks was amplified by al-Qaida's increasingly elaborate media strategy. For most of the 1990s, al-Qaida followed a rather old-fashioned media strategy based on issuing written statements and giving interviews to major news outlets. Apart from a media offensive in 1997 and 1998, during which Bin Ladin gave a long series of interviews to foreign journalists and Western TV networks, al-Qaida was initially quite passive on the propaganda front, at least by post-9/11 standards. The East Africa operation was accompanied only by poorly distributed written statements. However, from around 2000 onward, al-Qaida began producing its own audiovisual propaganda. In early 2001, al-Qaida produced its first recruitment video celebrating the USS *Cole* attack and the Palestinian intifada. While preparing the 9/11 attacks, al-Qaida introduced a new method borrowed from Hamas, namely video-recorded statements by each of the suicide bombers, as well as recordings from the preparation process. In 2001, al-Qaida also took steps towards establishing its own website, although it was never completed.[21]

[19] Fawaz Gerges, *The Far Enemy: Why Jihad Went Global* (Cambridge University Press: 2006).

[20] Anonymous, *Through our Enemies' Eyes*, 216.

[21] *al-Jazeera*, 15 April 2002, 9 September 2002; *tadmir al-mudammira al-amrikiyya kul* [Destruction of the American Destroyer *Cole*], 2001; Vik Iyer and Elsa McLaren,

The strong presence of Saudis in al-Qaida's attack teams – not least on 9/11 – has led to a widespread perception of al-Qaida as a Saudi-dominated organisation. This is a truth with modifications. Saudis were no doubt overrepresented among al-Qaida's suicide operatives. Al-Qaida's three main operations involved seventeen Saudis and two Saudi-raised Yemenis out of a total of twenty-four attackers. Moreover, in 2001, Saudis were in a clear majority in the training camps. However, in the upper levels of the organisation, Saudis were massively outnumbered by the Egyptians. There had been few Saudis among al-Qaida's founding members in 1988, and, as we shall see below, recruitment of Saudis did not really pick up until the very end of the 1990s. The Saudis' late arrival made them relatively less experienced and thus more expendable. Another factor for using them in international operations was the relative ease with which well-off Saudis obtained visas to foreign countries. A third rationale for using Saudis as suicide bombers was political communication, that is, to ensure that Bin Ladin's original cause, namely ending the US 'occupation' of the Arabian Peninsula, was not forgotten in Riyadh or Washington. But why not use the Saudis to attack in Saudi Arabia proper?[22]

Al-Qaida in Saudi Arabia

Bin Ladin came to Afghanistan in May 1996 with few Saudis in his entourage and a very limited organisational infrastructure inside the kingdom. During his stay in Sudan, he had lost touch with most of his Saudi friends from the early days of the Services Bureau, who disliked the revolutionary zeal of Bin Ladin's Egyptian comrades. Bin Ladin had also failed to gain a following among the Saudi Islamist grassroots, who were more interested in Bosnia or the Sahwa than Bin Ladin's East African adventures.

By all accounts, Bin Ladin himself did not intend to launch a major campaign in the kingdom prior to 1995. When Egyptian al-Qaida members proposed bombing the US embassy in Saudi Arabia in 1993

'New Bin Laden Video Aired', *The Times*, 7 September 2006; 'Letter from Abu Hudhayfa to Abu Abdallah'.

[22] For names and nationalities of the bombers in al-Qaida's three main operations, see *USA* v. *Usama bin Ladin et al*, 2014–17; *USA* v. *al-Badawi* – Indictment (Southern District of New York, 2003), 13; and *The 9/11 Commission Report*, 238–9. For an overview of core al-Qaida members and their nationalities, see *The 9/11 Commission Report*, 433–8 and Sageman, *Understanding Terror Networks*, 185–9. For more on Bin Ladin's entourage, see Ed Blanche, 'The Egyptians around Bin Laden', *Jane's Intelligence Review* 13, no. 12 (2001); for the rationale of using Saudis on 9/11 see *The 9/11 Commission Report*, 232.

in revenge for the arrest of Sheikh Omar Abd al-Rahman, the top al-Qaida leadership allegedly rejected the idea. However, the crackdown on the Sahwa in September 1994 convinced Bin Ladin of the futility of non-violent advocacy and made him consider a military campaign against US forces more seriously. The 9/11 Commission heard classified evidence of an alleged Bin Ladin plot to smuggle explosives from Sudan to eastern Saudi Arabia in 1994. Moreover, according to an Iraqi document captured by US forces in 2003, Bin Ladin met with an Iraqi government representative in Khartoum in early 1995 and discussed 'carrying out joint operations against foreign forces' in Saudi Arabia. However, these reports, even if accurate, do not suggest Bin Ladin was putting his full weight behind a terrorism campaign in the kingdom. He may have been held back somewhat by the Sudanese government, which was under pressure from Egypt, Saudi Arabia and the USA to contain the militants residing in Khartoum.[23]

In Afghanistan, on the other hand, Bin Ladin had no such political constraints. In 1996 he therefore declared jihad against the Americans on the Arabian Peninsula and began in earnest to build an al-Qaida network in the kingdom. Nasir al-Bahri has said that Bin Ladin 'opened branches of the al-Qaida organisation in Saudi Arabia' in 1996 and that 'many brothers' were responsible for al-Qaida's branches in Saudi Arabia. Bin Ladin focused his organisation-building efforts on what had been the heartland of the recruitment for the Afghan jihad and the region where his personal network was strongest, namely the Hijaz. Unfortunately we know very little about these early al-Qaida representatives. One of the few names that have emerged is that of a certain Abu Ahmad al-Tabuki, who was, according to his martyrdom biography, 'one of the most important wanted people in the kingdom, but he fled to Iraq. He was considered among the oldest leaders of the Sheikh [Usama bin Ladin]. The sabre Yusuf al-Uyayri [the founder of the QAP] also used to go to him.'[24]

However, Bin Ladin's network developed much more slowly than he had hoped. A key problem was that al-Qaida came to the Saudi scene just after the Riyadh and Khobar bombings, so many of Bin Ladin's sympathisers and potential helpers were in prison. Moreover, the United States became much more alert to the threat against its interests in Saudi Arabia and boosted the protection of potential targets. It

[23] Tom Hayes, 'Terror Chief's Followers Quit over Plans to Kill Civilians, Court Told', *Associated Press*, 21 February 2001; 'Overview of the Enemy – Staff Statement Number 15' (www.9–11commission.gov, 2004); Peter Bergen, 'Enemy of our Enemy', *New York Times*, 28 March 2006.

[24] *al-Quds al-Arabi*, 20 March 2005; Muhibb al-Jihad, *Martyrs of Mesopotamia*.

was not until the spring of 1997 that Bin Ladin recruited the man who would become al-Qaida's main operative leader on the Arabian Peninsula for the subsequent five years.

Abd al-Rahim al-Nashiri (b. 1966, aka Abu Bilal) was a Mecca-born Saudi of Yemeni origin who had fought in Afghanistan in the 1980s. In mid-1996 he had travelled with the so-called Northern group to Tajikistan. In January 1997, he passed through Jalalabad on the way back from the failed Tajik adventure and was invited by Bin Ladin to join al-Qaida, an offer he declined. A few months later he changed his mind, returned to Afghanistan and began working for Bin Ladin. Al-Nashiri would later gain notoriety as the coordinator of the USS *Cole* operation in October 2000 and the chief of al-Qaida's operations on the Arabian Peninsula before his arrest in the United Arab Emirates in November 2002.[25]

There is very little public information about al-Qaida operations inside Saudi Arabia between 1996 and 2001. As late as 2005, Western security officials interviewed by this author still referred cryptically to 'foiled attacks unknown to the general public' in Saudi Arabia in the 1996–2001 period. Whatever the precise level of operational activity, it seems clear that al-Qaida did not carry out any successful major operations in the kingdom between 1996 and 2001. There are no reports of violent attacks of any kind in Saudi Arabia between July 1996 and February 2000. A number of smaller attacks on Western targets occurred from August 2000 onward, but none of these seem to have been orchestrated by Bin Ladin.

However, there are indications that Saudi police prevented at least two major planned operations in 1998. The most significant and best-documented development took place in or around January 1998, when Saudi authorities arrested a group of militants in possession of Sagger antitank missiles somewhere in the south-west of the country. The intended target of the missile plot seems to have been the US consulate in Jidda, and the operation was allegedly timed to coincide with a visit to the kingdom by US Vice President Al Gore. The group behind the smuggling operation has been described by officials as the 'first al-Qaida cell in Saudi Arabia'. According to official US sources, the plot was sponsored by Bin Ladin and directed by Abd al-Rahim al-Nashiri with the assistance of the latter's cousin Jihad Muhammad Abu Ali, as well as a certain Abu Muhjin al-Shaybani. The story of the missile plot received an interesting twist in 2003, when Prince Turki al-Faisal said that Saudi authorities at the time had uncovered evidence that Khalid al-Mihdhar and Nawaf al-Hazmi – two of the future 9/11 hijackers – had also been involved in the operation and that Saudi intelligence had

[25] *The 9/11 Commission Report*, 152–3.

alerted the CIA about their identity as early as 1999, a claim US authorities vehemently denied.[26]

The Saudi authorities reacted by cracking down very hard on the jihadist community in the weeks and months following the discovery. Police arrested between 800 and 900 people across the country, especially in the Mecca area. The missile plot alerted Saudi authorities to the threat posed by al-Qaida and led the government to increase the pressure on the Taliban. In July 1998, Turki al-Faisal travelled to Qandahar in order to persuade Mulla Umar to extradite Bin Ladin. A declassified memo from the US National Security Council dated December 2000 mentions a foiled al-Qaida operation in Saudi Arabia in late 1997 – most likely a reference to the missile plot – which led the Saudi government to change its attitude to the threat from al-Qaida. The occurrence of this change was later confirmed by Turki al-Faisal, who said the missile plot led to the establishment of a 'joint [US–Saudi] terrorism task force' which would meet on a monthly basis.[27]

The 1998 missile plot remains well known in Saudi Islamist circles. Rumours of the incident reached the London-based opposition, who wrote in a mid-1998 newsletter that 'real operations have been foiled ... Groups loyal to Bin Ladin have succeeded in smuggling dangerous kinds of weapons into the kingdom.' As late as 2004, *Sawt al-Jihad* referred to a person 'who had been arrested in 1998 in connection with the famous missile case which led to the incarceration of many young mujahidin [who fought] in Bosnia'.[28]

Later the same year, there seems to have been a second missile-smuggling attempt involving Yemen-based Egyptian militants. The only available source for this is a US Presidential Daily Brief from 4 December 1998, which mentioned that the (Egyptian) Islamic Group acquired SA-7 missiles in Yemen in October 1998 and intended to bring them into Saudi Arabia, where they would be used against an Egyptian or an American aeroplane. The plot prompted the closure of the US embassy on 7 October 1998 and the arrest of around 300 Islamists in early 1999.

[26] *The 9/11 Commission Report*, 152 and 491; Pervez Musharraf, *In the Line of Fire: A Memoir* (London: Simon and Schuster, 2006), 213; George Tenet, *At the Center of the Storm: My Years at the CIA* (New York: HarperCollins, 2007), 105; Judith Miller, 'Killing for the Glory of God, in a Land far from Home', *New York Times*, 16 January 2001; John Solomon, 'Saudis, US Describe Intelligence Links', *Associated Press*, 17 October 2003; author's interview with Faris bin Huzzam.

[27] 'Strategy for Eliminating the Threat from the Jihadist Networks of al Qida: Status and Prospects' (National Security Council Memo, 2000 (www.gwu.edu/~nsarchiv/)); Solomon, 'Saudis, US Describe Intelligence Links'.

[28] *al-Islah*, no. 113 (1 June 1998); '*akhbar wa mushahadat* [News and Reports]', *Sawt al-Jihad*, no. 13 (2004): 5.

It is not clear, however, whether this second plot was orchestrated by al-Qaida.[29]

At a press conference in Afghanistan in May 1998, Bin Ladin acknowledged the seizure of the missiles in January and the arrest of the 800 suspects, but boasted that 'what was captured was much less than what was not captured'. In retrospect, it seems clear that he was bluffing, for the arrests had seriously complicated al-Qaida's plans for attacks in the kingdom. Not only were more potential collaborators imprisoned, the authorities were now also alerted to the identity and role of Bin Ladin's key deputy in the kingdom, Abd al-Rahim al-Nashiri. From then on, al-Nashiri's ability to operate inside the kingdom was somewhat circumscribed. From mid-1998 onward, he seems to have spent most of his time in Yemen and Afghanistan, planning operations in Yemen and making money from a honey-trade company. Although al-Nashiri remained Bin Ladin's main operative leader on the Arabian Peninsula, his value as an al-Qaida coordinator inside the kingdom itself had decreased by late 1998.[30]

This setback of the missile plot made Bin Ladin realise that premature operations were counterproductive and that he needed time to build an organisation in the kingdom. At some point in 1998, al-Qaida decided to unilaterally halt operations in Saudi Arabia and opt for a more long-term strategy. No explicit evidence of such a decision exists in open sources, but the prominent jihadi ideologue Abu Bakr Naji wrote in 2003 that 'the [al-Qaida] High Command used to consider the youth of the Arabian Peninsula as their striking force, but it did not select the Peninsula for change due to factors mentioned in previous studies'. Moreover, CIA director George Tenet wrote in his autobiography that 'Bin Ladin prior to 9/11 had imposed a ban on attacks in Saudi Arabia.' From 1998 onward, al-Qaida's strategy towards Saudi Arabia thus aimed at exploiting the kingdom as a recruitment base and source of funding. Instead of planning attacks, trusted representatives would work slowly but surely to build the infrastructure needed for a future campaign.[31]

The absence of major terrorist attacks in the kingdom between 1996 and 2001 was thus the result of perfectly explicable organisational factors: the pre-1998 lack of capability and the post-1998 lack of intention. This finding undermines the theory, put forward by Simon Henderson,

[29] *The 9/11 Commission Report*, 128–9; 'US Embassies in Saudi Arabia Closed for One Day', *ArabicNews.com*, 7 October 1998; 'Over 300 Bin Laden Companions'.

[30] Abu Shiraz, 'May 1998 Interview with Bin Laden Reported', *Pakistan*, 20 February 1999.

[31] Abu Bakr Naji, '*idarat al-tawahhush* [The Management of Savagery]' (www.tawhed.ws, 2004), 29; Tenet, *At the Center of the Storm*, 248.

Gerald Posner and others, according to which the Saudi regime had been paying protection money to al-Qaida since the early or mid-1990s. The theory is not supported by any publicly available evidence and is undermined by the very occurrence of the 1998 missile plots. It is also inconsistent with a 2000 US National Security Council memo which cites improved US–Saudi cooperation in the fight against al-Qaida after 1998. Until supported by more than cryptic references to classified intelligence sources, the pay-off hypothesis must be considered a conspiracy theory. Bin Ladin was serious about liberating the Arabian Peninsula and had no qualms about offending the royal family; he just needed more fighters.[32]

If Bin Ladin's military ambitions failed between 1996 and 2001, his recruitment efforts were an astounding success. By the summer of 2001, Saudis were crowding the training camps and queuing up to take part in suicide operations. According to senior al-Qaida leader Khalid Shaykh Muhammad, 70 per cent of all recruits in a given Arab training camp in Afghanistan were Saudis.[33]

It was not always like that, however. When al-Qaida first began recruiting actively in the kingdom in 1996, response was sluggish. In the absence of a local network of recruiters, Bin Ladin sent Afghanistan-based associates such as Abu Zubayda to Saudi Arabia, but these efforts were largely unsuccessful, presumably because these envoys lacked the necessary social networks. One of the best indications of Bin Ladin's recruitment problems is the testimony of Nasir al-Bahri, a Saudi-Yemeni who met Bin Ladin in Jalalabad in January 1997. He found the al-Qaida leader desperate to recruit Saudis into his organisation. Nasir al-Bahri recalled the conversation:

> 'I will not hide from you, Sheikh, that what you said is convincing and that you are putting forward a clear case, but it is clear to me you do not have anyone from the people of the land itself, that is, from the people of the Arabian Peninsula, whose cause this is.' He said to me: 'What you say is true. Most of the brothers around me are Egyptians, Algerians, and North Africans. That is why I invite you to join our caravan.'[34]

[32] Simon Henderson and Matthew Levitt, 'US–Saudi Counterterrorism Cooperation in the Wake of the Riyadh Bombing', in *Policy Watch* (Washington Institute for Near East Policy, 2003); Simon Henderson, *After King Abdullah: Succession in Saudi Arabia* (Washington, DC: Washington Institute for Near East Policy, 2009), 20–1; Gerald Posner, *Why America Slept: The Failure to Prevent 9/11* (New York: Ballantine Books, 2003), 45; 'Strategy for Eliminating the Threat'. Similar conspiracy theories have been put forward about other Gulf monarchies too, including Qatar and the UAE; see e.g. Uzi Mahnaimi, 'Qatar Buys off Al-Qaeda attacks with Oil Millions', *Sunday Times*, 1 May 2008.

[33] *The 9/11 Commission Report*, 233.

[34] *al-Quds al-Arabi*, 26 March 2005; 'Report of the Joint Inquiry into the Terrorist Attacks of September 11, 2001' (Washington, DC: US House of Representatives and US Senate, 2002), 131; *The 9/11 Commission Report*, 152.

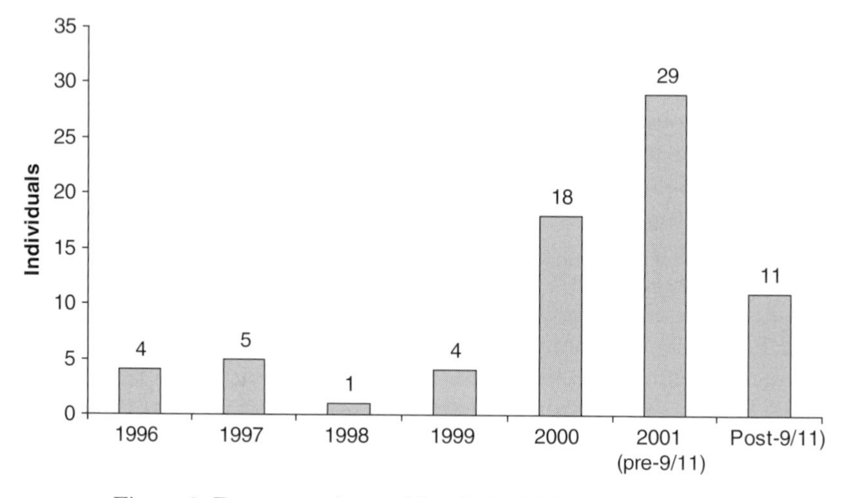

Figure 3: Departure dates of Saudis in Afghanistan, 1996–2001

In addition to this anecdotal evidence, the biographies of Saudi al-Qaida recruits collected for this study show that the vast majority of Saudi volunteers who trained in Afghanistan in this period arrived in 1999 or later (Figure 3).

The reasons for Bin Ladin's recruitment problems were the same that had prevented him from establishing an operational infrastructure, notably the imprisonment of many Saudi jihadists in the 1996–8 period and the controversial nature of Bin Ladin's global jihad project. In addition, the recruitment efforts in this early phase suffered from the lack of a clear al-Qaida media strategy.[35]

However, in 1998 the tide changed with Bin Ladin's growing media profile. The February 1998 release of the statement from the *World Islamic Front for Jihad against the Jews and the Crusaders* and the May 1998 press conference attracted significant attention in the Arab world. The East Africa bombings three months later proved to potential recruits that Bin Ladin was a man to be reckoned with. Finally, the US retaliation for the August attacks reinforced Bin Ladin's message about America's aggressiveness and the victimhood of the Muslim nation. Bin Ladin's popularity increased and the pool of potential recruits was growing – all Bin Ladin needed was someone on the ground to help him tap it. Luckily for Bin Ladin, an old friend was released from Dammam prison in mid-1998.

Yusuf bin Salih bin Fahd al-Uyayri was born in the early 1970s to an upper-middle-class family originally from the Qasim. His father's

[35] 'Letter from Abu Hudhayfa to Abu Abdallah'.

business had brought the family to Dammam where the young Yusuf grew up in the 1970s and 1980s. Former acquaintances have described him as a well-built, strong-willed teenager and a natural leader. While still in high school, he went to Afghanistan, where he allegedly excelled in the training camps and was appointed instructor at the al-Faruq camp in Khowst. He later became one of Usama bin Ladin's bodyguards and followed the al-Qaida leader to Sudan. He fought in Somalia before returning to Saudi Arabia in late 1993 or early 1994. Upon his return to the kingdom, al-Uyayri recruited for the Bosnian cause, and he personally trained jihad volunteers in the Dammam area.[36]

By 1996, al-Uyayri was a well-known figure on the jihadist scene in the Eastern province, so much so that he was arrested shortly after the Khobar bombing in June 1996 as one of many potential suspects. He was subjected to torture and imprisoned indefinitely, 'even after it became known that the *rafida* [Shiites] did it', as he later lamented. Al-Uyayri made use of his time in prison to read extensively in Islamic theology. He would later command great respect for his religious knowledge, and the fact that he was self-taught added to his heroic image. In June 1998, al-Uyayri was released by royal pardon, along with nearly 500 other prisoners in the Eastern Province, as part of the limited political liberalisation which began that year.[37]

Upon his release, he immediately reconnected with the Islamist community. He also took up writing, and by late July he had completed his first text, a pamphlet on how to acquire religious knowledge by self-study. In the first year or two after his release, he was mostly concerned with Kosovo and Chechnya, not with Afghanistan. This suggests that in the first two years after his release, al-Uyayri was in fact more of a classical than a global jihadist, and that he was closer to Khattab than to Bin Ladin. Al-Uyayri and Khattab had known each other personally since at least the early 1990s. They both grew up in the Eastern Province and al-Uyayri was a childhood friend of Abdallah al-Wabil, one of Khattab's close associates in Chechnya. In 1999 and early 2000, al-Uyayri followed the events in Chechnya closely and corresponded

[36] al-Salim, '*yusuf al-'uyayri*' (parts 1 and 2). For more on al-Uyayri, see Roel Meijer, 'Yusuf al-Uyairi and the Transnationalisation of Saudi Jihadism', in *Kingdom without Borders*, ed. al-Rasheed, 221–44; Roel Meijer, 'Yusuf al-Uyayri and the Making of a Revolutionary Salafi Praxis', *Die Welt des Islams* 47, nos. 3–4 (2007).

[37] al-Salim, '*yusuf al-'uyayri* (1)', 16–17; *al-Islah*, no. 22 (13 August 1996); author's interview with Faris bin Huzzam; Yusuf al-Uyayri, '*risala ila ra'is qism da'irat al-riqaba 'ala al-sujun fi'l-mintaqa al-sharqiyya 'an awda' sijn al-dammam* [Letter to the Head of the Department of Supervision of Prisons in the Eastern Province on the Conditions in Dammam Prison]' (www.qa3edoon.com, 2000); 'King Fahd Pardons 485 prisoners', *ArabicNews.com*, 31 August 1998.

directly with Khattab. Al-Uyayri also composed texts which were posted anonymously on the website of the Arab forces in Chechnya, *Sawt al-Qawqaz*. Some of these texts provided religious justifications for Khattab's increasingly brutal methods, such as suicide bombings and the killing of prisoners and hostages.[38]

In the course of the year 2000, Yusuf al-Uyayri gradually changed his focus from Chechnya to Afghanistan and began working for Bin Ladin. Al-Uyayri's relationship with al-Qaida seems to have blossomed after he made a trip to Afghanistan in July 2000 to assess the Taliban regime. In a subsequent report from this journey, he included the transcripts of interviews with very senior Taliban officials in both Kabul and Qandahar, including Mulla Umar himself. The fact that al-Uyayri had access to top Taliban officials suggests that he had come to Afghanistan on the invitation of, and with a recommendation from, Bin Ladin himself.[39]

From the autumn of 2000 onward, al-Uyayri devoted himself increasingly to the Afghan cause. Al-Uyayri's list of publications shows a shift in late 2000 from a focus on Chechen and domestic Saudi issues to a focus on the Taliban and the United States. It was also in late 2000 that the sheikhs of the al-Shu'aybi school began issuing fatwas on the need to support the Taliban, a development which was at least partly the result of al-Uyayri's influence. Bin Ladin's enlistment of al-Uyayri was indicative of the broader power shift that occurred in 2000 in the long-standing conflict between Khattab and Bin Ladin. Up until then, the classical jihadists had had the upper hand on the global jihadists; now setbacks on the Chechen front and Bin Ladin's growing media profile following the USS *Cole* attack turned the tables.[40]

Bin Ladin had known al-Uyayri well in the early 1990s and must have realised his value. Al-Uyayri was perfect for the job, for several reasons. First of all, he was a veteran jihadist with several years' experience as an elite training camp instructor. Second, his strong personal charisma commanded the admiration of younger recruits and enabled him to

[38] Yusuf al-Uyayri, '*tariqat talab al-'ilm* [The Way to Seek Knowledge]' (www.qa3edoon.com, 1998); al-Salim, '*yusuf al-'uyayri* (1)'; author's interviews with Nasir al-Barrak and Faris bin Huzzam; al-Salim, '*yusuf al-'uyayri* (1)', 18. Yusuf al-Uyayri, '*hidayat al-hayara fi jawaz qatl al-asara* [Guiding the Confused on the Permissibility of Killing Prisoners]' (www.qoqaz.com, 2000); Yusuf al-Uyayri, '*hal intaharat hawa am ustushhidat?* [Did Khava (Baraeva) Commit Suicide or Martyr Herself?]' (www.qoqaz.com, 2000).

[39] Yusuf al-Uyayri, '*al-mizan li-harakat taliban* [The Taliban in the Balance]' (www.tawhed.ws, 2001), 21.

[40] al-Salim, '*yusuf al-'uyayri* (1)', 18; al-Shu'aybi, '*hawla shar'iyyat hukumat taliban*'; '*qissat al-afghan al-'arab min al-dukhul ila afghanistan ila al-khuruj ma' taliban* [The Story of the Afghan Arabs from the Entry into Afghanistan to their Departure with the Taliban] (part 2)', *al-Sharq al-Awsat*, 9 December 2004.

convince many a financier and religious scholar to support jihadist causes. Third and most importantly, al-Uyayri's family was originally from Burayda, and this gave him unique access to the religious scholars and the donors in the Najd.[41]

Al-Uyayri's Najdi origin was highly significant, because up until 1999 the majority of Bin Ladin's agents in the kingdom, such as Abd al-Rahim al-Nashiri and Walid bin Attash, were Hijazis of Yemeni origin. Before al-Uyayri, al-Qaida's ability to mobilise resources in the central part of the country was circumscribed. With al-Uyayri, Bin Ladin finally had a foothold in the heartland of the Saudi Islamist landscape. Al-Uyayri had in fact already established close personal relationships with many of the most influential conservative clerics in Burayda. Al-Uyayri had known Salman al-Awda since 1993, and their mutual respect was reflected in the tone of al-Uyayri's many letters to al-Awda from 2000 onward. More important, al-Uyayri had moved to Burayda after his release from prison and married the sister of one of Sheikh Sulayman al-Ulwan's wives (who, incidentally, was from the highly respected al-Saq'abi family of religious scholars). He thus had a direct family connection to a key member of the al-Shu'aybi network, which was on the rise exactly at this time.[42]

Al-Uyayri's role in Bin Ladin's network was quite different from that of operators such as Abd al-Rahim al-Nashiri or Walid bin Attash. Al-Uyayri's function was not to mount international operations but to develop al-Qaida's recruitment and fundraising network in Saudi Arabia. By all accounts, he was not involved in the planning of the USS *Cole* or the 9/11 operations. However, he did travel to Afghanistan at least once more between his July 2000 visit and September 2001. He may also have travelled elsewhere; in one letter, he claims to have visited the Moro Islamic Liberation Front in Mindanao in the Philippines in August 2001.[43]

From mid-2000 onward, Yusuf al-Uyayri was, in the words of his jihadi biographer, 'preoccupied with recruiting youth and urging them to go to Afghanistan to join the camps and the training there'. He was also very active on the Internet, posting messages on the *al-Salafyoon* website and participating on the Internet-based radio forum *Paltalk* under the pseudonym 'Azzam'. Al-Uyayri's power as a recruiter lay probably less

[41] '*man huwa al-shaykh al-battar?* [Who is Sheikh Sabre?]' (www.qa3edoon.com, 2003); author's interviews with Faris bin Huzzam and Mansur al-Nuqaydan.

[42] '*man huwa al-shaykh al-battar?*'; author's interviews with Fahd al-Shafi, Sa'ud al-Sarhan and Mansur al-Nuqaydan.

[43] al-Uyayri, '*al-mizan li-harakat taliban*', 38; Yusuf al-Uyayri, '*hamsa fi udhn fadilat al-shaykh salman al-'awda*'.

in his own personal contact with young Saudis than in the influence he wielded over religious scholars. He convinced clerics that the Taliban regime was worth supporting, whereupon the scholars would encourage young Saudis to go to Afghanistan. We know for example that Abd al-Aziz al-Umari, one of the 9/11 hijackers, was recruited for Afghanistan by al-Uyayri's brother-in-law, Sheikh Sulayman al-Ulwan. Al-Uyayri's efforts were no doubt a very important factor behind the dramatic increase in the number of Saudis going to Afghanistan from 1999 onward.[44]

While al-Uyayri was undoubtedly important, he was by no means the only person contributing to the flow of volunteers between 1999 and 2001. In October 2005, the Saudi newspaper *al-Ukaz* published an interview with an anonymous 'repentant militant' who described how he was recruited in early 1999. The former militant said he was invited to lectures and meetings in specially allocated houses and desert camps. This suggests that as early as February 1999 there was an organised recruitment infrastructure in place, at least in the Riyadh area. In 2000 and 2001, recruiters seem to have been working in parallel in different parts of the country, although it is not clear to what extent they were working together or whether they all reported to Yusuf al-Uyayri. However, as we shall see later in this book, recruitment was not always a top-down process driven by a hierarchical network of professional recruiters. In many cases, recruits developed a motivation to go independently of a proactive recruiter, either by reading propaganda on the Internet, discussing politics with their friends, or hearing a sermon by a radical sheikh. For al-Qaida's purpose, it was often enough to have strategically placed 'gatekeepers' or 'fixers' who were reasonably well known in the local Islamist community.[45]

Al-Qaida's recruitment efforts were helped by the Internet, which was introduced in Riyadh, Jidda and Dhahran in January 1999 and in the rest of the country in July 1999. The kingdom rapidly became more digitalised than many of its neighbours. Very soon, the Web would prove to be an extremely powerful tool in the hands of the radical Islamist community in Saudi Arabia. The Internet provided a platform for cheap, anonymous, instantaneous and global distribution of written as well as audiovisual propaganda. For a clandestine and international community like the global jihadist movement, it was a godsend.[46]

[44] al-Salim, '*yusuf al-'uyayri* (2)', 15; *The 9/11 Commission Report*, 233.

[45] '*ta'ib ya'tarif: istakhdamna al-istirahat li-ghasl al-'uqul wa-tajnid al-irhabiyyin* [A Repentant Confesses: We Used Rest Houses for Brainwashing and Terrorist Recruitment]', *al-Ukaz*, 8 October 2005.

[46] 'General Internet Services in Saudi Arabia Next Month', *ArabicNews*, 10 June 1999.

Islamists were quick to exploit the enormous potential of the Internet to their political advantage. When the Web was introduced, a few jihadist websites were already available, notably *Sawt al-Qawqaz*, the webpage of the Chechen mujahidin. *Sawt al-Qawqaz* was one of the first jihadist sites to appear online and long remained one of the most sophisticated. Yusuf al-Uyayri began contributing articles for *Sawt al-Qawqaz* before establishing his own website, the well-known *al-Nida* site, shortly after 9/11. The first Saudi jihadi websites, such as the influential *al-Salafyoon*, started appearing in mid-1999. *Al-Salafyoon* seems to have been run by a group of young Saudis with links to clerics of the al-Shuʿaybi school in Burayda. Some of the people who later became involved in *Sawt al-Jihad* (the QAP's media office), like Abd al-Aziz al-Anzi, had begun their jihadist media career in *al-Salafyoon*. Around the year 2000, the first jihadist discussion forums such *al-Ansar* were launched. These forums included all kinds of jihadist propaganda, from theological treatises to pictures from Chechnya to training manuals. Participants could discuss political and religious issues with each other, pick up the latest news from the jihad fronts and ask for practical advice on bombmaking.[47]

The Internet would come to play a very important role in the mobilisation of Saudi jihadists because it allowed the most radical sheikhs to reach a wider audience, and because it facilitated the distribution of information and images from faraway jihad fronts such as Chechnya and Afghanistan. Over the years, Saudi jihadists would become extremely active on the Internet. In 2003 and 2004, the Internet was crucial for the QAP as an internal communications platform and external propaganda tool. Other new technologies, such as the mobile phone network, were also introduced in 1999. Add to this the fact that digital cameras became much cheaper and more widely available around this time, and it is fair to say that the year 1999 witnessed a quantum leap in the technological opportunities for clandestine activism in the kingdom.[48]

The story of the Saudi jihadists' use of the Internet between 1999 and 2004 is a classic example of how the introduction of new technologies can shift the balance of power between state and non-state actors. In this period, the Internet was the domain of the jihadists. They were much quicker and more dynamic in their exploitation of the possibilities of the Web than the Saudi state. The Internet had its limits, however,

[47] See '*al-ʿayn al-thalith: al-qissa al-kamila li "wazir iʿlam" al-qaʿida bi'l-saʿudiyya* [The Third Eye: The Complete Story of the 'Information Minister' of al-Qaida in Saudi Arabia]', *alarabiya.net*, 17 October 2005.

[48] '500 Lines for the Portable Phone in Saudi Arabia', *ArabicNews.com*, 23 July 1998.

and for other crucial tasks such as fundraising, virtual initiatives were not enough.

Fundraising was extremely important for al-Qaida in the late 1990s, because by the time Bin Ladin arrived in Afghanistan in 1996 there were only crumbs left of the former millionaire's private wealth. His assets in Saudi Arabia were frozen when he was stripped of his citizenship in 1994, and his expulsion from Sudan in 1996 cost him the businesses he had developed during his Khartoum years. At the same time, Bin Ladin had great ambitions for al-Qaida in Afghanistan and needed money to run his increasingly elaborate organisation.[49]

As we have seen, the rise of pan-Islamism in Saudi Arabia in the 1980s and 1990s had blurred the distinction between humanitarian and military support for Muslims in need. This had produced a Saudi charitable sector which could very easily be manipulated to channel money to militant groups abroad. Bin Ladin had established close links with key donors and charities during the Afghan jihad, the most important of whom were referred to as 'the Golden Chain' in a famous internal al-Qaida document.[50]

Saudi authorities had taken a number of steps to uproot fundraising infrastructure that could be traced directly to Bin Ladin. In 1993, Saudi authorities had taken IBC director Adil Batterjee in for questioning and closed the Jidda office of his charity. In 1997 they arrested Madani al-Tayyib (aka Abu Fadl al-Makki), al-Qaida's chief financial officer. In 1998, Saudi authorities arrested and deported Sa'id Sayyid Salama, an Egyptian who was working as a finance officer and international courier for al-Qaida. Donors inside Saudi Arabia therefore had to avoid appearing as dealing directly with Bin Ladin, for fear of attracting government attention. However, the structure and lack of oversight of the Saudi charitable sector made it very easy for donors to cover their traces, and for al-Qaida fundraisers to tap funds donated in good faith.[51]

Few knew the importance of fundraising better than the jihadist activists themselves. As Isa al-Awshan, an experienced Saudi fundraiser and later a prominent QAP member, wrote in 2003:

> There is no doubt that money is the lifeline of jihad, and from what is of greatest benefit to the jihad and the mujahidin is for a group of the umma – or the entire umma – to collect funds and send them to the people of the frontlines, and

[49] *The 9/11 Commission Report*, 170; Coll, *The Bin Ladens*.

[50] Burr and Collins, *Alms for Jihad*, 52; *The 9/11 Commission Report*, 170.

[51] Roe, Cohen and Franklin, 'How Saudi Wealth Fueled Holy War'; *The 9/11 Commission Report*, 122; Anonymous, *Through our Enemies' Eyes*, 211–12; *USA* v. *Usama bin Ladin et al*, 1288.

the impact of this on the jihad is not hidden from anyone ... Sheikh Yusuf al-Uyayri said that the one who has no income or wealth to spend should instead gather funds from those who do, including from women and children, and from private as well as public sources ... There are various methods in collecting money for the mujahidin which cannot all be mentioned here, but what is important is that you have complete determination to collect these donations. If this is your true concern and obsession, then you will find yourself coming up with countless and unlimited ways in which to do this, and you will pass unhurt through every obstacle placed in your way by the helpers of the Cross and the enemies of the mujahidin.[52]

The key to jihadist fundraising was the religious scholars, because private donors would nearly always consult clerics before making a donation. Many also entrusted sheikhs with money to pass on to good causes. A key task for jihadist fundraisers in Saudi Arabia was therefore to befriend religious scholars and convince them of the worthiness of the cause in question. This was why Yusuf al-Uyayri was so important to Bin Ladin. As a Burayda resident and brother-in-law of Sulayman al-Ulwan, al-Uyayri was very well placed to cajole the influential Najdi sheikhs into supporting jihadist causes. When al-Uyayri began raising funds for the Chechen jihad in 1999, he contacted the newly released Salman al-Awda, the Sahwist icon who had generated massive funds for the Bosnian, Tajik and Chechen jihad efforts in the first half of the 1990s. However, al-Uyayri was disappointed to find out that the sheikh had changed his views:

Commander Khattab told the brothers when he was in Dagestan, 'Give me a million dollars and we will stay until the end of the winter and be steadfast against the Russians.' So Sheikh Yusuf went to a wealthy man who agreed to give 8 million riyals, but only on the condition that Sheikh Salman write him a note or call him [to approve the donation]. So Sheikh Yusuf went to Salman al-Awda, but to no avail, because the sheikh skirted the issue and finally said 'I am actually not convinced by the Chechen issue.'[53]

When al-Uyayri realised that the former Sahwists were not going to be of much use, he turned his attention to the al-Shu'aybi school. These scholars were emerging as a more radical alternative to the Sahwa and were prepared to vouch for jihadist causes abroad. From 2000 onward, al-Uyayri lobbied hard to get these sheikhs interested in Afghanistan and the Taliban regime. During Hajj in late February 2001, al-Uyayri met with Taliban Ministers in Mecca in order to coordinate a telephone

[52] Muhammad al-Salim, *39 wasila li-khidmat al-jihad wa'l-musharaka fihi* [39 Ways to Serve Jihad and Take Part in It] (Sawt al-Jihad, 2003), 19–20.
[53] al-Salim, '*yusuf al-'uyayri* (2)', 18.

conference between Mulla Umar and Sheikh Hamud al-Shu'aybi. The conference call never took place because on the road from Mecca to Burayda, al-Uyayri, half asleep at the steering wheel, crashed into a camel and was arrested by police. For reasons that are not clear, he stayed in prison until August 2001.[54]

In addition to this kind of high-level lobbying, jihadist fundraisers also worked systematically on the ground to solicit funds directly from private donors. Representatives of various groups and causes would travel around the country in small delegations visiting wealthy donors and 'selling' their general or specific projects. Salesmanship was important because donors were critical and concerned with religious legitimacy. Most sponsors had two main criteria. First of all, the military campaign in question had to have the approval of a respected sheikh. Second, the money would have to be used for uncontroversial warfare or 'classical jihad' activity. Jihad donors would only fund specific guerrilla campaigns, not international terrorist operations against civilians. Fundraising therefore involved a considerable element of marketing and presentation skills, to ensure that donors saw the cause as legitimate and uncontroversial. For example, when fundraisers sought support for Bin Ladin in Afghanistan in the early 2000s, they would focus on the Taliban's war against the Northern Alliance and the need to defend the 'Islamic Emirate of Afghanistan', leaving out details about Bin Ladin's international terrorist ambitions.

The outbreak of the second Chechen war in 1999 created a very favourable environment for fundraising, because there was broad outrage in Saudi society over the images of civilian suffering coming out of Chechnya. Yusuf al-Uyayri and others started travelling across the country, visiting wealthy businessmen known for their jihadist sympathies. Al-Uyayri is said to have collected large sums of money for the Chechen cause in this way.

Another important fundraiser for Chechnya was Khalid al-Subayt, a veteran jihadist and close friend of Commander Khattab. Al-Subayt had fought in Afghanistan in the 1980s, and had accompanied Khattab to Tajikistan in the early 1990s before returning to Saudi Arabia for health reasons. He went to Chechnya in 1997 to teach in the 'Qawqaz Sharia Institute', the religious school set up by Khattab after the end of the first Chechen war. In 1999, shortly after the outbreak of the second Chechen war, al-Subayt was wounded in battle and had to return home. He came back to Saudi Arabia completely penniless, but he quickly made friends in the jihadist community. He notably became close to younger radicals such as future QAP media mogul Isa Al Awshan.[55]

[54] al-Salim, '*yusuf al-'uyayri* (1)', 18.

[55] Al Awshan, '*khalid bin 'abdallah al-subayt*'.

In 1999, shortly after his return to Saudi Arabia, al-Subayt became a very active fundraiser. He travelled around the country visiting donors together with Isa Al Awshan and other companions. Like salesmen, they brought portfolios with pictures and maps of Chechnya, and they updated the donors on the current status of the mujahidin in Chechnya. As Al Awshan later wrote:

> Khalid was a very likeable person, and none of the scholars or businessmen or other prominent people would stand in his way when he talked to them about the Chechen issue and of the need to support and back it. So they cooperated with him and supported the issue, which enabled him to recruit many people in the service of the mujahidin in Chechnya ... We would go with him on tours in many regions to visit scholars and wealthy people. Khalid had a map of Chechnya on which he showed the movement of the mujahidin, scenes of major operations and enemy bases. This gave the audience a clear picture of the Chechen issue. We would come back afterwards with hundreds and thousands [of riyals], which he would then send to Khattab – may God bless them both.[56]

In addition to this 'door-to-door approach', jihadist fundraisers also organised lectures and soirées on Afghanistan or Chechnya, with the aim of obtaining donations from the audience. Such sessions would be organised in private homes or in rest houses outside big cities. Because some meetings were open to a wider public – some accounts speak of hundreds and even thousands of attendees – the speakers had to be careful to conceal the real recipients of the money. Very often, there was outright deception, with fundraisers pretending to collect money for the building of mosques or hospitals. As a former QAP militant told the Saudi newspaper *al-Ukaz*:

> They would appeal to people's feelings. In the meetings in these tents and rest houses, which would be attended by thousands of people, Sultan Bijad [al-Utaybi] would exhort people to donate money to fictitious projects. He would say 'there is a charitable project to build a mosque' or something similar. Once he said one of the youth was passing through a difficult phase financially and needed support and help; and donations came from all corners. Invitations to these meetings were sent to many philanthropic businessmen, so it was very easy to get money.[57]

As al-Uyayri turned his attention away from the Chechen issue and started working more directly for Bin Ladin, his fundraising efforts also changed focus. Al-Uyayri began collecting money for Bin Ladin, and he used his growing leadership status in the Saudi jihadist community to influence other fundraisers to do the same. After 9/11 and the US-led

[56] Al Awshan, '*khalid bin 'abdallah al-subayt*'. [57] '*ta'ib ya'tarif*'.

invasion of Afghanistan, many of the people who had been preoccupied with the Chechen issue, such as Khalid al-Subayt and Isa Al Awshan, began focusing on Afghanistan instead. As Al Awshan explained:

> When the blessed raids on New York and Washington happened, he [Khalid al-Subayt] was in my house and we were following the event together through the Internet. He was happy and cheerful and the blessed strikes increased his enthusiasm for Afghanistan in addition to Chechnya. He collected large amounts of money for Afghanistan and sent it to the martyr Sheikh Yusuf al-Uyayri – may God bless them both.

At some point, Yusuf al-Uyayri also began to skim off money from the fundraising and use it in secret preparation for a future violent campaign inside Saudi Arabia. By placing himself on top of a large fundraising apparatus, and by becoming the key middleman for the cash flow from Saudi Arabia to Afghanistan, he was able to discreetly set aside significant sums of money that were used to build weapons stockpiles inside Saudi Arabia. Hence recruitment, fundraising and weapons collection efforts were closely connected and undertaken with a mid-term strategic objective in mind, the launch of a jihad on the Arabian Peninsula.[58]

As al-Qaida's infrastructure grew in both Saudi Arabia and Afghanistan, actors both inside and outside the organisation began pressing for attacks in the kingdom. In June 2001, the British secret service reported that Abu Zubayda was planning suicide car bomb attacks against US military targets in Saudi Arabia. There were also intelligence reports in mid-2001 about a group of Pakistanis who were planning to 'bomb the American community in Jeddah, possibly the US or British Schools there'. On 17 July 2001, sources close to al-Zawahiri told the CIA that an attack was about to take place inside Saudi Arabia within days. According to a Saudi martyr biography, a certain Fahd al-Sa'idi left his Afghan training camp for Saudi Arabia a few months before 9/11 to assess the potential for operations there. However, none of these attempts materialised. Al-Qaida's moratorium on operations in the kingdom was still in place – for now.[59]

The history of al-Qaida in the late 1990s is a classic example of how clandestine organisations may acquire military capabilities out of proportion to their political support in their alleged constituency. Unlike the classical jihadists, whose relatively restrained conception of warfare enjoyed broad support in the Islamist community, the global jihadist

[58] Author's interview with Faris bin Huzzam.
[59] Tenet, *At the Center of the Storm*, 146–7, 156; Fawwaz al-Nashmi, '*fahd bin samran al-sa'idi*', *Sawt al-Jihad*, no. 16 (2004).

agenda was highly controversial. However, access to a territory enabled al-Qaida to compensate for this weakness by establishing an elaborate training infrastructure in which recruits were socialised and indoctrinated into the global jihadist ideology. Another compensating factor was the presence of the highly charismatic Usama bin Ladin and capable mid-level entrepreneurs such as Yusuf al-Uyayri, who were able to enlist key allies, fundraisers and recruits by skilfully manipulating pan-Islamist sympathies in the Muslim world and by presenting their agenda as less radical than it really was.

In August 2001, the fruits of al-Qaida's Saudi mobilisation effort were clear for all to see. The training camps in Qandahar and the trenches on the Northern front were full of young, skinny Saudis, perhaps over a thousand in number. What on earth had brought them there?

6 Recruitment to al-Qaida

Who remembers the names of the Saudi 9/11 hijackers? While the story of Muhammad Atta and the Hamburg cell has been told in vivid detail, most of the Saudi hijackers remain an anonymous mass, collectively referred to as the 'muscle' of the operation. Much of the existing literature seems to presume the existence of a specifically Saudi extremism which ensures a permanent flow of recruits to war zones and terrorist groups. This assumption has diverted attention from the real puzzles of the Saudi recruitment to al-Qaida. Why did some Saudis and not others travel to Afghanistan? Why did people go in the late 1990s when there was no longer an officially sanctioned jihad in Afghanistan? How did they even get there, given how controversial jihadism had become in the mid-1990s? Using a sample of 197 biographies, this chapter takes a closer look at the backgrounds, motivations and recruitment patterns of Saudis who went to Afghanistan between 1996 and 2001.

Unemployment and 'Najdification'

Like the early jihadists, the Saudis in post-1996 Afghanistan were a diverse crowd. As a group, they were not losers, misfits or paupers, nor were they disgruntled graduates or ideologically driven rich kids. While these caricatures were probably all represented, the average al-Qaida recruits were middle- to lower-middle-class men in their early twenties from the big cities of Riyadh, Mecca and Jidda.

Nevertheless, Saudis in post-1996 Afghanistan were socio-economically less diverse and had a slightly lower level of education than the early jihadists. This reflects the fact that jihadism in the late 1990s was more dangerous and less common than in the 1980s, hence recruitment followed the jihad alumni's social networks to a greater extent than before. Many were linked by kinship or friendship to other militants. At least twenty-five people in this contingent had relatives who were jihadists, and presumably even more had jihadist acquaintances. People with jihad veterans in their social network were thus considerably more likely to travel to Afghanistan than those who did not.

Unemployment also seems to have been more common among the al-Qaida recruits than the early jihadists. There is extensive anecdotal information on unemployment in the biographies. One man who went to Afghanistan in September 2001 later said in an interview that 'I finished elementary school, and sat around without a job for many years prior to leaving for Afghanistan.' A Guantanamo prisoner who went to Afghanistan in March 2001 said, 'I read on the Internet about the Taliban. I was looking for a job. The page said they need Muslims and their help. So I thought they would have jobs helping Muslims.' These anecdotes are consistent with evidence that unemployment in the kingdom increased rapidly in the second half of the 1990s as a result of a rising youth population and decreasing oil revenues. Although difficult to confirm for lack of good data, the hypothesis that unemployment and idleness fuelled recruitment to al-Qaida's training camps is probably correct.[1]

Geographically, the al-Qaida recruits, like the early jihadists, came from the big cities, not from the rural peripheries. Residents of the Hijaz and the Najd were overrepresented. The central Najd region is much more strongly represented among al-Qaida recruits than the early jihadists, which suggests a process of 'Najdification' of the jihadist community in Saudi Arabia in the 1990s. This probably had to do with the emergence of the Najd-based al-Shu'aybi school of radical clerics and with the fact that police crackdowns in 1996 and 1998 affected the established Hijazi networks more than the emerging Najdi ones.

The south, however, remained very underrepresented. In fact, southerners were so rare in the al-Qaida camps that the 9/11 team, which featured eleven Saudis from the south, must have been carefully selected by Usama bin Ladin. The al-Qaida leader may have sought to show Riyadh that he had support from the south and its tribes. He may also have hoped to turn the negative trend in al-Qaida recruitment in

[1] Nayif Al Zahim, '*al-fatawa al-mudhallila naqalatni ila afghanistan li'l-jihad* [Misleading Fatwas Brought me to Afghanistan for Jihad]', *al-Riyadh*, 7 October 2006; 'Testimony of Detainees before the Combatant Status Review Tribunal' (US Department of Defense, 2006) (hereafter CSRT), 3045, 3246. For more on unemployment in the late 1990s, see Steffen Hertog, 'Segmented Clientelism: The Politics of Economic Reform in Saudi Arabia' (D.Phil. thesis, Oxford University, 2006), 218. For more on the possible link between idleness and al-Qaida recruitment, see e.g. Charles M. Sennott, 'Before Oath to Jihad, Drifting and Boredom', *Boston Globe*, 3 March 2002; Craig S. Smith, 'Saudi Idlers Attract Radicals and Worry Royals', *New York Times*, 17 December 2002; Raid Qusti, 'Riyadh Cracking Down on "Drifting Shababs"', *Arab News*, 2 May 2007, and 'Why Do they Drive around Aimlessly?', *Arab News*, 11 May 2007.

the south by making the hijackers from this region famous. The third and most plausible hypothesis is that the southerners in the 9/11 team represented particularly tight-knit groups of friends, a security advantage during long-winded operations on foreign territory. Several of the southern hijackers had travelled together to Afghanistan and thus knew each other very well. As rural southerners they may have been seen as outsiders by the Hijazi/Najdi majority in the camps, something which may have further strengthened their internal cohesion.[2]

The disproportionate presence of southern tribesmen, notably Ghamidis, in the 9/11 operation has led many observers to wrongly assume the existence of a 'southern radicalism' in Saudi Arabia and to exaggerate the role of tribal culture and tribal politics in al-Qaida recruitment. However, there are very few explicit indications in the jihadist literature prior to 2004 that tribal origin played a significant role in the recruitment or behaviour of Saudi jihadists. Most of the rare examples are related to the small contingent of southerners that took part in the 9/11 operation.[3]

We should certainly not disregard tribal dynamics in the study of Saudi Islamism, but there are three important reasons why the tribal factor is probably less important than many people think. First is that rapid social change, in particular urbanisation and internal migration, have rendered notions of particularly masculine or rebellious tribal cultures less relevant. Second, if there is a tribal factor in Saudi politics, it is more likely to be a force for order than for disorder. Tribalism is based on obedience to the tribal leaders, all of whom are closely integrated into, and generously paid by, the Saudi political system. This is why there are many more Ghamidis in the Saudi security services than in al-Qaida. Finally, tribalism to some extent runs counter to Islamist ideology, which emphasises the equality of believers before God and the unity of the Muslim nation above internal factionalism. For this reason, prominent radical ideologues such as Abu Muhammad al-Maqdisi have in fact condemned the promotion of tribal identity.[4]

One thing is clear, however: the Saudis in post-1996 Afghanistan represented a new generation of jihadists. In fact, the vast majority of the recruits left for Afghanistan in 2000 and 2001, making them too young to

[2] *The 9/11 Commission Report*, 232 and 524.

[3] See e.g. Charles M. Sennott, 'Why Bin Laden Plot Relied on Saudi Hijackers', *Boston Globe*, 3 March 2002; 'The Nineteen Martyrs (video)' (transcript available on www.jihadunspun.com, 2002).

[4] Mark N. Katz, 'Arabian Tribes in the 21st Century', *Middle East Times* (2007); Abu Muhammad al-Maqdisi, '*waqafat ma' thamarat al-jihad* [Stances on the Fruits of Jihad]' (www.tawhed.ws), chapter 5.

have prior jihad experience. Information on departure dates corroborates the anecdotal evidence that recruitment was sluggish until around 1999, after which it increased exponentially. This also shows that Saudi recruitment to al-Qaida remained at a very low level throughout the 1990s.

On the whole it is very difficult to pinpoint socio-economic factors with a strong predictive value for individual Saudi recruitment to al-Qaida. They were young, urban and perhaps unemployed, but so were thousands of other Saudis who did not go to Afghanistan. What motivated those who went?

Classical jihad exploited

Saudis went to Afghanistan for a number of declared reasons. First and most common was the pan-Islamist ideal of helping fellow Muslims in need. As one Saudi Guantanamo prisoner explained: 'I did not know exactly in which way I would help [the Afghans], but I went to help the people, not to fight.' The biographies convey the distinct impression that love for the in-group was much more important than hatred for the out-group, as was the case with the early jihadists. 'I went to train for jihad for God in order to fight whoever fights Muslims', said another Saudi prisoner.[5]

The second Chechen war played an extraordinarily important role in mobilising young Saudis for jihad. A large number of the Saudis who ended up in Afghanistan in this period had in fact intended to fight in Chechnya, but had been diverted to Afghanistan, where they were told they could train in anticipation of entry into Chechnya. One Saudi Guantanamo prisoner said he had decided to go to Chechnya after he learned his brother had died there. However, after a friend of his brother told him Chechnya was difficult to reach, he headed to Afghanistan instead. Another Saudi Guantanamo detainee explained that 'when I was in Saudi Arabia I met someone from Chechnya. And I wanted to go to Chechnya. So I went to Afghanistan. This person told me to go there and train for six months. Then after six months, they would be going to Chechnya.' These claims are credible because detainees had nothing to gain from them. To US authorities, volunteering for jihad in Chechnya would have seemed no less suspicious than attending al-Qaida camps in Afghanistan.[6]

[5] 'Testimony of Detainees – CSRT', 2704.

[6] See *The 9/11 Commission Report*, 233; and Sharon Curcio, 'Generational Differences in Waging Jihad', *Military Review* 85, no. 4 (2005): 84; 'Testimony of Detainees – CSRT', 1274, 2655; Chris Gourlay and Jonathan Calvert, 'Al-Qaeda Kingpin: I Trained 9/11 Hijackers', *Sunday Times*, 25 November 2007.

A particularly vivid account of how the Chechen cause mobilised Saudis is provided in the martyr biography of QAP militant Faysal al-Dukhayyil. One evening, before he had become religious, Faysal watched an interview with Commander Khattab on al-Jazeera together with some friends. He and his friends were allegedly so upset 'by the pictures of Chechen women and children under Russian missiles' that they went to see Faysal's cousin Ahmad al-Dukhayyil, who was a religious man with links in the jihadist community, in the hope that he could help them get to Chechnya. Ahmad was very surprised to see his unobservant cousin and said 'you still smell of cigarette smoke and you want to go to Chechnya?' Six months later, that is, in early or mid-2000, they went to Afghanistan. Faysal al-Dukhayyil would never make it to Chechnya, but instead ended up as one of the most active QAP militants in Saudi Arabia in 2003 and 2004. Al-Dukhayyil was one of several very prominent al-Qaida operatives who were initially brought to Bin Ladin's camps by outrage over Chechnya, not hatred for America. Several of the 9/11 hijackers, from Muhammad Atta and the Hamburg cell to the Saudi-muscle hijackers Ahmad and Sa'id al-Ghamidi, had initially wanted to fight with Khattab in Chechnya.[7]

The other main declared motivation, which seems to have eclipsed Chechnya in importance in 2001, was the desire to protect the Taliban, first against the Northern Alliance and then against the US-led invasion. At least eight – probably many more – of the people in our sample who travelled to Afghanistan before 9/11 said they went to fight against the Northern Alliance. For example, one volunteer who went in September 2000 said he wanted to defend the Taliban against the Northern Alliance, not fight Americans: 'I could have done that in Saudi Arabia', he insisted. He added that he believed Jihad was a duty when declared by a government, in this case the Taliban. Another young Saudi was not entirely certain about the legitimacy of the jihad, so he 'went to Afghanistan to see whether the fatwa conditions [for jihad in support of the Taliban] applied'.[8]

It is interesting that so many Saudis saw the Taliban's pre-9/11 struggle with the Northern Alliance as a jihad requiring their participation, when the Northern Alliance were Sunni Muslims. One reason for this conundrum is that the strong international pressure on the Taliban gave the impression that the latter were under threat from non-Muslim

[7] Bandar al-Dukhayyil, '*faysal bin 'abd al-rahman al-dukhayyil: musa'ir harb* [Faysal bin Abd al-Rahman al-Dukhayyil: Warrior]', *Sawt al-Jihad*, no. 28 (2004). *The 9/11 Commission Report*, 160, 165, 233.

[8] 'Testimony of Detainees – CSRT', 3116, 10.

forces. Another reason is that many recruits simply did not know what the Northern Alliance was. One volunteer said he went to Afghanistan 'to fight against the Shiites'. Another, who must have shirked his history classes, said he 'wanted to help his Muslim brothers fight the Russians'. 'I didn't know the Northern Alliance would be there', he insisted, 'I thought it was Russians.'[9]

One of the most surprising aspects about the declared motivations of Saudi al-Qaida recruits is the virtual absence of anti-Americanism and international terrorist ambitions. There is no doubt that anti-Americanism must have been a factor for those who went to Afghanistan after 9/11. In the biographies of those who went before 9/11, however, there are few if any examples of people who say their primary motivation was hatred for America or a desire to take part in international terrorist operations. There were of course exceptions. One Saudi who went to Afghanistan in August 2001 later bluntly told the Guantanamo tribunal: 'I fought the United States. I'm going to make it short and easy for you guys: I'm proud of what I did and there isn't any reason of hiding.' Such statements are nevertheless rather rare. This is not to say that Saudis who went to Afghanistan before October 2001 were friends of America – far from it – but they did not go to Afghanistan in order to take part in 9/11-style operations. Violent anti-Americanism, it seems, was cultivated in Bin Ladin's camps.[10]

The prevalence of motivations linked to conventional struggles in Chechnya and Afghanistan combined with the near-absence of anti-American motives suggest that most recruits were in fact driven by classical jihadist ideology, not global jihadism. This adds to the mounting evidence that al-Qaida's recruitment strategy relied on a conscious exploitation of the classical jihadist sympathies in the kingdom. Al-Qaida recruiters presented the camps as a necessary station on the way to classical jihad. Once in the camps, recruits were indoctrinated and socialised into Bin Ladin's global jihadism. This hypothesis is strengthened by the accounts of recruits from other countries, such as the group of Yemeni-Americans known as the 'Lackawanna Six', who broke off their training in al-Faruq in 2001 because they found the atmosphere much more anti-American than they had expected.[11]

[9] 'Testimony of Detainees – CSRT', 604, 3045; 'Testimony of Detainees before the Administrative Review Board' (US Department of Defense, 2006) (hereafter ARB), 828.

[10] ISN 682. 'Testimony of Detainees – CSRT', 2073; David Morgan, 'Saudi Man Admits Enemy Role at Guantanamo Trial', *Reuters*, 27 April 2006.

[11] Matthew Purdy and Lowell Bergman, 'Where the Trail Led: Between Evidence and Suspicion; Unclear Danger: Inside the Lackawanna Terror Case', *New York Times*, 12 October 2003.

Another telling account of al-Qaida's exploitation of classical jihadism is that of a Saudi named Nasir who was interviewed by the journalist Dexter Filkins in Mazar-e-Sharif in late 2001:

> [Nasir] had been on Hajj ... when a fellow Saudi named Abu Mali approached. It was the spring of 2001 ... The war against the infidels, Mali called it; would you fight against the infidels? Nasir said yes, he would go to Palestine to fight the Jews. Abu Mali said yes, of course, we will send you to Palestine ... Before fighting in Palestine, Abu Mali told him, Nasir would have to go first to Afghanistan to receive his training.

In Afghanistan, Nasir met Bin Ladin: 'Osama said, this is the way of jihad. If you are killed – in Palestine, in Chechnya, in Kashmir – you will help these people become free.' Later, the leaders 'told Nasir that he would not be going to Palestine after all. It was September 2001, and there was a jihad to be fought right there in Afghanistan. "I told them I wanted to go home", Nasir said. "I told them I did not fight against other Muslims."'[12]

Another point worth noting about motivations of al-Qaida recruits in this period is that discontent with the Saudi regime does not feature very prominently. There are a few exceptions, like Bosnia veteran and subsequent QAP member Ali al-Harbi, who went to Afghanistan after his release from al-Ruways prison in 1997 because he was afraid of being arrested and tortured again. It seems that socio-revolutionary motivations played a somewhat more important role in recruitment to post-1996 Afghanistan than it did for the early jihad zones, but pan-Islamism was clearly more important.[13]

Purely religious considerations were also at play. Many went to 'fulfil the duty of jihad' while having minimal knowledge and understanding of the political content and implications of this jihad. Some people went out of fear of ignoring a religiously sanctioned duty. One recruit insisted that he 'did not go there voluntarily, but to avoid punishment by God'. Others said they went to Afghanistan in order to assess the Taliban's implementation of Sharia law. Some of them seem to have intended to settle in Afghanistan because of the Taliban's strict social conservatism. Yet another type of religious motivation was a desire for martyrdom. A number of people seem to have gone to Afghanistan because they genuinely hoped to die as a martyr and go to heaven. A few had lost relatives or friends in Afghanistan and hoped to die as martyrs so they

[12] Dexter Filkins, *The Forever War* (New York: Alfred A. Knopf, 2008), 62–3.

[13] '*'ali al-ma'badi al-harbi: batal badr al-riyadh* [Ali al-Ma'badi al-Harbi: The Hero of the Badr of Riyadh]', *Sawt al-Jihad*, no. 24 (2004).

could meet their friends again. Political and religious motivations were often closely tied to more personal considerations.[14]

The third main type of motivation was more personal and social in nature, namely the quest for adventure and military experience. A number of people said more or less explicitly that they were drawn to the adventurous aspect of foreign travel, the masculine dimension of weapons training and the chivalry associated with being a mujahid.

For some, adventure was most important. One Saudi Guantanamo prisoner said he went alone to Afghanistan in late August 2001 'for training'. He said 'it was just a vacation I had', and his plan was to come back before school started. He did not cite any political or religious motivations. Another recruit saw the training camps almost as a leisure activity:

> In my mind I was thinking that the training there was going to be like a club where you can train anytime and you can leave anytime. You don't have any commitment to that club and at the same time you can take courses or school classes and study ... If I would have known about another place to get that training I would not have gone to Afghanistan.[15]

Others seem to have been mostly interested in the weapons training and the military experience. One Guantanamo detainee said he had wanted to learn how to defend himself. In Saudi Arabia, he said, 'there are no camps where civilians can learn to defend themselves. I offered my services to the Saudi Arabian Navy for the chance to train, but never heard back from them. That's when I began my quest to find a place where I could learn to defend myself, and ended up in Afghanistan.'[16]

For yet others, going to Afghanistan was a way to prove their manhood. One Saudi recruit explained how his brother, having already been to Afghanistan, would appeal to his masculine pride:

> I wasn't actually a dedicated Muslim. I wasn't dedicated or anything. [My brother] saw me and said 'Look at you! You are not a man, you are wasting your time.' He started talking to me and [said] 'You don't know how to do anything. No weapons, no training, no education. You have to be a man. You have to learn.' This kind of talking got to me.[17]

Like the early Saudi jihadists, post-1996 al-Qaida recruits were motivated by a combination of political, religious and mundane considerations. Again we see an absence of declared anti-Americanism or

[14] 'Testimony of Detainees – CSRT', 1115, 1275, 3071.
[15] 'Testimony of Detainees – CSRT', 2811; 'Testimony of Detainees – ARB', 20327.
[16] 'Testimony of Detainees – CSRT', 3021; 'Testimony of Detainees – ARB', 20540.
[17] 'Testimony of Detainees – CSRT', 2983; 'Testimony of Detainees – ARB', 1431.

regime hostility, but this time it is even more surprising given the activities in which the recruits would later engage. The secondary importance of anti-Americanism is testimony to the continued predominance of classical jihadist thought, as well as to the fact that the process of joining the jihad was primarily a social, not an ideological one.

Gatekeepers

The question of how people made it to al-Qaida's camps is particularly interesting because, unlike in the 1980s, jihadism was now a clandestine and perilous activitiy. Gone were the days when Abdallah Azzam could hold open-recruitment rallies for Afghanistan, and Barbaros could use local media to recruit volunteer fighters.

When radicalisation goes underground, it becomes even more difficult to study. To appreciate the complexity of radicalisation and recruitment, consider the story of Ahmad al-Shurfa, who allegedly first got the idea of going to Afghanistan after meeting a jihad veteran in Saudi Arabia. Al-Shurfa insisted that the person 'didn't influence me, he just spoke to me about jihad. It was my decision. Even after speaking with him I spoke to other sheikhs.' Al-Shurfa then made the final decision to go to Afghanistan after hearing a fatwa from a Saudi sheikh. He spoke to the scholar, read his book and followed an Internet jihad website. From another sheikh he received SAR 2,000 (US$533) and a letter containing instructions to fly to Karachi and call a local contact person. He headed out in the summer of 2001, was caught by US forces in late 2001 and sent to Guantanamo. Was al-Shurfa recruited or did he act on his own initiative? What was the defining factor – the jihad veteran, the sheikh, the Internet site or the facilitator? Or were there other factors that al-Shurfa did not mention, such as social pressure from his brothers or friends?

As we saw in the previous chapter, al-Qaida did have a rudimentary recruitment infrastructure in Saudi Arabia by 2000 and 2001. While the biographies in our sample rarely mention meetings with card-carrying al-Qaida recruiters, there are accounts of chance encounters with individuals who provided subtle or direct encouragement to go to Afghanistan. One recruit said he took an address for jihad in Kashmir from a man in Saudi Arabia who was 'from the mujahidin'. Another volunteer said he met a veteran of the Chechen jihad named Salih al-Harbi who convinced him to go to Chechnya, but told him he had to go to Afghanistan first. The recruiter then coordinated the whole journey to Afghanistan.[18]

[18] A possible exception may be Nawaf al-Hazmi, who went to Afghanistan after meeting Abu Zubayda in 1996; 'Report of the Joint Inquiry into the Terrorist Attacks of September 11, 2001', 131ff.; 'Testimony of Detainees – CSRT', 10, 2655.

Recruiters seem to have operated in two main arenas. One important recruitment arena was Mecca, notably during the period of Ramadan and Hajj, when the city is particularly crowded. One Saudi Guantanamo detainee described meeting what was undoubtedly a recruiter in Mecca during Ramadan (December) 2000. Like many other recruits, he was led to believe that he was entirely in charge of the situation:

> No one recruited me in Mecca. I met a man who told me about the idea of Jihad. After that I went to Jidda and met the man again who prepared me to go to Afghanistan. He gave me money and put me on a plane to the Arab Emirates first going to Pakistan. The man I met just gave me the idea. He didn't train me or anything like that. He just gave me the idea about fighting.[19]

Another important arena was the semi-formal religious study groups which are very widespread in Saudi Arabia. These forums come in many different shapes and forms, from evening get-togethers to summer camps in the desert. They could be organised by an older person like a teacher, or simply by groups of friends. Several Saudis in Afghanistan met recruiters in such study groups. One young Saudi explained how he became involved with a clique that gathered periodically to watch jihad videos and was allegedly encouraged by a mentor to go to Afghanistan. QAP member Talal al-Anbari was originally recruited for Afghanistan by someone in his religious study group in Jidda. Another QAP militant, Nayif al-Shammari, went to Afghanistan after spending time with a study group in Hafar al-Batin that would gather after school for lectures and screenings of jihad videos. After a while, the organisers suggested they train with weapons and encouraged them to go to Afghanistan. These study groups would often make use of 'rest houses' (*istirahat*) that are found in the thousands in the desert outside major cities. These picnic pavilions, which are very popular with Saudi families, offered complete privacy and were perfect for clandestine activities.[20]

There has been some debate in Saudi Arabia in recent years about the extent to which the school system is infiltrated by recruiters. Some have argued that organised religious youth activities such as summer camps play a role in radicalising Saudi teenagers. The information compiled

[19] 'Testimony of Detainees – CSRT', 3462; 'Testimony of Detainees – ARB', 624; see also Bergen, *The Osama bin Laden I Know*, 261–2.

[20] *The 9/11 Commission Report*, 526–7; Usama al-Najdi, '*talal al-anbari: haydara al-jiddawi* [Talal al-Anbari: Haydara from Jidda]', *Sawt al-Jihad*, no. 17 (2004); Raid Qusti and Munif al-Safuqi, 'Terror Teachers Target Rural Schools', *Arab News*, 11 July 2005; '*ta'ib ya'tarif*'; Frank Hairgrove and Douglas M. Mcleod, 'Circles Drawing Toward High-Risk Activism', *Studies in Conflict and Terrorism* 31, no. 5 (2008).

by this author does not corroborate such fears. There are cases of activists exploiting the many religious arenas for socialisation in Saudi Arabia, but it does not mean that these arenas or institutions are inherently radicalising or always manipulated by recruiters. The number of people taking part in such activities is so large and the number of Saudi jihadists so low that such a causal link cannot be established. The religious gatherings at which people were recruited to militancy were informal and not sanctioned by schools or local religious institutions.[21]

The other main type of top-down recruitment involved religious scholars. A considerable number of Saudis went to Afghanistan on the encouragement of a sheikh. A few people were inspired to go after hearing a sermon by a radical imam in a small local mosque. However, mosques were not as important as recruitment grounds as they had been in the 1980s because authorities no longer allowed public speeches calling for people to fight abroad. The influence of the religious scholars was therefore mostly confined to more private and informal settings. A number of scholars, notably the sheikhs of the al-Shuʿaybi school, encouraged their students to go to Afghanistan. Sheikh Sulayman al-Ulwan is said to have recruited 9/11 hijacker Abd al-Aziz al-Umari and many others for Afghanistan. Another hijacker, Muhammad al-Shihri, allegedly frequented religious circles in Burayda and may well have been encouraged by scholars there.[22]

Sometimes, sheikhs played a passive role and simply gave general fatwas authorising or encouraging the departure to Afghanistan. Several recruits said they were inspired by Hamud al-Shuʿaybi's fatwas on the Islamic nature of the Taliban regime and the need to support it. At other times, sheikhs also provided active logistical assistance. One recruit said religious scholars convinced him to fight in Afghanistan and told him how to get there. Another said he was inspired and helped in his travels by his Afghan Qur'an teacher. The same thing may have happened to 9/11 hijacker Wa'il al-Shihri, who was sent by his father to see a religious scholar in Medina after a period of deep depression. Only a few months later he left for Afghanistan together with his brother Walid.[23]

While encouragement 'from above' drove a number of Saudis to Afghanistan, many others sought out al-Qaida's camps on their own initiative or together with friends. The initial impetus came from a

[21] Mariam Al Hakeem, 'Do Not Allow Extremists to Exploit Students – Ministry', *Gulf News*, 3 June 2006; Y. Yehoshua, 'Are Saudi Summer Camps Encouraging Terrorism?', *MEMRI Inquiry and Analysis Series*, no. 241 (2005).

[22] 'Testimony of Detainees – CSRT', 1133; *The 9/11 Commission Report*, 232–3.

[23] 'Testimony of Detainees – CSRT', 1126, 1274, 1755, 2401, 2704, 3071; Sennott, 'Before Oath to Jihad, Drifting and Boredom'; Mutlaq al-Buqami, 'Al-Shihri Says Sons Missing for 10 Months', *Arab News*, 17 September 2001.

number of different sources, in most cases from friends and family. Another major source of inspiration was the Internet. As one former Guantanamo detainee told a Saudi newspaper after his release: 'I did not belong to any group or organisation, especially since I was not devout before I left. But there were some fatwas that called for jihad and were posted on certain websites. They influenced many young men, both devout and non-devout.'[24]

A widespread, but to a Western reader somewhat more surprising, catalyst was individual religious experiences like dreams or visions. Subsequent QAP fighter Talal al-Anbari, for example, claimed he turned to religion after a religious dream. Given the very strong emphasis that the jihadist literature puts on visions, it is of course possible that some of the accounts are post-facto reconstructions. Nevertheless, the number of people who claim to have become more religious after a religious experience is so significant that we cannot deny that many claims were genuine.[25]

Whatever the inspiration, recruits who sought to go to Afghanistan on their own initiative needed help to find a safe way to get there. They were helped by the vast network of helpers who provided logistical assistance to interested recruits. These 'gatekeepers' came in many types and were found in many places. Some of them were mosque imams. For example, Ghanim al-Harbi said he found his way to Afghanistan by asking around at a mosque in Dammam:

> I spoke to one of the Imams and they gave me the address. I was given a phone number and the man told me to meet him in Mecca. The person in Mecca told me about the camp and how it ran. I told him what I wanted from the training. I was given the address of a person in Lahore.[26]

Other gatekeepers were just ordinary people who were known in their local community for having contacts in jihadist circles. One recruit explained that after he decided to go to Chechnya, he went to see a man in his neighbourhood who helped him get to Afghanistan. Another good example of a local gatekeeper was the above-mentioned Ahmad

[24] 'Testimony of Detainees – ARB', 20327, 769; 'Testimony of Detainees – CSRT', 1645, 3045; Al Zahim, '*al-fatawa al-mudhallila*'; al-Najdi, '*talal al-anbari*'; Abdallah al-Subay'i, '*musa'id al-subay'i: rajul fi zaman qalla fihi al-rijal* [Musa'id al-Subay'i: A Man in a Time when Men are Scarce]', *Sawt al-Jihad*, no. 19 (2004).

[25] al-Najdi, '*talal al-anbari*'. For more on the importance of dreams in jihadist culture, see Iain R. Edgar, 'The Dream Will Tell: Militant Muslim Dreaming in the Context of Traditional and Contemporary Islamic Dream Theory and Practice', *Dreaming* 14, no. 1 (2004); and Iain R. Edgar, 'The True Dream in Contemporary Islamic/Jihadist Dreamwork: A Case Study of the Dreams of Taliban Leader Mullah Omar', *Contemporary South Asia* 15, no. 3 (2006).

[26] 'Testimony of Detainees – CSRT', 3021; 'Testimony of Detainees – ARB', 20540.

al-Dukhayyil, who helped his cousin Faysal get to Afghanistan after the latter begged him to show him the way to Chechnya. Yet another category of gatekeepers were Afghan expatriates in Saudi Arabia, who helped a number of al-Qaida recruits find their way to Afghanistan.[27]

Most people made the travel preparations as well as the journey itself together with friends or relatives. Group dynamics such as peer pressure, bidding games and intra-group affection were very important in driving the radicalisation process and preventing desertions. For some, social processes preceded ideological ones, as Marc Sageman has argued in his influential study on radicalisation.[28]

As we have seen, Saudis joined al-Qaida for a variety of reasons and not necessarily those we most expected. Some might find the analysis too kind or understanding towards the recruits. I do not dispute that most were responsible adults who knew they would be undertaking weapons training with outlaws. I also do not dispute that many ended up as fanatical anti-Western terrorists. What I have shown is that it was al-Qaida's camps, not people's backgrounds, which made them into global jihadists.

In early September 2001 there were close to a thousand Saudis in Afghanistan. Some were training in al-Qaida camps, others lingered in trenches in north-eastern Afghanistan. They had come for a variety of reasons and through a variety of routes. But they had one thing in common: they had no idea what was in store for them.

[27] 'Testimony of Detainees – CSRT', 1645, 3045, 3246; 'Testimony of Detainees – ARB', 769.

[28] Sennott, 'Before Oath to Jihad, Drifting and Boredom'; Sageman, *Understanding Terror Networks*.

7 Post-9/11 Saudi Arabia

At 5 p.m. local time on 11 September 2001, millions of Saudis watched the South Tower of the World Trade Center in New York collapse on live television. Few if any of them realised that this event thousands of miles away had just set in motion forces that would eventually bring bloodshed to the streets of Riyadh. The US-led invasion of Afghanistan would dislodge al-Qaida and lead Bin Ladin to actively plan for a campaign in Saudi Arabia. From late 2001 onward, global jihadists were focusing on a new project: Jihad on the Arabian Peninsula.

At the same time, 9/11 and the 'war on terror' had altered the context for militant Islamist activism in most corners of the world. How did this affect Saudi Arabia? We shall see that new international developments, polemics on the domestic Islamist scene and changes in policing combined to produce a highly beneficial context for mobilisation to global jihadism in Saudi Arabia between September 2001 and May 2003.

New symbols of Muslim suffering

It may seem curious that 9/11 – the most deadly terrorist attack in history – was followed by an increase in the level of anti-Americanism in the Muslim world. This paradox makes better sense when we recall that, at the time of the attack, a pan-Islamist renaissance had been underway in the Muslim world since around 1999. Moreover, the deep-seated culture of conspiracy thinking led many if not most Muslims in the Middle East to dismiss the 9/11 attacks as the work of Mossad or the CIA. Thus from the very beginning of the war on terrorism, many Muslims and most Islamists viewed all US actions in the war on terrorism as just the latest escalation in a long-term policy of discrimination, humiliation and oppression of Muslims.

The first development to fuel the view that the war on terror was a war on Islam was the US-led invasion of Afghanistan on 7 October 2001. While the invasion enjoyed a degree of support at the government level and in liberal circles in Saudi Arabia, the popular response was very negative. Many doubted Bin Ladin's responsibility for 9/11, while others believed his presence in Afghanistan did not justify a war. As the bombing proceeded, news of civilian deaths and the suffering of refugees rapidly eclipsed the memory of 9/11, and America came to be seen as the aggressor. Pan-Islamist rhetoric proliferated, and with it the usual public displays of pan-Islamic solidarity: condemnation at the OIC, fundraising campaigns for the suffering Afghans and so on. In the jihadist community the reaction was unequivocal: the US invasion was yet another example of infidel aggression against innocent Muslims. There was a new jihad in Afghanistan which required the participation of Saudis.

The invasion of Afghanistan brought anti-Americanism in the kingdom to new heights. A Saudi intelligence survey of educated Saudis between the ages of 25 and 41 from mid-October 2001, that is, a week into the bombing campaign, allegedly concluded that 95 per cent of them had 'sympathies' for Bin Ladin's cause. In January 2002, a former US ambassador to Saudi Arabia noted that 'for the first time since 1973, we actually have a situation in which the United States is so unpopular among the [Saudi] public that the royal family now thinks its security is best served by publicly distancing itself from the United States.' In radical Islamist communities, Bin Ladin's popularity soared, while more and more anti-American literature circulated on jihadist websites.[1]

The Afghanistan invasion revived the debate over the US military presence in Saudi Arabia. Despite efforts by Saudi authorities to impose – or appear as imposing – restrictions on the use of the American bases, they could not get away from the fact that the US Air Force was using Saudi Arabia as a pivot for the bombing campaign in Afghanistan. Global jihadist ideologues seized upon the opportunity to castigate the regime for its collaboration. The royals no doubt felt uncomfortable with the situation and in early 2002 there was diplomatic murmur about possible Saudi demands for a US withdrawal from its Saudi bases.[2]

The other major symbol of Muslim suffering to emerge was the detention facility for al-Qaida suspects at the US military base in Guantanamo Bay, Cuba. Set up in late 2001 to handle so-called 'enemy combatants' outside the framework of US and international law, Guantanamo became synonymous with the torture and humiliation of Muslims.

[1] Elaine Sciolino, 'Don't Weaken Arafat, Saudi Warns Bush', *New York Times*, 27 January 2002; '95 Percent of Saudis Supported Bin Laden's Cause', *ArabicNews.com*, 29 January 2002; David B. Ottaway and Robert G. Kaiser, 'Saudis May Seek US Exit', *Washington Post*, 18 January 2002.

[2] Ottaway and Kaiser, 'Saudis May Seek US Exit'.

Images of shackled prisoners in orange jumpsuits shocked TV spectators and spread like wildfire on the Internet, where they became an essential part of the iconography of Muslim suffering so important for the global jihadist propaganda. Guantanamo introduced a new theme to the pan-Islamist discourse, namely that of the innocently imprisoned Muslim. Websites such as *al-Asra* and *Cageprisoners*, set up by campaigners demanding the prisoners' release, gained a wide readership. The prisoner theme would later be strengthened by torture scandals in other US-run prisons such as Bagram in Afghanistan and Abu Ghraib in Iraq.[3]

In the kingdom, Guantanamo became a major public issue because so many of the prisoners were Saudi. The popular perception was that most of the Saudis in Guantanamo were victims of injustice. In 2002, Saudi media conveyed numerous interviews with families of prisoners who explained how their sons had gone to Pakistan for business, study or some other reason, only to be detained by Pakistanis and sold to the Americans. Saudi Islamists of all shades wrote about the detainees. By early 2002, many Saudis were already convinced that the war on terror was a war on Islam. At this point events in Palestine and Chechnya added to the sense of Muslim victimhood.[4]

In Palestine, the period from March to June 2002 represented arguably the tensest phase of the al-Aqsa intifada since late 2000. The most dramatic development was the so-called Jenin battle – better known in the Arab world as the 'Jenin massacre' – in early April 2002. Subsequent fact-finding missions concluded that the death toll was in the low fifties, considerably smaller than what had been claimed on the Arab and Palestinian side. Nevertheless, Jenin became an extremely potent and enduring symbol of Palestinian – and by extension Muslim – suffering under Israeli occupation.[5]

In Saudi Arabia the fury over Jenin was tangible. On 5 April, riot police were called in to disperse demonstrators who had gathered outside the US consulate in Dhahran. On 12 April, the Nayif-led 'Support Committee for the al-Aqsa Intifada' organised a three-day telethon

[3] See e.g. www.al-asra.com and www.cageprisoners.org.

[4] 'Nearly 100 Saudis Detained in Guantanamo Bay: Naif', *Arab News*, 29 January 2002; Abdul Rahman Almotawa, 'Carpet Trader Ends Up in Guantanamo', *Arab News*, 17 March 2002; Abdul Rahman Almotawa, 'Saudi Seeks Release of Son From US Jail', *Arab News*, 3 May 2002; 'US Troops Picked up Saudi in Pakistan', *Arab News*, 8 May 2002; 'Parents Happy over Efforts to Win Release of Guantanamo Prisoners', *Arab News*, 31 August 2002; Salman al-Awda, '*man li-asra al-muslimin?* [Who Will Help the Muslim Prisoners?]' (www.islamtoday.net, 2002).

[5] 'Israel and the Occupied Territories Shielded from Scrutiny: IDF Violations in Jenin and Nablus' (London: Amnesty International, 2002), 12.

which brought in a stunning SAR 600 million (US$160 million) in donations for the Palestinians. By mid-April, Internet forums and opinion pages were filled with loud condemnations and calls for action more serious than donations. Sales of American products allegedly decreased in March and April 2002 as many Saudis boycotted American products.[6]

In the midst of the Jenin crisis came a piece of important news from Chechnya, the other major symbol of Muslim suffering. On 26 April 2002, Russian authorities announced that Commander Khattab – the Saudi leader of the Arab contingent in the Chechen resistance – had been liquidated on the night between 19 and 20 March. Given Khattab's Saudi origin and heroic status in the Saudi Islamist community, the news of his death received considerable attention in the kingdom. Influential moderate Islamists like Salman al-Awda wrote obituaries praising him. The jihadist community was in mourning; in May 2002, the jihadist web forums were replete with postings about Khattab, and the *Sawt al-Qawqaz* and *al-Nida* websites posted articles eulogising the 'Lion of Islam'.[7]

Saudi interest in the Chechen cause was also fuelled by a new development, namely the adoption by Chechen rebels of spectacular and indiscriminate out-of-area operations. The new strategy was initiated on 22 May with the bombing of a military parade in the Dagestani city of Kaspiisk, escalated on 23 October 2002 with the Dubrovka theatre operation in Moscow and culminated in the Beslan massacre in September 2004. These terrorist attacks did not in themselves increase pan-Islamist sympathies in the broader Saudi population, but they served to

[6] 'Al-Faisal Says Israel Commited War Crimes against Palestinians', *ArabicNews.com*, 19 April 2002; 'A People Committee Organizes a Demonstration in al-Zahran Today, Saudi Authorities Ban Demonstration', *ArabicNews.com*, 5 April 2002; 'Saudi Police Disperse Massive Demonstration in Support of Palestinians', *ArabicNews.com*, 6 April 2002; 'Saudi Arabia Confirmed Arresting Abdul Hameed al-Mubarak Following Demonstration', *ArabicNews.com*, 16 April 2002; 'Organizer of Dhahran Demo Insane: Ahmad', *Arab News*, 16 April 2002; 'SR600 Million Raised for Palestinians in Three-Day Telethon'; 'Saudi Donation Campaign for Palestinians is Not a Provocation to Violence: US', *ArabicNews.com*, 15 April 2002; Nourah al-Khereiji, 'We Should Do More than Donate Money to Palestinians', *Arab News*, 15 May 2002; 'Saudis Boycott American Products and Services', *ArabicNews.com*, 8 May 2002; 'Saudi Arabians Boycott Coca Cola and Pepsi for Iranian Zamzam', *ArabicNews.com*, 23 August 2002.

[7] Salman al-Awda, '*khattab hayy yazraq*!! [Khattab is Alive and Well!!]' (www.islamtoday.net, 2002); Michael Wines, 'Russia Releases Tape to Support Claim of Chechen Rebel's Death', *New York Times*, 27 April 2002; '*al-qa'id khattab asad min usud al-islam* [Commander Khattab, One of the Lions of Islam]' (www.qoqaz.com, 2002); '*'aza' min al-mujahidin li'l-umma bi-ahad abtal al-jihad khattab* [Condolences from the Mujahidin to the Umma for (the passing of) Khattab, One of the Heroes of Jihad]' (www.alneda.com, 2002).

remind the Islamist community of the Chechen jihad. However, the developments in Chechnya were nothing compared to the international crisis which emerged in the autumn of 2002.[8]

In September 2002, the United States began to explicitly threaten Iraq with war over the latter's alleged weapons of mass destruction, and the subsequent deliberations at the United Nations dominated international media for months. Needless to say, the idea of an American invasion and subsequent occupation in the heart of the Arab and Muslim world were extremely controversial in Saudi Arabia. The Islamist community paid close attention to what they saw as preparations for yet another American aggression, at a time when the Muslim nation was facing more external threats than ever.

Iraq was an extremely delicate issue for the Saudi government. The official Saudi position was one of neutrality, but in reality it was one of ambiguity. On the one hand, the government expressed scepticism towards the military option in the disarmament crisis and publicly declared its refusal to let the Americans use its Saudi bases for the bombing campaign. On the other hand, Saudi Arabia was not among the most vocal opponents to the removal of Saddam Hussain, and in December 2002 it became clear that the kingdom would grant the US military limited use of Saudi territory in the war.[9]

The political atmosphere in the region in the spring of 2003 was one of extreme tension. The level of anti-Americanism had arguably never been higher in the history of the Middle East. At a time when the symbols of Muslim suffering in Palestine, Chechnya, Afghanistan and Guantanamo had already brought pan-Islamism to historic heights, the United States invaded Iraq, historic seat of the Abbasid caliphate and holder of enormous oil reserves. Clearly, it was not going to be difficult for the ideologues of global jihad to convince young Saudis of the need to fight America.

Al-Qaida's scholars

The political opportunities for mobilisation for jihad in Saudi Arabia in the 2001–3 period were also shaped by internal developments in the

[8] See Mark Kramer, 'The Perils of Counterinsurgency: Russia's War in Chechnya', *International Security* 29, no. 3 (2004): 50ff.

[9] 'Saudi Arabia would Oppose a US Attack on Iraq', *ArabicNews*, 16 February 2001; 'Al-Faisal: It is not Wise to Topple Saddam and Install Another', *ArabicNews.com*, 30 August 2002; 'Al-Rai al-Aam: Al-Faisal: Iraq's Acceptance of UN Inspectors won't Change War Fever', *ArabicNews.com*, 19 September 2002; '*al-sa'udiyya tulammih li'l-ta'awun 'askariyyan li-dharb al-'iraq* [Saudi Arabia Prepares to Cooperate Militarily to Strike Iraq]', *al-Quds al-Arabi*, 22 December 2002; Eric Schmitt, 'Saudis are Said to Assure US on Use of Bases', *New York Times*, 29 December 2002.

Saudi Islamist field, most notably the war of words between the old Sahwist scholars and the al-Shu'aybi school over how to deal with the United States and the West. From September 2001 onward, Nasir al-Fahd, Ali al-Khudayr and their comrades would take their pan-Islamist discourse much further, dramatically escalating their anti-Western rhetoric.

The sheikhs of the al-Shu'aybi school were important for the recruitment to the nascent QAP because they had a formal religious education. As such, they had the authority to issue fatwas and the social position to attract and maintain a following of students, something untrained activist ideologues like Yusuf al-Uyayri could not do. While al-Fahd and al-Khudayr were not involved in operational activities and were not part of the organisation built by al-Uyayri, they played an important indirect role as public agitators.

The post-9/11 period represented an opportunity for the ambitious and vocal preachers of the al-Shu'aybi school to impose themselves on the conservative side of the Saudi Islamist field. The first opportunity arose because the mainstream Saudi Islamist field, led by Sahwist leaders Salman al-Awda and Safar al-Hawali, condemned the 9/11 attacks. Even conservative clerics in Yusuf al-Uyayri's circles in Burayda were unsure of the wisdom and legitimacy of the operation.[10]

The sheikhs of the al-Shu'aybi school, on the other hand, were quick to issue statements legitimising the operations and praising the hijackers as martyrs. As early as 16 September 2001, Hamud al-Shu'aybi issued his *Statement on the Events that Happened in America*. In November, al-Shu'aybi argued that there was nothing wrong about terrorising (*irhab*) the enemy in certain circumstances as this was sanctioned by the Qur'anic verse, 'strike fear [*turhibuna*] in the enemies of God' (*al-Anfal*: 62). Abd al-Aziz al-Jarbu' followed up with a study entitled the *Foundation of the Legitimacy of the Destruction that Happened in America*. In September 2002, on the anniversary of the 9/11 attacks, Nasir al-Fahd would write an article called *Signs of the Merciful in the 'September Raid'*, echoing Abdallah Azzam's classic booklet *Signs of the Merciful in the Afghan Jihad*.[11]

The US invasion of Afghanistan represented another opportunity for the al-Shu'aybi school to fill the role as the most uncompromising

[10] Salman al-Awda, '*ru'ya fi ahdath amrika* [A View on the Events in America]' (www.islamtoday.net, 2001); al-Salim, '*yusuf al-'uyayri* (2)'.

[11] Hamud al-Shu'aybi, '*bayan 'amma jara fi amrika min ahadith* [Statement on the Events that Happened in America]' (www.aloqla.com, 2001); Hamud al-Shu'aybi, '*ma'na al-irhab wa haqiqathu* [The Meaning and Truth of Terrorism]' (www.aloqla.com, 2001); al-Jarbu, '*al-ta'sil li-mashru'iyyat ma hasal fi amrika min al-tadmir*'; Nasir al-Fahd, '*ayat al-rahman fi "ghazwat sibtimbar"* [Signs of the Merciful in the "September Raid"]', (www.tawhed.ws, 2002).

supporter of the umma in the face of infidel aggression. From October 2001 onward they would write numerous texts calling upon Muslims to take sides in the conflict between Islam and the Crusaders. The al-Shu'aybi school invoked the Wahhabi concept of 'Loyalty and Dissociation' (*al-wala' wa'l-bara'*) to say that it was time for Muslims to declare and show their loyalty to Islam and their hostility to the infidels. The implication of this Manichean principle was that any form of support for or association with non-Muslims in their war on Islam was deeply reprehensible and ultimately a cause for excommunication. This was the message in the declaration issued by Hamud al-Shu'aybi himself on 9 October entitled *Loyalty and Dissociation and the Obligation to Assist the Taliban*, which received considerable international media coverage. Al-Shu'aybi's statement was of course a thinly veiled criticism of the Saudi regime's alliance with the United States and the latter's use of Saudi airbases in the war in Afghanistan. The message was articulated even more explicitly a few weeks later in Nasir al-Fahd's book *Clarification on the Infidelity of Whoever Helps the Americans*. As the situation of the Taliban regime deteriorated, the radical sheikhs followed up with several statements urging Saudis to help the Taliban and expressing political support for Mulla Umar.[12]

As the al-Shu'aybi school gained prominence with their hawkish stances, they also grew more polemical vis-à-vis the rest of the religious community. They attacked the Sahwists for their soft stance on the issue of 9/11. They defended themselves vigorously against external criticism of their own writings. They were also not afraid to publicly criticise the most senior official clerics. However, these verbal skirmishes were negligible compared to the polemics that would arise a few months later.[13]

[12] Hamud al-Shu'aybi, '*al-wala' wa'l-bara' wa wujub nusrat taliban wa hukm man zahar al-amrikan 'alayha* [Loyalty and Dissociation and the Obligation to Assist the Taliban and the Ruling on Whoever Helps the Americans against them]' (www.aloqla.com, 2001); Nasir al-Fahd, '*al-tibyan fi kufr man a'an al-amrikan* [Clarification on the Infidelity of Whoever Helps the Americans]' (www.tawhed.ws, 2001); Hamud al-Shu'aybi, '*da'm al-imara al-islamiyya fi afghanistan wa ta'jil al-zakat laha* [Supporting the Islamic Emirate in Afghanistan and Directing Alms to it]' (www.aloqla.com, 2001); Hamud al-Shu'aybi, Ali al-Khudayr and Sulayman al-Ulwan, '*khitab li-amir al-mu'minin muhammad 'umar wa'l-mujahidin ma'hu* [Letter to the Commander of the Faithful Muhammad Umar and the Mujahidin with him]' (2001); Hamud al-Shu'aybi, Ali al-Khudayr and Sulayman al-Ulwan, '*khitab ila kafat 'ulama bakistan* [Letter to All Religious Scholars in Pakistan]' (2002). For more on *al-wala' wa'l-bara'* see Joas Wagemakers, 'Framing the "Threat to Islam": al-wala' wa al-bara' in Salafi Discourse', *Arab Studies Quarterly* 30, no. 4 (2008).

[13] Abd al-Aziz al-Jarbu', '*lam a'mur biha wa lam tasu'ni – radd 'ala maqal shaykh salman* [I did not Condone it and I was not Indifferent to it – Reply to Sheikh Salman's Article]' (www.tawhed.ws, 2001); Nasir al-Fahd, '*waqafat ma' al-waqafat* [Stances on the Stances]' (www.tawhed.ws, 2001); Hamud al-Shu'aybi, '*muqaddamat radd 'ala wazir*

The death of Hamud al-Shu'aybi on 18 January 2002 did not weaken the al-Shu'aybi school; on the contrary it emboldened it, because Nasir al-Fahd was now able to step forward as the leading figure of the radical side of the Saudi Islamist field. In the spring of 2002, he took advantage of the crisis in Palestine to publish a book implicitly criticising Crown Prince Abdallah's February 2002 peace initiative. However, al-Fahd was waiting for an opportunity to confront the still very popular Sahwists, especially Salman al-Awda, his arch-enemy from Ha'ir prison in the mid-1990s.[14]

The opportunity came in early May 2002, when Salman al-Awda, Safar al-Hawali and Nasir al-Umar put their names on a statement entitled 'How We Can Coexist' (also known as the 'Statement of the Intellectuals'). The statement, signed by 153 Saudi intellectuals and professionals, was a response to a declaration called 'What We are Fighting for' issued by a group of sixty prominent American intellectuals in February 2002. The conciliatory tone of the Saudi statement represented the exact opposite of the principle of 'Loyalty and Dissociation' promoted by the al-Shu'aybi school. The radical sheikhs were quick to capitalise on the Sahwists' 'soft' stance at a time when the dust from the Jenin battle had barely settled. Ali al-Khudayr lashed out verbally at the signatories, calling them 'defeatist traitors'. The month of May saw a steady stream of declarations by radical scholars condemning the statement in general and the Sahwists' participation in particular.[15]

The political pressure on the signatories led several of them to retract their support, claiming that they had not read the statement fully before signing. The three Sahwist leaders, unable to offer similarly bad excuses, produced a 'Clarifying Statement' intended to reassure their constituency of their firm attachment to the principle of 'Loyalty and Dissociation' – in practice disavowing the core content of the initial

al-shu'un al-islamiyya salih al al-shaykh [Introduction to the Answer to the Islamic Affairs Minister Salih Al al-Shaykh]' (www.saaid.net, 2001); Hamud al-Shu'aybi, '*bayan 'amma hasal min labs fi shurut al-ifta'* [Statement on the Confusion in the Conditions for Religious Rulings]' (www.aloqla.com, 2001).

[14] Nasir al-Fahd, '*al-tabyin fi makhatir al-tatbi' 'ala al-muslimin* [Clarification of the Dangers of Normalisation for Muslims]' (www.tawhed.ws, 2002).

[15] 'How We Can Coexist' (www.islamtoday.com, 2002). See also Mansur al-Nuqaydan, '*qissat bayan al-muthaqqafin al-sa'udiyyin* [The Story of the Statement of the Saudi Intellectuals]', *Elaph*, 13 November 2002; 'What We are Fighting for – A Letter from America' (Institute for American Values (www.americanvalues.org), 2002); Ali al-Khudayr *et al.*, '*ihya' millat ibrahim wa'l-radd 'ala al-mukhaddilin al-munhazimin* [Reviving the Creed of Abraham and Responding to the Defeatist Traitors]' (www.alkhoder.com, 2002); Stéphane Lacroix, 'Islamo-Liberal Politics in Saudi Arabia', in *Saudi Arabia in the Balance*, ed. Paul Aarts and Gerd Nonneman (London: Hurst, 2006), 48.

declaration. Hoping to leave the issue behind, Salman al-Awda then removed the original declaration as well as the clarification from the Arabic version of his website *Islam Today* (but left the original declaration on the English version of the site). The Sahwist leaders had suffered a massive political defeat.[16]

However, the sheikhs of the al-Shu'aybi school had no qualms about kicking an adversary who was lying down. Ali al-Khudayr published a text ridiculing the 'Clarifying Statement'. If Nasir al-Fahd stayed quiet in May, it was to prepare the knockout blow, namely the 400-page book entitled *Rebuttal of the Errors in the Statement of the Intellectuals*, which came out in June 2002. The following month, he concluded the verbal campaign against the signatories of the 'Statement of the Intellectuals' with an article bluntly reminding the readers that 'he who does not excommunicate an infidel is himself an infidel'. There was absolutely no middle ground in the conflict between Islam and the West – and certainly not in the new confrontation that arose in the autumn of 2002.[17]

The increasing international tensions over Iraq represented yet another opportunity for Nasir al-Fahd and his companions to grab attention with their uncompromising rhetoric. This time around they were more outspoken, because the political victories against the Sahwa had made them more confident. The verbal offensive began on 12 October, when a group of seven radical sheikhs led by Nasir al-Fahd published a fatwa explicitly stating that anyone who extends assistance to the Americans or its allies in an attack on Iraq would be considered an infidel. It was a clear warning to the regime on the issue of the US military bases in the kingdom. In early November, Abd al-Rahman al-Barrak, one of the few unifying figures on the conservative side of the Islamist field, tried to calm the situation somewhat by redacting a statement with a similar message expressed in softer language, and having both Sahwist leaders and Nasir al-Fahd sign it, along with over fifty other clerics. The Sahwist sheikhs, keen to

[16] Mirza al-Khuwaylidi, '*qissat bayan al-muthaqqafin al-sa'udiyyin: da'wat al-ta'ayush allati saqatat dahiyat al-hiwar al-dakhili* [The Story of the Statement of the Saudi Intellectuals: The Invitation to Coexistence which Fell Victim to the Internal Debate]', *al-Sharq al-Awsat*, 14 June 2002.

[17] Ali al-Khudayr, '*radd al-shaykh 'ali al-khudayr 'ala al-bayan al-tawdihi li-khitab al-ta'ayush* [Reply from Ali al-Khudayr to the Clarifying Statement to the Letter of Coexistence]' (www.tawhed.ws, 2002); Nasir al-Fahd, '*al-tankil bima fi bayan al-muthaqqafin min abatil* [Rebuttal of the Errors in the Statement of the Intellectuals]' (www.tawhed.ws, 2002); Nasir al-Fahd, '*tali'at al-tankil bima fi bayan al-muthaqqafin min abatil* [Early Excerpt of the Rebuttal of the Errors in the Statement of the Intellectuals]' (www.tawhed.ws, 2002); Nasir al-Fahd, '*hawla qa'idat man lam yukaffir al-kafir fa huwa kafir* [On the Rule that Whoever Fails to Excommunicate a Disbeliever is Himself a Disbeliever]' (www.tawhed.ws, 2002).

seem tough on America after their humiliation in the spring, signed up willingly. Nasir al-Fahd did too, but he was not prepared to let the al-Barrak statement remain the last word on the issue. Shortly afterward he published *The Crusade in its Second Stage: The Iraq War*, which was written as a sequel to the book published a year previously on the Afghanistan war entitled *Clarification on the Infidelity of Whoever Helps the Americans*. Al-Fahd followed up with more articles lambasting the US political manoeuvring at the UN, which he saw as thinly veiled preparations for an attack.[18]

In December 2002 the international press reported a secret deal between Saudi Arabia and the United States that would allow the latter access to airbases in the kingdom. Around the same time, as we shall see below, the police had started to sense that something was stirring in the grassroots of the jihadist community. To the regime, the preaching of al-Fahd and his comrades was no longer a nuisance on the fringe of the Islamist scene – it was a security threat.

In late February 2003, as part of a broader attempt to control the radical community before the Iraq war, the authorities decided to arrest the leading scholars of the al-Shu'aybi school. However, Nasir al-Fahd, Ali al-Khudayr and Ahmad al-Khalidi escaped and went underground. Over the next three months they would hide in a suburb in Medina, communicating with their followers through the Internet until they were captured on 27 May 2003.

As outlaws, the three sheikhs had nothing to lose. They could comment freely on the government's crackdown and on the situation in Iraq. Not surprisingly, therefore, it was in this period that the sheikhs produced their most radical texts. In early March they repeated their message – this time in clearer terms – that helping the US invasion was tantamount to apostasy. They issued several fatwas on various aspects relating to the Iraq war. Later, al-Fahd would notably rule on the legitimacy of attacking US targets outside Iraq. In late May 2003, Nasir al-Fahd would issue one of his last – and to a Western public most shocking – declarations, namely the *Treatise on the Use of Weapons of Mass Destruction against the Infidels*. The sheikhs of the al-Shu'aybi school would thus leave behind a trail of extremely anti-American

[18] Nasir al-Fahd *et al.*, '*fatwa fi kufr man a'an al-amrikan 'ala al-muslimin fi'l-'iraq* [Fatwa on the Infidelity of Whoever Helps the Americans against Muslims in Iraq]' (www.al-fhd.com, 2002); Abd al-Rahman Barrak *et al.*, '*bayan min 'ulama' din al-sa'udiyya* [Statement from the Religious Scholars of Saudi Arabia]' (www.mafhoum.com, 2002); Nasir al-Fahd, '*al-hamla al-salibiyya fi marhalatiha al-thaniyya: harb al-'iraq* [The Crusade in its Second Stage: The Iraq War]' (www.tawhed.ws, 2002); Nasir al-Fahd, '*ta'duw al-dhi'ab man la kilab lahu* [The Wolves Attack him who has no Dog]' (www.tawhed.ws, 2002).

writings which sanctioned the use of all means in all places in the jihad against the Crusaders.[19]

The WMD fatwa has naturally attracted a lot of attention in the West. It is worth noting that, at the time, the CIA believed it was issued in response to a specific request from senior al-Qaida officials, most likely in preparation for a mass-casualty attack which for some reason was called off. A former senior CIA official interviewed by this author said this hypothesis was supported by substantial classified evidence.[20]

In this period the three renegade scholars also published texts sanctioning violence against Western targets and Saudi security forces in Saudi Arabia. Al-Fahd issued a fatwa stating that a visa did not constitute a security guarantee for Western visitors to Saudi Arabia. By refuting the 'visa argument' – the main objection of moderate religious scholars to anti-Western violence in the kingdom – al-Fahd essentially declared Westerners in Saudi Arabia legitimate targets for violence. On 7 March 2003, al-Fahd, al-Khudayr and al-Khalidi also published a text entitled *Letter to You the Mujahidin*, which told 'all those wanted and detained' to be patient and steadfast, and all those not detained to 'continue your work in God's name'. Another text released on the same day was addressed to the 'Men in the Mabahith', warning the security services that 'chasing and arresting mujahidin for doing jihad is one of the greatest services one can extend to the Crusaders', and that 'whoever helps the Crusaders against the mujahidin ... is an infidel and an apostate'. These fatwas were very important for the mobilisation for the QAP because they could be used to dispel doubts among potential recruits and hesitant fighters at the lower levels of the organisation.[21]

[19] Ali al-Khudayr, Nasir al-Fahd and Ahmad al-Khalidi, '*nasiha fi bayan hukm man wala al-kuffar wa a'anahum fi harbihim 'ala al-muslimin wa kalam 'ala al-raya* [Advice on the Statement on Whoever Shows Loyalty to the Infidels and Helps them in their War on the Muslims, and a Word on the Banner]' (www.alkhoder.com, 2003); Nasir al-Fahd, '*hawla ahadith al-sufyani* [On the Sufyani Incidents]' (www.tawhed.ws, 2003); Nasir al-Fahd, '*hawla ahadith "al-qahtani"* [On the al-Qahtani Incidents]' (www.tawhed.ws, 2003); Nasir al-Fahd, '*hukm mujahadat al-amrikan kharij al-'iraq* [The Ruling on Fighting the Americans Outside Iraq]' (www.tawhed.ws, 2003); Nasir al-Fahd, '*risala fi hukm istikhdam aslihat al-dimar al-shamil didd al-kuffar* [Treatise on the Use of Weapons of Mass Destruction against the Infidels]' (www.tawhed.ws, 2003); Reuven Paz, 'Global Jihad and WMD: Between Martyrdom and Mass Destruction', *Current Trends in Islamist Ideology* 2 (2005).

[20] Tenet, *At the Center of the Storm*, 272–4; interview with Rolf Mowatt-Larsen, Cambridge, MA, June 2009.

[21] Nasir al-Fahd, '*hal tu'tabar ta'shirat al-fiza 'aqd aman?* [Is the Visa Considered a Security Guarantee?]' (www.tawhed.ws, 2003?). For the 'visa argument', see Abdallah al-Rashid, *intiqad al-i'tirad 'ala tafjirat al-riyadh* [Criticism of the Objection to the Riyadh Bombings] (www.qa3edoon.com, 2003); Stéphane Lacroix, 'Le champ politico-religieux en Arabie Saoudite après le 11 septembre' (Master's thesis (*mémoire de DEA*), Institut d'Etudes Politiques de Paris, 2003).

The precise nature of the relationship between the sheikhs of the al-Shu'aybi school and the operational networks of the nascent QAP remains unclear. On the one hand, there was certainly personal contact and interaction. Al-Uyayri had entertained close relations with these sheikhs since at least 1999, and he regularly posted their texts on the *al-Nida* website which he supervised from late 2001 onward. Several of the students of these clerics were later found in the QAP's ranks. After the publication of the list of nineteen wanted militants on 8 May 2003, the sheikhs issued a declaration confirming that they knew the wanted men personally (and stressing that the latter were jihad veterans, not terrorists). Moreover, when the sheikhs were underground between February and May 2003 they must have sensed that something was brewing.[22]

On the other hand, contact does not necessarily imply complicity. The sheikhs most likely did not know – and did not want to know – details about the operational planning. Al-Fahd and his companions were public figures who operated in the ideological field of Saudi Islamism, not in the militant underground. There are no indications in the QAP literature that these sheikhs were directly involved in the operational planning, logistical support or recruitment efforts that were going on in 2002 and 2003. A few days after the 12 May 2003 attacks, the three runaway clerics issued a statement claiming ignorance of the existence of any kind of organisational structure in the kingdom. Moreover, in November and December 2003, the three imprisoned clerics appeared on television repenting, retracting their previous rulings and saying they did not realise the consequences of their declarations. Although most commentators agreed that Nasir al-Fahd's repentance was insincere, Ali al-Khudayr's retraction seemed genuine. Yusuf al-Uyayri and the operational QAP network most likely did not inform the sheikhs of the details and scope of their military activities. QAP military strategists later wrote about the need to keep religious scholars separate from the military infrastructure of a jihadist organisation.[23]

[22] For example, QAP militants Abd al-Latif al-Khudayri and Turki al-Fuhayd studied with Ali al-Khudayr; see Sa'd al-Anzi, '*'abd al-latif bin hamad al-khudayri*', *Sawt al-Jihad*, no. 27 (2004) and *al-Sharq al-Awsat*, 18 June 2003; Ali al-Khudayr, Nasir al-Fahd and Ahmad al-Khalidi, '*bayan fi nusrat al-mujahidin alladhina nushirat asma'uhum wa suwaruhum* [Statement in Support of the Mujahidin whose Names and Pictures Have Been Released]' (www.alkhoder.com: 2003).

[23] Ali al-Khudayr, Nasir al-Fahd and Ahmad al-Khalidi, '*bayan hawla al-ahdath* [Statement on the Incidents]' (www.alkhoder.com, 2003), cited in Lacroix, 'Le champ politico-religieux'; Muhammad al-Harbi, 'Khudair Repents Supporting Terror Attacks', *Arab News*, 18 November 2003; Khaled al-Awadh, 'Another Scholar Recants', *Arab News*, 23 November 2003; Adnan Malik, 'Third Saudi Cleric Renounces Militancy', *Associated Press*, 14 December 2003; author's interviews with Sa'ud al-Sarhan and Yusuf al-Dayni. Nasir al-Fahd later released a statement from prison in which he

Although the sheikhs of the al-Shu'aybi school were probably not part of Yusuf al-Uyayri's military infrastructure, they facilitated recruitment and mobilisation for the nascent QAP in 2002 and early 2003 in several important ways. First, they contributed to an increase in anti-Western attitudes in the Saudi religious community. By producing extremely anti-American discourse and distributing it very efficiently on the Internet, Nasir al-Fahd and his fellows increased the pool of potential recruits for global jihadist activism in Saudi Arabia. Second, the fatwas provided religious justification for the killing of Westerners as well as Saudi security forces if the latter interposed, and this was essentially all the sanction the QAP needed for their military campaign. Al-Fahd and al-Khudayr were bright and articulate clerics with formal religious training and considerable knowledge. Their fatwas thus carried considerably more weight than those of the second-rate clerics who would later emerge within the QAP such as Abdallah al-Rushud or Faris al-Zahrani. Finally the escalation of the rhetoric of the al-Shu'aybi school signalled to the authorities the unrest that was in the making.

From soft to hard policing

The third major dynamic shaping the political opportunities of the global jihadists in Saudi Arabia was the relative hardening of the policing of the jihadist community in late 2002. For about a year after 9/11, policing was relatively non-confrontational, as it had been since around 1999. Although arrests were made, there was no systematic attempt to uproot al-Qaida's networks in the kingdom in this period. Returnees from Afghanistan were not treated as a particularly serious security risk. Most of those arrested were not held for long, and many returnees were not detained at all, but rather requested to report to their local police station. Upon their release, most suspects were not supervised by the security services; several of the most prominent and active QAP militants had in fact been arrested and released in 2002.[24]

retracted his retraction; see Nasir al-Fahd, '*al-taraju' 'an al-taraju' al-mafrud* [Retraction of the Supposed Retraction]' (www.tawhed.ws, 2005); al-Muqrin, *dawrat al-tanfidh*.

[24] 'Saudi Security Forces Arrest Several Sympathizers with Osama Bin Laden', *ArabicNews.com*, 22 October 2001; 'Yemen Extradites 21 Saudi Fugitives', *Arab News*, 28 October 2001; 'Sanaa Hands over to Riyadh a Saudi Belongs to al-Qaida', *ArabicNews.com*, 28 February 2002; 'Saudi Arabia Handed over 16 al-Qaida Members from Iran', *ArabicNews.com*, 13 August 2002; Faisal Saeed, 'Al-Qaeda Suspects Won't be Extradited to US: Saud', *Arab News*, 13 August 2002. See also Fawwaz al-Nashmi, '*khalid al-baghdadi (abu ayub al-najdi)* [Khalid al-Baghdadi (Abu Ayub al-Najdi)]', *Sawt al-Jihad*, no. 18 (2004); Hasin al-Binayyan, 'Al-Qaeda Arrests "Idle Speculation"', *Arab News*, 12 November 2001. See also 'Riyadh Frees 160 Returnees from Afghanistan',

When confronted with the failure to detain the people who would later run the QAP, Saudi police officers later argued that there was nothing else they could do, since the militants had not yet committed any crimes. This apparent concern for the legal rights of detainees is unconvincing. A more likely explanation is poor intelligence; in many cases police simply did not know the detainee's record. Another factor was domestic politics; in the pan-Islamist atmosphere of 2002 it was politically difficult for the regime to imprison jihad veterans. The third reason was the flawed assessment that the returnees would reintegrate into society like most classical jihadists had done in the past and not engage in violence on Saudi territory. The security establishment did not realise that the Saudi returnees had radicalised in a very different way from that of previous veterans. Key officials had tended to see previous plots in 2001 and 2002 primarily as the work of outside agents and thus did not expect a major campaign waged by Saudis.[25]

For the same reasons, there was an attitude of denial in important parts of the Saudi security establishment towards the participation of Saudis in al-Qaida and towards the possibility of an al-Qaida presence in the kingdom. The public record is full of rather curious statements by top Saudi officials on this issue in 2001 and 2002. A number of officials publicly expressed doubts about Bin Ladin's responsibility for 9/11 several months after the attack. In December 2001, the Saudi embassy in Pakistan claimed it did not know of Saudis having died in Afghanistan. In late October 2001, Interior Minister Prince Nayef said with a straight face that al-Qaida did not have links in the kingdom. In August 2002, the police said none of the people arrested in the kingdom in the preceding months had links to al-Qaida. In the late summer of 2002, probably as the result of plots uncovered in the spring and summer of 2002, the attitude seems to have changed somewhat, at least in parts of the intelligence community.[26]

In the autumn of 2002, the police approach to the jihadist community became gradually more confrontational. In September 2002, the

Arab News, 18 June 2002; Ibn al-Mawsul, '*istishhad ahad shabab al-jawf fi bilad al-rafidayn* [One of the Jawf Youth Martyred in Mesopotamia]' (http://topforums.net, 2005). Among the militants arrested and released in 2002 were Abd al-Ilah al-Utaybi, Musaid al-Subay, Nasir al-Khalidi, Isa al-Awshan and Talib al-Talib.

[25] Author's interview with Interior Ministry Spokesman Mansur al-Turki, Riyadh, January 2007.

[26] See e.g. 'Saudi Official Denies Bin Laden to Have Been Involved in Saudi Explosions', *ArabicNews.com*, 30 October 2001; Tenet, *At the Center of the Storm*, 234; 'Riyadh Denies Killing of Saudis in Afghanistan', *ArabicNews.com*, 7 December 2001; Khaled Al-Maeena and Javid Hassan, 'Prince Naif Denies Al-Qaeda Links in Kingdom', *Arab News*, 21 October 2001; 'None Arrested in Kingdom Have Direct Link to Al-Qaeda', *Arab News*, 27 August 2002.

London-based opposition newsletter *al-Islah* wrote that 'a list of wanted people belonging to the jihadist current has been issued, and police have orders to arrest them – and to shoot to kill if they refuse to surrender'. By late November 2002, the Saudi authorities had allegedly detained around a hundred people on suspicion of links with terrorism.[27]

The jihadists responded in kind. Radical scholars allegedly issued fatwas in private telling people not to surrender to police and to carry weapons in self-defence. November 2002 saw the first ever exchange of gunshots between Sunni militants and police since 1979. These early confrontations broke barriers on the use of violence in the kingdom, strengthened the internal cohesion of the nascent QAP and gave the project of 'jihad on the Arabian Peninsula' a sense of urgency within the jihadist community.[28]

The change in police approach was motivated by several factors. First was the discovery of attempted attacks at Prince Sultan Airbase and Ra's Tanura in the spring and summer of 2002 (see next chapter), which convinced parts of the security establishment of the reality of the threat. Another factor was heavy American pressure for a tougher Saudi stance against al-Qaida. A third factor was the real increase in the level of jihadi activity from September 2002 onward, as the returnees from Afghanistan were settling in, the Iraq controversy escalated and the al-Uyayri network began to get organised.

However, rather than contain the security threat, the moderate hardening of police methods helped the mobilisation effort, because the crackdown was inconsistent and partial. Put simply, the police approach was confrontational enough to affect the militants' intentions – by fuelling their sense of victimhood and belief in the urgency of their project – but not effective enough to dent their operational capabilities.

From the jihadists' perspective, two specific events in late 2002 marked the end of the post-1999 modus vivendi with the police. First was the so-called 'Ifta' incident' on 2 November 2002. Frustrated with the unwillingness of the official scholars to address the burning political issues of the day, a group of around 100 young Islamists, led by future QAP ideologues Abdallah al-Rushud and Ahmad al-Dukhayyil, decided to go to the Dar al-Ifta' (the central authority for religious

[27] *al-Islah*, no. 334 (30 September 2002); 'Prince Nayef: More than 100 Convicts under Terrorism Charges', *ArabicNews.com*, 21 November 2002; 'Saudi Opposition: Hunger Strike by Detained Islamists', *ArabicNews.com*, 4 January 2003.

[28] *al-Islah*, no. 334 (30 September 2002). It is not clear exactly who issued these rulings, but it is highly likely that it was someone from the al-Shu'aybi school, for example Nasir al-Fahd or Ali al-Khudayr. Hamud al-Uqla al-Shu'aybi is said to have issued a similar fatwa before his death in January 2002; *al-Islah,* no. 340 (18 November 2002); author's interview with Mansur al-Nuqaydan.

decrees) in Riyadh and confront the Grand Mufti of Saudi Arabia, Abd al-Aziz Al al-Shaykh, with a number of contentious questions. At the entrance they were met by riot police, and their request to meet the Grand Mufti was ignored. The petitioners refused to leave and, after some negotiation, fifty people were let in. However, their audience with the Mufti was very brief, and they left frustrated not to have been taken seriously. Upon leaving the Dar al-Ifta' complex, a large number of them were detained by the police, though al-Rushud and al-Dukhayyil were able to escape and go underground. As a direct result of the Ifta' incident, some jihadists began carrying weapons for their personal protection.[29]

The second watershed event occurred two weeks later, when a militant fired what journalist Faris bin Huzzam has described as 'the first bullet' against a Saudi police officer. On 16 November the police were able to locate a wanted suspect named Muhammad al-Sahim by wiretapping his telephone. Al-Sahim was in a house in the al-Shifa district in Riyadh together with a number of other soon-to-be-famous militants, including Faysal al-Dukhayyil, Bandar al-Dukhayyil and Nasir al-Sayyari, who had gathered to listen to Ahmad al-Dukhayyil speak. As the police stormed the house, a shoot-out erupted and Muhammad al-Sahim was shot in the right leg and arrested. The remaining militants escaped in a car. The incident was later described in the QAP's magazine, *Sawt al-Jihad*:

> In Ramadan occurred the al-Shifa' incident, and this was the first confrontation between the mujahidin youth and their sympathisers and the dog security services. By this event, God removed the barrier of fear from the people. Until then, young men would be invited to the security services by telephone, and they would go and see them by their own choice, without considering resistance or going into hiding. Then came this incident and induced them to carry weapons and defend their religion and themselves.[30]

From this point onward the tension escalated. In early December, a new secret wanted list was issued, and the following months saw a

[29] Abdallah al-Rushud, '*bayan hawla ahdath al-ifta*' [Statement on the Ifta' Events]' (www.tawhed.ws, 2002); see also *al-Islah*, no. 339 (4 November 2002); *al-Islah*, no. 340 (11 November 2002); al-Dukhayyil, '*faysal bin 'abd al-rahman al-dukhayyil*', 14–15.

[30] *al-Hayat*, 25 January 2005; al-Dukhayyil, '*faysal bin 'abd al-rahman al-dukhayyil*'; *al-Islah*, no. 341 (18 November 2002); *al-Islah*, no. 342 (25 November 2002); see also Nasir al-Sayyari's account in the film *badr al-riyadh*; *al-Riyadh*, 19 November 2002; 'Operations in Riyadh in Search for al-Qaida Members, 8 Saudi Soldiers Wounded in Clashes', *ArabicNews.com*, 18 November 2002; 'Saudi Ministry Denies Wounding of Security Men in Clashes with Bin Laden's Supporters', *ArabicNews.com*, 19 November 2002. See also *al-Islah*, no. 342 (25 November 2002).

series of armed confrontations. By mid-February, over 400 people had allegedly been arrested on suspicion of al-Qaida links. The change in the Saudi approach to counterterrorism was noted by the United States who praised the 'new effort'.[31]

In late February 2003, the confrontation was brought to a new level with the arrest of sheikhs suspected of helping the jihadists. Many radical scholars had already been banned from preaching in late 2002, but their imprisonment represented a dramatic escalation. The arrest wave began on 20 February with the detention of Sheikh Hamad al-Humaydi in Zulfi. On 27 February, a certain Sheikh Usama Uqayl al-Kawhaji was arrested in Riyadh. On 1 March, as mentioned above, police made an unsuccessful attempt at arresting Nasir al-Fahd, Ali al-Khudayr and Ahmad al-Khalidi. Other scholars such as Sulayman al-Ulwan also started feeling the heat and allegedly went into hiding for a period in mid-March. In early May, the pressure on the scholars was lifted somewhat, perhaps due to the end of the major hostilities in Iraq. Hamad al-Humaydi was released on 6 May and Sulayman al-Ulwan was reportedly allowed to teach again. However, the damage had already been done – the militants now considered themselves past the point of no return.[32]

The immediate prelude to the QAP campaign began on 18 March 2003 with an explosion in an anonymous house in the Jazira district of Riyadh. As the police investigated the blast site, they realised they were standing in a safe house for militants. The destruction had been caused by the premature explosion of a bomb intended for a large-scale attack in Riyadh. Investigators discovered a massive arms cache and numerous documents pointing to the existence of a cell poised on launching a violent campaign. They also found the remains of a person who had died in the blast, presumably while assembling the bomb. The unlucky bombmaker was Fahd al-Sa'idi, a recent returnee from Afghanistan.[33]

The chance discovery of the Jazira safe house put the police on the trail of the militant network that was planning the spring 2003 offensive. The next month and a half saw several clashes. On 23 March, police raided a house in the al-Rayan district of eastern Riyadh and made several arrests. On 5 April, police arrested the Polish-German

[31] *al-Islah*, no. 349 (13 January 2003); 'Prince Nayef Announces Bringing 90 Saudis to Court over Joining al-Qaida', *ArabicNews.com* (2003); 'Powell Welcomed Declared Saudi Measures on Fighting Terrorism', *ArabicNews.com* (2002).

[32] *al-Islah*, no. 355 (24 February 2003); *al-Islah*, no. 356 (3 March 2003); *al-Islah*, no. 358 (17 March 2003); Lacroix, 'Le champ politico-religieux'.

[33] *al-Sharq al-Awsat*, 19 March 2003; *al-Islah*, no. 359 (24 March 2003); al-Nashmi, '*fahd bin samran al-sa'idi*'.

convert and suspected al-Qaida operative Christian Ganczarski. On 22 April, another major shoot-out occurred west of Riyadh as police attempted to arrest a group of militants at a rest house in Wadi Laban. The militants were able to escape after a short exchange of gunfire. By the end of April 2003, the intelligence picture had become so ominous that the US embassy in Riyadh issued an official warning about the risk of imminent terrorist attacks.[34]

The most frightening discovery of all was made on 6 May 2003, when Saudi police raided the safe house belonging to the al-Qaida operative Turki al-Dandani in Riyadh. After a gun battle during which the militants were able to escape, the police conducted a routine search of the house. In addition to the 'usual' inventory – explosives, weapons, money, fake documents etc. – the police found something truly alarming: handwritten wills of suicide bombers. Realising there was no time to lose, the authorities published a list with names and pictures of nineteen wanted individuals on 8 May. They initiated a frantic search for the candidate suicide bombers, but unfortunately it was too late.[35]

[34] *al-Islah*, no. 359 (24 March 2003); M. Ghazanfar Ali Khan, 'German Arrested in Riyadh for Alleged Al-Qaeda Link', *Arab News*, 6 April 2003; *Der Spiegel*, 12 May 2003; *al-Islah*, no. 364 (28 April 2003); Roger Harrison, 'US Warns of Terror Plans, but Kingdom has no Information', *Arab News*, 1 May 2003; 'US Warns Citizens of Al-Qaeda Threat', *Arab News*, 3 May 2003.

[35] Raid Qusti, 'Al-Qaeda Plot Foiled', *Arab News*, 8 May 2003; '*ghazwat al-hadi 'ashar min rabi' al-awwal: 'amaliyyat sharq al-riyadh wa-harbuna ma' amrika wa 'umala'iha* [The 12 May Raid: The East Riyadh Operation and our War with America and its Agents]' (www.qa3edoon.com, 2003), 46; Javid Hassan, 'SR300,000 Offered for Capture of Fugitives', *Arab News*, 9 May 2003; Douglas Jehl, 'Saudis Seek 19 Suspected of Terrorist Plot', *New York Times*, 10 May 2003; 'Checkpoints Set up near Riyadh to Track Down Terror Suspects', *Arab News*, 10 May 2003.

8 The mujahidin on the Arabian Peninsula

> Today your brothers and sons, the sons of the Two Sanctuaries, have started their jihad in the cause of Allah, to expel the occupying enemy from the Land of the Two Sanctuaries.
>
> Usama bin Ladin, *Declaration of War against the Americans*, 1996

> What we are doing today is but an answer to God's call and his Prophet, who say, 'Expel the infidels from the Arabian Peninsula.'
>
> Muhammad al-Shihri, martyrdom video, 12 May 2003[1]

By launching the QAP campaign in May 2003, Bin Ladin returned to the original cause of his global jihad project, namely the eviction of US forces from Saudi Arabia. This meant that the al-Qaida leadership had reversed its 1998 decision to postpone military operations in the kingdom. It also meant that the group was prepared to compromise its most important fundraising and recruitment base. What had caused this change? And how did al-Qaida implement the new strategy?

Returning from Afghanistan

When the planes struck the World Trade Center and the Pentagon on 11 September 2001, Usama bin Ladin and his fellow commanders were fully aware that a US military invasion of Afghanistan was imminent. They had therefore taken a number of preparatory steps, ranging from emergency evacuation plans from the training camps to strategic moves such as the assassination, on 9 September, of Northern Alliance commander Ahmad Shah Mas'ud. As soon as the news of the 9/11 attacks was confirmed, the al-Qaida leadership evacuated the main training camps and started assigning foreign recruits to Arab units at Taliban military fronts. Boosted by volunteer fighters who had started pouring into Afghanistan in late September 2001, al-Qaida and the rest of

[1] '*wasaya al-abtal: shuhada' al-haramayn* [Wills of the Heroes: Martyrs of the Two Sanctuaries]' (Saudi Arabia: al-Sahhab Foundation for Media Production, 2003).

the Arab community were getting ready for full-scale military conflict. At this point, Bin Ladin seems to have been genuinely optimistic. He believed the United States would get bogged down in Afghanistan in a guerrilla war in which it would 'bleed to death', much like the Soviet Union did in the 1980s.[2]

When the US-led coalition initiated 'Operation Enduring Freedom' on 7 October 2001, it soon became clear that Arab and Taliban forces would not be able to withstand the lethal combination of Western aerial bombardment and Northern Alliance ground forces. Al-Qaida had misjudged not only the power, but also the nature of the US intervention. The Arab fighters, who expected a massive deployment of US ground forces, found themselves before an elusive and intangible enemy. On 12 November, Northern Alliance forces entered the capital Kabul, bringing the conventional part of the war to an end. In two months, 110 CIA officers and 350 US Special Forces, combined with airpower, Afghan allies and US$70 million, had evicted the Taliban in what President Bush called 'one of the biggest bargains of all time'.[3]

After the battle of Tora Bora and the fall of Qandahar in mid-December 2001, the Arab military infrastructure collapsed and the process of decentralisation of al-Qaida accelerated. Bin Ladin and al-Zawahiri went into hiding in the border areas, others slipped into Pakistan and yet others kept on fighting. In January and February 2002, most of the remaining Arab fighters, some 600–700 in total, regrouped in the Shahi Kot area in the Paktia province, in response to which US-led forces launched 'Operation Anaconda' in March 2002. The so-called 'battle of Shahi Kot' (3–18 March) was the final confrontation involving significant numbers of Arab fighters in Afghanistan. By mid-March 2002, al-Qaida's infrastructure in Afghanistan was in tatters, and the organisation, or what remained of it, found itself in an entirely new strategic situation.[4]

[2] Bergen, *The Osama bin Laden I Know*, 311, 326; Sayf al-Adl, '*risala ila ahlina fi'l-'iraq wa'l-khalij khassatan wa ummatina al-islamiyya 'amma*', www.drasat.com, 2003; Alan Cullison and Andrew Higgins, 'Forgotten Computer Reveals Thinking behind Four Years of al Qaeda Doings', *Wall Street Journal*, 31 December 2001; 'Testimony of Detainees – CSRT', 1002; Gary Berntsen and Ralph Pezzullo, *Jawbreaker* (New York: Crown, 2005), 128; Alan Cullison, 'Inside Al-Qaeda's Hard Drive', *The Atlantic Monthly*, September 2004.

[3] Tom Downey, 'My Bloody Career', *Observer*, 23 April 2006; 'Operation Enduring Freedom – Operations', www.globalsecurity.org; Bob Woodward, *Bush at War* (New York: Simon and Schuster, 2002), 317.

[4] Paul Hastert, 'Operation Anaconda: Perception Meets Reality in the Hills of Afghanistan', *Studies in Conflict and Terrorism* 28, no. 1 (2005); Sean Naylor, *Not a Good Day to Die* (London: Penguin, 2005); Michael Scheuer, *Imperial Hubris: Why the West is Losing the War on Terror* (Washington, DC: Brassey's, 2004), 92; Abd al-Aziz Hifz, *ahdath*

The US-led invasion of Afghanistan changed the operational environment of Bin Ladin's organisation in three fundamental ways. First and most importantly, al-Qaida lost access to its most important asset, namely its territory in Afghanistan. For the first time since its foundation, the organisation no longer had a safe meeting-place in which to quietly plan operations and train new recruits. Second, Arab fighters in general, and the al-Qaida leadership in particular, were being hunted in Afghanistan and Pakistan like never before. Finally, the many security measures and international cooperation in the so-called 'war on terror' made it much more difficult for al-Qaida to move personnel, money and messages across borders and distances.

This new reality forced the al-Qaida leadership to reconsider both the structure and the strategy of their organisation, particularly with regards to Saudi Arabia. The aim of evicting the Crusaders from the Arabian Peninsula was integral to the global jihadist doctrine and the idea had been cultivated in the al-Qaida leadership for a long time. Between 1998 and 2001, Bin Ladin's view had been that a premature terrorist campaign on the Peninsula would do more harm than good given Saudi Arabia's importance as a source of recruits, money and ideology.

In late 2001, however, the new strategic environment had altered the cost-benefit analysis. Saudi Arabia's usefulness as a source of money and recruits had decreased. Having been evicted from Afghanistan, al-Qaida was no longer able to accommodate new Saudi volunteers, while money transfers from wealthy Saudi donors could now be traced more easily. At the same time, Saudi Arabia's relative attractiveness as a theatre of operations had increased, because in 2002 jihadists were pursued less vigorously in the kingdom than in perhaps any other country in the region, with the possible exception of Yemen.

It took some time for al-Qaida to realise the scope of the changes brought about by the invasion. As late as October 2001, Saudis were still encouraged to leave the kingdom and come to Afghanistan and help fight the Americans. Bin Ladin's change of mind did not come until late 2001, and was at least partially encouraged by impatient Saudi mujahidin. In late November 2001, mid-level Saudi fighters were beginning to feel disillusioned with the fighting in Afghanistan and asked Bin Ladin for permission to return to the Peninsula and launch operations there.[5]

shay kut riwayatan wa tahlilan [The Events at Shahi Kot Told and Analysed] (www.alemarh.com, May 2002).

[5] al-Nashmi, '*fahd bin samran al-sa'idi*'.

There had long been pressure from below in the al-Qaida organisation to start operations in Saudi Arabia. The above-mentioned Fahd al-Sa'idi had been particularly eager and had gone from Afghanistan to Saudi Arabia shortly before 9/11 to assess the potential for operations there. Another driving force for the launch of a jihad on the Peninsula was Mit'ib al-Muhayyani, who would later lead an important QAP cell in Mecca. In the late summer of 2001, he and a group of friends, all of whom had met in the al-Faruq camp, allegedly made a vow between themselves to wage jihad in Saudi Arabia one day. Other sources refer to a similar vow being taken in January or February 2002:

> Haydara stayed fighting the crusaders with his brothers until the withdrawal from Qandahar ... Then Haydara made a vow together with some of his brothers to work on the Arabian Peninsula to cleanse it of polytheists. In that group was the hero Mit'ib al-Muhayyani. The heroes arrived on the Peninsula which had longed so much for their coming, and he was one of the founders of the work inside the Peninsula. From day one the two heroes Mit'ib and Talal undertook work in one of the preparation groups.

Similarly, the QAP member Khalid al-Farraj said he went to Afghanistan after 9/11, where he received a proposal to 'operate within Saudi Arabia' from fellow Saudis. 'Later I returned, and after contacting them, I joined the cells here,' he said.[6]

The pressure from low- and mid-level Saudi al-Qaida fighters for the launch of a jihad in Saudi Arabia increased considerably after mid-December 2001 because they saw the order of the Taliban commanders to withdraw from Qandahar to Shahi Kot as the end of the meaningful resistance in Afghanistan. As Turki al-Mutayri later wrote, 'the order to retreat came; we left and decided to work to strike the rear bases of the enemy in the land of Muhammad'. The biographies in *Sawt al-Jihad* suggest that several of the Saudis who were in Afghanistan and later came to play key roles in the nascent QAP had been in Qandahar in December 2001 and moved to Shahi Kot in early 2002. The social bonds forged through this shared experience were thus an important factor in the subsequent formation of the QAP.[7]

[6] al-Nashmi, '*fahd bin samran al-sa'idi*'; Abu Muhammad al-Makki, '*mit'ib al-muhayyani*', *Sawt al-Jihad*, no. 4 (2003); al-Najdi, '*talal al-anbari*'. See also '*'amir al-shihri: himma wa anafa ... wa thabbat hatta al-shahada* [Amir al-Shihri: Loftiness and Pride ... and Trustworthiness until Martyrdom]', *Sawt al-Jihad*, no. 12 (2004); P. K. Abdul Ghafour, 'Al-Qaeda Controls Young Operatives by Torture Threats', *Arab News*, 23 September 2004.

[7] '*turki bin fuhayd al-mutayri* [Turki bin Fuhayd al-Mutayri]', *Sawt al-Jihad*, no. 20 (2004).

While some Saudi fighters started pushing for action in the kingdom as soon as things became difficult in Afghanistan, the majority stayed until Usama bin Ladin himself issued direct orders to leave. These general orders seem to have been issued some time in the first three months of 2002. The biographer of Turki al-Dandani, one of the most important subsequent QAP leaders, later wrote:

> One of the brothers met him in Zarmat, his last stop in Afghanistan, and said to him: 'Don't you want to head down with your brothers?' – i.e. leave Afghanistan – because the order to leave had been issued. His eyes filled with tears and he said: 'I have not known the real life except here with these heroes.' But in the end he went, because it was an order issued by the commander.[8]

By the early spring of 2002, a small exodus from Afghanistan had been put in motion as foreign fighters returned to their home countries. Many of the Saudis fled through Iran, where they were often detained for a few weeks or months before moving on. Some also fled through Pakistan. For some, the return journey was strenuous and included incarceration in several countries and a less-than-warm welcome by Saudi security services upon arrival in the kingdom. Others slipped quietly into the country.[9]

Al-Qaida was very serious about its new Saudi strategy. The original plan seems to have been to send none other than Sayf al-Adl – al-Qaida's chief military commander following the death of Muhammad Atif – to the kingdom to direct the military effort. Al-Adl never made it, because he was detained in Iran after fleeing Afghanistan, but his belongings were later recovered in a QAP safe house in Riyadh.[10]

By May 2002 the majority of the surviving Saudi mujahidin – somewhere between 300 and 1,000 individuals – had made it back to the kingdom. The young men that Bin Ladin had sent home were highly motivated for action. Now he needed to ensure that the planning efforts were coordinated and professionally executed. In late May 2002, the US National Security Agency allegedly intercepted a message containing orders from Usama bin Ladin to Yusuf al-Uyayri to start preparing for

[8] Downey, 'My Bloody Career'; Ibn al-Mawsul, '*istishhad ahad shabab al-jawf*'; '*'ali al-ma'badi al-harbi*'; Abu Hajir al-Jawfi, '*turki al-dandani: 'azima wa shuja'a* [Turki al-Dandani: Greatness and Courage]', *Sawt al-Jihad*, no. 7 (2004).

[9] al-Dukhayyil, '*faysal bin 'abd al-rahman al-dukhayyil*'; al-Nashmi, '*khalid al-baghdadi (abu ayub al-najdi)*'; '*qabilat al-'utayba tazuff ahad abna'iha shahida* [The Utayba Tribe Celebrates One of its Sons as a Martyr]', *Sawt al-Jihad*, no. 4 (2003); al-Subay'i, '*musa'id al-subay'i*'.

[10] 'Summary of Evidence for Combatant Status Review Tribunal – al-Shib, Ramzi bin' (US Department of Defense, 2007), 2. Author's email correspondence with Nawaf Obaid, 16 March 2007.

a full-blown terrorist campaign in Saudi Arabia. CIA director George Tenet met with Prince Bandar, the Saudi ambassador to Washington, and told him, 'bad news, Bin Laden has changed his focus. Now it's you. It's Saudi Arabia.'[11]

Al-Nashiri and al-Qaida's failed 2002 offensives

When the top al-Qaida leadership gave the green light for operations in Saudi Arabia in early 2002, there were several semi-independent networks and cells working in parallel on different projects inside the kingdom. While Yusuf al-Uyayri and his lieutenants adopted a long-term approach focusing on organisation-building and recruitment in this period, others favoured immediate action and planned operations already in 2002. Most of the independent operations planned in this period were relatively small-scale, but some were decidedly more ambitious.

The first ominous sign that al-Qaida had set its eyes on Saudi Arabia came in early May 2002 with the discovery of an empty tube from a shoulder-fired surface-to-air missile near the Prince Sultan Airbase. Someone had penetrated the security perimeter and fired a missile, presumably in an attempt to down a US military aircraft. In mid-May, Saudi authorities identified the main suspect as a Sudanese veteran from Afghanistan, a certain Abu Hudhayfa, who had recently been to Saudi Arabia. On 18 June 2002, the Saudi Interior Ministry announced the arrest of the Sudanese suspect, an Iraqi and eleven Saudi citizens in connection with the plot. Abu Hudhayfa was said to have led an al-Qaida cell in Saudi Arabia which included six of the arrested Saudis. The remaining five Saudis and the Iraqi were accused of hiding the Sudanese man and smuggling him out of the country, allegedly through Iraq. The suspects had allegedly procured explosives and two missiles from Yemen. It later emerged that the missiles used at Prince Sultan Airbase were from the same production batch as the one fired at the Israeli aeroplane in Mombasa, Kenya in November 2002.[12]

[11] Ron Suskind, *The One Percent Doctrine* (New York: Simon and Schuster, 2006), 146–7.

[12] Jamie McIntyre, 'FBI Warns Portable Missiles a Threat', *CNN.com*, 31 May 2002; 'Kingdom Arrests 7 Al-Qaeda Men', *Arab News*, 19 June 2002; Jamie McIntyre, 'Officials: Man May Have Fired on US Planes', *CNN.com*, 12 June 2002; 'Saudis Arrest al-Qaeda Suspects', *BBC News Online*, 18 June 2002; *al-Hayat*, 19 June 2002; 'Saudis Bar Access to Terror Suspects', *www.cbsnews.com*, 19 June 2002; John J. Lumpkin, 'Evidence Growing that al-Qaida Sponsored Kenya Attacks', *Associated Press*, 3 December 2002.

Many aspects of the Abu Hudhayfa missile plot remain unclear, including the identity of Abu Hudhayfa himself. One might speculate that he is the same as the author of the very important 'Letter from Abu Hudhayfa to Abu Abdallah' from 2000 in which a Saudi-based jihadist advised Usama bin Ladin on a future al-Qaida strategy for the kingdom. However, Abu Hudhayfa is a common nickname which has been used by many militants, including Saudis, in the past. What seems more certain is that the Abu Hudhayfa cell was operating relatively independently of both the al-Nashiri and the al-Uyayri networks. The operation does not feature on the long lists, issued by US and Saudi authorities, of operations allegedly planned by Abd al-Rahim al-Nashiri in 2002. Neither the name Abu Hudhayfa nor the missile episode itself is referenced in the QAP literature. Whatever the truth about the missile plot, the announcement of the arrests on 18 June 2002 was highly significant, because it amounted to the first public admission by Saudi authorities since the mid-1990s that Bin Ladin-linked militants were operating in the kingdom. However, there were much bigger fish in the pond than Abu Hudhayfa.[13]

The flagship of al-Qaida's operational efforts in Saudi Arabia in 2002 was the network headed by Abd al-Rahim al-Nashiri. Al-Nashiri had worked for Bin Ladin since 1997 and had risen to al-Qaida stardom as the mastermind of the USS *Cole* attack in 2000 and a facilitator of several other operations on and around the Arabian Peninsula. In the spring of 2002, al-Nashiri fled from Afghanistan via Pakistan to Yemen, from where he allegedly 'oversaw recruitment and logistics, including the purchase of weapons, and plotted a new wave of attacks in the region'. Judging by the information released by Saudi and US authorities, al-Nashiri was extremely busy in 2002. A biography of al-Nashiri published by the US Defense Department alleged that in 2002 al-Nashiri was involved in a plot to crash an aeroplane into a Western navy vessel in Port Rashid (UAE), a plan to attack warships in the Hormuz Strait and in the Port of Dubai, as well as an operation against oil tankers in the straits of Gibraltar. The biography, which was presumably based on harsh interrogations of al-Nashiri himself, also stated that he was involved in plans to attack 'land-based targets' in Morocco, Qatar and Saudi Arabia.[14]

[13] 'Letter from Abu Hudhayfa to Abu Abdallah [AFGP-2002–003251]' (Department of Defense Harmony Database); 'Biographies of High Value Terrorist Detainees Transferred to the US Naval Base at Guantanamo Bay', *Press Release, Office of the Director of National Intelligence*, 6 September 2006.

[14] Philip Shenon, 'A Major Suspect in Qaeda Attacks is in US Custody', *New York Times*, 22 November 2002; 'Biographies of High Value Terrorist Detainees'.

The precise scope and nature of al-Nashiri's activities inside Saudi Arabia in 2002 are not publicly known, but US and Saudi authorities have mentioned several large-scale plots. In May 2003, Saudi authorities claimed that al-Nashiri had planned several attacks in the kingdom in 2002, notably at the Tabuk air base, the Ra's Tanura oil facility, the Ministries of Interior and Defence, and an expatriate compound in Jidda. American sources have confirmed this extensive list of alleged plots. However, these claims must be treated with caution, because al-Nashiri, like other 'high-value detainees', was tortured by his American captors. Moreover, one might wonder how one man could possibly be involved in such a large number of operations in such a short space of time.[15]

The only conspiracy to have been described in some detail in the media was the alleged plan to attack Ra's Tanura in the late summer of 2002. On 14 October 2002, ABC News reported that US and Saudi intelligence had recently averted a major attack on the Ra's Tanura oil terminal. It quoted intelligence sources as saying that 'several dozen' suspects had been detained, but that the existence of the plot had been kept secret 'because of its potential to embarrass the Saudi government and its possible impact on oil prices'. It later emerged that the suspects were employees at the oil company Aramco. However, the precise nature of the operation was never revealed.[16]

The role of al-Nashiri himself seems to have been that of a supervisor, not a hands-on operative. Given al-Nashiri's status and past record, it is not entirely clear whether he even took the risk of entering the kingdom in this period. We do know that al-Nashiri was in Afghanistan and Pakistan in early 2002, in Yemen in mid-2002 and in the UAE in November 2002. The sheer number, size and geographical span of his alleged operations make it hard to see how al-Nashiri would have been able to spend much time on the detailed planning of attacks inside Saudi Arabia. It follows from this that al-Nashiri must have relied to a large extent on subordinates inside the kingdom. Al-Nashiri's main contacts inside Saudi Arabia in this period seem to have been Khalid al-Juhani and Khalid al-Haj (aka Abu Hazim al-Sha'ir). Outside the kingdom, one of al-Nashiri's closest partners was his old friend Walid

[15] Alan Sipress and Peter Finn, 'Terror Cell had Recent Gun Battle with Police', *Washington Post*, 14 May 2003; 'Biographies of High Value Terrorist Detainees'; 'Verbatim Transcript of Combatant Status Review Tribunal Hearing for ISN 10015' (www.defenselink.mil, 2007).

[16] John McWerthy, 'Pipeline Targeted', *ABCNews.com*, 14 October 2002. Later reports said between seven and ten people were arrested, including an American national of Saudi origin; Tabassum Zakaria, 'American in Qaeda Cell in Oil Co. – Saudi Official', *Reuters*, 17 October 2003.

bin Attash (aka Khallad) who was based in Pakistan. According to US authorities, Khallad moved from Afghanistan to Karachi in early 2002, where he served as the communications link between al-Qaida's senior leadership and the network in Saudi Arabia. He also allegedly 'assisted in the movement of operatives from South and Southeast Asia to the Arabian Peninsula. He is also said to have aided efforts by Khalid Sheikh Muhammad to recruit Saudi hijackers for the al-Qaida plot to hijack airliners to attack Heathrow airport.'[17]

Very interestingly, al-Nashiri seems to have operated more or less independently of Yusuf al-Uyayri and his network. For a start, the QAP literature, which is otherwise very generous with names and descriptions of events, contains virtually no references to Abd al-Rahim al-Nashiri, Walid bin Attash, Khalid al-Juhani or Khalid al-Haj. This suggests that al-Nashiri's men did not interact very much with al-Uyayri's lieutenants, at least not until the spring of 2003.

Another reason to believe that the two networks were independent is that the al-Uyayri network was unaffected by the surveillance of al-Qaida chief of operations Khalid Sheikh Muhammad in late 2002 and early 2003. In the autumn of 2002, a Swiss-led intelligence operation led to the successful identification of Sheikh Muhammad's telephones, which enabled US intelligence to map and track his network of contacts. This operation was instrumental in bringing about the series of important arrests that occurred in this period. On 8 November 2002, Abd al-Rahim al-Nashiri was captured in the United Arab Emirates on his way to Malaysia. In the early morning on 1 March, Khalid Sheikh Muhammad himself was arrested in Rawalpindi. On 29 April 2003, Walid bin Attash was captured in Karachi. This investigation allegedly also led to the identification of al-Qaida cells inside the kingdom. Remarkably, however, it does not seem to have affected the al-Uyayri network to any significant degree.[18]

By all accounts, the separation was entirely intentional and part of a clever two-track strategy for al-Qaida's jihad in Saudi Arabia. Keeping

[17] 'New Al Qaeda Terror Chief in Persian Gulf', *FoxNews.com*, 1 October 2003; 'Biographies of High Value Terrorist Detainees'.

[18] See P. K. Abdul Ghafour, 'Swiss Uncover Al-Qa'ida Cells Planning Attacks in Kingdom', *Arab News*, 13 December 2003; Don Van Natta Jr and Desmond Butler, 'How Tiny Swiss Cellphone Chips Helped Track Global Terror Web', *New York Times*, 4 March 2004. For the details of al-Nashiri's arrest, see Patrick E. Tyler, 'Qaeda Suspect was Taking Flight Training Last Month', *New York Times*, 23 December 2002; Musharraf, *In the Line of Fire*, 240. For al-Attash's arrest, see James Risen, 'A Top Qaeda Member, Tied to 9/11, is Captured', *New York Times*, 1 May 2003; Van Natta Jr and Butler, 'How Tiny Swiss Cellphone Chips Helped Track Global Terror Web'; Scott Shane, 'Inside a 9/11 Mastermind's Interrogation', *New York Times*, 22 June 2008.

al-Nashiri and al-Uyayri apart had several advantages. First, if one network collapsed, there would be a second structure to fall back on. This may well have been what happened after al-Nashiri's capture. US intelligence sources have said that at the time of his capture, al-Nashiri was planning an attack against a US compound in Riyadh for mid-2003. If this is correct, it is reasonable to assume that al-Nashiri was originally charged with directing the 2003 Riyadh operation. Al-Nashiri's capture may have forced the al-Qaida leadership to fall back on the back-up structure. This would also explain why a senior figure such as Khalid al-Juhani was used as a suicide bomber in the 12 May 2003 operation; as a remnant of the now identified al-Nashiri circle he was a long-term liability for the al-Uyayri network.[19]

The second and most important advantage of Bin Ladin's two-track strategy was that it allowed one network to work in the shadow of the other. By all accounts, Western and Saudi intelligence services devoted most of their attention and resources to the more established and high-profile al-Nashiri network, while practically overlooking the activities of al-Uyayri and his men. The hyperactive al-Nashiri thus served as a lightning rod for the scrutiny of intelligence services; he drew attention away from the strategically more significant effort of the mysterious figure long known simply as *al-battar* – 'the Sabre'.

The al-Uyayri network

The backbone of the organisation which subsequently became known as 'al-Qaida on the Arabian Peninsula' was built not by Abd al-Rahim al-Nashiri, but by Yusuf al-Uyayri. In the course of 2002 and early 2003, Yusuf al-Uyayri worked below the radar of Saudi and US intelligence services and succeeded in recruiting, organising and training a formidable number of operatives. In the course of some twelve months he mobilised a militant network whose size stunned most observers when it started to unravel in the summer of 2003.[20]

When al-Uyayri began actively mobilising al-Qaida sympathisers in the kingdom in the spring of 2002, he was not starting from scratch. Al-Uyayri was a veteran jihadist who had been one of Bin Ladin's main assets in the kingdom since about 2000. His Qasimi family background had given him access to key scholars and donors in the Najd and made him the most influential al-Qaida recruiter and fundraiser in Saudi

[19] 'Biographies of High Value Terrorist Detainees'.

[20] Former CIA official Bruce Riedel has confirmed that the QAP campaign took American intelligence services by surprise; see Bruce Riedel, *The Search for Al Qaeda* (Washington, DC: Brookings Institution Press, 2008), 107.

Arabia. In late 2001 and early 2002, he had gained even more respect and authority in the global jihadist community by founding and editing the *al-Nida* website and by authoring a number of very popular and influential ideological texts.

The key to al-Uyayri's success was discretion and patience. He published extensively on the Internet, but never signed his works by his own name. In the Saudi jihadist underground he was referred to simply as 'the Sabre'. Fellow jihadists referred to him posthumously as the 'unknown soldier' (*al-jundi al-majhul*). So discreet was al-Uyayri that, according to American journalist Ron Suskind, the CIA did not know the Sabre's real name until April 2003, and Saudi authorities allegedly briefly arrested and released him in early March 2003 without realising who he was. Al-Uyayri adopted a slow and patient approach to the jihad on the Arabian Peninsula. He discouraged his lieutenants from getting involved in premature plots that might attract unwanted attention. While al-Nashiri's men were trying hard to mount attacks, al-Uyayri was quietly building an organisation.[21]

Although he was killed early in the campaign, on or around 31 May 2003, 'the Sabre' was celebrated in the QAP literature as the spiritual father of the mujahidin on the Arabian Peninsula, and for good reason. Yusuf al-Uyayri was the single most important individual in the Saudi branch of al-Qaida. His entrepreneurship and talent for organisation-building were vital for the emergence of the QAP and the occurrence of the 2003 campaign.

A crucial component of al-Uyayri's organisation-building strategy was information and propaganda. Al-Uyayri made an enormous contribution to the media effort of the global jihadist movement, not only in Saudi Arabia. He developed new propaganda methods and infrastructure, and he produced very influential texts. The initiative which would earn al-Uyayri the most fame within the movement was the establishment of the 'Centre for Islamic Studies and Research' (CISR) which published propaganda material on a website known as *al-Nida* ('the call') – on the website www.alneda.com – from September 2001 onward (the web address would subsequently change frequently). Directed by al-Uyayri himself, the CISR was essentially a Saudi-based media office and virtual publishing house which produced a variety of propaganda material relating to al-Qaida and the global jihadist movement. Judging from both the design and content of the website, Yusuf al-Uyayri was inspired by *Sawt al-Qawqaz*, the website of the Arabs in Chechnya,

[21] '*liqa' ma' ahad al-matlubin al-tisa' 'ashar* (2) [Interview with One of the Nineteen Wanted Men]', *Sawt al-Jihad*, no. 2 (2003): 23; Suskind, *The One Percent Doctrine*, 217–18.

which had existed since the late 1990s. *Al-Nida* presented news about militant Islamist activity around the world, notably in Afghanistan. The website also contained advertisements for books, articles and fatwas by radical sheikhs, notably those of the al-Shuʿaybi school. The CISR also produced its own studies and ideological texts, mostly written by al-Uyayri himself.[22]

Al-Nida quickly became the closest thing there was to an official al-Qaida website. Al-Uyayri was in direct contact with Bin Ladin, who began using *al-Nida* in early 2002 to distribute written and recorded statements. For example, in April 2002, it posted several statements signed *Qaʿidat al-Jihad* which were believed to emanate from the top al-Qaida leadership (although its precise authors have never been identified). It also posted an audio recording by the Kuwaiti al-Qaida spokesman Sulayman Abu Ghayth about the bombing of the Djerba synagogue in Tunisia.[23]

Because of its association with al-Qaida, *al-Nida* received considerable media attention in the West and became the target of Internet hackers. In a curious development, al-Uyayri lost the domain name www.alneda.com on 12 July 2002 to an American Internet pornographer named Jon David Messner, who had used an Internet service called *Snapback* to 'hijack' the site after the Internet provider realised al-Uyayri's contact details were fictitious. Within a few weeks, the CISR was back online on another internet address, www.drasat.com. In late 2002 and early 2003, it came under increasingly heavy fire, but survived by moving between Internet addresses.[24]

The CISR was very important for the evolution of the global jihadist community in Saudi Arabia for two principal reasons. First, it helped spread global jihadist propaganda and raise awareness of the global jihadist cause in Islamist circles. Along with discussion forums such as *al-Sahat* and *al-Ansar*, the CISR website relayed information about al-Qaida's activities at a time when anti-Americanism was rising steeply and at a time when many of the returnees from Afghanistan had lost touch with their old friends. Second, the CISR served as the nursery for the people who would later run the QAP's media activities under the name *Sawt al-Jihad*. Isa al-Awshan, Abd al-Aziz al-Anzi and other key

[22] Muhammad al-Shafiʿi, *'usuliyyun: al-ʿuyayri kan al-mas'ul ʿan mawqaʿ "al-nida"' al-intirniti al-natiq bi-ism "al-qaʿida"* [Fundamentalists: Al-Uyayri was in Charge of the 'al-Nida' Website, al-Qaʿida's Mouthpiece]', *al-Sharq al-Awsat*, 4 June 2003.

[23] Hegghammer, *Dokumentasjon*, 167–70 and 173–8.

[24] See declaration on www.alneda.com. See also Mike Boettcher, 'Pornographer Says He Hacked al Qaeda', *CNN.com*, 9 August 2002; Patrick Di Justo, 'How Al-Qaida Site was Hijacked', *Wired.com*, 10 August 2002.

members of the QAP's media committee had all worked together with Yusuf al-Uyayri in the CISR.[25]

In addition to administering the website, Yusuf al-Uyayri was also a very active contributor. His ideological production between September 2001 and May 2003 was remarkable, in quantity as well as quality. Al-Uyayri wrote about a wide range of topics in this period, but most significant were his so-called 'strategic studies' about the US encroachment in the Gulf region and the need to resist the American presence with a sophisticated military strategy. Three of his works proved particularly influential. The first was the 100-page booklet called *The Truth of the New Crusade* which he wrote in the course of a few weeks in September 2001. This text became widely read in jihadist circles, so much so that Bin Ladin himself mentioned it in his interview with al-Jazeera in October 2001. In the autumn of 2002, al-Uyayri co-wrote his arguably most influential work, *The Crusade on Iraq Series*. Published as a series of thirteen articles on the CISR website, this text was a strategic study of the upcoming Iraq war and how the mujahidin could best resist the Americans. Third was *The Future of Iraq and the Arabian Peninsula after the Fall of Baghdad*, written in April 2003 as a follow-up to the *Crusade on Iraq Series*.[26]

Al-Uyayri was one of the founders of the genre of strategic studies in modern jihadi literature, a genre characterised by its secular, pragmatic and objective style. In the anonymously authored study entitled *Iraqi Jihad: Hopes and Dangers*, which became known for having possibly inspired the March 2004 Madrid bombings, al-Uyayri is cited as a key intellectual inspiration.[27]

Al-Uyayri's works were also very important for the formation of the QAP because they articulated a strategic rationale for the need to expel the Americans from the Gulf and the Arabian Peninsula. Al-Uyayri brought the focus of the global jihadist movement back to its original cause, namely the US military presence in Saudi Arabia. Al-Uyayri also contributed numerous writings on military tactics and training. He

[25] See Majid al-Qahtani, '*'isa bin sa'd bin muhammad al 'awshan: faris al-'ilam al-jihadi* [Isa bin Sa'd bin Muhammad Al Awshan: The Knight of Jihadi Media]', *Sawt al-Jihad*, no. 30 (2007) and '*al-'ayn al-thalith: al-qissa al-kamila*'.

[26] Yusuf al-Uyayri, '*haqiqat al-harb al-salibiyya al-jadida* [The Truth of the New Crusade]' (www.alneda.com: 2001); Yusuf al-Uyayri, '*silsilat al-harb al-salibiyya 'ala al-'iraq* [The Crusade on Iraq Series]' (www.drasat.com, 2002); Yusuf al-Uyayri, '*mustaqbal al-'iraq wa'l-jazira al-'arabiyya ba'd suqut baghdad* [The Future of Iraq and the Arabian Peninsula after the Fall of Baghdad]' (www.tawhed.ws, 2003).

[27] Brynjar Lia and Thomas Hegghammer, 'Jihadi Strategic Studies: The Alleged Policy Study Preceding the Madrid Bombings', *Studies in Conflict and Terrorism* 27, no. 5 (2004).

placed great emphasis on the need for military training, which is why his successors named their training camps and their magazine for military affairs after him 'Camp of the Sabre' (*mu'askar al-battar*). He knew that to build an effective military organisation, ideology and propaganda were not enough.[28]

Another key component of al-Uyayri's organisation-building effort was therefore recruitment. Al-Uyayri established a relatively centralised and hierarchical recruitment infrastructure in 2002 and early 2003. The formation of the al-Uyayri network occurred in three distinct phases, each characterised by different recruitment dynamics. The first phase, from about May 2002 till about August 2002, saw the spontaneous formation of a number of relatively independent cells in different parts of the country, though mainly in Riyadh and the Hijaz. These cells typically consisted of one or two entrepreneurial figures who had recently returned from Afghanistan with Bin Ladin's orders fresh in mind and who encouraged friends to join in. Some of these entrepreneurs, such as Faysal al-Dukhayyil, Turki al-Mutayri or Mit'ib al-Muhayyani, would later become important mid-level commanders or regional cell leaders in the QAP. However, in this early phase there was limited communication between the groups because the returnees had been separated on their way back from Afghanistan.[29]

In the second phase, from about September till about December 2002, al-Uyayri and his men established contact with the proto-cells which had formed in different parts of the country. The purpose was to make the latter coalesce into a larger organisation and to avoid premature offensives which might endanger the jihadist community as a whole. One of the best illustrations of this coordination effort is found in the martyr biography of Faysal al-Dukhayyil:

> Before Ramadan that year [i.e. before November 2002], [Faysal al-Dukhayyil] was preparing an operation, and he had conducted surveillance of some sites which he intended to strike. However, before the operation, God wanted that he meet Turki al-Dandani. Abu Ayub [Faysal al-Dukhayyil] suggested that he take part in the operation, but al-Dandani asked him to wait and suspend [the operation]. Then Abu Ayub said: 'There is no point in waiting – the personnel is ready, the surveillance is completed, so all we need to do is strike.' Then al-Dandani informed him that there was a rapid coordination effort going on to

[28] See e.g. Yusuf al-Uyayri, '*al-riyada al-badaniyya qabl al-jihad* [Physical Exercise before Jihad]' (www.qa3edoon.com, undated); Yusuf al-Uyayri, '*thawabit 'ala darb al-jihad* [Guidelines for Jihad Training]' (www.tawhed.ws, undated); Yusuf al-Uyayri, '*la takun ma' al-'aduw diddna! risala 'amma 'an amn al-ma'lumat* [Don't Help the Enemy Against Us: General Note on Information Security]' (www.drasat.com, 2002?).

[29] See al-Dukhayyil, '*faysal bin 'abd al-rahman al-dukhayyil*'; '*turki bin fuhayd al-mutayri*'; al-Makki, '*mit'ib al-muhayyani*'.

form an organisation for jihad on the Peninsula and that it was better to unite the efforts. The latter [al-Dandani] was in contact with Abu Hajir [Abd al-Aziz al-Muqrin] and informed him about the situation. Then Abu Hajir asked to meet Abu Ayub to know more about his work and coordinate with him. So they met and merged into one group.[30]

Among al-Uyayri's most important recruiters was Abd al-Aziz al-Muqrin, a veteran jihadist who would later become the leader of the QAP. In 2002 and early 2003, al-Muqrin and his assistant Turki al-Mutayri travelled 'to every corner of the Peninsula' to enlist new cells. Another important networker was Ahmad al-Dukhayyil, a preacher who attracted a number of followers through his fiery sermons in various small Riyadh mosques in the summer and autumn of 2002.[31]

The main vehicle for al-Qaida's recruitment efforts was the Afghan alumni networks. Al-Uyayri and his men targeted the community of returnees from Afghanistan very systematically. Recruitment to the QAP thus remained largely restricted to the Arab Afghan community, their acquaintances and relatives. Al-Uyayri knew that these people were the most likely to join his controversial project. He also knew that the internal loyalty in these networks was strong and that many friends had been separated on the way back from Afghanistan. Several biographies recount the pleasure of reuniting with old friends in the militant underground.[32]

The third phase of the building of the QAP lasted from January to May 2003 and was characterised by the consolidation of the central leadership and by the transition from simple networking to more active recruitment. Recruitment in this phase focused on a broader target audience than in the earlier phase. Until late 2002, the al-Uyayri network attracted mainly the most able and most motivated of the recent returnees from Afghanistan. In early 2003, it sought to recruit other Saudi radicals who had thus far remained passive. Recruitment was also delegated to the various regional cell leaders, while the top leadership could focus on training and logistics.

The third main component of the Sabre's organisation-building effort was the training infrastructure. Al-Uyayri, like other top al-Qaida strategists, had realised that training was crucial for any serious

[30] al-Dukhayyil, '*faysal bin 'abd al-rahman al-dukhayyil*', 14.

[31] '*turki bin fuhayd al-mutayri*'; Dhayyab al-Utaybi, '*abd al-rahman bin abdallah al-harbi* [Abd al-Rahman bin Abdallah al-Harbi]', *Sawt al-Jihad*, no. 26 (2004): 12. For more on al-Muqrin, see Norman Cigar, *Al-Qaida's Doctrine for Insurgency: Abd al-Aziz al-Muqrin's 'A Practical Course for Guerrilla War'* (Washington, DC: Potomac Books, 2008).

[32] al-Nashmi, '*fahd bin samran al-sa'idi*'.

military project. He understood that training camps not only improved the recruits' physical shape and technical know-how, but also generated organisational coherence and strong social bonds between recruits. Thus in 2002 and early 2003, Yusuf al-Uyayri worked systematically to set up a training infrastructure inside Saudi Arabia.[33]

The earliest indications of the existence of such camps came in February 2003 with reports that Saudi police had discovered two training camps with adjacent weapons caches, one in Asfan between Jidda and Medina and another in Namas south of Ta'if. In January 2004, news agencies reported that Saudi authorities had discovered a number of camps outside Saudi cities. Around the same date, captured QAP militants appeared on Saudi television repenting and describing their experiences as militants. They said recruits were brought to safe houses in Riyadh where they learned to handle and clean guns, before being taken out to the desert for training. Some also went to Mecca, where they would spend three or four days in a camp learning to assemble and fire weapons with the militants.[34]

These reports were later confirmed by the QAP literature, which is full of references to training in this period. For example, one biography explains that Abd al-Muhsin al-Shabanat 'joined the mujahid Abu Ayub Faysal al-Dukhayyil immediately after the al-Shifa incident [on 16 November 2002] and trained with him for a while. Then he trained with Abu Hajir and took the executive course with him. He learned a lot about military sciences and the art of war in a short period.' Other accounts mention people being appointed as instructors; Talal al-Anbari, for example, 'moved to the Camp of the Sabre to supervise military exercises, and the brothers benefited greatly from his expertise'.[35]

The best evidence of training is in the QAP's many film productions. The film called *Martyrs of the Confrontations* from early December 2003 showed Yusuf al-Uyayri addressing a crowd with subtitles saying 'during one of the training sessions in the Arabian Peninsula'. The end of the film included extensive footage of indoor military training sessions inside a house described as 'The Amana Safe House' (Amana is

[33] See e.g. Abd al-Qadir Bin Abd al-Aziz, *risalat al-'umda fi i'dad al-'udda* [Treatise on the Pillar of Military Preparation] (www.tawhed.ws, 1988?) and al-Suri, *da'wat al-muqawama*.

[34] *al-Islah*, no. 355 (24 February 2003); 'Saudis Discover al-Qaida Training Camps', *Associated Press*, 15 January 2004; Dominic Evans, 'Saudi Militants Shown Repenting on State TV', *Reuters*, 12 January 2004.

[35] Al Awshan, '*khalid bin 'abdallah al-subayt*', 27; '*shuhada' al-muwajahat* [Martyrs of the Confrontations]' (Al-Sahhab Foundation for Media Production, 2003); Turki al-Mutayri, '*'abd al-muhsin al-shabanat: shahid fi yawm 'id* [Abd al-Muhsin al-Shabanat: Id Martyr]', *Sawt al-Jihad*, no. 23 (2004): 20; al-Najdi, '*talal al-anbari*'.

a neighbourhood in north Riyadh). The pictures showed men in black combat gear exercising, playing with weapons and practising indoor combat manoeuvres. The film *Badr of Riyadh* issued in February 2004 also contained long recordings of indoor military training sessions inside a building described as the 'Camp of the Sabre'. The first pictures of outdoor training appeared in March 2006 in a film about the life of QAP operative Fahd al-Juwayr. It showed recruits going through an obstacle course at a desert location also described as the 'Camp of the Sabre'. The most revealing pictures appeared in the film called *The Quds Squadron* which appeared in June 2006. It showed extensive indoor training activities, notably footage of a man assembling a bomb device, accompanied by the following screen caption: 'assembling and experimenting with explosives – Battar Camp'. The film also showed pictures of outdoor training. One clip showed a deserted pick-up truck being blown up for practice. At another point in the film, a masked man described as Abd al-Aziz al-Muqrin was shown addressing a group of ten people at night-time. All these videos were most likely recorded in 2003 or 2004.[36]

The camp infrastructure was based on the template of the Afghan camps in Saudi Arabia. Practically all aspects about the Saudi camps, physical as well as social, echoed the atmosphere of al-Qaida's Afghan camps. The camps had symbolic names, were led by appointed instructors and offered semi-formal courses in spartan conditions. Given the many references to the Afghan training camps in the QAP literature, it is reasonable to assume that the camps served not only a military purpose, but also a social one, namely to satisfy the nostalgia of the Arab Afghan community. Al-Uyayri was essentially offering a 'little piece of Afghanistan' inside Saudi Arabia.

The total number and precise location of the camps are not clear. The descriptions in the QAP literature are too vague to provide a detailed overview of the training infrastructure and its evolution. What we know is that by late 2002 it was elaborate and organised. In November 2002, recruits could take 'courses' and competent members could be 'appointed as instructors'. It also seems clear that the most extensive and sophisticated training took place in the first four months of 2003. After May 2003, the police crackdowns made it much more difficult to organise training sessions, at least in the open air.[37]

[36] '*shuhada' al-muwajahat*'; 'The Battle of Istirahat al Amana' took place on 10 August 2003; '*badr al-riyadh*'; '*dima' lan tadi' – al-juz' al-awwal* [Blood Not Spilt in Vain – Part One]' (Sawt al-Jihad Foundation for Media Production, 2006); '*sariyat al-quds* [The Quds Squadron]' (Sahhab Foundation for Media Production, 2006).

[37] al-Mutayri, ''*abd al-muhsin al-shabanat*', al-Najdi, '*talal al-anbari*'.

The fourth component of Yusuf al-Uyayri's organisation-building project was the accumulation of material resources, in particular safe houses, weapons and money. In the beginning, militants would simply meet in their own homes, but they soon moved to establish a network of safe houses. They rented apartments and houses under fake names, using either forged papers or stolen ID cards (such cards were typically stolen from petrol stations, where people leave cards as deposits). Some of the houses were used as living quarters for militants. Some jihadists lived together for up to six months prior to the beginning of the campaign. While most militants had left their families and gone underground, some brought their wives to stay in the safe house, in order not to awaken the suspicion of neighbours. Other houses were not used at all, but rather kept as a reserve hideout in case of an emergency.[38]

Most of the early infrastructure seems to have been located in the Najd and the Hijaz, and the seemingly most important safe houses were discovered in the cities of Riyadh, Mecca, Medina and in the Qasim countryside. However, cells would later be discovered in a wide variety of locations from Jizan in the south to Ha'il in the north, Jidda in the west to Dammam in the east. The crackdown in the spring and summer of 2003 uncovered a number of apartments, houses and farms that were being used as hideouts by groups of sometimes up to twenty to thirty militants. In 2006, a Saudi security source said that since the outbreak of the campaign, police had dismantled twelve major safe houses in Riyadh (4), Hijaz (3), Qasim (2), Eastern Province (2) and Najran (1) respectively.[39]

Another essential commodity was of course weapons. In 2002 and 2003, returnees from Afghanistan were amassing explosives and weapons of all calibres. Yusuf al-Uyayri appointed 'preparation groups' (*majmu'at al-tajhiz*) that were tasked with weapons acquisition. For example, a *Sawt al-Jihad* biography explains that 'Mit'ib [al-Muhayyani] and Talal [al-Anbari] worked in one of the preparation groups and were able to bring a large weapons delivery to the brothers.' In early 2003, another militant, Khalid al-Subayt, 'was busy collecting and buying weapons'. Saudi security sources have revealed that the QAP used four main routes to smuggle personnel, weapons and equipment

[38] 'Two Saudi Detainees Speak on "Illegitimate" Methods Used by "Terrorist Cells"', *al-Arabiya Television (from World News Connection)*, 2 October 2004; '*'ali al-ma'badi al-harbi*'; author's interview with Mansur al-Turki.

[39] Nawaf Obaid, 'Remnants of al-Qaeda in Saudi Arabia: Current Assessment' (Presentation at the Council of Foreign Relations, New York, 2006). In the QAP campaign, arrests were made in and near the cities of Jizan, Abha, Baha, Ta'if, Mecca, Jidda, Medina, Yanbu, Tabuk, Sakaka, Hail, Burayda, Unayza, Zulfi, Riyadh, Hofuf, Dammam and others.

in and out of the country. The precise location of these routes is not publicly known, but the main source for weapons was no doubt Yemen. With its history of civil war, weak state, tribal weapons culture and maritime accessibility, Yemen has long been the illegal weapons hub of the Arabian Peninsula and much of the Middle East. The flow of illegal weapons across the southern border region of Ghat had been a problem for decades, and practically all Saudi militants since Juhayman had obtained their weapons from Yemen. Border guards regularly seize large quantities of arms and explosives at the Saudi–Yemeni border. In 2002 alone, they allegedly seized 176,000 sticks of dynamite and 4.1 million rounds of ammunition.[40]

As already mentioned, the quantities of arms and explosives discovered by police in mid-2003 stunned most observers. Although specific figures from the Saudi Interior Ministry must always be taken with a pinch of salt, we may note that in January 2004 the police said that since May 2003 they had seized a total of 24 tons of explosive materials, 300 rocket-propelled grenades, 430 hand grenades, 300 explosive belts and 674 detonators. Informed diplomats in Riyadh have said the quantities discovered in the summer of 2003 were enough to equip 'an army of several thousand men'.[41]

In fact the quantities were so large that it is unlikely they were acquired by the al-Uyayri network alone in just twelve months. Weapons were widely available on the black market for purchase in small quantities, but large shipments were difficult to come by in 2002, as even arms dealers admitted. Two factors account for the mysteriously large weapons discoveries. One is that jihadists had been collecting weapons for many years, perhaps since as early as 1994 according to some sources. Second, not all the weapons belonged to the militants. Some of the weapons caches, especially the buried containers uncovered in mid-2003, seem to have belonged to professional arms dealers and not the QAP.[42]

There has been periodic speculation that the QAP got some of its weapons from corrupt elements of the Saudi security services, but there is no substantial evidence to this effect. With weapons so widely

[40] al-Najdi, '*talal al-anbari*', 52; Al Awshan, '*khalid bin 'abdallah al-subayt*', 27; Obaid, 'Remnants of al-Qaeda'; 'Paper: Saudis Seize Arms at Yemen Border Every Hour', *Reuters*, 21 August 2003; Stephen Ulph, 'Shifting Sands: Al-Qaeda and Tribal Gun-Running along the Yemeni Frontier', *Terrorism Monitor* 2, no. 7 (2004); Ibrahim al-Mutawa, 'Smuggling on Saudi–Yemeni Border', *Arab News*, 15 February 2003.

[41] 'Terror Hunt Nets Huge Quantities of Explosives', *Arab News*, 13 January 2004.

[42] al-Mutawa, 'Smuggling on Saudi–Yemeni Border'; author's interviews with Faris bin Huzzam and Sa'ud al-Sarhan; Fahd Frayyan, 'Saudi Arabia Says Terror Plot Foiled, 16 Detained', *Reuters*, 21 July 2003; 'Saudi Authorities Report Terror Arrests', *Associated Press*, 20 October 2003.

available in Yemen, and with the QAP's weapons caches already too big for the number of recruits, it is difficult to see why they would take the risk of trading weapons with national guardsmen or police officers. However, there are indications of the existence of a black market for army and police equipment such as uniforms. Several of the QAP's later operations, such as the Khobar shooting spree in May 2004 or the kidnapping of the American engineer Paul Johnson in Riyadh in June 2004, were carried out by operatives wearing National Guard or police uniforms. Such markets exist in many countries and need not be indicative of al-Qaida infiltration of these institutions.[43]

For all of the above-mentioned activities, money was essential. Whenever a strategic safe house was discovered or a senior operative arrested, stacks of cash were never far away. In 2002 and 2003, al-Uyayri and his lieutenants clearly had access to significant amounts of money. Several QAP members are described in their martyr biographies as having been involved in collecting funds in 2002 and 2003. Unfortunately there is not much public information about the financial sources of the QAP. Some of the money came from the exploitation of the Zakat system. Militants would place collection boxes at mosques to solicit donations from unknowing benefactors. They also obtained money from private donors who were tricked into believing they were giving money for a different cause, such as 'Iraqi families'.[44]

By the spring of 2003, al-Uyayri's organisation-building efforts were starting to bear fruit. Arms and money were piling up, safe houses were ready and camps were churning out recruits. As one militant noted at the time, 'the situation on the Arabian Peninsula is like a volcano that can erupt at any moment'.[45]

Launching the jihad

The precise details of the decision-making behind the launch of the 12 May attack are not known, because we lack the testimony of the most

[43] Peter Finn, 'Al Qaeda Arms Traced to Saudi National Guard', *Washington Post*, 19 May 2003; 'Police Dragnet Yields 34; Army Uniforms Seized', *Arab News*, 3 April 2007; Michael Knights, 'The Khobar Rampage, May 2004' (JTIC Terrorism Case Study (Jane's Information Group), 2005); '*qissat al-asir al-amriki muhandis al-abatshi bul marshal* [The Story of the American Captive, the Apache Engineer Paul Marshall]', *Sawt al-Jihad*, no. 19 (2004).

[44] See e.g. Al Awshan, '*khalid bin abdallah al-subayt*', and al-Anzi, ''*abd al-latif bin hamad al-khudayri*'; Abd al-Rahman al-Muttawa, '[Prince Nayif Urges Citizens not to Help Kill Innocent People Unknowingly by Paying Contributions to Suspicious Boxes]', *al-Sharq al-Awsat*, 22 July 2003; Fahd al-Frayyan, 'Saudi Arabia Says Terror Plot Foiled, 16 Detained', *Reuters*, 21 July 2003; Mahmoud Ahmad, 'Al-Qaeda Operatives are an Ignorant Lot, Say Former Members', *Arab News*, 3 October 2003.

[45] Al Awshan, '*khalid bin abdallah al-subayt*', 27.

important actors. Yusuf al-Uyayri, Turki al-Dandani, Khalid al-Haj and Abd al-Aziz al-Muqrin all died before they could be interrogated, and Usama bin Ladin, Ayman al-Zawahiri and Sayf al-Adl are still on the loose at the current time of writing. Moreover, the jihadist literature is practically silent on the specifics of this decision-making process. Hence almost everything that is known about this process comes from unverifiable intelligence sources.

At the time of the launch of the campaign, the al-Uyayri network consisted of an operational core of some 50 people and a wider network of between 300 and 700 people who were prepared to take up arms. However, the organisational structure was not fully developed. It has been claimed that al-Uyayri presided over a structure of five autonomous cells in this period. However, the five-cell structure was just a plan which was never actually implemented. At this time, the al-Uyayri network was best described as a loose cluster of cells. The militants did not even have a proper name: they referred to themselves simply as the 'mujahidin on the Arabian Peninsula', and it would take another six months until the name 'al-Qaida on the Arabian Peninsula' was first used. None of the media for which the QAP would later become famous were in place either – the magazine *Sawt al-Jihad* was not launched until September 2003 and *Mu'askar al-Battar* a few months later.[46]

The underdeveloped nature of the organisation strongly suggests that the campaign was launched prematurely. This hypothesis is further strengthened by reports about an alleged polemic between Yusuf al-Uyayri and the central al-Qaida leadership in the spring of 2003 over the timing of the campaign. As the Saudi security consultant Nawaf Obaid explained:

> Even in Afghanistan there were disagreements among the leadership regarding the timing and potential targets of the attack. Al-Ayeri maintained that al Qaeda members were not yet ready and lacked the time, resources and necessary supply routes from Yemen. Furthermore, recruitment proved to be more difficult than expected. Ayman al-Zawahiri ... dismissed these objections,

[46] These estimates are the author's own, based on an overall assessment of QAP biographies, a reading of the texts in *Sawt al-Jihad*, and author's interviews with Saudi and Western security officials. Obaid and Cordesman put the number of Saudi al-Qaida members at 500–600. Of these, roughly 250 were diehards; Obaid and Cordesman, *Al-Qaeda in Saudi Arabia*, 20. In late May 2003, Prince Bandar estimated that a core of 50 Afghanistan veterans had recruited up to 300 more people; see Don Van Natta Jr and Neil MacFarquhar, 'Al Qaeda Still Plotting in Saudi Arabia, Officials Say', *New York Times*, 20 May 2003; author's interview with Nawaf Obaid, Riyadh, January 2007; Anthony H. Cordesman and Nawaf E. Obaid, *National Security in Saudi Arabia: Threats, Responses, and Challenges* (Westport, CT: Praeger Security International, 2005), 112.

> arguing that the time was right for operations to begin. Al-Zawahiri made the case that attacking soft targets and Americans (who would flee the kingdom) would paralyze and consequently topple the Saudi Government ... Abdul Kareem al-Majati, a Moroccan national and main deputy and general strategist of al-Ayeri agreed with his commander's assessment, but was overruled by Bin Laden. Soon after, Majati left Saudi Arabia with the belief that attacking prematurely was a huge miscalculation and would compromise the existence and establishment of future al Qaeda cells.[47]

A European intelligence official and an American diplomat interviewed by this author have independently confirmed the broad lines of this account. They added – independently – that the debate also involved Saudi-based clerics and private sponsors who threatened to cut off funding to al-Qaida if an all-out campaign was launched on Saudi soil.[48]

Saudi sources have alleged that Iran-based al-Qaida operatives played a crucial role in the planning of the 12 May attack. Less than a week after the attack, fingers of blame were pointed at the al-Qaida leader Sayf al-Adl, who was known to be based in Iran. According to a September 2003 article in the *Washington Post*, Saudi authorities 'obtained a trove of evidence – phones, computer hard drives, documents and cash – that pointed back to Iran and [Sayf al-] Adel. In addition, one of al Qaeda's local leaders in Saudi Arabia, Ali Faqasi Ghamdi, turned himself in and confessed that Adel and his associates were behind the bombings.' Other sources said Bin Ladin's son Sa'd, who was also believed to be based in Iran, had placed phone calls to the cell members two days prior to the 12 May attacks. The Saudis allegedly reacted by dispatching two delegations to Iran, demanding that the Iranians hand over key Saudi al-Qaida members and that Sayf al-Adl be returned to Egypt. Iran refused the requests but allegedly placed the al-Qaida group under a form of house arrest.[49]

Unfortunately we do not know exactly when the above-mentioned debates took place or when the orders to launch the campaign were issued. Nawaf Obaid has said that the order and subsequent debate happened as late as in April 2003. However, the premature explosion involving Fahd al-Sa'idi on 18 March 2003 suggests the order may have

[47] Cordesman and Obaid, *National Security in Saudi Arabia*, 113; Craig Whitlock, 'Al Qaeda Shifts its Strategy in Saudi Arabia', *Washington Post*, 19 December 2004.

[48] Author's interview with European intelligence source, March 2006; author's interview with US diplomat, May 2006.

[49] Dana Priest and Susan Schmidt, 'Al Qaeda Figure Tied to Riyadh Blasts', *Washington Post*, 18 May 2003; Peter Finn and Susan Schmidt, 'Iran, al Qaeda and Iraq', *Washington Post*, 6 September 2003; John R. Bradley, 'Clues Tie al Qaeda to Saudi Bombings', *Washington Times*, 18 August 2003.

been given even earlier. Usama bin Ladin's statement on 16 February 2003, the so-called 'Sermon on the First Day of Id al-Adha', has been interpreted by some as a signal to launch the campaign.[50]

There are indications that the decision to strike may have been taken even earlier. Former CIA director George Tenet noted in his memoirs that the debate within al-Qaida over conducting attacks in Saudi Arabia dated back to the autumn of 2002. Tenet further wrote that after the debate, Bin Ladin instructed Abu Hazim al-Sha'ir (Khalid al-Haj) to move forward with the attacks at any price. Another official US document stated that when Abd al-Rahim al-Nashiri was captured in early November 2002 he had been planning a major attack on a Riyadh compound for the summer of 2003. Moreover, in late November 2002, the newspaper *al-Quds al-Arabi* reported that an al-Qaida-affiliated website had posted a message allegedly written by Bin Ladin urging the 'People of the Peninsula' to 'grab your weapon' and prepare for an upcoming 'ordeal'. The message, whose authenticity has not been confirmed, had allegedly been brought from Afghanistan to Saudi Arabia by a senior mujahid who had recently returned from Afghanistan.[51]

Given that we do not know exactly when the order was issued, it is difficult to identify the factors which informed the tactical timing of the campaign. There are at least five possible explanations. One possibility is that al-Qaida wanted to capitalise on the high levels of anti-Americanism in the kingdom following the Iraq war. Another theory is that the arrest of Khalid Sheikh Muhammad in February 2003 and Walid bin Attash in April led al-Qaida to speed up preparations for fear that its networks in the kingdom would be compromised. A third possibility is that the attacks were timed to coincide with the May visit of senior US officials to Saudi Arabia. Fourth, the central al-Qaida leadership may have wanted to coordinate the Riyadh operation with the Casablanca operation which was in the planning around the same time (and occurred on 17 May 2003). A final factor may have been sheer impatience. We know that Ayman al-Zawahiri and

[50] Author's interview with Nawaf Obaid. The statement opened with the so-called 'sword verse' of the Qur'an, namely 'When the sacred months are over, kill the idolaters wherever you find them.' In 2003 the end of the so-called 'sacred months' (Dhu al-Hijja, Muharram, Safar and Rabi al-Awwal) fell at the end of May, and this has brought suggestions that the text was a form of official announcement of the launch of the jihad. There is evidence of at least one militant who interpreted Bin Ladin's February declaration in this way; see Khalil al-Makki, '*sami al-luhaybi: 'azimat al-rijal*', *Sawt al-Jihad*, no. 6 (2003).

[51] Tenet, *At the Center of the Storm*, 248; 'Biographies of High Value Terrorist Detainees'; '*bin ladin fi risala khassa ila ahl al-jazira: ihmilu al-silah li'l-difa' 'an 'aradikum* [Bin Ladin in a Special Message to the "People of the Peninsula": Grab your Weapon and Defend your Honour]', *al-Quds al-Arabi*, 28 November 2002.

other Egyptians in the central al-Qaida leadership had been pushing for operations inside the kingdom for some time. It may have become difficult for Bin Ladin to continue to postpone the attack. The reason for the precise timing may not be of crucial importance; what matters is that the strategic decision to attack had been taken in early 2002, long before the Iraq war.[52]

Another interesting but unsolved question about the 12 May operation is whether it was announced in advance. On 7 April and on 10 May 2003, the magazine *al-Majalla* published messages from a certain Abu Muhammad al-Ablaj, an alleged al-Qaida spokesman, warning about upcoming attacks in Saudi Arabia. The 7 April report quoted al-Ablaj as saying that al-Qaida 'had finished preparations to attack the Saudi regime and the rear of the US Army'. The 10 May report said 'al Qaeda will move the battle to the Gulf and Arabian Peninsula, and air bases, warships and military bases will be targeted'. These messages proved conspicuously prescient, although they emerged during the Iraq crisis, when such threats were very common, and the specific targets mentioned were not attacked in the end.[53]

The tactical aspects about the operation are somewhat better known. The targets were carefully chosen to fit the QAP's declared anti-American agenda. Compounds were seen by radicals as symbols of Christianity and moral corruption. One treatise described the compounds as containing 'churches and bars, mixed nightclubs and swimming pools, basically all kinds of infidelity and debauchery'. Moreover, the QAP argued, compounds could not really be considered Saudi territory, but rather part of America. This allowed QAP ideologues to dismiss the objection by moderate scholars that foreigners carry Saudi visas and are thus formal guests who should be protected. The specific compounds were chosen because of their association with American defence contractors. The Vinnell compound may have been chosen to echo the

[52] Joel Brinkley, 'Saudis Blame US and its Role in Iraq for Rise of Terror', *New York Times*, 14 October 2004; 'Rumsfeld, Powell, and Spencer to visit Saudi Arabia', *ArabicNews.com*, 29 April 2003; Kathy Gannon, 'Al-Qaeda Claims Riyadh Attacks', *Associated Press*, 22 June 2003.

[53] *al-Majalla*, 7 April 2003; Mahmud Khalil, '*al-qa'ida: ajrayna taghyirat fi haykaliyyat al-tanzim wa natafawwaq 'ala al-amrikiyyin istratijiyya* [Al-Qaida: We Have Made Changes in the Organisational Structure and We Prevail over the Americans Strategically]', *al-Majalla*, 10–17 May 2003. Immediately after the 12 May attack, al-Ablaj sent a message assuming responsibility for the bombing; see Mahmud Khalil, '*al-qa'ida: hadafna irbak amn al-khalij* ["Al-Qaida": Our Aim is to Undermine Security in the Gulf]', *al-Majalla*, 18–24 May 2003. A week later, al-Ablaj issued new threats which were not followed up; see Mahmud Khalil, '*al-qa'ida tutliq silsilat tahdidat jadida wa miyah al-gharb muhaddada bi-tasmim* [Al-Qaida Issues a Series of New Threats and the West's Water is Threatened with Poisoning]', *al-Majalla*, 25–31 May 2003.

1995 Riyadh bombing. As Abd al-Aziz al-Muqrin later wrote, 'we struck Vinnell in 1995 and we did it again in 2003'.[54]

The main coordinator of the attack was al-Uyayri's close associate Turki al-Dandani. Al-Dandani supervised a team of fourteen attackers divided into three teams led by Muhammad al-Shihri, Khalid al-Juhani and Hazim al-Kashmiri respectively. The operation involved five vehicles, two of which were used to pave the way for the bomb vehicles. Despite early claims by authorities that all bombers died, it later emerged that several, perhaps as many as six of the attackers, actually survived and escaped from the scene.[55]

The operation was initially supposed to take place a little later in the month, but it was moved forward due to the disruptive 6 May raid. The composition of the teams was also changed right before the attack. Younger candidates were scrapped for more experienced personnel at the last minute. From the point of view of the survival of the organisation, this may seem strange, but it was most likely motivated by the desire to ensure a successful first operation or 'opening shot'. And successful it was: the three bombs went off within minutes of each other, with devastating effect: 35 people were killed and over 160 wounded.[56]

Al-Uyayri's men had embarked on an extremely ambitious and completely unprecedented project. Who were these people and what drove them?

[54] '*ghazwat al-hadi 'ashar min rabi' al-awwal*', 46; Michael Knights, 'The East Riyadh Operation, May 2003' (JTIC Terrorism Case Study (Jane's Information Group), 2005); al-Muqrin, *dawrat al-tanfidh*, 39.

[55] '*turki al-dandani: rahil al-abtal* [Turki al-Dandani: The Departed Hero]', *Sawt al-Jihad*, no. 8 (2004); Knights, 'The East Riyadh Operation'. See also Abd al-Aziz al-Ghamidi, '*min abtal ghazwat sharq al-riyadh* [Heroes from the East Riyadh Raid]', *Sawt al-Jihad*, no. 22 (2004); al-Nashmi, '*khalid al-baghdadi (abu ayub al-najdi)*'; and '*wasaya al-abtal*'. See also '*ghazwat al-hadi 'ashar min rabi' al-awwal*', 47.

[56] Abu Yasir al-Khalidi, '*nasir al-sayyari: batal badr al-riyadh* [Nasir al-Sayyari: The Hero of the Badr of Riyadh]', *Sawt al-Jihad*, no. 25 (2004); Cordesman and Obaid, *National Security in Saudi Arabia*, 269. There have been conflicting reports on the number of fatalities and their nationalities. A detailed study by *Jane's* analyst Michael Knights concluded that the dead included eight Americans, seven Saudis, three Filipinos, two Australians, two Jordanians, one Briton, one Irishman and one Swiss citizen; Knights, 'The East Riyadh Operation'.

9 Recruitment to the QAP

War on the Arabian Peninsula was a radical project even by Saudi jihadist standards. While the early jihadists had joined conventional conflicts and the al-Qaida recruits explored training camps, the QAP members were to launch suicide bombings in the streets of Riyadh. The militants also knew that domestic activism was likely to attract a much harsher government response than would fighting abroad. In short, the QAP's project was vastly more controversial and dangerous than anything previously undertaken by Saudi Islamists. Why did it still attract hundreds of people?

To answer this question, we shall look at the backgrounds, motivations and trajectories of individual QAP recruits, as we did with the previous activists. The following analysis is based on a collection of 259 biographies of people involved in the QAP campaign between 2002 and 2006. To address the issue of varying depth of involvement, the analysis distinguishes between the full sample of 259 and a core sample of 69 of the most active militants.[1]

Boys of Riyadh

The QAP consisted primarily of Saudi nationals, but there were also foreigners, especially from Yemen, Chad, Morocco, Kuwait, Syria and Mauritania. Some non-Saudis in the QAP, such as the Yemeni Khalid al-Haj and the Moroccans Karim al-Majati and Yunus al-Hayyari, held positions of leadership, but most foreigners played marginal roles in the movement, which remained a distinctly Saudi phenomenon.

[1] Other scholars have studied the profiles of QAP members using smaller samples; e.g. Abdallah al-Khalifa, ed., *al-tatarruf wa'l-irhab fi'l-mujtama' al-'arabi al-sa'udi: dirasa ijtima'iyya wa ithnughrafiyya* [Extremism and Terrorism in Saudi Arab Society: A Sociological and Ethnographical Study] (Riyadh: King Faisal Centre for Research and Islamic Studies, 2004) and Meijer, 'The "Cycle of Contention"'. Saudi authorities have conducted several classified studies on the backgrounds of militants; see e.g. Mohamed Al-Ghamdi and Shahid Ali Khan, 'Study Gives Insight on Terrorists' Lives', *Saudi Gazette*, 1 May 2008.

Interestingly, there were virtually no South Asians. With a few exceptions, the large Asian expatriate population has not been involved in militancy in the kingdom's history. One explanation may be that Asians in the kingdom work very hard and under tight supervision. A more important factor is probably the absence (until the mid-2000s) of a strong global jihadist current in South Asia. Local Saudi militants have also been reluctant to collaborate with Asians because of racism, language barriers and fear of infiltration.[2]

QAP militants were relatively old by militant Islamist standards. Their average age was 27 years at the start of the campaign, which is higher than both earlier Saudi jihadists and militant Islamists in other countries, who have tended to be in the low twenties. These figures debunk the view of Saudi militants as young and gullible teenagers. There were teenagers too, but they played a marginal role.[3]

It is worth noting that at least fourteen in the core sample were married; this weakens the hypothesis, popular in some circles, that sexual frustration and the desire for the seventy-two virgins of paradise drives Islamist terrorism. While most QAP militants had left their families behind, some wives accompanied their husbands in their underground existence in order to deflect suspicion from neighbours and police. Some militants' wives seem to have performed minor logistical and media-related tasks. *Sawt al-Jihad* included several articles signed with female pseudonyms, and the magazine *al-Khansa'* was allegedly produced by the 'Women's Information Office in the Arabian Peninsula'. No women were involved in operations, however.[4]

In terms of geographical background, there was a clear predominance of people from the city and region of Riyadh. In fact, the percentage of Riyadh residents in this sample is more than twice as high as in the overall population. Riyadh's predominance was linked to the previously

[2] Exceptions include an alleged plot by Pakistanis to bomb a US target in Jidda in mid-2001; see Tenet, *At the Center of the Storm*, 147. A Saudi-born Pakistani was a very active contributor on jihadist websites in 2002 and 2003; see '*fi ma'lumat khassa hasalat 'alayha al-sharq al-awsat ... ashhar al-muta'assibin min kuttab al-intirnit ghayr sa'udiyyin* [According to Exclusive Information Obtained by *al-Sharq al-Awsat* ... the Most Notorious Internet Writers are not Saudi]', *al-Sharq al-Awsat*, 2 October 2005. The many arrests in 2007 and 2008 allegedly included some Asians; see e.g. Andrew Hammond, 'Saudi Arabia Says Arrests 520 Terrorism Suspects', *Reuters*, 25 June 2008.

[3] The average age of the two militant Egyptian groups studied by Saad Eddin Ibrahim in the late 1970s was 22 and 24 years respectively; see Ibrahim, 'Anatomy of Egypt's Militant Islamic Groups', 439. The Hizbollah militants studied by Alan Krueger were on average 22 years old when they died; see Krueger and Malečková, 'Education, Poverty and Terrorism', 132.

[4] Donna Abu Nasr, 'Suspected Militants Killed in Saudi Clash', *Associated Press*, 13 October 2004.

noted 'Najdification' of Saudi jihadism which can be explained by the presence of key ideologues (such as the al-Shu'aybi school) and QAP recruiters (such as Yusuf al-Uyayri) in the Najd from the late 1990s onward. The southern regions of Baha, Asir, Jizan and Najran continued to be markedly underrepresented.

As in the case of al-Qaida recruits, there is relatively little anecdotal evidence about tribal ties affecting recruitment, and the absence of good national statistics makes it impossible to say whether certain tribes are over- or underrepresented. Interestingly, there were markedly more references to tribes and tribal identity in the QAP literature from the later stages in the campaign, that is, from 2004 onward. However, at that point, most of the recruitment had already taken place.[5]

Socio-economically, the QAP members were mostly lower middle class. A handful came from very rich or influential families while a small minority had a record of delinquency before they radicalised. QAP militants had a lower average level of education than both the early Saudi jihadists and the Saudis in post-1996 Afghanistan, despite being on average three to five years older and thus having had more time to complete their studies. Moreover, many seem to have been unemployed or working in temporary jobs. It is worth noting, however, that few if any of the people in our sample seem to have been significantly overqualified for their job, and few studied prestigious subjects such as medicine or engineering. This suggests that social-mobility closure was not an important grievance, unlike among Egyptian militants in the 1970s.

Unlike earlier Saudi jihadists, a relatively high proportion of QAP militants had been employed in religious professions, in places such as the religious police, Islamic charities, religious schools and courts. In most cases, the jobs in question were low-level or part-time positions. Moreover, QAP militants included relatively fewer students than the earlier jihadists. These occupational tendencies most likely reflect the problems of socio-economic reintegration of the returnees from Afghanistan. The student rate was probably low because few of the returnees went back to university, while the proportion of religious professionals reflected the increase in religiosity that accompanied the al-Qaida camp experience.

Interestingly, there were hardly any engineers, doctors or economists in the QAP. Notable exceptions included Turki al-Dandani who studied medicine, Abd al-Rahman al-Jubara who studied engineering in Canada and Ali al-Ghamidi who studied economics. However, none of them practised their profession. This is in contrast to militant Islamist

[5] For a rare exception, see '*qabilat 'utayba tazuff ahad abna'iha*'.

groups in other countries, such as Egypt, which included a disproportionately high number of people educated in prestigious natural science disciplines. The absence of these professions in the QAP may at least partly be explained by the structure of the Saudi labour market. Unlike Egyptian engineering students in the 1970s, most Saudi engineering graduates in the 2000s were all destined for prestigious and well-paid positions in the private sector.[6]

On the whole, these militants cannot be described as poor or underprivileged. However, their relatively low level of education and high rate of unemployment make them the least privileged group of the three samples studied thus far. Moreover, their problems on the job market were no doubt compounded by their jihadi CVs.

The Afghanistan factor

There is one clear common denominator in the life stories of the QAP members, namely previous jihad experience. At least thirty-eight people (i.e. 55 per cent) – probably more – of the core sample of sixty-nine trained or fought abroad before joining the QAP. The high proportion of jihad veterans is crucial for understanding the emergence as well as the radicalism of the QAP. We know from other contexts and periods that exposure to violence and military training is conducive to violent behaviour. We also know that al-Qaida's camps in post-1996 Afghanistan had a particularly strong radicalising effect on recruits because the training was so systematic and the culture of violence so pronounced. The Saudis who returned from Afghanistan in 2002 had radicalised in a very particular way and represented an alien element on the Saudi Islamist scene.[7]

While this was an advantage in the early phase, it was a serious problem in the long run, because the QAP would prove largely unable to recruit outside the Arab Afghan community. To the vast majority of Islamists in the kingdom, the concept of a jihad at home was alien; those who did not consider it illegitimate saw it as counterproductive. The returnees from Afghanistan, on the other hand, viewed things differently after having been indoctrinated in training camps and battle-hardened by combat. They came back with a more global, anti-American and intransigent ideological vision than Islamists who had never left the kingdom.

[6] Diego Gambetta and Steffen Hertog, 'Engineers of Jihad', *University of Oxford: Sociology Working Papers*, no. 10 (2007).

[7] See e.g. Dave Grossman, *On Killing: The Psychological Cost of Learning to Kill in War and Society* (Boston: Little, Brown, 1995).

Equally important were the indirect consequences of taking part in jihad abroad, notably the experience of imprisonment and torture. A number of QAP militants – at least fourteen in our core sample of sixty-nine – had spent time in prison before 2003. Some, like Ali al-Harbi and Yusuf al-Uyayri, had been caught in the 1996 or 1998 crackdowns. Others, like Abd al-Aziz al-Muqrin or Khalid al-Baghdadi, had been imprisoned abroad in the late 1990s in countries such as Ethiopia or Pakistan. Yet others, like Amir al-Shihri and Isa al-Awshan, spent time in Iranian or Syrian prisons on the way back from Afghanistan in late 2001. A few of those who returned from Afghanistan in late 2001 or early 2002 were arrested upon arrival in Saudi Arabia and held for periods of one to six months. Most of the militants who spent time in prison said they were subjected to physical and psychological torture. The radicalising effect of imprisonment and torture on political activists is well known from other contexts and periods, not least from Nasser's Egypt and early 1990s Algeria. It is difficult to assess exactly how many of the QAP members suffered torture and how serious the abuse may have been. However, the number of victims in a community need not be very large for torture accounts to become a cause of radicalisation. Tales of abuse can be spread widely with modern media, and because repressive acts have deep social embeddedness, so the imprisonment and torture of one person may cause resentment in that person's entire social network.[8]

Another consequence of fighting abroad was socio-economic reintegration problems at home. As noted above, many of the returnees from Afghanistan seem to have had problems reintegrating into society, not only because they were radicalised, but also because their absence had made them less attractive on the labour market. Moreover, their arrest and interrogation left many feeling betrayed by state and society. Faced with these and other adaptation problems, many of them ended up socialising mostly with other Afghan veterans. Hence the internal social networks in the jihadist community strengthened at the expense of their links with the rest of the Islamist community.[9]

The jihad veterans in the QAP belonged to two different generations: those who went before 1996 and those who went after 1999. The former constituted a heterogeneous group in terms of their jihad experience. Some fought in 1980s Afghanistan, others in Bosnia or Chechnya.

[8] *'liqa' ma' ahad al-matlubin al-tisa' 'ashar* (1)' and al-Nashmi, '*khalid al-baghdadi (abu ayub al-najdi)*'; al-Salim, '*yusuf al-'uyayri* (1)'; or the interview with Ali al-Harbi in the film *Badr of Riyadh*; James Moody, 'Fighting a Hydra: A Note on the Network Embeddedness of the War on Terror', *Structure and Dynamics: eJournal of Anthropological and Related Sciences* 1, no. 2 (2006).

[9] See e.g. al-Nashmi, '*khalid al-baghdadi (abu ayub al-najdi)*'.

These older veterans pursued one of two different paths after their first jihad ended. Some, like Sa'ud al-Utaybi and Hamad al-Humaydi, returned to Saudi Arabia and led quiet lives until 2003. Others, like Abd al-Aziz al-Muqrin and Yusuf al-Uyayri, became lifestyle jihadists and developed close links with the al-Qaida leadership. The experience of the second generation of jihad veterans was more homogeneous. Most went to Afghanistan between 1999 and 2001 and trained at the Faruq camp in Qandahar. Many of them fought alongside the Taliban on the Kabul front in late 2001 and left Afghanistan through Iran or Pakistan. These shared experiences most likely strengthened the internal cohesion of the group.[10]

Interestingly, the role of the individual militants in the QAP organisation during the campaign turned out to be closely linked to the nature and timing of their jihad experience. One might discern three categories of QAP members: the 'top commanders', the 'ideologues' and the 'fighters'. The top commanders such as al-Uyayri and al-Muqrin were 'lifestyle jihadists' from the first generation of veterans. They had left for Afghanistan at a very young age in the late 1980s or early 1990s, had distinguished themselves by their physical abilities and leadership skills and worked as instructors in training camps. They had remained active militants throughout the 1990s, spent years in prison and suffered torture.

The ideologues, on the other hand, had little or no practical jihad experience. The principal ideologues in the QAP included Abdallah al-Rushud, Faris al-Zahrani, Ahmad al-Dukhayyil, Isa al-Awshan, Sultan al-Utaybi, Abd al-Aziz al-Anzi, Abd al-Latif al-Khudayri, Abd al-Majid al-Munay' and Hamad al-Humaydi. Apart from al-Humaydi, who was in Afghanistan for a short while in the 1980s, al-Dukhayyil who was briefly in Afghanistan in the late 1990s and al-Awshan who made it to the Iranian–Afghan border in late 2001, the ideologues never went abroad for jihad. They had all studied religion, either officially at Imam Muhammad bin Sa'ud University or privately with sheikhs. Most of them had mediocre résumés or failed careers in the religious sector, and none of them were particularly well known as religious scholars before the outbreak of the campaign.

The fighters represented a more heterogeneous group which can be broken down into three subcategories. The first and operationally most

[10] See e.g. '*qabilat 'utayba*'; al-Makki, '*mit'ib al-muhayyani*'; al-Jawfi, '*turki al-dandani*'; al-Nashmi, '*fahd bin samran al-sa'idi*'; al-Najdi, '*talal al-anbari*'; al-Nashmi, '*khalid al-baghdadi (abu ayub al-najdi)*'; '*turki bin fuhayd al-mutayri*'; ''*ali al-ma'badi al-harbi*'; al-Dukhayyil, '*faysal bin abd al-rahman al-dukhayyil*'; '*liqa' ma' ahad al-matlubin al-tisa' 'ashar* (2)'; '*liqa' ma' al-mujahid salih bin muhammad al-'awfi* [Interview with the Mujahid Salih bin Muhammad al-Awfi]', *Sawt al-Jihad*, no. 8 (2004) and ''*abd al-rahman al-yaziji yurawi waqa'i ma'rakat hayy al-nahda fi liqa' khass* [Abd al-Rahman al-Yaziji Recounts the Events of the Battle of Nahda in a Special Interview]', *Sawt al-Jihad*, no. 28 (2004).

important category consisted of the young jihad veterans who had gone to Afghanistan after 1999 and returned in late 2001 see above). They had trained in Bin Ladin's camps during al-Qaida's 'peak' and had left Afghanistan against their own will, hence they returned highly trained and motivated. Most of the core QAP members, such as (Turki al-Dandani, Mit'ib al-Muhayyani and Faisal al-Dukhayyil, were drawn from this category. The second subcategory consisted of older jihad veterans who had 'retired' in the mid- or late 1990s and were mobilised by the QAP campaign in 2003. These men, such as Ibrahim al-Rayis, Khalid al-Subayt, Ali al-Harbi, Sa'ud al-Utaybi and Bandar al-Ghamidi were experienced and respected fighters, but lacked the leadership skills to become top commanders. The third subcategory consisted of the new recruits, that is, people who had been too young to go to Afghanistan, but who were recruited into the QAP from 2002 onwards. Many of them, such as Bandar al-Dukhayyil and Mansur Faqih, were friends and relatives of jihad veterans or QAP members.

In fact, it seems that a large number of the QAP recruits who had not been to Afghanistan themselves were friends or relatives of jihad veterans. A striking number of QAP militants had relatives in the organisation. The following are the most prominent examples:

- Faysal al-Dukhayyil, his brother Bandar and their cousin Ahmad al-Dukhayyil
- Fahd al-Juwayr and his cousin Khalid al-Farraj (who seem to have had two other militant cousins)
- Mansur Faqih and his brother Hasan
- Muhammad al-Suwaylimi and his brother Ahmad
- Mustafa al-Ansari, his brother Ayman and their cousins Samir and Sami al-Ansari
- Fayiz al-Juhani, his brother Id al-Juhani and their cousin Turki al-Huzaymi
- Abd al-Karim al-Yaziji and his cousin Abd al-Rahman

If we include people who had relatives in the broader jihadist community, the list becomes even longer. Examples include

- Isa Al Awshan, who had a brother in Guantanamo and another brother who died in Afghanistan in 2001
- Fayez and Id al-Juhani, who lost three cousins in Falluja in Iraq in 2004
- Abd al-Rahman al-Jubara, whose brother Muhammad al-Jubara was in Guantanamo
- Mansur and Hasan Faqih, whose brother Fahd was killed in Afghanistan in 1998

- Amir al-Shihri, whose brother Zaydan died in Afghanistan in late 2001
- Abd al-Muhsin al-Shabanat, whose brother Badr died in Afghanistan in late 2001

It is reasonable to assume that the number of pre-existing friendship links within the QAP was even higher than the number of family links. In other words, the QAP consisted mainly of jihad veterans and their acquaintances. But why would they get involved in terrorism in their home country?

Anti-Americanism and companionship

While previous Saudi militants had not cited anti-Americanism as a primary motivation, all QAP fighters were very anti-American. The most commonly cited motivation was the same as the QAP's declared aim, namely to end the perceived US military occupation of Saudi Arabia. Some emphasised the political justification for this struggle, namely the need to stop the US military from using Saudi Arabia as a base for attacks on Muslims in Afghanistan and Iraq. Others emphasised the religious dimension, quoting the injunction by the Prophet that 'there shall not be two religions on the Arabian Peninsula' or the need to 'expel the polytheists from the Arabian Peninsula'.

Interestingly, a number of people who joined the QAP, usually individuals who had not been to Afghanistan, initially wanted to go and fight in Iraq, but were convinced to stay by QAP recruiters (see below). This suggests that some recruits had an initial preference for classical jihadism, not global jihad or revolutionary activism.

We also find somewhat more anti-regime views expressed by QAP militants than among earlier jihadists. Nevertheless, revolutionary motivations seem to have played a much smaller role than anti-Americanism in driving QAP recruits. Many were of course hostile to the police and the security services and may have joined the QAP to escape imprisonment, as we shall see below. Moreover, as the campaign proceeded, the QAP's discourse became more regime-critical, and most active QAP fighters no doubt came to see themselves as being at war both with the Crusaders and with the Saudi security establishment. However, only a few QAP members seem to have been driven primarily by ideological regime hostility from the very start.[11]

[11] One such person was Ahmad al-Dukhayyil, who in 2002 worked on 'raising awareness on the infidelity of the tyrant', wrote letters to the ulama and gave fiery speeches in mosques around Riyadh; al-Qa'qa' al-Najdi, '*al-shaykh ahmad bin nasir al-dukhayyil* [Sheikh Ahmad bin Nasir al-Dukhayyil]', *Sawt al-Jihad*, no. 5 (2003).

A second type of motivation for joining the militant underground was the desire for companionship and a sense of loyalty towards comrades-in-arms from Afghanistan. Some of the early members of the al-Uyayri network emphasised the fact that they had sworn an oath in Afghanistan to continue their jihad on the Arabian Peninsula. Many returnees had great affection for their friends from Afghanistan and were longing for the special atmosphere of companionship and chivalry which they had experienced in the 'Land of Honour', that is, Afghanistan.[12]

The companionship factor was important not only for the jihad veterans, but also for others in the extended jihadist network who found themselves under increasing pressure from the authorities. Because the jihadist community was relatively closed and tight-knit, a person could find himself in a situation where several or even most of his friends had joined the QAP. Many chose to follow them into the militant underground. The importance of loyalty increased as police pressure on the QAP members mounted. A number of people joined the QAP after seeing a friend or relative appear on the wanted list. For many of these people, joining the QAP was a declaration of loyalty to their friends more than a statement of ideology.[13]

The notions of companionship and loyalty were closely associated with those of chivalry and heroism. Judging from the discourse of the QAP's publications, it is clear that the militants saw themselves as part of a pioneering vanguard of holy warriors. Many recruits, particularly those who had already been to Afghanistan, seem to have been attracted to the chivalrous dimension of the QAP's jihad. In a TV interview, a former militant noted that the QAP recruitment effort 'taps into the romanticism of youth. They rely on dashing elements who love adventure ... particularly the 20-year-olds who wish to prove themselves.'[14]

A third type of motivation for joining the QAP was fear and anger over the police crackdown. As seen above, police began a campaign of arrests in late 2002 which would escalate rapidly in 2003, particularly after the QAP campaign broke out. A number of people found themselves on wanted lists and would hear about friends and relatives who had been arrested by police. Given the many stories of torture that circulated in the Islamist community, some people were no doubt afraid of capture and saw involvement with the militants as a strategy of self-

[12] al-Makki '*mit'ib al-muhayyani*'; al-Najdi, '*talal al-anbari*'.

[13] '*majmu'at maqalat al-shahid muhammad bin 'abd al-rahman al-suwaylimi* [Collection of Articles of the Martyr Muhammad bin Abd al-Rahman al-Suwaylimi]' (www.al-hesbah.org, 2006).

[14] Rawya Rageh, 'Ex-Militants: al-Qaida Preys on Young Men', *Associated Press*, 22 September 2004.

defence. A significant number of people in the broadly defined 'jihadist community' who were initially not directly involved with the al-Uyayri network joined the QAP only after they realised they were on the radar of the authorities. This was notably the case with a number of radical preachers (who would later become QAP ideologues) such as Ahmad al-Dukhayyil, Abdallah al-Rushud and Hamad al-Humaydi. It was only after being chased by police that they joined the militant underground, where they found protection. Muhammad al-Suwaylim, for example, joined the QAP in mid-2003 after being sought by the Interior Ministry. Another good example is the case of Khalid al-Subayt, a veteran of the Chechen jihad, who was involved with fundraising for Afghanistan and Chechnya but not with the QAP proper. In September 2003, shortly after Crown Prince Abdallah's return from a visit to Moscow which likely included intelligence exchange on Saudis formerly in Chechnya, Khalid became wanted by the police. He then decided to go underground and 'joined a safe house with around eighty other mujahidin'. These accounts suggest that the wanted lists issued by the authorities in May 2003, December 2003 and July 2005 may have been counterproductive (although their publication did have the positive effect of encouraging informants and legitimising police operations).[15]

Other recruits seem to have been driven more by anger and a desire for vengeance for the perceived injustice they or their friends had suffered at the hands of the security services. Some QAP recruits were themselves torture victims. In the film *Badr of Riyadh*, Ali al-Harbi (one of the suicide bombers in the November 2003 Muhayya bombing) spoke at length about the torture he and his friends had suffered in al-Ruways prison in the mid-1990s. Another example is Khalid al-Baghdadi (one of the suicide bombers in the May 2003 Riyadh bombing) who had been detained by police in 2002. His martyr biography claimed that shortly after his arrival from Afghanistan he was approached by officials from the Interior Ministry who politely requested him to come over for 'five minutes of questioning'. Instead he was imprisoned for five months and allegedly subjected to torture. 'When he was released', his biography noted, 'he joined the mujahidin on the Peninsula.' A number of people who had not been detained themselves joined the QAP after learning of the death or arrest of a close friend or relative. For example, Mansur al-Faqih joined the QAP when his brother Hassan was arrested in May

[15] See al-Najdi, '*al-shaykh ahmad bin nasir al-dukhayyil*'; al-Rushud, '*bayan*'; and Abdallah al-Rashid, '*al-'alim al-mujahid hamad bin 'abdallah al-humaydi* [The Mujahid Scholar Hamad bin Abdallah al-Humaydi]', *Sawt al-Jihad*, no. 29 (2005); al-Mutayri, '*abd al-muhsin al-shabanat*'; '*majmu'at maqalat al-shahid muhammad bin 'abd al-rahman al-suwaylimi*'; Al Awshan, '*khalid bin 'abdallah al-subayt*'.

2003. Fahd al-Juwayr joined the QAP in early 2005 after two of his brothers or cousins were killed by police a year earlier.[16]

Persuasion, incrimination and protection

Because few recruits transcended social networks on their way into the QAP, it is more difficult to distinguish between top-down and bottom-up recruitment processes. The recruitment narratives contain very few examples of random encounters with recruiters or inspiration from public sermons. There are no examples of people being lured into the QAP in 2002 or 2003 by shady recruiters at summer camps or in schools. Conversely, relatively few joined the QAP entirely on their own initiative. There are some exceptions, such as the case of Sami al-Luhaybi, who carried out an attack on the US marine base in Jubayl on his own initiative before joining the QAP. Some operations, such as the Yanbu shooting spree on 1 May 2004, were carried out by independent cells that had not been in close contact with the QAP organisation. There were also indications of people being inspired by the QAP's massive Internet media campaign to provide various forms of assistance, but few if any became core militants in this way. It may be that the grass-roots interest was not large enough or that the QAP was reluctant, for security reasons, to integrate people without recommendations. Either way, few people entered the QAP without knowing someone in the jihadist community.[17]

The available biographies suggest that there were three principal ways into the QAP, neither of which can easily be classified as 'top-down' or 'bottom-up' recruitment, namely persuasion, incrimination and protection. The first consisted of QAP activists simply persuading other people in the jihadist community to join them. This typically occurred at informal social gatherings in the homes of people in the Arab Afghan community. Some people, such as Abd al-Latif al-Khudayri, were known for hosting regular evening receptions for jihad veterans. For example, Bandar al-Dukhayyil recalled meeting Ali al-Harbi at a gathering for jihad youth in 2002 and remembered that 'Ali was

[16] *'badr al-riyadh'*; al-Nashmi, *'khalid al-baghdadi (abu ayub al-najdi)'*. See Raid Qusti, 'Background of the Most Wanted Terrorists: Part 4', *Arab News*, 14 December 2003. Fahd al-Juwayr deepened his involvement in the QAP after two of his brothers were killed by Saudi police; see Abdullah al-Shihri, 'Leader of al-Qaida in Saudi Arabia Killed', *Associated Press*, 28 February 2006; *al-Sharq al-Awsat*, 4 July 2005.

[17] al-Makki, *'sami al-luhaybi'*; Abd al-Aziz al-Muqrin, *'li-kull al-raghibiyyin fi'l-jihad 'ala ard al-jazira al-'arabiyya* [To all those who Desire Jihad on the Arabian Peninsula]', *Mu'askar al-Battar*, no. 10 (2004). See e.g. the 'Letters to the editor' in *Sawt al-Jihad* nos. 8, 20, 21, 26, 27 and 28.

arguing strongly in favour of jihad on the Arabian Peninsula.' Another veteran jihadist, Ibrahim al-Rayis, wanted to go to Iraq in the spring of 2003, but 'he met one of the brothers who suggested that he join the mujahidin on the Arabian Peninsula instead'. A particularly illustrative example of these recruitment processes is found in the biography of Musa'id al-Subay'i, a recent returnee from Afghanistan. In early 2003,

> Musa'id, Abdallah al-Subay'i and Abd al-Ilah al-Utaybi were trying together to get hold of travel documents to go to Iraq. At this point Musa'id met Abd al-Muhsin Shabanat, and they became good friends. Abd al-Muhsin was in contact with the people doing jihad work inside Saudi Arabia, and he introduced Musa'id to one of the mujahidin. Musa'id consulted with his friends Abdallah al-Subay'i and Abd al-Ilah al-Utaybi and together they decided to join.[18]

From late 2002 onward, the advocates of jihad in Saudi Arabia also organised get-togethers specifically intended to persuade others in the Arab Afghan community to join the nascent QAP. Radical sheikhs such as Ahmad al-Dukhayyil gave clandestine lectures for small groups of people in the jihadist community. The famous al-Shifa police raid on 16 November 2002 (see previous chapter) interrupted one such lecture. Some people, such as Abd al-Rahman al-Harbi, joined the mujahidin after meeting Ahmad al-Dukhayyil. It is still not clear whether the most prominent radical Saudi sheikhs (such as Nasir al-Fahd and Ali al-Khudayr) were directly involved in this mobilisation effort. On the one hand, there are no explicit references in the QAP literature to secret meetings or recruitment rallies involving these sheikhs. On the other hand, several of their students were later found in the militants' ranks.[19]

The 'incrimination' pattern consisted of people becoming unwittingly implicated in the organisation after extending assistance to old friends already in the QAP. Militants on the run from police would ask friends and relatives for various forms of help, such as shelter, money or transport. This often led to the helper himself becoming wanted by the police and persuaded by the cause and eventually choosing to join the militants. While most of these processes were natural, in the sense that the militant asking for help was genuinely acting out of desperation, there are indications that some QAP members purposely asked for favours from friends and relatives specifically to implicate them and

[18] '*'ali al-ma'badi al-harbi*'; Sa'ud al-Utaybi, '*ibrahim al-rayis: thabat hatta al-mamat* [Ibrahim al-Rayis: Steadfastness to the Death]', *Sawt al-Jihad*, no. 9 (2004); al-Subay'i, '*musa'id al-subay'i*.

[19] al-Utaybi, '*abd al-rahman bin 'abdallah al-harbi*'; al-Anzi, '*'abd al-latif bin hamad al-khudayri*'.

complicate their extraction from the group. In the TV programme *Inside the Cell*, imprisoned militants explained how QAP members would consciously try to implicate acquaintances: 'They would say that some youths were wanted [by the security services] or were mujahidin on their way to Iraq and were in need of money or a rented flat for a short period of time. In this way, a person [extending help to these mujahidin] could find himself enrolled in the cell without knowing.' Another thing worth noting about this testimony is the way in which the QAP exploited sympathy for the jihad in Iraq for their own purposes. This echoed al-Qaida's exploitation of the Chechen issue between 1999 and 2001 and illustrated the parasitic relationship between global jihadism and classical jihadism.[20]

The third main type of entry path to the QAP consisted of people actively seeking out acquaintances in the QAP in order to get protection from the police. As explained above, a number of people in the jihadist community who were initially not involved with the QAP decided to join after becoming wanted by the authorities. Precisely for this reason, QAP insiders systematically worked to fuel fear of the police within the organisation. Former militants have explained how QAP leaders would provide graphic descriptions of the horrific torture which would befall militants if they were captured. This not only served to demonise the enemy, but also to decrease the risk of defection and increase the willingness of militants to fight to the death rather than surrender.[21]

Those who joined the jihad on the Arabian Peninsula were extremely optimistic about their prospects. They were well trained, heavily armed and strongly motivated. Their leaders promised them victory and their ideologues assured them the jihad was divinely ordained. The outcome would be quite different.

[20] *'liqa' ma' al-shaykh al-mujahid sa'ud bin hamud al-'utaybi* [Interview with the Mujahid Sheikh Sa'ud bin Hamud al-Utaybi]', *Sawt al-Jihad* 2003; Rageh, 'Ex-Militants'.

[21] Rageh, 'Ex-Militants'; Abdul Ghafour, 'Al-Qaeda Controls'.

10 The failure of the jihad in Arabia

The East Riyadh operation was just the beginning. The May 2003 attack was followed by a seemingly endless series of shoot-outs and attacks, each of which raised concern about the security situation in the kingdom. For a long time, the view of many Western analysts was pessimistic. In the early summer of 2004, when the atmosphere was at its most tense, many believed that the situation was spinning completely out of control. Then, to the surprise of many, the violence subsided. By late 2006 the QAP campaign had petered out. Why?

The aims of the QAP

Before looking at the campaign in more detail, it is worth reflecting briefly on what the QAP was fighting for. A key question which has divided analysts is whether the militants were aiming to topple the Saudi government or merely to evict the Western presence. In other words, was the QAP a revolutionary or pan-Islamist phenomenon? The conventional way of looking at terrorist groups' intentions consists of establishing a list of aims derived from the groups' declarations. However, the 'manifesto approach' can be misleading, because groups often mix short-, mid- and long-term aims in their statements, depending on context. Group leaders may also describe their objectives differently, according to whether they are speaking to other leaders, to their footsoldiers or to a wider audience. As we shall see, this was indeed the case with the QAP, and we therefore need a slightly more nuanced approach.

A useful way to analyse ideologically ambiguous actors such as the QAP is to distinguish between *secret aims*, *declared aims* and *discursive themes*. Secret aims are those that only the leaders know. Declared aims are those openly declared in propaganda material. Discursive themes are broad messages conveyed through the systematic use of semantically connected words and examples. Discursive themes represent an indirect way of gauging intentions because in radical literature they usually represent the central grievance that the group hopes will mobilise followers. As argued in the Introduction, one can speak of an ideal-type 'revolutionary theme' and an ideal-type 'pan-Islamist theme' in radical Islamist propaganda. The former highlights the corruption of the Muslim ruler through examples of domestic repression, torture and corruption. The latter emphasises the global suffering of Muslims at the hands of non-Muslims by listing 'occupied territories' (Palestine, Kashmir, Chechnya), alleged massacres (Qana, Falluja) and prisoner abuse (Guantanamo, Abu Ghraib).

In the QAP's case, there is no doubt that the declared aim was to evict the Crusaders, and that the dominant discursive theme was pan-Islamist. For example, in a 2002 book entitled *This is How We View the Jihad and How We Want It*, the Saudi author placed the 'Jews and the Crusaders' on the top of a list of enemies, and noted that 'this is the enemy against which we must act at this stage'. An early *Sawt al-Jihad* editorial also stated that 'our number-one enemy is the Jews and the Christians'. Conversely, the group repeatedly stressed that it would not target the security forces unless the latter interfered to protect the Crusaders. The group was very keen to rid itself of the 'takfiri' label and explicitly dismissed accusations that they wanted to attack Muslims. Moreover, one does not need to review much QAP propaganda to see that the discursive theme was more pan-Islamist than revolutionary.[1]

As the campaign proceeded, the group's declarations became more hostile to the government. The QAP literature from early 2004 onward is full of verbal attacks against the security establishment in particular, but also against the royal family and the ulama. No strangers to humour and irony, QAP writers used terms such as *kha'in al-haramayn* (Traitor of the Two Holy Mosques) instead of *khadim al-haramayn* (Custodian of the Two Holy Mosques) and *hay'at kibar al-umala* (Council of Senior Agents) instead of *hay'at kibar al-ulama* (Council of Senior Scholars).

[1] Hazim al-Madani, '*hakadha nara al-jihad wa nuriduhu* [This is How We View the Jihad and How We Want It]' (www.qa3edoon.com, 2002); Sulayman al-Dawsary, '*al-iftitahiyya* [Opening Word]', *Sawt al-Jihad* 2003. In September 2003, Abd al-Aziz al-Muqrin was quoted in *Sawt al-Jihad* as saying that 'the brothers try as much as possible to avoid clashes with the military and the security forces'; '*liqa' ma' ahad al-matlubin al-tisa' 'ashar* (1)'. Sulayman al-Dawsary wrote '[we must] avoid, as much as possible, confronting the state's armies and forces, so that we can deliver knock-out blows to the occupiers', al-Dawsary, '*al-iftitahiyya*'. In May 2003, Yusuf al-Uyayri stated: 'How logical is it that we should sacrifice our blood and our throats for those far away, and then decide to terrorise and shed the blood of our own people?'; '*ghazwat al-hadi 'ashar min rabi' al-awwal*'.

Despite the relative increase in socio-revolutionary discourse, however, the declared main purpose of the QAP campaign remained the eviction of the Crusaders.[2]

At the same time there is also strong evidence to suggest that the top al-Qaida leadership and at least some QAP leaders ultimately intended to topple the Saudi government. Khalid Sheikh Muhammad allegedly told interrogators that Bin Ladin's highest priority was to spur a revolution in Saudi Arabia and overthrow the government. Former prison mates of captured QAP ideologue Faris al-Zahrani have said the latter spoke incessantly about the infidelity (*kufr*) of the regime. Other captured QAP militants have revealed that QAP leaders envisaged a two-stage campaign: a first phase aimed at mobilising the Saudi people for jihad against the Crusaders, and a second stage in which the enthusiastic masses would turn against the Al Sa'ud. This strategy is consistent with that articulated in internal al-Qaida documents prior to 2001, as we saw in chapter 5.[3]

Interestingly, the revolutionary agenda was not widely known among low-level operatives. The QAP leadership went to great lengths to conceal their aims both from its members and, more importantly, from the Saudi public. As we saw in the previous chapter, new recruits joined the organisation primarily out of a desire to fight Americans, not the regime. Moreover, as we shall see, most of the QAP's premeditated operations were directed against Western targets. When the militants began the controversial task of attacking Saudi police targets, they claimed these operations in the name of a fictitious entity called the 'Haramain Brigades'. This was to preserve the clarity of the QAP's 'Americans first' strategy and to avoid staining the QAP's reputation with Muslim blood.[4]

The QAP was in other words both a pan-Islamist and a revolutionary phenomenon, and the tension between these two projects shaped the organisation's behaviour. The pan-Islamist dimension was nevertheless more important, because the success of the group's mobilisation depended on its declared anti-Americanism. The movement came into being despite, not because of, the revolutionary aims of its leaders. The QAP leaders concealed their long-term plan because they knew

[2] For a particularly harsh verbal attack on the security forces, see Abu Bakr al-Husni, *hidayat al-sari fi hukm istihdaf al-tawari'* [The Prophet's Guidance on Targeting Emergency Forces] (www.qa3edoon.com, 2004), which was published in the aftermath of the al-Washm bombing in April 2004.

[3] Tenet, *At the Center of the Storm*, 248; Rageh, 'Ex-Militants'.

[4] Interview with Saudi security source, Riyadh, November 2005; Mahmoud Ahmad, 'Al-Qaeda Operatives are an Ignorant Lot, Say Former Members', *Arab News*, 3 October 2003.

that revolutionary discourse and violence would not mobilise sufficient followers in Saudi Arabia. They thus strove to use pan-Islamist propaganda and deal clean blows to Western targets for as long as possible. However, this would prove easier said than done.

Evolution of the campaign

Broadly speaking, the QAP campaign began in strength, gradually decreased and eventually failed. However, the level of violence oscillated throughout the campaign, and it is possible to discern five major phases between May 2003 and late 2009 (when this book went to press). A first phase of reorganisation after initial setbacks; a second period of consolidation and revenge on security forces; a third phase marked by the QAP's final offensive; a fourth phase witnessing the death throes of the original QAP; and a fifth phase characterised by the new generation's failed attempts to revive the campaign.[5]

Setback and reorganisation (May–November 2003)

The East Riyadh bombing on 12 May 2003 provoked a massive police crackdown on the Saudi jihadist community. The summer of 2003 saw a large number of arrests and shoot-outs across the country (see Text Box 1). The crackdown dented the al-Uyayri network very severely. Between 13 May and 8 November, at least twenty-six militants died, including top leaders Yusuf al-Uyayri, Turki al-Dandani and Ahmad al-Dukhayyil. An unknown number of people (at least 100) were detained, including key operatives such as Ali al-Ghamidi. The renegade Burayda sheikhs were picked up in Medina, and a large number of other scholars were discreetly detained throughout the summer, leaving the militants without clerical backing. Moreover, the network lost crucial resources and infrastructure as police uncovered more and more safe houses.

The crackdown led the remaining militants to scrap the original five-cell structure envisaged by al-Uyayri and start a process of improvised

[5] For other overviews of the QAP campaign, see e.g. Riedel and Saab, 'Al Qaeda's Third Front'; Andrzej Ancygier, *Al-Qa'ida in Saudi Arabia 2003 and 2004* (Berlin: Grin Verlag für akademische Texte, 2005); and Bouchaib Silm, 'Notes on al Qaeda in Saudi Arabia', *Asian Journal of Social Science* 35, nos. 4/5 (2007) and Ali Bakr, *tanzim al-qa'ida fi jazirat al-'arab* [Al-Qaida on the Arabian Peninsula] (http://islamyoon.islamonline.net, 30 August 2009).

Text Box 1: Major crackdowns and shoot-outs, May–November 2003

- *28 May – Arrests of the sheikhs*: Fifteen people – including Ali al-Khudayr, Nasir al-Fahd and Ahmad al-Khalidi – were arrested in Medina.
- *31 May – Killing of Yusuf al-Uyayri*: Police killed Yusuf al-Uyayri and his companion during a car chase near Turba in the Ha'il province. Two police officers were killed and two were wounded.
- *14–15 June – Khalidiyya events*: Police raided an apartment in the Khalidiyya neighbourhood of Mecca, killing five militants and arresting five. Two policemen were killed, while nine others were wounded. On 15 June, another seven people from the Khalidiyya flat were arrested in a different location in Mecca.
- *3 July – Killing of Turki al-Dandani*: Senior militant Turki al-Dandani and two accomplices died during a siege and gunbattle with police in a safe house in the Jawf province.
- *28 July – Killing of Ahmad al-Dukhayyil*: Militant ideologue Ahmad al-Dukhayyil was killed during a shoot-out with police at a farm in the Qasim province. Four other militants and two policemen died. One militant and eight policemen were wounded.
- *12 August – First battle of Suwaydi*: A five-hour shoot-out in the Suwaydi district of Riyadh led to the death of four policemen and a militant. Five militants were arrested, but seven escaped.
- *15 August – Jizan arrests*: 200 policemen stormed a weapons storage facility and arrested twenty-one people in a village in the Jizan province.
- *23 September – Jizan hospital siege*: A gunbattle at a hospital compound in Jizan led to the death of a police officer and three militants, including senior militant Sultan al-Qahtani. Two militants and four policemen were wounded.
- *6 November – Second battle of Suwaydi*: A fierce gunbattle erupted in Riyadh's Suwaydi district as police tried to raid a safe house for militants. One militant was killed and eight policemen were wounded

reorganisation. A key concern was to convey the impression to the outside world that the QAP was a large and formalised organisation. In September 2003 the militants established a specialised media unit under the name *Sawt al-Jihad* which was charged with producing propaganda magazines and videos. In November 2003 they also began using the name 'al-Qaida on the Arabian Peninsula' for the first time. The image overhaul was most likely an attempt at compensating for the weakness and disarray caused by the mid-2003 crackdown. And it worked; from late 2003 to late 2004, the QAP's very sophisticated media campaign made the organisation look much larger and more coherent than was really the case on the ground.[6]

Details of the organisational structure of the QAP in this period remain sparse. A Western diplomatic source said the view in intelligence circles at the time was that three major clusters of militants had crystallised in late 2003: two in the Riyadh area and one in the Hijaz. However, it is not clear how each cluster was organised or whether there was a central strategic leadership. Al-Uyayri's successor as Bin Ladin's main man in the kingdom was most likely the Saudi-Yemeni Khalid al-Haj, but the latter's degree of involvement in operational planning is uncertain. His name is conspicuously absent from the QAP's publications in this period. What we do know is that the network's centre of gravity was in Riyadh – for this was where most major operations would take place over the next twelve months.[7]

By the late autumn of 2003, the organisation had regrouped and was ready to launch a new offensive. On 8 November 2003 came the second major operation in the kingdom, namely the so-called Muhayya bombing. Two suicide bombers, later described in QAP propaganda as the 'Truth Brigades', drove an explosives-filled van painted as a police van into the Muhayya residential compound, killing 17 people and wounding over 120. The attack was timed to coincide with the anniversary of the seventh-century battle of Badr (17 Ramadan), and the bombing vehicle carried registration number 313, evoking the number of Muslim participants in the historic battle. The QAP video *Badr of Riyadh* later documented the preparation and execution of the attack in extraordinary detail.[8]

However, the Muhayya operation turned out to be a public-relations disaster for the militants. Most of the casualties were Arabs and Muslims, many of them children, and the attack happened during Ramadan, the holy month of fasting. By all accounts, the militants did not realise that the compound housed mainly Arabs; in their statements, the QAP insisted that the government media were lying about the casualties being Arab and Muslim. Muhayya was widely considered a turning point in the campaign because it shifted popular opinion firmly against the militants. Nevertheless, the QAP planned another major compound bombing in Riyadh for late 2003. On 25 November, police raided a

[6] '*bayan hawla al-taraju'at al-akhira* [Statement on the Recent Retractions]', *Sawt al-Jihad*, no. 5 (2003).

[7] Author's interview with Western diplomatic source, Riyadh, November 2005.

[8] Badr is a symbol of Muslim victory and therefore a popular label for modern jihadi operations. On most jihad fronts since the 1980s Arab fighters have undertaken 'Badr operations' on the *hijri* date 17 Ramadan.

Text Box 2: Major shoot-outs, December 2003–March 2004

- *8 December – al-Rayyis killing*: Police shot and killed veteran jihadist (and former Bayt Shubra member) Ibrahim al-Rayyis at a petrol station in Riyadh's Suwaydi district.
- *29 January – The Farraj patricide*: Hamud al-Farraj notified police that his son Khalid was hiding weapons in a house in Riyadh. When the police and the father went to inspect the house, they came under heavy fire by a group of militants which included Khalid al-Farraj. Six policemen and the father died. Seven militants were subsequently arrested.
- *18 February – Riyadh killing*: An unidentified militant was shot and killed by police in Riyadh.
- *15 March – al-Haj killing*: Leading QAP member Khalid al-Hajj and his aide were shot and killed by police in Riyadh.

house and discovered a vehicle laden with even more explosives than was used in the Muhayya attack. They also found a video containing surveillance footage of the Seder compound in Riyadh. PR backlash or not, the QAP was set to continue its struggle.[9]

Consolidation and revenge (December 2003–March 2004)

From December 2003 to March 2004 there was a relative lull in the violence. The summer crackdown and the November operations had drained the QAP's resources, and the group needed time to restructure. Moreover, public hostility combined with the publication of a new list of twenty-six wanted men on 6 December forced the militants to lie low. The gunfights between police and militants continued, but with reduced frequency (see Text Box 2). With the exception of the 29 January clash, the militants were rarely found in groups of more than three people, and they were discovered on the road more often than in safe-houses. Moreover, practically all of the clashes and arrests took place in the Riyadh area.

December 2003 saw a new and interesting development, namely the first attacks against Saudi security forces (see Text Box 3). This was significant because such attacks were historically rare. Militants had

[9] See '*al-'amaliyya al-'askariyya 'ala mujamma' al-salibiyyin bi-iskan muhayya* [The Military Operation on the Crusader Compound in Muhayya]', *Sawt al-Jihad*, no. 5 (2003); Neil MacFarquhar, 'Among Saudis, Attack has Soured Qaeda Supporters', *New York Times*, 11 November 2003.

Text Box 3: Attacks on security services, December 2003

- *4 December – Huwayrini attack*: Gunmen wounded Major-General Abd al-Aziz al-Huwayrini, a senior Interior Ministry official, in an attack in Riyadh.
- *Mid-December – Mabahith car bomb attempt*: Police defused a car bomb near the headquarters of the Saudi intelligence services.
- *29 December – Mabahith car bomb*: A bomb exploded in the parked car of Ibrahim al-Dhali, a major in the intelligence services.

never before targeted the heart of the Saudi security establishment in this way. The attacks were no doubt motivated by a desire for revenge for the police crackdown in the previous months. QAP texts and videos from this period suggest that the militants felt frustrated with the police obstructing their efforts to attack Western targets. The QAP was becoming gradually more socio-revolutionary in both discourse and behaviour.

Very interestingly, these attacks were not claimed by the QAP, but rather attributed to a mysterious organisation called the 'Haramain Brigades'. At the time, the appearance of a new group caused much speculation among analysts. It has since emerged that the attacks were in fact carried out by core QAP members, and that the Haramain Brigades was a fictitious entity invented to prevent the QAP from being associated with the 'dirty work' of attacking Saudi policemen. This shows that the QAP feared being perceived as socio-revolutionaries, realising no doubt that attacks on Saudis would undermine whatever public support was left for their campaign. The name QAP had to be reserved for the declared 'Westerners first' strategy.[10]

Spring offensive and QAP collapse (April–July 2004)

In April 2004 the level of violence increased again. The period from April to June 2004 constituted the peak of the QAP campaign in terms of attack frequency and media impact. The offensive marked Abd al-Aziz al-Muqrin's assumption of the leadership of the QAP following the death of Khalid al-Hajj on 15 March. The QAP notably planned a series of suicide car bombs for the spring of 2004, evidenced by the

[10] '*bayan kata'ib al-haramain* [Statement of the Haramain Brigades]' (www.hostinganime.com/kataeb, 2004); Ahmad, 'Al-Qaeda Operatives are an Ignorant Lot'; author's interview with unidentified Saudi Islamist and Saudi security source.

Text Box 4: Major shoot-outs, April–May 2004

- *5 April – Rawda shoot-out*: Saudi security forces shot dead a suspected militant after a car chase in the Rawda area of Riyadh. The dead militant's companion sought refuge in a nearby house and was wounded and arrested after a seven-hour siege.
- *12 April – Fayha incident*: A policeman and a militant were killed and four policemen wounded in a gunbattle at a safe house in the Fayha area of Riyadh.
- *22 April – Jidda shoot-out*: Three militants were killed and a policeman was wounded in a protracted gunbattle and siege on a safe house in the al-Safa area of Jidda.
- *20 May – Burayda siege*: Four militants and a policeman were killed in a shoot-out and siege at a rest house in the Khudayra area of Burayda. Two policemen were injured.

discovery, in April, May and June, of almost ten vehicles in the process of being rigged with explosives.

In April and May, the intensified hunt for militants resulted in several shoot-outs and sieges of militant safe houses (see Text Box 4).

One of the most striking new developments in April 2004 was the considerably more aggressive attitude of the militants vis-à-vis the police (see Text Box 5). In addition to being more 'trigger happy' in confrontations with police, militants also started using heavier weaponry, such as rocket-propelled grenades.

The unrestrained nature of the war between the militants and the police was firmly underlined on 21 April, when a suicide car bomb exploded in front of the headquarters of the traffic police in the Washm area of central Riyadh. Six people were killed and almost 150 were wounded. The Washm bombing was another PR setback for the militants, because all of the casualties were Muslims. Again the QAP undertook a carefully choreographed act of media manipulation to dissociate itself from the attack. On the day of the bombing, it issued a statement in the name of the Haramain Brigades claiming the attack; a week later followed a statement in the name of the QAP distancing the latter from the bombing. Later, a video entitled *Echo of Jihad*, also attributed to the Haramain Brigades, documented the preparation of the attack. Little did the public know that the QAP and the Haramain Brigades were one and the same, and that it was al-Muqrin who had ordered the Washm bombing.[11]

[11] '*al-bayan al-rabi'* [Statement no. 4]' (www.qal3ah.org, 2004); Abd al-Aziz al-Muqrin, *27 April Audio Statement* (Sawt al-Jihad, 2004).

Text Box 5: Main attacks on security forces, April–June 2004

- *5 April – Jidda*: A police officer was shot dead at point-blank range during questioning of a suspect outside a shop.
- *9 April – Jidda*: A policeman in Jidda was shot and killed by gunmen in a car he had stopped to inspect.
- *13 April – Unayza*: Gunmen in a car attacked two separate police patrols on the Riyadh–Qasim road, killing four policemen before escaping.
- *14 April – Uyayna*: Militants attacked a checkpoint 35 km north-west of Riyadh, killing a policeman and injuring another, before escaping into the hills.
- *20 April – Burayda*: A militant opened fire at a checkpoint in Burayda, wounding two policemen before escaping.
- *1 June – Ta'if*: Two militants opened fire at police at a checkpoint on the Mecca–Ta'if highway. They were killed twelve hours later after fleeing and hiding in a nearby mountainous area.

The scale of the Washm bombing – the largest ever against a government target in the kingdom – also called for ideological clarification and justification. In late April, the QAP therefore published a book called *The Prophet's Guidance on Targeting Emergency Forces*, which blamed the police for provoking the violence and explained that the aggression of the security forces had prompted another organisation, the Haramain Brigades, to step in and defend the mujahidin.[12]

As if to emphasise the message that the QAP was only after Western targets, the militants launched a wave of simple but spectacular attacks on Western expatriates in May and June 2004. The offensive began on 1 May, when a group of four militants infiltrated the head office of the company ABB in the city of Yanbu on the west coast and opened fire on random employees of Western complexity. Five people died, in addition to the four attackers. The attack marked a significant tactical and geographical shift by the militants, and it raised fears that al-Qaida was targeting the oil industry. It later emerged that the Yanbu attack was perpetrated by a cell operating independently from the core QAP leadership. However, the blueprint for the Yanbu operation would soon be adopted and applied on a bigger scale by al-Muqrin and his men.[13]

On 29 May 2004, a very similar operation targeted a compound in Khobar, at the opposite end of the kingdom. A group of four militants referring to themselves as the 'Jerusalem Squadron' infiltrated

[12] al-Husni, *hidayat al-sari*. [13] al-Muqrin, *'li-kull al-raghibiyyin'*.

Text Box 6: Assassinations of Westerners, May–June 2004

- *22 May*: German citizen Jonathan Hermann Bengler was shot by gunmen in a car as he came out of a bank in Riyadh.
- *2 June*: An American and a Saudi bystander were wounded when gunmen opened fire outside a compound in Riyadh.
- *6 June*: Irish cameraman Simon Cumbers was killed and British journalist Frank Gardner critically wounded by gunmen in Riyadh's Suwaydi district while researching a documentary about the QAP.
- *8 June*: US citizen Robert Jacobs was killed by gunmen inside his own house in Riyadh.
- *12 June*: US citizen Kenneth Scroggs was shot and killed as he parked his car by his house in Riyadh.

a residential complex and went on a shooting spree, killing random Westerners and other non-Muslims before barricading themselves in a building with a small number of hostages. The attackers seemed to be inspired by the October 2002 Dubrovka theatre operation in Moscow and hoped to create an international hostage drama. They allegedly called the TV station al-Jazeera demanding to be given airtime, something the latter refused. When the drama ended a day later, twenty-two people were dead, while three of the militants had escaped.[14]

Shortly before the Khobar attack, militants in Riyadh had embarked on a different, but no less attention-grabbing strategy, namely assassinations of individual Westerners in Riyadh. The five such attacks which occurred in late May and early June shook the Western expatriate community in the kingdom to the core (see Text Box 6).

The pinnacle of this wave of violence was reached on 12 June, when a cell led by Abd al-Aziz al-Muqrin took the American citizen Paul Johnson hostage in Riyadh. The incident, which was to be the QAP's

[14] Knights, 'The Khobar Rampage, May 2004'; Abdul Hameed Bakier, 'Lessons from al-Qaeda's Attack on the Khobar Compound', *Terrorism Monitor* 4, no. 16 (2006). The attack was amply documented by the QAP itself; see '*bayan bi-sha'n ghazwat sariyyat al-quds* [Statement on the Raid of the Quds Squadron]' (www.qa3edoon.com, 2004); '*al-taqrir al-ikhbari al-hadi 'ashar bi-sha'n tafasil 'amaliyyat sariyat al-quds* [News Report Eleven on the Details of the Quds Brigade Operation]' (www.qa3edoon.com, 2004); '*liqa' khass ma' qa'id sariyat al-quds – fawwaz bin muhammad al-nashmi* [Special Interview with the Leader of the Quds Squadron Fawwaz bin Muhammad al-Nashmi]', *Sawt al-Jihad*, no. 18 (2004); and '*sariyat al-quds* [The Quds Squadron]'; *al-Ra'i al-Amm*, 31 May 2004.

first and last kidnapping, received enormous media attention, not least because the militants released videos on the Internet showing Johnson begging for his life. On 18 June, he was decapitated on camera and the gruesome video was posted online. All these relatively simple operations seriously undermined the sense of security among Western expatriates, many of whom left the kingdom at this point. Western media and foreign observers believed the Saudi authorities had lost the ability to maintain security, and some even believed the stability of the regime itself was at stake.[15]

In reality, however, it was the QAP that was on the brink of collapse. Spectacular as they seemed, the new tactics were a sign of weakness. The militants had been forced to use handguns creatively because they lacked explosives. Moreover, there was no broad uprising because most of the violence was the work of al-Muqrin's cell alone. The structural weakness of the QAP organisation became clear in the summer of 2004 when Saudi security services, helped by US intelligence, inflicted two crippling blows on the QAP. On 18 June the police located and killed Abd al-Aziz al-Muqrin and three of his closest companions at a gas station in Riyadh. This stripped the organisation of its most skilled militant entrepreneur. Then, on 20 July 2004, police raided a Riyadh house which had served as the organisation's de facto headquarters and the centre for the QAP's media production. The police allegedly seized a treasure trove of documents, computers and videos which would enable investigators to track down much of the remaining QAP network. This discovery effectively broke the back of al-Qaida on the Arabian Peninsula.[16]

Death rattle of the old QAP (August 2004–May 2005)

The period from August 2004 to May 2005 saw the elimination of the last remaining leaders of the original QAP – including al-Muqrin's successor Sa'ud al-Utaybi. Despite two major attacks in Jidda and Riyadh in December 2004, the QAP was unable to sustain and reconstitute itself. After the final gunbattle at al-Rass in early April 2005, the QAP was severely weakened as an organisation, although scattered cells of junior operatives would continue the fight.

[15] '*bayan bi-khusus al-asir al-amriki pul marshal junsun wa shurut itlaq sirahihi* [Statement on the American Prisoner Paul Johnson and the Conditions for his Release]' (www.qa3edoon.com, 2004); Ewan MacAskill and Brian Whitaker, 'Shaken Expatriates Rethink Saudi Future', *Guardian*, 2 June 2004.

[16] Author's interview with Nawaf Obaid; author's interview with former Saudi inmate who learned about the devastating impact of the 20 July raid directly from imprisoned QAP ideologue Faris al-Zahrani himself.

Initially it was difficult to see that the QAP was under heavy pressure. Assassinations of individual Westerners continued into August and September 2004. On 3 August, Irishman Anthony Higgins was killed by gunmen in his Riyadh office. On 15 September, Briton Edward Muirhead-Smith was shot and killed at a parking lot outside a shopping centre in Riyadh. Later the tactic spread to Jidda, where the French citizen Laurent Barbot was shot and killed on 26 September. However, these were the last assassinations of Westerners in Saudi Arabia for a long time – such attacks would not take place again until February 2007.

The intelligence successes of mid-2004 had given the Saudi security services a significant advantage over the QAP. Information discovered in the QAP headquarters as well as interrogations of captured militants enabled the police to identify a large number of operatives and facilitators across the country. Thus, in the autumn of 2004, the frequency of arrests and shoot-outs increased considerably (see Text Box 7). From late November onward, there were significantly fewer gunbattles between militants and police. With the exception of a 9 January 2005 shoot-out near the city of Zulfi, arrests and raids were met practically without resistance.

However, in December 2004 it became clear that some cells had escaped the dragnet. On 6 December, a group of five gunmen calling themselves the 'Falluja Squadron' attacked the US consulate in Jidda in a very well-planned operation. As the entrance gate opened to let in a diplomatic vehicle, the militants forced their way into the compound. The ensuing gunbattle left six Asian and African consulate employees dead and at least twelve others wounded.[17]

Meanwhile, another operational cell by the name 'al-Muqrin Squadron' had been preparing for a major operation involving two coordinated attacks on police targets in Riyadh. In the evening of 29 December, a car bomb exploded at the exit of a traffic tunnel near the Interior Ministry, killing the operative driving the car and wounding five bystanders. Half an hour later, a suicide car bomb blew up prematurely as it was heading full speed towards the entrance of a training facility for the National Guard. Two attackers died and twelve guardsmen were wounded in the blast. An hour later, police located

[17] Michael Knights, 'Operation Conquest of Falluja: Assault on the US Consulate in Jeddah, December 2004', in *JTIC Terrorism Case Study* (Coulsdon: Jane's Information Group, 2006); '*bayan hawla 'amaliyyat al-qunsuliyya al-amrikiyya fi jidda (ghazwat falluja)* [Statement on the American Consulate Operation in Jidda (The Falluja Raid)]' (www.qa3edoon.com, 2004); '*ghazwat al-qunsuliyya al-salibiyya al-amrikiyya* [Raid on the American Crusader Consulate]' (Sawt al-Jihad Media Production, 2006).

Text Box 7: Major crackdowns, August–November 2004.

- *11 August*: A militant was killed and policeman wounded in a shoot-out in Mecca.
- *31 August*: A militant was killed and three militants wounded in a shoot-out at a checkpoint in Ahsa.
- *3 September*: A policeman was killed and three others wounded in a clash with militants in Burayda.
- *5 September*: Three Saudi security officers chasing suspected extremists in Burayda died when their patrol car caught fire after being hit by gunfire.
- *20 September*: A militant and three policemen were wounded in a shoot-out in Tabuk.
- *12 October*: Three militants were killed in a shoot-out during a police raid on a hideout in Riyadh.
- *3 November*: Two policemen and a militant were wounded in a shoot-out in Burayda.
- *5 November*: A militant was killed and three police were wounded in a raid on an apartment in the Jamia district of Jidda.
- *9 November*: A militant was killed and another wounded during a raid on another house in the Jamia district of Jidda.
- *16 November*: A policeman was killed and eight others wounded in a shoot-out in Unayza.
- *27 November*: A militant was killed in a clash with police in the Jamia district of Jidda.

the remnants of the cell and initiated a gunbattle which left as many as seven militants dead.[18]

Although the 29 December operation was large in terms of weaponry and casualty toll, it was widely perceived as a failure for the QAP.[19] Neither of the two bombs detonated in the right location, and only militants were killed. The ability of the QAP to carry out large-scale bombing had clearly diminished. Indeed, it would take over a year until another significant bombing was attempted. The lack of militant activity in early 2005 combined with the discontinuation, since late 2004, of the QAP's Internet publications such as *Sawt al-Jihad* seemed to confirm the view that the organisation was incapacitated. However, many

[18] '*bayan hawla 'amaliyyat al-dakhiliyya fi'l-riyadh* [Statement on the Interior Ministry Operation in Riyadh]' (www.qa3edoon.com, 2004).

[19] Stephen Ulph, 'Al-Qaeda's Diminishing Returns in the Peninsula', *Terrorism Focus* 2, no. 1 (2005).

unanswered questions lingered, not least concerning the whereabouts of senior leaders still on the run.

The questions were answered in early April 2005 when a local resident in the town of al-Rass alerted the police to suspicious activity at a nearby farm. When security forces tried to search the farm on 3 April, they were met with heavy armed resistance. The three-day gunbattle that followed was the bloodiest to take place during the QAP campaign. Its ferocity reflected the importance of the location. Holed up inside the farm was practically the entire leadership of the QAP – or what remained of it. Realising that they represented the nerve centre of the organisation, they fought until the end using their gigantic weapons store. When the dust settled on 5 April, 14 militants – including top leaders Karim Majati and Saʿud al-Utaybi – were dead, while 5 more were wounded. On the police side, there were almost 100 casualties. The al-Rass event effectively marked the end of the original QAP. By now, practically all of the militants who had been part of Yusuf al-Uyayri's original network were dead or captured.

Nevertheless, the jihadists had a final surprise in store. In late April 2005, the twenty-ninth issue of *Sawt al-Jihad* appeared on the Internet after a six-month hiatus. The magazine's continued appearance despite QAP setbacks had puzzled many observers in 2004. Now it seemed to defy logic again, by reappearing after the al-Rass incident with vivid accounts from inside the siege. However, the mystery was largely solved in May 2005, when police arrested Abd al-Aziz al-Anzi, a previously unknown figure. It turned out that al-Anzi was the last remaining member of the original *Sawt al-Jihad* editorial committee and that he had single-handedly produced the April 2005 'bonus issue'. A similar development occurred in January 2007 when a jihadist Internet entrepreneur named Abu Abdallah al-Najdi produced a thirtieth issue of *Sawt al-Jihad*, only to be arrested later in the spring. The al-Anzi and al-Najdi cases illustrate how single media-savvy individuals can dramatically increase the perceived size and strength of an organisation.[20]

The new generation (June 2005–December 2008)

The people who continued the jihad on the Arabian Peninsula from mid-2005 onward represented a new generation of QAP militants. Gone were the senior operatives who had trained in Afghanistan and

[20] Shaun Waterman, 'Saudi Arrests are Effort against Web Jihad', *United Press International*, 18 June 2007. For more on Abu Abdallah al-Najdi, see Faris bin Huzzam, '*amir al-lajna al-iʿlamiyya* [Commander of the Media Committee]', *al-Riyadh*, 18 July 2006.

known Yusuf al-Uyayri. Their successors had been recruited to the organisation in late 2003 or 2004 and had usually no jihad experience abroad. This generational change was visible on the new list of thirty-six most wanted militants which was published by the Interior Ministry on 28 June 2005. More important, the remaining networks were fragmented and had no central leadership. After Sa'ud al-Utaybi's death at al-Rass, Salih al-Awfi was declared the official QAP leader. When the latter died on 18 August 2005, no new leader was announced, though the authorities later suggested Fahd al-Juwayr was the most senior figure. After al-Juwayr's death on 27 February 2006, no leadership figure seemed to emerge.

The fragmentation on the ground was illustrated by the occasional appearance of Internet statements by obscure organisational entities and previously unknown individuals. Between October 2005 and March 2006 a short series of statements were released under the name 'Echo of Tuwayq Brigades in Zulfi'. In mid-2006 another obscure entity entitled 'Good Tidings Foundation for Media Production' published a video (*Breaking Captivity*) and a series of statements before being officially 'included' in the al-Qaida organisation. These statements were most likely posted by scattered individuals or cells with few or no connections to the al-Uyayri network.[21]

In the second half of 2005, the new generation of Saudi militants was clearly on the defensive. In fact, during all of 2005, the QAP only successfully executed two minor attacks, both of which were directed at security forces. On 19 June 2005, a group of militants killed Mubarak

[21] Abdullah al-Shihri, 'Leader of al-Qaida in Saudi Arabia Killed', *Associated Press*, 28 February 2006; Abu Hajir al-Zulfawi, '*awwal bayan rasmi li-kata'ib sada tuwayq bi'l-zulfi* [First Official Statement by the Echo of Tuwayq Brigades in Zulfi]' (2005); Abu Hajir al-Zulfawi, '*al-radd 'ala takahhunat jaridat al-watan* [Response to the Speculations of *al-Watan* Newspaper] (Statement 3)' (2006). For an analysis of the Echo of Tuwayq phenomenon, see Ali al-Qahtani, '*bayan "kata'ib al-zulfi" yatadamman al-'ilan 'an ta'sis al-jama'a al-munasira li'l-qa'ida* [Statement from "Zulfi Brigades" Announces the Foundation of a Support Group for al-Qaida]', *al-Watan*, 19 October 2005; and Stephen Ulph, 'Another al-Qaeda Group Forms in Saudi Arabia', *Terrorism Focus* 2, no. 19 (2005); '*mu'assasat al-basha'ir li'l-intaj al-i'lami tuqaddim al-asdar al-awwal: kasr al-asr* [The Good Tidings Foundation for Media Production Presents First Publication: "Breaking Captivity"]', (www.w-n-n.com, 2006); '*bayan man nahnu wa madha nurid wa ma 'alaqatuna bi-tanzim al-qa'ida fi jazirat al-'arab* [Statement on Who We Are, What We Want and What is Our Relationship with al-Qaida on the Arabian Peninsula]' (www.al-hesbah.org, 2006); '*bayan min tanzim al-qa'ida fi jazirat al-'arab yubashshir bi-indhima' mu'assasat al-basha'ir li'l-intaj al-i'lami taht liwa'ihi* [Statement from the al-Qaida Organisation on the Arabian Peninsula Announcing the Inclusion of the Good Tidings Foundation for Media Production under its Banner]' (www.al-boraq.com, 2006); Chris Heffelfinger, 'Statement to the Saudi Mujahideen Summons Iraq Returnees', *Terrorism Focus* 3, no. 26 (2006); 'Group Vows Revenge after Saudi Shoot-Out: Web', *Reuters*, 24 June 2006.

Text Box 8: Major gunbattles, July–October 2005

- *3 July – al-Hayyari killing*: Senior militant Yunus al-Hayyari was killed in a police raid on a hideout in Riyadh. Two militants and six policemen were injured.
- *18 August – al-Awfi killing*: Alleged QAP leader Salih al-Awfi and another militant were killed in a police raid on a safe house in Medina.
- *18 August – Riyadh raid*: A militant was killed in a gunbattle with police in Riyadh.
- *4–6 September – Dammam siege*: Five militants were killed in a three-day gunbattle and siege at a safe house in Dammam. The militants were allegedly planning an attack on an oil target in the Eastern province.
- *30 October*: A gunman killed a police officer in a shoot-out in Mecca.

al-Sawat – a police interrogator infamous for his alleged brutality towards prisoners – at his house in Riyadh. On 27 December, two wanted QAP militants went on a shooting rampage against random police patrols in the Burayda area, killing five policemen. Both perpetrators were eventually also killed.

The militants were unable to carry out attacks in this period because the police held the initiative. In the second half of 2005, police discovered numerous weapons caches and safe houses while continuing to conduct arrests. Most of the police operations were met with little resistance, but a few developed into gunbattles (see Text Box 8).

By early 2006, the shoot-outs had become even less frequent, and once again it seemed that the QAP campaign was dying out. But yet again, the militants had a card up their sleeve. On 24 February 2006, a group of militants calling themselves 'the Usama bin Ladin Squadron' tried to drive two explosives-laden vehicles into the Abqaiq oil refinery through one of the side gates. Both cars blew up prematurely during the gunbattle with the guards at the gate. The police were then able to locate the planners of the operation, all of whom were killed in a gunbattle in Riyadh on 27 February. This was the QAP's first attack on an oil facility and it sent shockwaves through the global oil markets. However, spectacular as it may have been, the Abqaiq operation was essentially an overly ambitious attack that ended in failure. As such, it illustrated the operational weakness from which the QAP had suffered since mid-2004.[22]

[22] Michael Knights, 'Abqaiq Attack Underscores Terrorist Failings and Highlights Growing Focus on Oil Targets', *Olive Group Special Report*, March 2006. For the

The Abqaiq operation was the only significant attack in 2006 to reach execution stage. This is not to say that the militants lacked the intention. In the course of 2006, the police foiled several large-scale plots in the making. On 21 April, police discovered a car full of weapons, forged papers and maps of vital installations in the Eastern province. On 23 June, police raided a Riyadh flat, setting off a gunbattle in which six militants and a police officer died. Inside the apartment they found martyrdom videos and other evidence indicating that the cell was on the verge of executing a suicide operation, allegedly on a 'security target', in Riyadh. In July and August, Saudi police arrested as many as eighty suspected militants across the kingdom. On 12 August another gunbattle erupted in the Jamia district in Jidda, leaving two militants dead.

The last lethal attack to take place in Saudi Arabia before this book went to press was the killing by gunfire of four French tourists near the archaeological site of Mada'in Salih north of Medina on 26 February 2007. It was perpetrated by a four-man cell from Medina who escaped the scene but were hunted down over the course of the following six months. Since then the Saudi authorities have periodically announced the arrests of large numbers of people. For example, a news report in June 2008 said 701 suspects had been arrested earlier that year. These announcements reflected both a change in communication strategy (based on 'saving up' arrests rather than announcing them as they happen) as well as a tougher approach to Internet propagandists and Saudis supporting the jihad in Iraq, people who tended not to be arrested in the past. However, some of the cells uncovered in 2007 and 2008 were allegedly preparing large and ambitious plots to strike at oil facilities.[23]

militants' own account, see '*al-taqrir al-ikhbari al-hadi 'ashar bi-sha'n tafasil 'amaliyyat sariyat al-shaykh usama bin ladin* [Eleventh News Report on the Details of the Operation by the Sheikh Usama bin Ladin Squadron]' (www.qa3edoon.com, 2006). See also Michael Scheuer, Stephen Ulph and John C. K. Daly, *Saudi Arabian Oil Facilities: The Achilles Heel of the Western Economy* (Washington, DC: The Jamestown Foundation, 2006); Khalid R. al-Rodhan, *The Impact of the Abqaiq Attack on Saudi Energy Security* (Washington, DC: Center for Strategic and International Studies, 2006); Simon Henderson, 'Al-Qaeda Attack on Abqaiq: The Vulnerability of Saudi Oil', in *Policy Watch* (Washington, DC: Washington Institute of Near East Policy, 2006); Stephen Ulph, 'Mujahideen Explain Away Failures of the Abqaiq Attack', *Terrorism Focus* 3, no. 9 (2006).

[23] Hassan M. Fattah, 'Gunmen Kill 3 French Sightseers on Road Near Saudi Holy City', *New York Times*, 27 February 2007; Michael Slackman, 'Saudis Arrest 172 in Anti-terror Sweep', *New York Times*, 27 April 2007; Sulayman Nimr, 'Saudi Detains 208 Suspects in Plot Targeting Oil Facility', *Agence France Presse*, 28 November 2007; Donna Abu Nasr, 'Saudi: 701 Suspected Militants Arrested this Year', *Associated Press*, 25 June 2008.

Although shoot-outs, low-level attacks and arrests continued, it was fairly clear in late 2009 that the jihad on the Arabian Peninsula had lost its momentum. The rate and quality of operations had gradually decreased since the beginning of the campaign. All of the original QAP leaders were gone. The number of active militants had decreased to somewhere in the low tens. There was a small trickle of new recruits, but these did not nearly have the skills and capabilities of the QAP pioneers. *Sawt al-Jihad* and *Mu'askar al-Battar* were defunct, and the level of jihadist Internet activity in Saudi Arabia had decreased considerably. For all intents and purposes, the campaign had failed.

Explaining the downfall of the QAP

Three factors undermined the jihad on the Arabian Peninsula. First was the power of the state, whose unlimited resources and efficient counterterrorism strategy made the QAP's campaign militarily unviable. Second was the lack of popular support for the QAP's project and the popular perception of the militants as revolutionaries bent on creating disorder. Third was the Iraq war which split the Saudi jihadist movement and undermined mobilisation to the QAP.

If Saudi Arabia's policing of its militant Islamist community had been periodically complacent or inefficient in the past, it all changed with the East Riyadh bombing. From May 2003 onward, the state devoted its full resources to combating Islamist militants. The resources allocated to counterterrorism were colossal: the total security budget in 2004, 2005 and 2006 was estimated at US$8.5, 10 and 12 billion respectively. The Interior Ministry was practically given a blank cheque for personnel recruitment and equipment purchases. It constructed state-of-the-art training facilities and electronic surveillance systems. Training of special forces was intensified with considerable assistance from the United Kingdom. CIA analysts and technical experts came to Riyadh to work side by side with their Saudi counterparts, bringing crucial expertise in advanced intelligence collection and analysis. The seriousness of the violence and the many casualties in police ranks also changed the culture and attitudes within the security services. The determination and morale of police and intelligence officers increased, as did their salaries. In short, the May 2003 bombing sparked a total overhaul of the Saudi security establishment.[24]

[24] For details of Saudi counterterrorism efforts since May 2003, see Anthony Cordesman and Nawaf Obaid, *Saudi National Security: Military and Security Services – Challenges and Developments* (Washington, DC: CSIS, 2004), 144–7; Obaid, 'Remnants of al-Qaeda'; 'Saudi–US Cooperation in War on Terror Sharply Up: Official', *Arab*

The result of these efforts was a dramatic increase in the so-called 'hard counterterrorism' capability of the Saudi security apparatus. SWAT (Special Weapons and Tactics) teams were much more efficient, and the intelligence services became more professional. Advances in technical surveillance gave the police de facto hegemony over the Internet, the telephone network and the road network. Admittedly, the change did not happen overnight, for the first year or two of the campaign saw many examples of poorly handled situations. Nevertheless, the overall trend was one of considerable improvement – perhaps the most spectacular capability increase of any counterterrorism apparatus in modern history.

However, the Saudi handling of the QAP was not based on hard counterterrorism alone. In fact, the state's use of force was relatively measured and targeted, at least compared with other Arab countries' handling of militant Islamists. The 'soft' Saudi approach worried many foreign commentators, some of whom even criticised Saudi Arabia for not using repressive measures of the Egyptian and Algerian kind. In retrospect, it is clear that it was precisely the restrained and diversified nature of Saudi counterterrorism which made it so effective.[25]

Saudi soft counterterrorism had many different components, three of which are crucial for understanding the QAP's downfall. One was the circumscription of the organisation's resources. The authorities filled the many loopholes in the charitable and financial sectors which had enabled the militants to obtain funds. They cracked down on the huge illegal arms market and boosted border control, making explosives and detonators less available. These measures, combined with the seizure of safe houses and weapons stores, slowly but surely dried up the QAP's resources.

The second key element to the 'soft' counterterrorism strategy was the creation of exit options for the militants. The regime opened communication channels and established 'ports of call' for potential deserters. A month-long general amnesty was declared in mid-2004 and mid-2006, and militants were encouraged to surrender throughout the campaign. Low-profile semi-official mediation initiatives involving influential Islamists such as Safar al-Hawali and Muhsin al-Awaji were also launched. Surrenders were highly publicised and repentant

News, 25 October 2003; Abdullah F. Ansary, 'Combating Extremism: A Brief Overview of Saudi Arabia's Approach', *Middle East Policy* 15, no. 2 (2008); E. Glass and Y. Yehoshua, 'Saudi Arabia's Anti-Terror Campaign', *MEMRI Inquiry and Analysis Series*, no. 425 (2008).

[25] Teitelbaum, 'Terrorist Challenges'; Christopher Boucek, *Saudi Arabia's 'Soft' Counterterrorism Strategy* (Washington, DC: Carnegie Endowment for International Peace, 2008).

militants regularly appeared on television, in order to give the impression that desertions were common (which, in fact, was not the case).

To further encourage desertions, the state attempted to appear as merciful and forgiving towards repentant militants. This began with de facto abstention from prisoner abuse. By most available accounts, it seems that the police really did not torture captured QAP militants, at least not with the methods and on the scale it had done in the mid-1990s. In order to counter the lingering torture stories from the mid-1990s, the authorities sought to create a degree of transparency about prisoner treatment by broadcasting interviews with detainees praising the prison conditions in more or less convincing fashion. The government also launched a much-publicised prisoner re-education programme designed to deradicalise detained militants and reintegrate them into society. While the soft treatment of detainees produced only negligible desertions from the QAP, it had the much more important effect of stemming new recruitment and of preventing further radicalisation of detainees. A less savoury part of the strategy to appear as non-repressive was the regime's decision to avoid public terrorism trials. Almost a thousand people were arrested during the campaign, yet none were tried in court until secret trials began in 2009.[26]

The third and most important component of the soft Saudi counter-terrorism strategy was the propaganda campaign. Saudi authorities ran a vast and highly sophisticated campaign for the hearts and minds of the population in general and the Islamist community in particular. The state used all available outlets, from the media to the official religious sector to the education system to convey one overarching message, namely that the militants were confused rebels bent on killing Muslims and creating disorder.

The genius of the Saudi information strategy was that it portrayed the militants as revolutionaries, thereby exploiting the taboo of domestic rebellion in Saudi political culture to delegitimise the militants in the eyes of the population. The media notably used every available

[26] 'Terrorists Offered Amnesty', *Arab News*, 24 June 2004; 'Saudi's Qaeda Rejects Renewed Amnesty by King: Web', *Reuters*, 4 July 2006. It was even rumoured at one point that the Egyptian Islamist lawyer Muntasir al-Zayyat would come to Saudi Arabia to mediate, though this never happened; 'The Lawyer of the Egyptian Islamic Groups Mediates to Stop Violence in Saudi Arabia', *ArabicNews.com*, 20 May 2004; John Solomon, 'Saudi Interrogators Try Gentler Approach', *Associated Press*, 30 November 2003; James Sturcke, 'Come on in ... the Bread and Water is Fine', *Guardian*, 15 December 2004; 'Saudi Terror Trials Reach Verdict', *Reuters*, 8 July 2009. For more on prisoner rehabilitation, see Christopher Boucek, 'Extremist Reeducation and Rehabilitation in Saudi Arabia', *Jamestown Terrorism Monitor* 5, no. 16 (2007) and Lawrence E. Cline, 'Changing Jihadist Behaviour: The Saudi Model', *Small Wars Journal*, 10 April 2009.

opportunity to highlight and magnify the effect of the violence on Muslim life and property, thereby discrediting the militants' claim to focus on Westerners. After the Muhayya bombing, for example, TV and newspapers showed close-up pictures of wounded Arab children. Media also highlighted the death of an 11-year-old Syrian girl in the Washm bombing in April 2004 and that of a 10-year-old Egyptian boy in the Khobar attack the following month.

The authorities also used so-called 'black propaganda' (i.e. fabricated information) about alleged QAP plans to kill Muslim civilians and about the militants' alleged desecration of mosques and the Qur'an. Practically every year since 2003, Saudi authorities have claimed to have foiled al-Qaida plots to attack Mecca during the pilgrimage. One particularly implausible report claimed militants had booby-trapped copies of the Qur'an in preparation for a Hajj attack.[27]

Another part of the information strategy consisted of parading repentant militants on television and having them explain how they had been wrong in taking up arms. In November and December 2003, Ali al-Khudayr, Nasir al-Fahd and Ahmad al-Khalidi were shown repenting on television. In January 2003 came the first in a series of three programmes entitled *Inside the Cell* in which captured QAP militants spoke of how they had been lured into terrorism by cunning al-Qaida leaders.

The government propaganda campaign exacerbated a crucial problem facing the QAP, namely the lack of public support, even in the Islamist community, for a violent campaign on Saudi soil. The disconnection between the QAP and its alleged constituency was laid bare from day one of the campaign. The 12 May 2003 operation was met with widespread condemnation in Saudi society as a whole, including in conservative Islamist circles. Newspapers were full of editorials and op-eds condemning the attacks. The entire religious establishment as well as the heavyweight Sahwist clerics decried the bombings. Those who did not condemn it cited conspiracy theories exonerating the jihadist community. However, all such doubts disappeared with the Muhayya bombing in November 2003. The grim pictures of wounded Muslim children on the front pages of Saudi newspapers turned the domestic public opinion decisively against the militants. Even militant Islamist organisations abroad – including Hamas and the Egyptian al-Jama'a al-Islamiyya – criticised the violence. From then on, the broad

[27] 'Official: Saudis Foil Terror Attack on Pilgrims', *Reuters*, 4 November 2003; P. K. Abdul Ghafour, 'Cell Was Targeting Muslims', *Arab News*, 5 November 2003; Mohammed Alkhereiji, 'Abdullah Tells Citizens to Report Suspects', *Arab News*, 22 June 2003.

consensus in the kingdom was that the militants were terrorists who posed a threat to Saudi society. The QAP's PR defeat underlined the weakness of global jihad ideology compared to classical jihad as well as the relative ideological success of the state's religious discourse in the domestic arena.[28]

The chronic legitimacy deficit created a hostile operational environment. The number of sympathisers prepared to extend assistance to militants decreased while the number of people willing to report suspicious behaviour to the police increased. With eyes and ears everywhere around them, the militants' mobility was restricted and their access to money and hideouts was limited. In October 2003, a *Sawt al-Jihad* editorial noted that 'the number of those who give good advice has become smaller, and the mujahidin have become strangers among family, relatives and friends; the mujahidin can rarely find helpers in doing good, and do not find support along the path except from those whom God has spared.'[29]

More significantly, the QAP experienced serious recruitment problems once the campaign was launched. Numerous articles in *Sawt al-Jihad* lamented the lack of a response to the call for jihad and called on former acquaintances of the militants to join. For example, Abd al-Aziz al-Muqrin appealed to those who trained with him in Afghanistan, while Isa al-Awshan called on his old friends from the religious summer camps. Others hoped to mobilise their local communities with articles entitled 'To the People of Zulfi' and the like. Yet others left QAP propaganda on the doorsteps of former friends. The QAP's propaganda efforts to enlist the support of women – a relatively unusual initiative for a jihadist group – also reflected the organisation's recruitment problems. The increasingly frequent appeals to tribal identity in the QAP's texts from late 2003 onward must also be understood in this perspective.[30]

[28] See for example 'The Enemy Within [Editorial]', *Arab News*, 14 May 2003 and Raid Qusti, 'Cleaning Up Our Own Backyard', *Arab News*, 21 May 2003; '*bayan hawla hawadith al-tafjirat* [Statement on the Bombing Incidents]' (www.islamtoday.net, 16 May 2003); Salman al-Awda, '*al-tafjirat wa tada'iyatuhu* [The Bombings and their Falterings]' (www.islamtoday.net, 2003); 'Hamas Condemns Riyadh Bombing as Harmful to Islam', *Reuters*, 13 November 2003; and Karam Zuhdi, ed., *tafjirat al-riyadh: al-ahkam wa'l-athar* [The Riyadh Bombings: Rulings and Effects] (Cairo: Maktabat al-Turath al-Islami, 2003).

[29] *Sawt al-Jihad*, no 1 (2003).

[30] '*liqa' ma' ahad al-matlubin al-tisa' 'ashar* (2)', 27; Isa Al Awshan, '*risala maftuha ila shabab al-marakiz al-sayfiyya* [Open Letter to the Youth of the Summer Camps]', *Sawt al-Jihad*, no. 19 (2004); Fahd al-Juwayr al-Farraj, '*ya ahl al-zulfi* [Oh People of Zulfi]', *Sawt al-Jihad*, no. 18 (2004); Ra'id bin Abdallah al-Bahlal, '*ya ahl al-zulfi … ayna ghayratukum?* [Oh People of Zulfi … Where are the Rest of You?]', *Sawt al-Jihad*, no.

Another symptom of the QAP's legitimacy deficit were their constant attempts to open a debate with more mainstream Islamist figures. The mid-2003 imprisonment of the sheikhs of the al-Shu'aybi school had deprived the QAP of a crucial legitimising resource. The people who served as QAP ideologues during the campaign, such as Faris al-Zahrani and Abdallah al-Rushud, were obscure and intellectually mediocre figures who commanded very little respect and influence in the wider Islamist community. This was a serious disadvantage in the Saudi arena where political legitimacy is intimately tied to scholarly credibility. Realising that they would need the support of more influential clerics, al-Zahrani and the other QAP ideologues wrote a number of open letters to the ulama as well as personal letters to figures such as Safar al-Hawali. These initiatives failed, because it was inconceivable for mainstream Islamists to support the QAP. The old Sahwist figures had never espoused violent methods and had moved closer to the regime after their release in the late 1990s.[31]

As often happens in clandestine organisations, the QAP responded to political adversity with denial and introversion. The militants dismissed all news reports that contradicted their world-view – such as reports of Muslim casualties – as fabrications. Their own accounts of attacks and shoot-outs became increasingly exaggerated and unrealistic. The failure of the people to respond to the call for jihad was blamed on government manipulation. To maintain the purity of this ideological universe, QAP call leaders actively prevented their followers from accessing mainstream media or contacting friends and family. The militants drifted out of touch with reality and into an increasingly delusional ideological universe. As a result, QAP cells became completely disconnected from the social and political setting in which they operated. Unable to understand the political repercussions of their violence, they undertook operations which further isolated them. They

27 (2004); Muhammad al-Salim, '*ya ahl kuwayt*! [People of Kuwait!]', *Sawt al-Jihad*, no. 13 (2004); Al Awshan, '*khalid bin 'abdallah al-subayt*'; Muna bint Salih al-Sharqawi, '*ya nisa' dawrukun – fa-qad nama al-rijal* [Women, it's Your Turn, for the Men have Slept]' (www.qa3edoon.com, 2004). For the QAP's tribal discourse, see Madawi al-Rasheed, 'The Local and the Global in Saudi Salafism', *ISIM Review* 21 (2008).

[31] See e.g. Abdallah al-Najdi, '*risala ila al-'ulama wa'l-du'at* [Letter to the Scholars and the Preachers]' (www.qa3edoon.com, 2004); Abdallah al-Rushud, '*talab munazara ma' al-shaykh nasir al-'umar* [Request for Debate with Sheikh Nasir al-Umar]' (www.qa3edoon.com, 2004); and Faris al-Zahrani, '*talab munazara ma' safar al-hawali* [Request for Debate with Safar al-Hawali]' (www.qa3edoon.com, 2004); Faris al-Zahrani, '*bayan hawla al-da'awa al-kadhiba min safar al-hawali wa ashbahihi* [Statement Regarding the False Claims by Safar al-Hawali and his Ilk]' (www.tawhid.ws, 2004).

thus became caught in a vicious circle which, to use Donatella Della Porta's expression, drove them deeper and deeper underground.[32]

The third key reason for the failure of the QAP campaign was the parallel jihad in Iraq, which accentuated the split between the 'classical' and the 'global' currents of the Saudi jihadist movement.

Post-2003 Iraq attracted classical jihadists from Saudi Arabia and elsewhere because it was a textbook case of defensive jihad. Foreign military forces occupied Muslim territory after what was widely perceived as an unjustified act of aggression. The Iraqi insurgency thus enjoyed considerable support in pan-Islamist Saudi Arabia. The mainstream Saudi Islamist position – articulated by old Sahwists as well as some establishment clerics – was that the jihad in Iraq constituted a collective obligation (*fard kifaya*), that is, a duty for Iraqis but optional for Saudis. Classical jihadists went a step further and viewed the jihad as an individual obligation (*fard 'ayn*) for all Muslims including Saudis. For the classical jihadists, there was no jihad more important than Iraq. In addition to being a theologically clear-cut case, Iraq was also much closer to Saudi Arabia, both geographically and culturally, than previous jihad zones such as Afghanistan, Bosnia or Chechnya. Thus from early 2003 onward, classical jihadists worked hard to mobilise young Muslims to fight in Iraq. Thousands of foreign fighters, including over a thousand Saudis, travelled to Iraq and continue to do so at the current time of writing (although the flow has abated since 2005). Many commentators rightly described Iraq as the 'new Afghanistan' for the jihadist movement.[33]

The global jihadists such as the QAP held a slightly different view on the jihad in Iraq. While they considered Iraq an extremely important cause, they saw it as only one of several legitimate battlegrounds in the overall jihad against the Crusaders. Because resources for violent Islamist activism were scarce in Saudi Arabia after May 2003, classical and global jihadists quickly found themselves in a state of competition over recruits and money. This drove the two camps into a heated ideological debate over which battlefront was preferable: Iraq or Saudi Arabia.

[32] Abdul Ghafour, 'Al-Qaeda Controls Young Operatives by Torture Threats'.

[33] '*jam' min al-'ulama' al-sa'udiyyin yuwajjihun khatiban maftuhan li'l-sha'b al-'iraqi* [Group of Saudi Scholars Direct Open Letter to the Iraqi People]' (www.islamtoday.com, 2004). See also Ayidh al-Qarni's statement on al-Jazeera on 14 November 2004, Salman al-Awda's article in *al-Riyadh*, 20 November 2004, and Safar al-Hawali's interview with *al-Ukaz*, 19 May 2005. Nawaf Obaid and Anthony Cordesman, *Saudi Militants in Iraq: Assessment and Kingdom's Response* (Washington, DC: Center for Strategic and International Studies, 2005); Thomas Hegghammer, *Saudi Militants in Iraq: Backgrounds and Recruitment Patterns* (Kjeller: Norwegian Defence Research Establishment (FFI/Report), 2007).

The controversy emerged almost immediately after the May 2003 bombings when critics suggested that the QAP go to Iraq if they really wanted to fight the Crusaders. The disagreement was visible on jihadist Internet forums throughout the summer of 2003. In the first issue of *Sawt al-Jihad* in October, Abd al-Aziz al-Muqrin felt obliged to explain why he had not gone to Iraq. The controversy escalated significantly in December 2003, when the Chechnya-based Saudi ideologue Abu Umar al-Sayf released an audio recording in which he publicly criticised the QAP and called on Saudis to fight in Iraq instead. Al-Sayf and other classical jihadists argued that the violence in Saudi Arabia diverted attention and resources away from the jihad in Iraq. The QAP countered with articles in *Sawt al-Jihad* arguing that the jihad in Saudi Arabia was not at all incompatible with the jihad in Iraq and that Saudis should fight the Crusaders close to home, where they could have a stronger impact. The QAP was clearly struggling to counter the forceful arguments of the classical jihadists, for in the spring of 2004 they published a series of articles addressing common 'misconceptions' and 'doubts' about the jihad in Saudi Arabia, foremost of which was the Iraq argument. However, in mid-2004 the debate seemed to settle firmly in favour of the classical jihadist position. Interestingly, Bin Ladin and Ayman al-Zawahiri never took part in the debate, but they certainly spoke more about Iraq than about Saudi Arabia in their statements in this period.[34]

The ideological conflict between classical and global jihadists manifested itself in a de facto organisational separation between the two parts of the Saudi jihadist community. People involved in recruitment and fundraising for Iraq seem to have held the QAP at arm's length for fear of attracting police attention. Conversely, the QAP had little to gain from interacting with activists who were sending recruits and money out of the country. This is not to say that the two networks were completely isolated from one another. There were personal contacts and declarations of mutual support between the QAP and al-Qaida in Iraq. A few QAP fighters also left Saudi Arabia for Iraq as the situation

[34] al-Rashid, *intiqad al-i'tirad 'ala tafjirat al-riyadh*; Sada al-Da'wa, '*ma lakum la tuqatilun fi'l-'iraq wa jami' al-turuq maftuha?* [Why Are You Not Fighting in Iraq When All the Roads are Open?]' (www.sadaaljihad.net, 2003); '*liqa' ma' ahad al-matlubin al-tisa' 'ashar* (1)'; 'Al-Qa'ida Leader Calls for Attacks on Americans in Iraq Rather than on the Saudi Government in Saudi Arabia', *MEMRI Special Dispatch*, no. 635 (2003); Muhammad al-Salim, '*la tadhhabu ila al-'iraq*! [Don't Go to Iraq!]', *Sawt al-Jihad*, no. 7 (2003); Muhammad al-Salim, '*labayka ya 'iraq* [Woe to you, Iraq]', *Sawt al-Jihad*, no. 11 (2004); '*tasa'ulat hawla al-jihad didd al-salibiyyin fi jazirat al-'arab* [Questions about the Jihad against the Crusaders on the Arabian Peninsula]', *Sawt al-Jihad*, no. 11 (2004).

in the kingdom became more difficult. Nevertheless, the examples of interaction are very few considering the size of the two networks. For all intents and purposes, the QAP and the Saudi Iraq network were independent entities.[35]

The split in the Saudi jihadist movement greatly undermined support for and recruitment to the QAP. Aspiring Saudi jihadists keen on fighting in defence of the Islamic nation saw Iraq as a vastly more attractive battleground than the streets of Riyadh and Mecca. No Saudi donor would fund weapons that would be used literally outside their doorstep when he or she could support the mujahidin in Iraq instead. The advantage of the 'Khattabists' over the 'Bin Ladinists' manifested itself very clearly in the outcome of their recruitment efforts. While the QAP only recruited a small number of relatives and acquaintances, the classical jihadists mobilised an entire new generation of Saudis for Iraq.

Iraq was not the only battlefront which attracted Saudi classical jihadists in this period. In early 2006 there were several indications of a renewed flow of Saudi fighters (although very few, most likely in the tens) to Afghanistan. In April 2006 a Saudi citizen tried to infiltrate the Jordanian–Israeli border to fight for the Palestinians. In the summer of 2006 came reports of Saudi money and fighters (allegedly some thirty to forty individuals) reaching Somalia to support the struggle against US-backed Ethiopia. During the violence in Lebanon in the spring of 2007, there were reports of Saudis fighting alongside the jihadist group Fatah al-Islam. This continued flow of Saudis to foreign jihad zones suggested that the classical jihadist movement was still very much alive in the kingdom, despite the weakening of the QAP. The victory of the classical jihadists supports the hypothesis that Bin Ladin's global jihadism has been far more controversial in Saudi Arabia than often assumed, and that the mainstream of the militant Islamist community in Saudi Arabia has been driven by the slightly more moderate classical jihadist ideology.[36]

[35] QAP operative Yunus al-Hayyari was said to have been an old friend of Abu Anas al-Shami, the main ideologue of Abu Mus'ab al-Zarqawi's group al-Tawhid wa'l-Jihad until his death in September 2004. Examples of declarations of support include the June 2004 symbolic funeral and three-day mourning session in a radical Baghdad mosque in honour of the death of Abd al-Aziz al-Muqrin; see Nir Rosen, *In the Belly of the Green Bird: The Triumph of the Martyrs in Iraq* (New York: Free Press, 2006), 191. In a July 2005 statement, Abu Mus'ab al-Zarqawi praised QAP ideologue Abdallah al-Rushud who had allegedly died in Iraq. On 6 September 2005, the Iraqi jihadi ideologue Abu Maysara al-Iraqi issued a statement of support for the QAP.

[36] Author's interviews with Mariam Abou Zahab and Nawaf Obaid; Faris bin Huzzam, '*shababuna ila afghanistan mujaddada* [Our Youth are Going to Afghanistan Again]', *al-Riyadh*, 3 October 2006; Faris bin Huzzam, '*limadha 'adu ila afghanistan?* [Why Did They Return to Afghanistan?]', *al-Riyadh*, 10 October 2006; Raid Qusti, 'Saudi

The great irony about the QAP campaign is that it was launched only weeks after the United States and Great Britain announced that they would withdraw most of their military personnel from the kingdom. The declared aim of the QAP, the eviction of the Crusaders from the Land of the Two Sanctuaries, had essentially been reached before the confrontation had started. Curiously, this fact virtually never featured in Saudi debates, jihadist or public, about the QAP campaign. The militants treated reports of the withdrawal as false and continued to speak of the Peninsula as occupied by American forces, while Saudi authorities never used political arguments, only religious ones, in its war of ideas against QAP.[37]

The QAP experiment was a disaster for al-Qaida. Not only did it fail by a wide margin, it also provoked state countermeasures which destroyed Saudi Arabia as a source of money, recruits and ideology for the global jihadist movement. As *al-Sharq al-Awsat* editor Abd al-Rahman al-Rashid accurately and eloquently predicted in May 2003: 'If they say that by targeting New York on September 11th, the extremists have shot themselves in the foot, in the Riyadh bombings the same extremists have shot themselves in the head.'[38]

Being Held in Israel: Saud', *Arab News*, 5 April 2006; Sue Pleming, 'US Says Funds Flow in from Saudi Arabia to Somalia', *Reuters*, 29 June 2006; '10 Saudi Islamists Killed in Lebanon Unrest', *Agence France Presse*, 9 July 2007.

[37] Eric Schmitt, 'US to Withdraw All Combat Units from Saudi Arabia', *New York Times*, 30 April 2003. The decision had allegedly been taken by the Saudi leadership in January 2003; Patrick E. Tyler, 'Saudis Plan End to US Presence', *New York Times*, 9 February 2003.

[38] Abd al-Rahman al-Rashid, '*bayna nyu yurk wa'l-riyadh* [Between New York and Riyadh]', *al-Sharq al-Awsat*, 26 May 2003.

Conclusion

In the morning of 13 May 2003, forensic experts began trawling the blast sites of the Riyadh bombing for body parts. In the Vinnell compound lay the scattered remains of Khalid al-Juhani, a suicide bomber whose biography encapsulated the story behind the QAP campaign. In 1992, at age 18, Khalid had travelled to Bosnia to become a mujahid, inspired by the constant calls in mosques and the media for Saudis to help their suffering Muslim brothers in Bosnia. When Khalid returned to the kingdom a couple of years later, his sacrifice for the Muslim nation was no longer recognised by the state. In 1996, perhaps to escape the arrest and torture which befell jihad veterans after the bombings in Riyadh and Khobar, Khalid travelled to Afghanistan, at a time when Usama bin Ladin began rebuilding the al-Qaida organisation to wage global jihad against America. Khalid became a prominent al-Qaida member and recorded a martyrdom video in 2001 in the hope of one day taking part in an operation against the Crusaders. However, when al-Qaida unexpectedly found itself evicted from Afghanistan in early 2002, Bin Ladin decided to open a new battlefront in Saudi Arabia. Khalid was given a new task: go home and prepare for jihad on the Arabian Peninsula. A year later he led one of the attack teams in the 12 May operation.[1]

While the task of the blast investigators finished long ago, this study has attempted to piece together a bigger puzzle, that of why the QAP campaign happened in 2003 and not before. In a sentence, the answer is that revolutionary Islamism and global jihadism have never thrived in the kingdom and that the 2003 violence was due to the sudden and massive influx of global jihadists from Afghanistan in 2002.

The QAP campaign was a result of the fundamental transformation of al-Qaida's strategic environment after the fall of the Taliban regime in late 2001. From al-Qaida's perspective, the loss of a safe haven in

[1] 'Saudi Sought by FBI may have Died Years Ago, Relatives Say', *Arab News*, 20 January 2002; Sipress and Finn, 'Terror Cell'.

Afghanistan and the launch of the 'Global War on Terror' altered the cost-benefit analysis of preserving Saudi Arabia as a support base. Thus in early 2002, long before the prospect of a US invasion of Iraq, Bin Ladin gave the green light for a jihad on the Arabian Peninsula. Over the following year, Bin Ladin's deputy Yusuf al-Uyayri built an organisation with the help of the many Saudis who had recently returned from Afghanistan. Al-Uyayri's remarkable mobilisation was possible because the Saudi security apparatus was incapable of handling the sudden and massive influx of highly trained and motivated militants. The high capability of the militants and the low capability of the security services created a window of opportunity which Yusuf al-Uyayri was able to exploit through expert social movement entrepreneurship. He was helped in the process by Bin Ladin's two-track strategy for the Saudi jihad, which diverted police attention to the hyperactive al-Nashiri network so that al-Uyayri could mobilise in tranquillity. Domestic and international political developments helped al-Uyayri's recruitment efforts, but violence was almost inevitable because the returnees were so numerous and so determined.

Why, though, were there so many Saudis in Afghanistan in the first place? The strong Saudi presence in al-Qaida's camps was linked to the successive rise of classical jihadism and global jihadism in the kingdom. In the mid-1980s, a Saudi jihadist movement emerged as a result of the Muslim Brotherhood-driven mobilisation of Arabs for Afghanistan and the Saudi state's promotion of pan-Islamism for domestic legitimacy purposes. In the early 1990s the Saudi regime was caught in a double game of one-upmanship of declared solidarity towards oppressed Muslims, which in turn created broad social acceptance for classical jihadist activism. Only after the Islamist opposition had been silenced in 1994 did the regime take serious steps to stem the flow of Saudis to conflict zones, which it now realised might backfire. However, by then pan-Islamism had been cemented as a crucial force in Saudi politics and the Saudi jihadist movement had gained a momentum of its own. Large constituencies in Saudi Arabia continued to view classical jihadism – that is, private participation in other Muslims' struggles of national liberation – as entirely legitimate.

Usama bin Ladin's global jihadist project, which was launched in the mid-1990s, enjoyed considerably less support in Saudi Arabia because it involved extreme tactics as well as violence inside the kingdom. The doctrinal footing for these tactics and this strategy was also considered dubious by most conservative Wahhabis. However, because the global jihadist discourse was also rooted in pan-Islamism, Bin Ladin could easily exploit the widespread popular Saudi support for classical jihadism for his own purposes. Al-Qaida's recruitment strategy between 1996 and 2001 relied on presenting the training camps in Afghanistan as a station on the way to a classical jihad, notably in Chechnya. Once in the camps, recruits were socialised into and indoctrinated with global jihadism. The flow of Saudis to the al-Qaida camps increased exponentially from 1999 onward as a result of four crucial and near-simultaneous developments: the pan-Islamist renaissance caused by the Chechen war and the Palestinian intifada; the rise of the al-Shu'aybi school of radical clerics; the introduction of the Internet; and the release of Yusuf al-Uyayri from prison.

The reason for the low level of violence inside the kingdom before 2003 was, simply put, that the classical jihadists did not have the intention and the global jihadists did not have the capability. Classical jihadism was about fighting outside enemies in conflicts that were sanctioned as jihad by senior Saudi religious scholars. Classical jihadists such as Khattab disliked the US military presence in the kingdom, but they did not consider it legitimate to fight in Saudi Arabia because the government and the senior scholars opposed it. The global jihadists, on the other hand, wanted to fight the Americans on Saudi soil, because they saw the US presence as unacceptable and because they viewed the Saudi government and its scholars as illegitimate and thus not in a position to decide on the question of jihad. However, Bin Ladin initially did not have many Saudi followers and the al-Qaida infrastructure in the kingdom prior to 1999 was very weak. After a series of failed operations in Saudi Arabia in 1998 which proved counterproductive to his effort, Bin Ladin decided to indefinitely postpone the jihad on the Arabian Peninsula. Instead he began to cultivate it as a recruitment and fundraising ground, a strategy which proved very successful.

The crucial role of pan-Islamism in Saudi politics and the 1999 quantum leap in al-Qaida recruitment represent significant findings because they imply that the large Saudi presence in the early jihad zones and in al-Qaida's camps was the product of temporary political developments and not of some essential and timeless Saudi radicalism. Moreover, this should serve to attenuate the widespread perception of Saudi Arabia as 'al-Qaida country'. It also suggests that, before 9/11, Bin Ladin's global jihadism was a much more marginal and controversial doctrine within the worldwide jihadist community than much of the literature on al-Qaida has thus far suggested. My findings are thus more in line with those of Fawaz Gerges and Brynjar Lia, who demonstrated that global jihadism was a fringe view in the Arab Afghan community right up until 9/11. The late 2000s criticism of al-Qaida by prominent veteran jihadists, heralded by many commentators as a major breakthrough in the ideological war against al-Qaida, thus represents nothing more than a return to the *status quo ante*.[2]

Following the strategic failure of the QAP campaign, Saudi Arabia has reverted to a security situation more similar to that prior to 9/11. The 2003 violence was in many ways an exception which confirms the rule of Saudi Arabia's relative internal stability. The campaign was the result of a unique momentary discrepancy between, on the one hand, the very high organisational capability of the 2002 returnees from Afghanistan, and on the other hand, the weakness and non-confrontational attitude of the Saudi security services. That gap is now closed, and mobilisation for organised nationwide activism in the kingdom has become more difficult. The downfall of the QAP confirms a broader historical tendency, namely that large-scale mobilisation for violent Sunni activism inside Saudi Arabia is extremely difficult.

This points to what this book contends is the most significant specificity of Saudi jihadism, namely its pan-Islamist orientation. Compared with the Arab republics, the kingdom has experienced much less socio-revolutionary violence and much more violence directed against non-Muslims. Saudi Arabia has in fact never been home to a strong socio-revolutionary Islamist movement of the Egyptian or the Algerian type. Conversely, the kingdom has had a comparatively strong classical jihadist movement since the mid-1980s. This is not to say that socio-revolutionary tendencies do not exist in the kingdom; they do, and sometimes, such as in the case of the 2002 Sakaka assassinations, they produce violence. Moreover, some of the anti-Western militancy may well be socio-revolutionary activism in disguise. Torture in Saudi prisons in the mid-1990s pushed many classical jihadists into al-Qaida's arms, and unemployment was a factor in jihadi recruitment from the mid-1990s onward. However, in the larger picture we are dealing with a relatively clear pattern which can hardly be coincidental.[3]

What our analysis suggests is that there are different ideal types of militant Islamism that manifest themselves at different levels in different countries. This opens up for the possibility that different types of activism have different root causes and that specific forms of activism are correlated with specific socio-political features of a given country. Such a line of inquiry, which one might call the 'comparative politics of

[2] Gerges, *The Far Enemy*; Lia, *Architect of Global Jihad*; Peter Bergen and Paul Cruickshank, 'The Unraveling', *The New Republic* (2008); Lawrence Wright, 'The Rebellion Within', *New Yorker* (2008).

[3] Madawi al-Rasheed observed the same pattern in 'The Minaret and the Palace: Obedience at Home and Rebellion Abroad', in *Kingdom Wthout Borders*, ed. al-Rasheed, 199–220.

Islamist contestation', would seem to provide for more nuanced thinking about the causal dynamics of Islamist violence. Rather than look for correlations between, for example, regime types or poverty on levels of terrorism or Islamism in general, we may examine their effects on different types of Islamist activism. For example, it may well be that poverty and state repression are more strongly correlated with socio-revolutionary Islamism than with pan-Islamist militancy. Conversely, chronological variations in the number and visibility of international conflicts pitting Muslims versus non-Muslims may affect levels of pan-Islamist activism more strongly than socio-revolutionary Islamism.

At least four explanations may account for the peculiar 'extroversion' of Saudi militancy. One is that the main drivers of socio-revolutionary Islamism, namely violent regime oppression and socio-economic problems, have been less pronounced in Saudi Arabia than in the Arab republics. There have been economic downturns in the kingdom, but they had a lesser impact than those of 1970s Egypt and late 1980s Algeria. Moreover, the level of violent state repression has also been lower in Saudi Arabia than in most Arab republics.

A second possibility is that the Saudi polity contains certain structural obstacles for socio-revolutionary contestation that one does not find in the Arab republics. The continuity of rule by the Al Sa'ud and the absence of a revolutionary precedent may have made it more difficult to mobilise for regime change. The rentier economy may have afforded the government more power of co-optation with which to pacify aspiring social movement entrepreneurs. Tribalism seems to promote obedience to political authority and prevent class-based identity formation. The religious profile of the Saudi state has offered it a somewhat higher degree of protection against accusations of apostasy than the secular Arab republics. As Madawi al-Rasheed has shown, the Saudi religious establishment was long able to restrict the ideological space of contesting subjects. A third possible explanation is that Saudi Islamists may be particularly hostile to non-Muslims, as a result of either Wahhabi puritanism or of the social distance between Saudis and non-Muslims. The Wahhabi imperative of *al-wala' wa'l-bara'* (loyalty and disassociation) encourages believers to actively distance themselves from non-Muslims and their world. The absence of tourism and the confinement of expatriates to compounds means that most Saudis, apart from a liberal elite, have historically had limited interaction with non-Muslims. Of the almost 800 Saudi militants studied in this book, only a handful seem to have ever met a Westerner. The fourth theory is that the Saudi regime has given pan-Islamist activists more political space than have the Arab republics, as part of a strategy to divert Islamist contestation away from the regime. While all explanations have some validity, the political diversion hypothesis is probably the most significant.[4]

This book has generated a number of findings with broader implications for neighbouring academic fields. Those interested in Saudi politics and society will note at least three insights. The first concerns the way in which the Saudi state manages political opposition. Interestingly, the regime has succeeded in making mass mobilisation very difficult without resorting to the same level of violent repression as many of its neighbours in the region. As we have seen, Saudi policing of the Islamist community prior to 2003 was relatively soft and non-confrontational, with the exception of the 1996–8 crackdown. Instead, the state has perfected a complex formula of social control based on the use of rent, tribes and religion to co-opt opponents, undermine class formation and prevent politicisation. However, this delicately balanced political ecosystem worked only so long as Saudi society remained relatively isolated from the rest of the world. The media revolution broke the state monopoly of information, enabled opposition groups to grow strong in exile and empowered small domestic actors. Moreover, as al-Rasheed has argued, globalisation undermined the Saudi state ulama's monopoly on religious authority, weakening its ability to mould consenting subjects. The QAP campaign was to some extent a consequence of the Saudi state's failure to realise the full implications of these changes. At the same time, the QAP's failure indicates that despite the many challenges, the ulama still command a great deal of authority in the kingdom.[5]

A second and related point concerns the role of religion in Saudi society. Islamist militancy has been widespread in Saudi Arabia, not because of the high level of religiosity *per se*, but because the religious sphere offers considerable, and, since the early 1980s, increasing, opportunities for political mobilisation. The ideological nature of the Saudi state has ensured political support for religious activity, and the oil rent enables the state to afford the luxury of a massive unproductive religious sector. In its ideal, isolated form, the Saudi religious sphere is self-regulating and keeps citizens apolitical and obedient. For this reason, and for those mentioned above, the religious sector has not been subject to direct, intrusive control by the state. Jihadist entrepreneurs therefore found in the religious sphere a vast range of arenas and tools (local mosques, private lessons, summer camps, charities, etc.) which

[4] al-Rasheed, *Contesting the Saudi State*; Thomas Hegghammer, 'Jihad, Yes, but not Revolution: Explaining the Extroversion of Islamist Militancy in Saudi Arabia', *British Journal of Middle Eastern Studies* 35, no. 3 (2009).

[5] al-Rasheed, *Contesting the Saudi State.*

they could use more or less freely for political mobilisation. The state continued to tolerate even these activities so long as they did not involve violence at home. However, it was relatively easy for the global jihadist entrepreneurs to use the same arenas and tools to mobilise clandestinely for violence in the kingdom when they so decided. This illustrates what Guilain Denoeux and Stéphane Lacroix have referred to as the double-edged nature of religious networks. However, without broad support in the Islamist community, these arenas can only be exploited for a short period of time, after which rebels will be excluded from the same spheres and be unable to sustain their campaign, as was the case with the QAP.[6]

A third set of observations pertains to the political geography of Saudi Arabia. It is often assumed that Islamist radicalism is stronger in certain parts of the country than others, particularly in 'neglected peripheries', 'tribal areas' and 'hotbeds of religious extremism'. Many of these assumptions turn out to be incorrect. The south – seen after 9/11 as a major al-Qaida recruitment ground – was in fact the most underrepresented region in the Saudi jihadist movement. Southerners were so rare in al-Qaida that the 9/11 hijackers must have been picked for very specific reasons, one of which may have been a desire to redress the recruitment problems in the south. Similarly, the socially very conservative region of Qasim was not particularly overrepresented. Most Saudi jihadists, in both absolute and relative terms, were from Riyadh, Khobar and the Mecca–Medina–Jidda triangle, that is, the kingdom's big urban conglomerates. A handful of medium-sized cities such as Zulfi and big city neighbourhoods such as Thuqba in Dammam provided disproportionately many Saudi militants, often as a result of the 'social network effect'. Interestingly, the geographical centre of gravity of the Saudi jihadist movement shifted over time from the Hijaz – where the Muslim Brotherhood-driven mobilisation for the Afghan jihad started – to the Najd, where the main al-Qaida clerics and recruiters operated from the late 1990s onward.

This book has also generated at least two important findings with relevance to the study of political Islam. First is the usefulness of analytical concepts grounded in political behaviour as opposed to concepts grounded in theology. By avoiding essentialist terms such as 'salafi' and 'takfiri', and relying instead on categories reflecting immediate political

[6] Guilain Denoeux, *Urban Unrest in the Middle East: A Comparative Study of Informal Networks in Egypt, Iran and Lebanon* (Albany: State University of New York Press, 1993); Stéphane Lacroix, 'The Double-edged Role of Islamic Networks in Saudi Politics' (paper presented at the Annual Meeting of the Middle East Studies Association, Montreal, 19 November 2007).

preferences such as 'pietist' and 'socio-revolutionary', I was able to distinguish between previously conflated phenomena and provide more powerful causal explanations than those hitherto available. The rationale-based conceptual framework outlined in the Introduction worked well in the Saudi context. My analysis confirmed that militants were usually linked, sociologically, discursively or both, to the non-violent actors sharing the same dominant rationale. Most global jihadists came from a classical jihadist background, and the early classical jihadists had strong links to the international Islamic organisations. Although further research is required to test this typology in other contexts, it seems intuitively relevant; socio-revolutionary militants in Egypt and Algeria emerged from non-violent state-oriented movements (Muslim Brotherhood and the FIS), not from pietist salafi communities. In Pakistan, militant sectarian groups such as Lashkar-e Janghvi emerged from more moderate sectarian interest groups such as Sipah-e Sahaba, not from state-oriented groups like Jamaat-e Islami.

A second and related point is the utility of the concept of pan-Islamism for the analysis of transnational Islamist militancy. The view of classical and global jihadism as expressions of extreme pan-Islamism, and as having structural similarities with ethno-nationalist ideologies, has important implications for our understanding of the causes of al-Qaida's growth, and by extension for counterterrorism policy. The discourse and action of Saudi jihadists were consistently focused on the external enemy, and their violence was nearly always rationalised as an act of solidarity towards Muslims oppressed by non-Muslims, not as an effort to correct the malgovernance or corruption of Muslim rulers. Moreover, mobilisation to Saudi jihadism was considerably easier when there were more available international symbols of Muslim suffering. Put very simply, this suggests that symbols of Muslim suffering – especially Muslim struggles of national liberation such as Palestine and Chechnya, but also captivity symbols such as Guantanamo and Abu Ghraib – play a much more important role than domestic socio-economic problems in recruitment to classical and global jihadism.

Ultimately, this means that in the fight against al-Qaida, addressing the symbols of Muslim suffering is more urgent than political and economic reform in the Arab world. Solving the Palestinian and Chechen conflicts will obviously not make al-Qaida militants put down their arms, but addressing them more seriously than today will reduce the resonance of Bin Ladin's discourse in the broader Muslim population and thus narrow al-Qaida's recruitment base. Of course, jihadism is not a linear expression of the objective level of suffering in Muslim countries, particularly since new technology and media enable jihadist propagandists to produce symbols of Muslim suffering from small and seemingly innocuous events. Nevertheless, the concept of pan-Islamism at least helps us identify the language and rhetorical mechanisms with which al-Qaida fights for the hearts and minds of the Muslim population.

Scholars specialising in the study of political violence more generally will also have found points of interest in this book. For a start, the analysis illustrated the contingency of small-scale violence and the limits of macro-level structural theories in explaining the behaviour of terrorist groups. While we can identify certain necessary socio-economic causes behind, for example, the Saudi regime's decision to promote pan-Islamism in the 1980s or behind the flow of Saudis to al-Qaida and the QAP in the late 1990s, these factors are not sufficient to explain the mobilisation for Afghanistan in those periods, much less the outbreak of the 2003 violence. Instead, individual entrepreneurs (such as Yusuf al-Uyayri) and coincidences (such as Azzam's chance encounter with Kamal al-Sananiri) played a crucial role in shaping the course of events. For political actors the size of the QAP or the Saudi jihadist movement, the key to explaining timing and variations in the level and form of the violence is located most often at the organisational level and in the ability of agents to mobilise resources in given political circumstances. Donatella Della Porta's dynamic tri-level framework facilitated the identification of constellations of factors at different levels at particular points in time, such as the 1999 turning point in Saudi recruitment to al-Qaida. The framework also highlighted how the interplay between the Saudi state and the classical jihadists, notably the state's oscillation between repression and leniency, stimulated the growth of global jihadism. The analysis also demonstrated the utility of theories on framing, notably for demonstrating the relationship between international political developments and the mobilising power of pan-Islamist groups. In periods of growth in the number and visibility of conflicts pitting Muslims versus non-Muslims, such as in the periods from 1982 to 1987, from 1992 to 1995 and from 1999 to 2003, pan-Islamist groups have tended to prosper.

A second important finding is that the distinction between nationalist and socio-revolutionary ideologies, known from other forms of political violence, also seems to apply in the world of militant Islamism. This suggests that there is a generic difference between conflict dynamics based on religion and ethnicity on the one hand and those based on socio-economic cleavages on the other. We already know from the European context that ethno-nationalist groups such as the IRA and ETA were usually larger in size, more embedded in the population and had a broader recruitment base (in socio-economic terms) than did socio-revolutionary groups such as Rote Armé Fraktion or Brigate Rosse. Studies of nationalist-type Islamist groups such as Hamas and Hizbollah seem to confirm this tendency. This book has shown that pan-Islamist groups display many of the same discursive and behavioural traits as ethno-nationalist groups. Moreover, pan-Islamists also have a broader recruitment base than socio-revolutionary ones. Classical jihadists have an even broader recruitment base than global jihadists, which suggests a correlation between the perceived legitimacy of a cause in a given population and the breadth of the recruitment base.

Interestingly, despite the many apparent idiosyncrasies of Saudi society, the meso- and micro-level social dynamics were largely the same in the Saudi jihadist groups as in other militant groups. Saudi jihadism was an urban phenomenon attracting young males. Group dynamics such as in-group loyalty and bidding games were extremely important for individual recruitment, often more so than ideological ones, a tendency which echoes Marc Sageman's observations on small-group radicalisation. Exposure to violence through training and combat was crucial to individual radicalisation; it increased the likelihood of subsequent militancy more than any other factor. The core of the QAP represented the remains of a gradually thinned down and radicalised community of jihadists. The QAP also shared the tendency for isolated clandestine groups to go 'deeper and deeper underground' and to get caught in cycles of revenge with the police to the point of losing sight of their alleged constituencies and declared grievances, as was the case with the leftist extremists studied by Della Porta.

The bombing on 12 May 2003 has been called 'the mother of all wake-up calls' for the Saudi regime about the dangers of leaving the jihadist community unchecked. Since 2003, there has been a general realisation in the Saudi government and the security establishment that the QAP campaign does represent a form of 'blowback' from the state's promotion and acceptance of private military participation in foreign conflicts. The subsequent culture change and the capability increase in the police and the intelligence services have been remarkable, and Saudi Arabia is now a country where violent mobilisation is considerably more difficult than in 2002. What is perhaps even more remarkable is the fact that this change was not accompanied by a massive overreaction by the state. Unlike the brutal repression of the Islamist opposition in early 1990s Algeria and Egypt, the Saudi crackdown on the QAP was relatively measured and targeted. This policy is not only commendable from a human rights perspective, it also constituted effective counterterrorism.

At the current time of writing, the QAP is rightly considered defunct as an organisation, although continued arrests suggest there are still communities bent on launching operations in the kingdom. The release, on 2 February 2009, of a new wanted list of eighty-five suspects, all of whom are supposed to be abroad, suggests that the most pressing threat is posed by the return of hardened fighters from abroad. Saudis in Iraq constitute a particularly important source of concern, with many observers warning against a surge in violence similar to that caused by the returnees from Afghanistan in 2002. However, while returnees from Iraq must be watched closely, a replay of the 2002–3 mobilisation is unlikely because Saudis in Iraq are fewer, they will return in trickles and they face a revamped Saudi security apparatus.[7]

Another source of concern is Yemen, where a local al-Qaida branch has been gaining strength since 2006. A number of Saudi militants have fled from Saudi Arabia to Yemen, from where they hope to continue the jihad on the Arabian Peninsula. On 19 January 2009, some of these escapees appeared in a video together with Yemeni militants to announce that the Saudi and Yemeni branches of al-Qaida had merged under the old name al-Qaida on the Arabian Peninsula. While this merger proves that al-Qaida's networks in the kingdom have been weakened, it is also disconcerting, because Yemen represents a potentially formidable launching-pad for ad hoc operations inside the kingdom. This became clear on 27 August 2009 when a Saudi suicide operative dispatched from Yemen came very close to assassinating Deputy Interior Minister Muhammad bin Nayif in the latter's Jidda office.[8]

[7] For the state of the QAP in 2008, see Michael Knights, 'The Current State of al-Qa'ida in Saudi Arabia', *Sentinel* 1, no. 10 (2008). For returnees from Iraq, see Michael Knights, 'Saudi Terrorist Cells Await Return of Jihadists from Iraq', *Jane's Intelligence Review* 17, no. 12 (2005); Michael Knights, 'A New Afghanistan? Exploring the Iraqi Jihadist Training Ground', *Jane's Intelligence Review* 18, no. 7 (2006); 'Blowback Time Beckons as Saudi Jihadists are Squeezed in Iraq', *Gulf States Newsletter* 29, no. 767 (2005); Sulayman Nimr, 'Saudi Fears Iraq Returnees Will Boost Qaeda', *Agence France Presse*, 5 December 2006; Megan Stack, 'Iraqi Strife Seeping into Saudi Kingdom', *Los Angeles Times*, 26 April 2006. For the wanted list, see 'Kingdom Unveils List of 85 Wanted Militants Abroad', *Arab News*, 3 February 2009.

[8] Michael Slackman, 'Would-be Killer Linked to Al Qaeda, Saudis Say', *New York Times*, 29 August 2009. For indications of Saudi presence in al-Qaida in Yemen, see '*muqabala ma' ahad al-matlubin, abu hammam al-qahtani* [Interview with One of the Wanted, Abu-Hammam al-Qahtani]', *Sada al-Malahim*, nos. 1 and 2 (2008); Gregory Johnsen, 'Tracking Yemen's 23 Escaped Jihadi Operatives – Part 1', *Terrorism Monitor* 5, no. 18 (2007); Gregory Johnsen, 'Tracking Yemen's 23 Escaped Jihadi Operatives – Part 2', *Terrorism Monitor* 5, no. 19 (2007). For the Saudi–Yemeni merger, see Thomas Hegghammer, 'Saudi and Yemeni Branches of al-Qaida Unite', www.jihadica.com, 24 January 2009.

At the end of the day, the jihad in Saudi Arabia cannot be un-launched. The QAP is unlikely to be forgotten, particularly since its propaganda will continue to circulate indefinitely on the Internet. Future militants may redefine the purpose of the struggle in a more revolutionary direction, making the Saudi jihad more similar to the Algerian, Egyptian or Syrian campaigns. The QAP's successors might also settle for less than a countrywide insurgency, opting instead for sporadic but spectacular ad hoc attacks. Although the global jihadists are currently few and marginalised, their ranks may refill with returnees from Iraq or with recruits drawn from the friends and families of 'martyred' al-Qaida militants. As David Cook has pointed out, there is no such thing as failure in jihad – only deferred success.[9]

The big question in the long term is whether Saudi Arabia is able and willing to curb the strong pan-Islamist sentiment in Saudi society, something which will require bold anti-populist stances on key international issues as well as a systematic promotion of local Saudi nationalism. It will not be an easy task. As a Saudi intelligence official observed in 2005: 'We encouraged our young men to fight for Islam in Afghanistan. We encouraged our young men to fight for Islam in Bosnia and Chechnya. We encouraged our young men to fight for Islam in Palestine. Now we are telling them you are forbidden to fight for Islam in Iraq, and they are confused.'[10]

[9] David Cook, *Failed Jihad*, Cambridge University Press, forthcoming, Introduction.

[10] Robert Windrem, 'Saudi Arabia's Ambitious al-Qaida Fighter', *NBC News*, 11 July 2005.

Appendix 1 – Socio-economic data on Saudi militants

ABOUT THE DATASET

- The dataset contains 539 unique biographies of Saudi militants active between 1980 and 2006. The sum of all sub-samples is higher because some individuals fought in more than one location.
- The dataset has been constructed by extracting as much biographical information as possible on as many individuals as possible using publicly available sources such as jihadist literature, press reports, secondary literature and legal documents.
- It includes individuals whose participation in violent activism – that is, fighting, training or weapons acquisition – can be established with a reasonable degree of certainty. In most cases the criterion for inclusion is either death/injury in combat, self-declared activism, or arrest and public accusation. Individuals arrested and not tried (such as Guantanamo detainees) have not been included unless they publicly admitted to training or fighting.
- No survey work or interviews with militants were conducted as part of the compilation process. The biographies are therefore very uneven in their length, focus and level of detail. The individuals for whom we have the best information are not a random sample, but rather the most active and prominent fighters.
- The dataset is coded according to thirty different variables, but for many variables there are too many missing values to allow for meaningful analysis. Below I have included data on those variables for which information is the most complete, namely age, geographic origin, education level and profession.

AGE

	All	Known birth year	Known age at joining	Average birth year	Average age at joining
Early jihad fronts	161	53	30	1968	20
Afghanistan	113	42	22	1967	20
Bosnia	53	23	8	1969	21
Chechnya/ Tajikistan	37	8	n/a	1971	n/a
Al-Qaida 1996–2001	197	67	32	1975	22.5
QAP	260	73	73	1976	27
Core	69	40	40	1977	26

GEOGRAPHIC ORIGIN

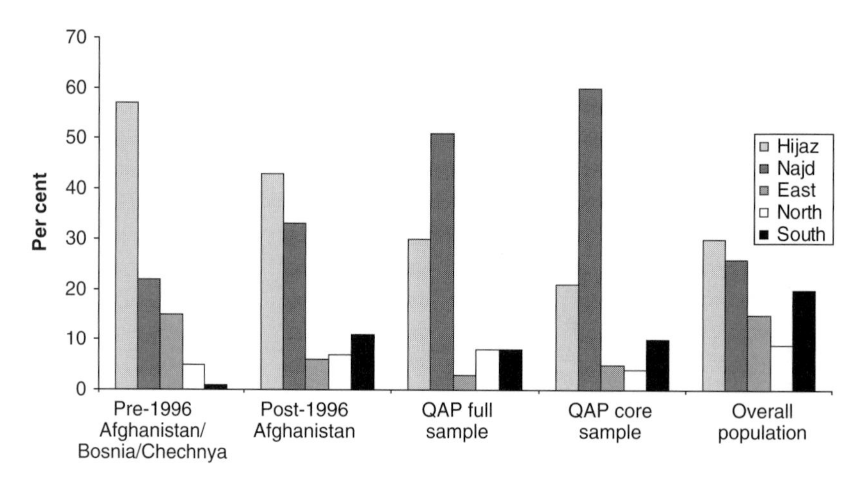

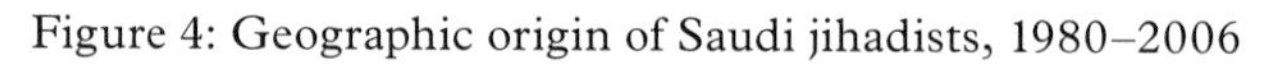

Figure 4: Geographic origin of Saudi jihadists, 1980–2006

BY MACRO-REGION

	All	Known	Hijaz	Najd	East	North	South
Early jihad fronts	161	137	78	30	20	7	2
Afghanistan	113	95	58	17	16	3	1
Bosnia	53	48	28	12	5	2	1
Chechnya/ Tajikistan	37	27	11	6	6	3	1
Al-Qaida 1996–2001	197	140	60	47	8	10	15
QAP	260	92	28	47	3	7	7
Core	69	57	12	34	3	2	6

BY ADMINISTRATIVE REGION

	All	Known	Mecca	Medina	Riyadh	Qasim	Eastern
Early jihad fronts	161	137	52	26	28	2	20
Afghanistan	113	95	36	22	16	1	16
Bosnia	53	48	22	6	12	0	5
Chechnya/ Tajikistan	37	27	7	4	5	1	6
Al-Qaida 1996–2001	197	140	49	11	42	5	8
QAP	260	92	16	12	37	10	3
Core	69	57	7	5	28	6	3

BY ADMINISTRATIVE REGION (CONT.)

	North	Jawf	Ha'il	Tabuk	Baha	Asir	Jizan	Najran
Early jihad fronts	1	1	2	3	1	1	0	0
Afghanistan	0	1	1	1	1	0	0	0
Bosnia	0	0	2	0	0	1	0	0
Chechnya/ Tajikistan	1	0	0	2	1	0	0	0
Al-Qaida 1996–2001	2	3	1	4	4	10	1	0
QAP	0	6	1	0	2	3	2	0
Core	0	1	1	0	1	3	2	0

EDUCATION LEVEL

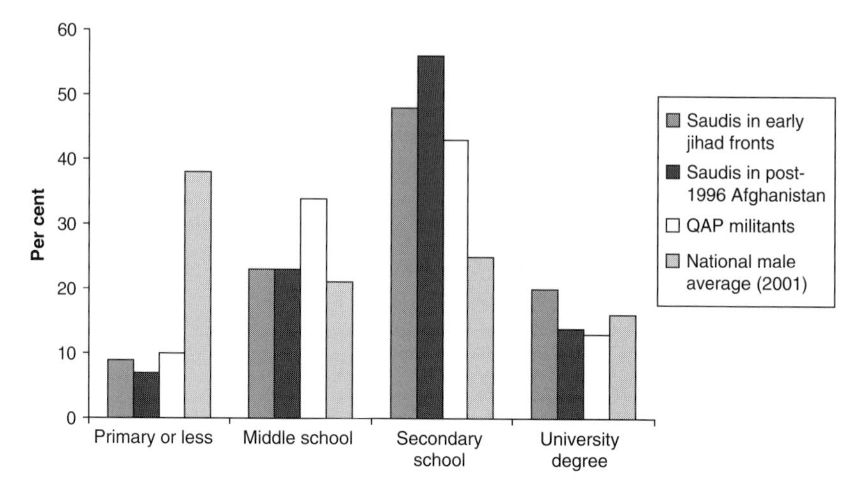

Figure 5: Evolution of education level of Saudi jihadists

	All	Known	Grad.	Ugrad.	Unfin.	High	Mid.	Prim.
Early jihad fronts	161	35	1	6	11	6	8	3
Afghanistan	113	—	—	—	—	—	—	—
Bosnia	53	—	—	—	—	—	—	—
Chechnya/ Tajikistan	37	—	—	—	—	—	—	—
Al-Qaida 1996–2001	197	44	0	6	18	7	10	3
QAP	260	—	—	—	—	—	—	—
Core	69	30	0	4	11	2	10	3

Data sorted according to individuals' highest completed level of education.
Grad.: Ph.D. or master's degree; Ugrad.: bachelor's degree or equivalent;
Unfin.: higher education without degree; High: high school; Mid.: middle school;
Prim.: primary school.

PROFESSIONAL STATUS

	All	Known	Student	Manual	Agricult.	Sm. trade
Early jihad fronts	161	37	13	4	1	4
Afghanistan	113	—	—	—	—	—
Bosnia	53	—	—	—	—	—
Chechnya/ Tajikistan	37	—	—	—	—	—
Al-Qaida 1996–2001	197	37	13	2	1	5
QAP	260	—	—	—	—	—
Core	69	29	1	0	0	3

Data refers to sector of last job held before militancy. Student: student; Manual: manual/blue-collar work; Agricult.: agriculture; Sm. trade: small trade.

PROFESSIONAL STATUS (CONT.)

	Teaching	Health	Pol./mil.	Gov't	Business	Religious
Early jihad fronts	1	0	1	1	8	4
Afghanistan	—	—	—	—	—	—
Bosnia	—	—	—	—	—	—
Chechnya/ Tajikistan	—	—	—	—	—	—
Al-Qaida 1996–2001	1	0	4	1	4	6
QAP	—	—	—	—	—	—
Core	2	0	4	0	2	12

Teaching: non-religious teaching; Health: health sector; Pol./mil.: police or military; Gov't: non-religious public sector; Business: white-collar private sector; Religious: religious sector.

Appendix 2 – Chronology of Islamist violence in Saudi Arabia, 1979–2009

Note: The list draws on press reports, jihadist literature, personal interviews and J. E. Peterson's *Saudi Arabia: Internal Security Incidents Since 1979*. Full bibliographic references are available in Hegghammer, 'Violent Islamism in Saudi Arabia'. For the most eventful period between May 2003 and December 2006, space considerations forced me to exclude all but the most serious incidents.

21 November–5 December 1979: Hundreds of members of an apocalyptic sect led by Juhayman al-Utaybi seized the Great Mosque in Mecca, initiating a two-week siege causing hundreds of deaths.

19 May 1985: Two bombs placed in dustbins exploded in Riyadh, killing one and wounding three bystanders. Shiite militants suspected.

15 August 1987: An explosion at Ra's Tanura gas plant was claimed by Hizbollah of Hijaz, while authorities said it was due to an electrical failure.

28 and 30 March 1988: Bombs went off at a refinery at Ra's Tanura and a petrochemical plant in Jubayl. Four Shiites were arrested and beheaded for the attacks.

August 1988: According to unconfirmed reports, three Saudi police officers were killed by Shiite militants in Qatif.

October 1989: Two bombs were defused near the Ministry of Interior. Shiite militants suspected.

3 February 1991: Unknown people fired shots at a US military bus in Jidda, injuring three US soldiers and a Saudi guard. The same day a US transport bus was doused with kerosene by unknown perpetrators in Jidda.

28 March 1991: At least six shots were fired at a US Marine vehicle, injuring three marines.

Mid-1991: Over a period of several months, Islamists invoking *hisba* (moral policing) conducted around ten attacks against video stores, women's centres and empty cars of people suspected of leading 'sinful lives' in Riyadh and in Burayda. No human casualties.

11 November 1994: Islamist Abdallah al-Hudhayf threw acid in the face of a police officer in Riyadh.

13 November 1995: An explosives-filled car (not a suicide bomb) detonated outside the US-run Office of the Programme Manager for the Saudi National Guard (OPM/SANG) in downtown Riyadh, killing five Americans and two Indians.

27 March 1996: An Egyptian plane was hijacked on the way from Jidda to Egypt and diverted to Libya by three Saudis who allegedly acted to 'pass on a message from God about the problems in Palestine and Sudan'.

April 1996: Several Saudi Shiites were arrested trying to smuggle advanced explosives from Jordan into Saudi Arabia by car.

25 June 1996: An explosives-filled tanker truck (not a suicide bomb) exploded by US Airforce barracks in Khobar, killing nineteen Americans.

January 1998: Saudi authorities seized a batch of antitank missiles being smuggled from Yemen into Saudi Arabia by al-Qaida-linked activists. The incident was followed by the arrest of several hundred suspected militants.

December 1998: Unconfirmed reports mentioned a failed attempt by Yemen-based Egyptian militants to smuggle missiles into Saudi Arabia. Three hundred suspected militants were allegedly arrested in Saudi Arabia as a result.

17 March 2000: Shots fired from a moving car at the Russian consulate in Jidda, wounding a guard.

9 August 2000: A lone gunman wounded a Briton near Khamis Mushayt airbase.

14 October 2000: Two Saudis hijacked a plane and took it to Baghdad.

17 November 2000: Briton killed and his wife wounded by small car bomb in Riyadh.

22 November 2000: Three Britons injured by small car bomb in Riyadh.

16 December 2000: Briton injured by booby trap on his car in Khobar.

14 January 2001: Car bomb defused in Riyadh.

15 March 2001: Bomb exploded in front of al-Jarir bookstore in Riyadh.

16 March 2001: Three Chechens hijacked a plane from Istanbul to Moscow and diverted it to Medina.

18 April 2001: Home-made bomb discovered outside Jordanian embassy in Riyadh.

2 May 2001: American doctor in Khobar injured by parcel bomb.

6 October 2001: One American killed and at least four people wounded in possible suicide bombing in Khobar.

15 November 2001: An acid-filled bottle hurled at the car of a German family in Riyadh.

Early May 2002: An empty SA-7 missile tube was discovered outside Prince Sultan Airbase.

5 June 2002: Australian BAE employee targeted by a sniper in Tabuk.

20 June 2002: British banker killed by small car bomb in Riyadh.

29 June 2002: Bomb found under the car of US hospital employee in Riyadh.

11 July 2002: Saudi man detained after entering the Qatari consulate in Jidda with a loaded gun.

Late summer 2002: Arrests in connection with planned attack on Ra's Tanura oil terminal.

September 2002: Saudi judge shot and killed in Sakaka.

29 September 2002: German killed by small car bomb in Riyadh.

16 November 2002: The first shoot-out between Islamist militants and police took place in Riyadh. One militant injured.

20 November 2002: Man fired shots and threw a Molotov cocktail in an American fastfood restaurant in al-Kharj.

30 November 2002: Crude bomb exploded under car of a Dutch family, nobody hurt.

Early February 2003: Shots fired at an Australian expatriate jogging near his compound in Khamis Mushayt.

6 February 2003: Gunmen fired at the car of a Briton in Riyadh, causing minor injuries.

17 February 2003: Deputy Governor of al-Jawf killed by gunman in Sakaka.

20 February 2003: Briton shot dead in his car in Riyadh.

26 February 2003: Man arrested after trying to firebomb a McDonald's restaurant in Dammam.

18 March 2003: Al-Qaida bombmaking factory in Riyadh discovered after a bomb went off prematurely.

25 March 2003: Gunman killed a policeman and wounded another at a traffic light in Sakaka.

21 April 2003: A police chief in Jawf shot dead in his car.

1 May 2003: American shot and killed in an attack by a lone gunman on a marine base in Jubayl.

6 May 2003: Major gun battle in Riyadh led to the publication of the list of nineteen wanted militants two days later.

8 May 2003: Saudi authorities issued a wanted list of nineteen militants.

12 May 2003: Three car bombs devastated three residential compounds for Western expatriates in Riyadh, killing thirty-five people.

Late September 2003: First issue of QAP magazine *Sawt al-Jihad* published. Another magazine, *Mu'askar al-Battar*, was launched three months later.

8 November 2003: A suicide car bomb at the Muhayya residential compound killed 17 people and wounded over 120, primarily Arab and Muslim expatriate workers.

4 December 2003: Gunmen wounded Maj.-Gen. Abd al-Aziz al-Huwayrini.

6 December 2003: Saudi authorities issued a wanted list of twenty-six militants.

29 December 2003: A vehicle belonging to a major from the Interior Ministry exploded in eastern Riyadh.

15 March 2004: QAP leader Khalid al-Hajj and another militant were killed by police in the Nasim area of Riyadh.

21 April 2004: Washm bombing. A suicide car bomb targeted a general security building in Riyadh. Six people were killed and 145 were wounded.

1 May 2004: Yanbu attack. Four militants went on a shooting spree in Yanbu.

22 May 2004: German citizen Jonathan Hermann Bengler was killed by unidentified gunmen in Riyadh.

29–30 May 2004: Khobar attack. Four militants went on a shooting spree at several locations in Khobar. Many casualties.

2 June 2004: Gunmen fired on two Americans in separate cars leaving a compound in Riyadh. One of the Americans and a Saudi bystander were wounded.

6 June 2004: BBC correspondent Frank Gardner was wounded and his Irish cameraman was killed in an attack by gunmen in the Suwaydi neighbourhood in Riyadh.

8 June 2004: US citizen Robert Jacobs was killed in his house in Riyadh's al-Khalij neighbourhood.

12 June 2004: US citizen Kenneth Scroggs was shot and killed as he parked his car by his house in Riyadhs (al-Malazz neighbourhood).

12 June 2004: US citizen Paul Johnson was kidnapped in Riyadh. He was decapitated on 18 June.

18 June 2004: Security forces killed Abd al-Aziz al-Muqrin and three other militants in Riyadh.

23 June 2004: Saudi authorities declared one-month amnesty for militants wanting to surrender.

20 July 2004: Saudi security forces killed two militants, wounded three others and arrested at least two in a raid on the residence of Salih al-Awfi.

3 August 2004: Irish national Anthony Christopher Higgins was shot dead by militants who stormed into his Riyadh office firing machineguns.

30 August 2004: Shots fired at a US diplomatic car near the US consulate in Jidda, no casualties.

11 September 2004: An explosion, apparently from inside a moving taxi, went off near a branch of the Saudi-American bank in the al-Bawady district of Jidda, at around 9 a.m., wounding one attacker.

15 September 2004: British national Edward Muirhead-Smith was shot and killed in Riyadh.

26 September 2004: French engineer Laurent Barbot was shot in his car and killed near Giant Stores in the al-Zahra district in Jidda early in the morning.

1 October 2004: Gunshots were fired from a moving car at Seder village compound in Riyadh.

Early November 2004: QAP magazines *Sawt al-Jihad* and *Mu'askar al-Battar* were discontinued. Two more issues of *Sawt al-Jihad* subsequently appeared in April 2005 and January 2007, but these were produced by lone individuals.

6 December 2004: Gunmen stormed the US consulate in Jidda, triggering a bloody three-hour siege in which six non-American staffers and four attackers were killed.

29 December 2004: Militants directed suicide car bomb attacks at the Interior Ministry and a National Guard training facility in Riyadh. The bombs detonated prematurely and left ten militants and one bystander dead.

3–5 April 2005: A violent three-day gunbattle in al-Rass left fourteen militants dead and several wounded.

19 June 2005: Police interrogator Mubarak al-Sawat shot dead by militants at his house.

28 June 2005: Saudi authorities issued a wanted list of thirty-six militants.

24 February 2006: Militants in two explosives-laden cars tried to enter the Abqaiq oil facility through a side gate. The attack was foiled and the cars exploded by the gate, killing the two drivers and two security guards.

20 November 2006: A British man was stabbed and injured at a petrol station in Jubayl in the Eastern Province.

2 December 2006: Saudi authorities announced that they had arrested 136 militants in several cities over a period of two months.

7 December 2006: Gunmen firing from a nearby building killed two security guards outside the al-Ruways prison in Jidda.

26 February 2007: Four French tourists were shot dead by militants near the Mada'in Salih archaeological site north of Medina.

27 April 2007: Saudi authorities announced the recent arrest of 172 suspected militants.

9 August 2007: Saudi authorities announced the recent arrest of 135 suspected militants.

28 November 2007: Saudi authorities announced the recent arrest of 208 suspected militants.

3 March 2008: Saudi authorities announced the recent arrest of fifty-six suspected militants.

25 June 2008: Saudi authorities announced the recent arrest of 701 suspected militants.

19 January 2009: Saudi and Yemeni branches of al-Qaida announced their merger under the name al-Qaida on the Arabian Peninsula.

2 February 2009: Saudi authorities issued a list of eighty-five wanted militants believed to be abroad.

26 May 2009: Shots were fired at a minibus carrying foreigners in Jubail; no casualties.

19 August 2009: Saudi authorities announced the recent arrest of forty-four suspected militants.

27 August 2009: A suicide bomber blew himself up in the Jidda office of Deputy Interior Minister Muhammad bin Nayif, wounding the Prince lightly. The wanted militant had avoided security by expressing his intention of personally surrendering to Bin Nayif.

13 October 2009: Two militants and a policeman were killed in a clash at a security checkpoint near Jizan by the Yemeni border.

Bibliography

SOURCES CONSULTED

ISLAMIST MAGAZINES

al-Ansar (1990s London version), 1994–8 – paper
al-Ansar (post-9/11 Internet version), 2002–3 – digital
al-Bayan (al-Muntada al-Islami), 1986–2003 – digital
al-Bunyan al-Marsus (Ittihad/Sayyaf), 1985–90 – paper
al-Fajr (Libyan Islamic Fighting group), 1998 – digital
al-Huquq (Committee for the Defence of Legitimate Rights), 1994–6 – paper
al-Islah (Movement for Islamic Reform in Arabia), 1996–2003 – digital
al-Jihad (Services Bureau), 1984–9 – paper
al-Khansa' (QAP), 2004 – digital
al-Mujahid (Jamil al-Rahman), 1989–90 – paper
al-Mujahidun (Egyptian Islamic Jihad), 1995 – digital
al-Mujtama' (Muslim Brotherhood), 1969–2003 – digital
al-Rabita (Muslim World League), 1979–89 – paper
al-Sirat al-Mustaqeem (USA), 1994 – digital
CDLR Monitor (Committee for the Defence of Legitimate Rights), 1994–5 – paper
Journal of the Muslim League, 1973–90 – paper
Mu'askar al-Battar (QAP), 2003–4 – digital
Nida' al-Islam (Australia), 1997–2003 – digital
Sada al-Malahim (al-Qaida in Yemen), 2008 – digital
Sawt al-Jihad (QAP), 2003–7 – digital

ISLAMIST STATEMENTS

Bayanat (Committee for the Defence of Legitimate Rights), 1995–6 – paper
Bayanat (QAP), 2003–6 – digital
Taqarir Ikhbariya (QAP), 2003–6 – digital
Miscellaneous statements by Saudi militants, 2003–7 – digital

ISLAMIST WEBSITES

Note: URL addresses change frequently – in each case I have provided the most commonly used address at the time when I collected my data (various periods between 2001 and 2007).

Abd al-Aziz al-Jarbu' website (www.geocities.com/aljarbo)
Abd al-Rahman al-Barrak website (http://albarrak.islamlight.net)
Aflam Online (http://almagribi.blogspot.com)

al-Anfal (www.anfaal.net)
al-Ansar (www.al-ansar.biz)
al-Boraq (www.al-boraq.com)
al-Diyar al-Arabiyya (http://topforums.net)
al-Firdaws (www.alfirdaws.org)
al-Haqa'iq (www.hakayk.org)
al-Hikma (www.al-hikma.net)
al-Hisba (www.al-hesbah.org)
al-Ikhlas (www.alekhlaas.net)
al-Islah (www.yaislah.org)
al-Mourabitoune (www.ribaat.org)
al-Qa'idun (www.qa3edoon.com)
al-Qal'a (www.qal3ah.org)
al-Sahat (http://alsaha.fares.net)
al-Salafyoon (http://alsalafyoon.com)
al-Saqifa (www.alsakifa.org)
al-Tajdid (www.tajdeed.org.uk)
Ali al-Khudayr website (www.alkhoder.com)
Ana Muslim (www.muslm.net)
Azzam Publications (www.azzam.com)
Baghdad al-Rashid (www.baghdadalrashid.com)
Cihad (www.cihad.com)
Hamud al-Shu'aybi website (www.aloqla.com)
Islam Today (www.islamtoday.net)
Islamic Awakening (www.islamicawakening.com)
Kata'ib al-Haramayn website (www.hostinganime.com/kataeb)
Kavkazcenter (www.kavkazcenter.com)
Mafhum (www.mafhoum.com)
Markaz al-Dirasat wa'l-Buhuth al-Islamiyya (www.alneda.com; www.drasat.com)
Minbar al-Tawhid wa'l-Jihad (www.tawhed.ws)
Nasir al-Fahd website (www.al-fhd.com)
Risalat al-Umma (www.al-ommh.net)
Sada al-Jihad (www.sadaaljihad.net)
Safar al-Hawali website (www.alhawali.com)
Sawt al-Jihad website (www.hostinganime.com/sout)
Sawt al-Qawqaz (www.qoqaz.com)
Sayyid al-Fawa'id (www.saaid.net)
Shabakat Hadramawt al-Arabiyya (www.hdrmut.net)
Tibyan Publications (http://tibyaan.atspace.com)
World News Network / Shabakat al-Akhbar al-Alamiyya (www.w-n-n.com)

VIDEO MATERIAL

al-Qaida

[The Nineteen Martyrs], 2002
tadmir al-mudammira al-amrikiyya kul [Destruction of the American Destroyer *Cole*], 2001 (a version with English subtitles distributed in London under the title *State of the Umma*).

Various video clips featuring 9/11 hijackers, 2002–6
Various statements and interviews with Usama bin Ladin, 2001–5
Various statements and interviews with other al-Qaida spokesmen (Ayman al-Zawahiri, Sulayman Abu Ghayth, Adam Gadahn), 2002–6

QAP

badr al-riyadh (Badr of Riyadh), 2004
dima' lan tadi (Blood not Spilt in Vain) (parts 1 and 2), 2006
ghazwat falluja (The Falluja Raid), 2006
jahim al-amrikan fi ard al-hijaz (The Hell of Americans in the Hijaz), 2005
kasr al-asr (Breaking Captivity), 2006
muhammad shaddaf al-shihri (Tribute video), 2006
sada al-jihad (Echo of Jihad), 2004
salih al-'awfi (Tribute video), 2006
sariyat al-quds (The Quds Squadron), 2006
shuhada' al-jawf (The Martyrs of Jawf), 2006
shuhada' al-muwajahat (Martyrs of the Confrontations), 2003
Untitled (Al-Muqrin Announcement on Paul Johnson), 2004
Untitled (Burial of Rakan al-Saikhan), 2004
Untitled (Decapitation of Paul Johnson), 2004
Untitled (Interview with two Chadian QAP fugitives in Iraq), 2006
Untitled (Killing of Robert Jacob), 2004
wa harridu al-mu'minin (And Incite the Believers), 2005
wasaya al-abtal (Wills of the Martyrs), 2003
Various short video clips, 2004–6

Miscellaneous

al-ansar al-'arab fi afghanistan [Arab Followers in Afghanistan], 1988
Saudi TV recording of captured Juhayman Rebels, 1979
Various lectures by Abdallah Azzam, 1985–9
Various video clips from Bosnia, 1992–5
Various video clips from Chechnya, 1999–2007
Various video clips from Iraq, 2002–7
Various video clips from post-2001 Afghanistan, 2002–7

AUDIO MATERIAL

Various recordings of QAP operations
Various recorded statements and lectures by:

Salih al-Awfi
Isa al-Awshan
Abdallah Azzam
Faysal al-Dukhayyil
Hamad al-Humaydi
Abd al-Aziz al-Jarbu'
Jamal Khalifa
Ibn Khattab
Ali al-Khudayr
Usama bin Ladin
Abd al-Majid al-Munay'
Abd al-Aziz al-Muqrin
Umar Abd al-Rahman
Abdallah al-Rushud
Abdallah al-Sa'd
Abu Umar al-Sayf
Hamud al-Shu'aybi
Sulayman al-Ulwan
Yusuf al-Uyairi
Faris al-Zahrani
Ayman al-Zawahiri
Sa'id bin Zu'ayr

INTERVIEWS

First-hand sources

Muhsin al-Awaji
Abu Abdallah al-Balkhi
Nasir al-Barrak
Muhammad al-Dawsary
Yusuf al-Dayni
Mishari al-Dhaydi
Sulayman al-Duwaysh
Abd al-Rahman al-Hadlaq
Muhammad al-Hudhayf
Nasir al-Huzaymi
Abd al-Rahman al-Lahim
Hasan al-Maliki
Khalid al-Mushawwah
Mansur al-Nuqaydan
Abd al-Aziz al-Qasim
Muhammad al-Rashid
Abd al-Aziz al-Rubaysh
Ibrahim al-Sakran
Sa'ud al-Sarhan
Fahd al-Shafi
Abd al-Aziz al-Subayyil
Abdallah al-Thabit
Adil al-Turayfi
Mansur al-Turki
Abdallah Bijad al-Utaybi
Fahd al-Utaybi
Abdallah al-Yahya
Abdallah Anas
Hudhayfa Azzam
Frank Gardner
Jamal Isma'il
Ahmad Zaydan

Second-hand sources

Mariam Abou Zahab
Awad al-Badi
Asiem al-Difraoui
Ibrahim al-Gharaybeh
Abd al-Rahman al-Hakimi
Abdallah al-Mu'jil
Muhammad al-Sayf
Muhammad al-Shafi'i
Katib al-Shammari
Ali al-Umaym
Turki al-Utaybi
Muhammad al-Zulfa
Faiza Salih Ambah
Camille Ammoun
AbdurRahmaan Anderson
Khalid Batarfi
Peter Bergen
Faris bin Huzzam
Christopher Boucek
Douglas Brown
James Buchan
Benjamin Dyal
Dominic Evans
Sian Evans
Scott Fagan
Mamoun Fandy
Gregory Gause
Kim Ghattas
Alain Gresh
Mohammed Hafez
Andrew Hammond
Bernard Haykel
Steffen Hertog
Andrew Higgins
Gregory Johnsen
Sean Keeling
Gilles Kepel
Michael Knights
Evan Kohlmann
Robert Lacey
Stéphane Lacroix
Clyde Leamaster
Amélie Le Renard
Brynjar Lia
William McCants
Pascal Ménoret
Nabil Mouline
Rolf Mowatt-Larsen
Petter Nesser
Tim Niblock
Nawaf Obaid
Reuven Paz
Thomas Pierret
Magnus Ranstorp
Bernard Rougier
Omar Saghi
Guido Steinberg
Stig Stenslie
Camille Tawil
Dominique Thomas
Arne Walther
Christoph Wilcke
Lawrence Wright
May Yamani

Some security officials and Islamist sources have been anonymised.

JUDICIAL AND GOVERNMENT DOCUMENTS

'*Almrei* v. *Canada* (2005 FC 1645).' Federal Court of Canada, Ottawa, 2005.

'Bin Laden/Ibn Khattab Threat Reporting.' *Defendant's exhibit 792 – US vs Moussaoui* (www.rcfp.org, 2001).

'Biographies of High Value Terrorist Detainees Transferred to the US Naval Base at Guantanamo Bay', *Press Release, Office of the Director of National Intelligence*, 6 September 2006.

'Expert Report Concerning the Area Financial Investigations relating to the judicial assistance request, ref. no. INV/10289/T09-PH (245), dated 8/27/2002 of the "Office of the Prosecutor" (OTP) of the International Court of Criminal Justice for the former Yugoslavia relating to the "Third World Relief Agency" (TWRA), Vienna, Austria', Federal Office of Criminal Investigation (Germany), 28 August 2003 (http://documents.nytimes.com).

Harmony Database, Various documents (www.ctc.usma.edu/harmony_docs.asp).

National Security Archive, Various documents (www.gwu.edu/~nsarchiv/index.html).

'Substitution for the Testimony of Khalid Sheikh Mohammed.' *Defendant's exhibit 941 – US vs Moussaoui* (www.rcfp.org).

'Substitution for the Testimony of Muhammad Manea Ahmad al-Qahtani (Phase 2).' *Defendant's exhibit ST001 – US* v. *Moussaoui* (www.rcfp.org).

'Summary of Evidence for Combatant Status Review Tribunal – al-Shib, Ramzi bin.' US Department of Defense, 2007.

'Summary of Interviews with Muhammad al-Awhali.' *Defendant's exhibit 767 – US vs Moussaoui* (www.rcfp.org, 1998).

'Testimony of Detainees before the Administrative Review Board.' United States Department of Defense (www.dod.mil, March/April 2006).

'Testimony of Detainees before the Combatant Status Review Tribunal.' United States Department of Defense (www.dod.mil, March/April 2006).

USA v. *Ahmed al-Mughassil et al*, Eastern District of Virginia (2001).

USA v. *al-Badawi – Indictment*, Southern District of New York (2003).

USA v. *Enaam Arnaout – Government's Evidentiary Proffer*, Northern District of Illinois (2003).

USA v. *Haouari*, Southern District of New York (2001).

USA v. *Usama bin Ladin et al*, District Court of Southern New York (2001).

'Verbatim Transcript of Combatant Status Review Tribunal Hearing for ISN 10011' (www.defenselink.mil, 2007).

'Verbatim Transcript of Combatant Status Review Tribunal Hearing for ISN 10015' (www.defenselink.mil, 2007).

SOURCES CITED

'820 Mujahideen Imprisoned in Saudi Arabia, March 1998.' www.azzam.com, 1998.

The 9/11 Commission Report. New York: W. W. Norton, 2004.

"*abd al-rahman al-yaziji yurawi waqa'i ma'rakat hayy al-nahda fi liqa' khass* [Abd al-Rahman al-Yaziji Recounts the Events of the Battle of Nahda in a Special Interview].' *Sawt al-Jihad*, no. 28 (2004: 25–31).

Abu Rumman, Bashir and Abdallah Sa'id. *al-'alim wa'l-mujahid wa'l-shahid al-shaykh 'abdallah 'azzam* [The Scholar, Mujahid, Martyr and Sheikh Abdallah Azzam]. Amman: Dar al-Bashir, 1990.

'*akhbar wa mushahadat* [News and Reports].' *Sawt al-Jihad*, no. 13 (2004): 4–6.
al-Adl, Sayf. '*risala ila ahlina fi'l-'iraq wa'l-khalij khassatan wa ummatina al-islamiyya 'amma*.' Markaz al-Dirasat wa'l-Buhuth al-Islamiyya, 2003.
'*al-'amaliyya al-'askariyya 'ala mujamma' al-salibiyyin bi-iskan muhayya* [The Military Operation on the Crusader Compound in Muhayya].' *Sawt al-Jihad*, no. 5 (2003): 6–9.
al-Anzi, Sa'd. "*abd al-latif bin hamad al-khudayri* [Abd al-Latif bin Hamad al-Khudayri].' *Sawt al-Jihad*, no. 27 (2004): 11–12.
al-Awda, Salman. '*al-tafjirat wa tada'iyatuhu* [The Bombings and their Falterings].' www.islamtoday.net, 2003.
'*khattab hayy yazraq!!* [Khattab is Alive and Well!!].' www.islamtoday.net, 2002.
'*man li-asra al-muslimin?* [Who Will Help the Muslim Prisoners?].' www.islamtoday.net, 2002.
'*ru'ya fi ahdath amrika* [A View on the Events in America].' www.islamtoday.net, 2001.
'*ya ibn (al-watan) la taftari 'ala ahlak* [Oh Son of the Nation, Do Not Bring Calumny on your People].' www.islamtoday.net, 2004
al-Azdi, Abu Jandal. *tahrid al-mujahidin al-abtal ala ihya' sunnat al-ightiyal* [Encouraging the Heroic Mujahidin to Revive the Practice of Assassinations]. www.tawhed.ws, 2004.
usama bin ladin: mujaddid al-zaman wa qahir al-amrikan [Usama bin Ladin: Renewer of the Century and Victor over the Americans]. www.qa3edoon.com, 2003.
wujub istinqadh al-mustad'afin fi sujun al-tawaghit [The Obligation to Rescue the Oppressed in the Tyrants' Prisons]. www.tawhed.ws, 2004.
al-Bahlal, Ra'id bin Abdallah. '*ya ahl al-zulfi ... ayna ghayratukum?* [Oh People of Zulfi ... Where are the Rest of You?].' *Sawt al-Jihad*, no. 27 (2004): 26–30.
al-Barrak, Abd al-Rahman *et al.* '*bayan min 'ulama' din al-sa'udiyya* [Statement from the Religious Scholars of Saudi Arabia].' www.mafhoum.com, 2002.
'*al-bayan al-rabi'* [Statement no. 4].' www.qal3ah.org, 2004.
al-Dawsary, Sulayman. '*al-iftitahiyya* [Opening Word].' *Sawt al-Jihad* (2003): 2–4.
al-Dukhayyil, Bandar. '*faysal bin 'abd al-rahman al-dukhayyil: musa'ir harb* [Faysal bin Abd al-Rahman al-Dukhayyil: Warrior].' *Sawt al-Jihad*, no. 28 (2004): 12–17.
al-Fahd, Nasir. '*al-dawla al-uthmaniyya wa mawqif da'wat al-shaykh muhammad bin 'abd al-wahhab minha* [The Ottoman State and the Position of the Call of Sheikh Muhammad ibn Abd al-Wahhab on it].' Manuscript, 1993.
'*al-hamla al-salibiyya fi marhalatiha al-thaniyya: harb al-'iraq* [The Crusade in its Second Stage: The Iraq War].' www.tawhed.ws, 2002.
'*al-qasimi: min al-tawhid ila al-ilhad* [Al-Qasimi: From Tawhid to Unbelief].' www.al-fhd.com, undated.
'*al-radd 'ala maqal hadm al-tamthil min manzur islami li-katibihi sulayman bin 'abdallah al-turki* [Answer to the Article "Destruction of Statues from an Islamic Viewpoint" by Sulayman bin Abdallah al-Turki.' www.tawhed.ws, 2001.

(al-Fahd, Nasir, cont.)

'*al-tabyin fi makhatir al-tatbi' 'ala al-muslimin* [Clarification of the Dangers of Normalisation for Muslims].' www.tawhed.ws, 2002.

'*al-tankil bima fi bayan al-muthaqqafin min abatil* [Rebuttal of the Errors in the Statement of the Intellectuals].' www.tawhed.ws, 2002.

'*al-taraju' 'an al-taraju' al-mafrud* [Retraction of the Supposed Retraction].' www.tawhed.ws, 2005.

'*al-tibyan fi kufr man a'an al-amrikan* [Clarification on the Infidelity of Whoever Helps the Americans].' www.tawhed.ws, 2001.

'*ayat al-rahman fi "ghazwat sibtimbar"* [Signs of the Merciful in the "September Raid"].' www.tawhed.ws, 2002.

'*hal tu'tabar ta'shirat al-fiza 'aqd aman?* [Is the Visa Considered a Security Guarantee?].' www.tawhed.ws, 2003?

'*haqiqat al-hadara al-islamiyya* [The Truth of Muslim Civilisation].' Manuscript, 1993?

'*hawla ahadith "al-qahtani"* [On the al-Qahtani Incidents].' www.tawhed.ws, 2003.

'*hawla ahadith al-sufyani* [On the Sufyani Incidents].' www.tawhed.ws, 2003.

'*hawla qa'idat man lam yukaffir al-kafir fa huwa kafir* [On the Rule that Whoever Fails to Excommunicate a Disbeliever is Himself a Disbeliever].' www.tawhed.ws, 2002.

'*hukm al-'uturat al-kuhuliyya* [Ruling on Perfumes with Alcohol].' www.al-fhd.com, 1999.

'*hukm mujahadat al-amrikan kharij al-'iraq* [The Ruling on Fighting the Americans Outside Iraq].' www.tawhed.ws, 2003.

'*iqamat al-burhan 'ala wujub kasr al-awthan* [Establishing the Proof for the Obligation to Break the Statues].' www.tawhed.ws, 2001.

'*kashf shubhat hasan al-maliki* [Exposing Hasan al-Maliki's Deception].' www.al-fhd.com, 2001.

'*libas al-mar'a amam al-nisa'* [Women's Dressing before Women].' www.tawhed.ws, 2000.

'*ma'jam al-ansab al-usar al-mutahaddira min 'ashirat al-asa'ida* [Genealogy of the Sedentary Families of the Asa'ida Branch].' www.al-fhd.com, 1999.

'*manhaj al-mutaqaddimin fi'l-tadlis* [The Modernists' Method of Deceit].' www.al-fhd.com, 2000.

'*mas'alat al-tasfiq* [The Issue of Clapping].' www.al-fhd.com, 1999.

'*risala fi hukm al-ghana' bi'l-qur'an* [Letter on the Ruling of Singing the Qur'an].' www.tawhed.ws, 2001.

'*risala fi hukm istikhdam aslihat al-dimar al-shamil didd al-kuffar* [Treatise on the Use of Weapons of Mass Destruction against the Infidels].' www.tawhed.ws, 2003.

'*risala ila 'asrani* [Letter to a Modernist].' www.al-fhd.com, undated.

'*shi'r ahmad shawqi fi'l-mizan* [The Poetry of Ahmad Shawqi in the Balance].' Manuscript, 1994.

'*sirat samahat al-shaykh muhammad bin ibrahim al al-shaykh* [Biography of His Excellency Sheikh Muhammad bin Ibrahim Al al-Shaykh].' www.al-fhd.com, 1999.

(al-Fahd, Nasir, cont.)
'*ta'duw al-dhi'ab man la kilab lahu* [The Wolves Attack him who Has no Dog].' www.tawhed.ws, 2002.
'*tali'at al-tankil bima fi bayan al-muthaqqafin min abatil* [Early Excerpt of the Rebuttal of the Errors in the Statement of the Intellectuals].' www.tawhed.ws, 2002.
'*waqafat ma' al-waqafat* [Stances on the Stances].' www.tawhed.ws, 2001.
al-Fahd, Nasir, Ali al-Khudayr, Ahmad al-Khalidi, Abdallah al-Sa'd, Hamad al-Humaydi, Hamad al-Rayis and Ahmad al-Sanani. '*fatwa fi kufr man a'an al-amrikan 'ala al-muslimin fi'l-'iraq* [Fatwa on the Infidelity of Whoever Helps the Americans against Muslims in Iraq].' www.al-fhd.com, 2002.
al-Farraj, Fahd al-Juwayr. '*ya ahl al-zulfi* [Oh People of Zulfi].' *Sawt al-Jihad*, no. 18 (2004): 34–5.
al-Ghamidi, Abd al-Aziz. '*min abtal ghazwat sharq al-riyadh* [Heroes from the East Riyadh Raid].' *Sawt al-Jihad*, no. 22 (2004): 25–6.
al-Hadhlul, Ziyad Salih, and Muhammad Abdallah al-Humaydhi. *al-qissa al-kamila li'l-dawr al-sa'udi fi'l-busna wa'l-harsak* [The Full Story of the Saudi Role in Bosnia-Herzegovina]. Riyadh: Al-Homaidhi Printing Press, 1998.
al-Harfi, Abd al-Rahman. '*al-sira al-dhatiyya li-samahat al-shaykh hamud bin 'uqla al-shu'aybi* [The Biography of Sheikh Hamud bin Uqla al-Shu'aybi].' www.saaid.net, 2001.
al-Hawali, Safar. *kashf al-ghumma 'an 'ulama al-umma* [Revealing the Sorrow to the Scholars of the Nation]. Riyadh: Dar al-Hikma, 1991.
'*mafhum al-jihad* [The Concept of Jihad].' www.alhawali.com, 1989.
al-Husni, Abu Bakr. *hidayat al-sari fi hukm istihdaf al-tawari'* [The Prophet's Guidance on Targeting Emergency Forces]. www.qa3edoon.com, 2004.
al-Jafn, Abd al-Rahman. '*inas al-nubala' fi sirat shaykhina al-'uqla* [Noble People in the Life of our Sheikh al-Uqla].' www.saaid.net, 2002.
al-Jarbu', Abd al-Aziz. '*al-i'lan bi-wujub al-hijra min dar al-kufr ila dar al-islam* [Declaration on the Need to Emigrate from the Abode of Infidelity for the Abode of Islam].' www.tawhed.ws, 2001.
'*al-mukhtar fi hukm al-intihar khawf ifsha' al-asrar* [Selected Sayings on the Ruling on Suicide for Fear of Divulging Secrets].' www.tawhed.ws, 2001.
'*al-ta'sil li-mashru'iyyat ma hasal fi amrika min al-tadmir* [The Foundation of the Legitimacy of the Destruction that Happened in America].' www.tawhed.ws, 2001.
'*lam a'mur biha wa lam tasu'ni – radd 'ala maqal shaykh salman* [I did not Condone it and I was not Indifferent to it – Reply to Sheikh Salman's Article].' www.tawhed.ws, 2001.
al-Jasir, Jasir. '*mu'azzam al-afghan al-sa'udiyyin yumarisun hayatihim bi-sura tabi'iyya ba'd 'awdatihim* [Most Saudi Afghanis Lead Normal Lives after their Return].' *al-Majalla*, no. 847 (1996): 23.
'*qissat al-afghan al-sa'udiyyin* [The Story of the Saudi Afghans].' *al-Majalla*, 11 May 1996, 18–23.
al-Jawfi, Abu Hajir. '*turki al-dandani: 'azima wa shaja'a* [Turki al-Dandani: Greatness and Courage].' *Sawt al-Jihad*, no. 7 (2004): 33–5.

al-Khalidi, Abu Yasir. '*nasir al-sayyari: batal badr al-riyadh* [Nasir al-Sayyari: The Hero of the Badr of Riyadh].' *Sawt al-Jihad*, no. 25 (2004): 11–13.

al-Khalifa, Abdallah, ed. *al-tatarruf wa'l-irhab fi'l-mujtama' al-'arabi al-sa'udi: dirasa ijtima'iyya wa ithnughrafiyya* [Extremism and Terrorism in Saudi Arabian Society: A Sociological and Ethnographical Study]. Riyadh: King Faisal Centre for Research and Islamic Studies, 2004.

al-Khudayr, Ali. '*al-qawa'id al-arba' allati tufarriq bayna din al-muslimin wa din al-'almaniyyin* [The Four Rules which Separate the Religion of Muslims and the Religion of the Secularists].' www.tawhed.ws, undated.

'*al-wijaza fi sharh al-usul al-thalatha* [An Abridged Explanation of the Three Foundations].' www.tawhed.ws, 1994.

'*bayan fi hasan bin farhan al-maliki* [Statement on Hasan bin Farhan al-Maliki].' www.tawhed.ws, 2001.

'*fatwa fi ta'yid hadm al-asnam* [Fatwa on Supporting the Destruction of the Statues].' www.tawhed.ws, 2001.

'*fi turki al-hamad* [On Turki al-Hamad].' www.alkhoder.com, 2001.

'*radd al-shaykh 'ali al-khudayr 'ala al-bayan al-tawdihi li-khitab al-ta'ayush* [Reply from Ali al-Khudayr to the Clarifying Statement to the Letter of Coexistence].' www.tawhed.ws, 2002.

'*risala fi bayan hal ta'ifat al-'asraniyyin al-dalla* [Letter regarding the Statement on the Status of the Misled Faction of Modernists].' www.tawhed.ws, undated.

al-Khudayr, Ali, Nasir al-Fahd and Ahmad al-Khalidi. '*bayan fi nusrat al-mujahidin alladhina nushirat asma'uhum wa suwaruhum* [Statement in Support of the Mujahidin whose Names and Pictures have been Released].' www.alkhoder.com, 2003.

'*bayan hawla al-ahdath* [Statement on the Incidents].' www.alkhoder.com, 2003.

'*nasiha fi bayan hukm man wala al-kuffar wa a'anahum fi harbihim 'ala al-muslimin wa kalam 'ala al-raya* [Advice on the Statement on Whoever Shows Loyalty to the Infidels and Helps them in their War on the Muslims, and a Word on the Banner].' www.alkhoder.com, 2003.

al-Khudayr, Ali, and Ahmad al-Khalidi. '*bayan fi riddat mansur al-nuqaydan* [Statement on the Apostasy of Mansur al-Nuqaydan].' www.alkhoder.com, 2003.

al-Khudayr, Ali, and Muhammad al-Rushudi, Hamad al-Rayis and Muhammad al-Saqabi. '*ihya' millat ibrahim wa'l-radd 'ala al-mukhaddilin al-munhazimin* [Reviving the Creed of Abraham and Responding to the Defeatist Traitors].' www.alkhoder.com, 2002.

al-Libi, Abu Anas. '*al-shaykh al-'uqla 'alam shamikh fi zaman al-inhitat* [Sheikh al-Uqla – Eminent Personality in an Era of Decline].' www.almuqatila.com, 2002.

al-Majdhub, Muhammad. *ma' al-mujahidin wa'l-muhajirin fi bakistan* [With the Mujahidin and the Emigrants in Pakistan], 1st edn. Medina: Nadi al-Madina al-Munawwara al-Adabi, 1984.

al-Makki, Abu Muhammad. '*mit'ib al-muhayyani* [Mit'ib al-Muhayyani].' *Sawt al-Jihad*, no. 4 (2003): 33–6.

al-Makki, Khalil. '*sami al-luhaybi* [Sami al-Luhaybi].' *Sawt al-Jihad*, no. 6 (2003): 30–1.

al-Maliki, Hasan. *manahij al-ta'lim* [Education Curricula]. Manuscript, undated.

nahwa inqadh al-tarikh al-islami [Towards Saving Islamic History]. Manuscript, undated.

'*naqs kashf al-shubuhat* [The Imperfection of "Unveiling the Deceptions"].' Manuscript, undated.

al-Maqdisi, Abu Muhammad. *al-kawashif al-jaliyya fi kufr al-dawla al-sa'udiyya* [The Obvious Proofs of the Saudi State's Impiety], 1989.

al-Muqrin, Abd al-Aziz. *27 April Audio Statement*. Sawt al-Jihad, 2004.

dawrat al-tanfidh wa harb al-'isabat [A Course in Operational Execution and Guerrilla Warfare]. www.qa3edoon.com, 2004.

'*li-kull al-raghibiyyin fi'l-jihad 'ala ard al-jazira al-'arabiyya* [To all those who Desire Jihad on the Arabian Peninsula].' *Mu'askar al-Battar*, no. 10 (2004): 17–19.

al-Mutayri, Turki. ''*abd al-muhsin al-shabanat: shahid fi yawm 'id* [Abd al-Muhsin al-Shabanat: Id Martyr].' *Sawt al-Jihad*, no. 23 (2004): 20–1.

al-Najdi, Abdallah. '*risala ila al-'ulama wa'l-du'at* [Letter to the Scholars and the Preachers].' www.qa3edoon.com, 2004.

al-Najdi, al-Qa'qa'. '*al-shaykh ahmad bin nasir al-dukhayyil* [Sheikh Ahmad bin Nasir al-Dukhayyil].' *Sawt al-Jihad*, no. 5 (2003): 34–5.

al-Najdi, Usama. '*talal al-anbari: haydara al-jiddawi* [Talal al-Anbari: Haydara from Jidda].' *Sawt al-Jihad*, no. 17 (2004): 50–3.

al-Nashmi, Fawwaz. '*fahd bin samran al-sa'idi*.' *Sawt al-Jihad*, no. 16 (2004): 45–6.

'*khalid al-baghdadi (abu ayub al-najdi)* [Khalid al-Baghdadi (Abu Ayub al-Najdi)].' *Sawt al-Jihad*, no. 18 (2004): 53–4.

al-Nowaiser, Mowaffaq. 'Khattab, the Man who Died for the Cause of Chechnya.' *Arab News*, 4 May 2002.

al-Nuqaydan, Mansur. '*al-hijra ila al-mustahil: maqati' min sira ruhiyya* [Emigrating to the Impossible: Excerpts from a Spiritual Life].' *al-Majalla*, 2 May 2000.

'*al-kharita al-islamiyya fi'l-sa'udiyya wa mas'alat al-takfir* [The Islamist Map in Saudi Arabia and the Question of Takfir].' *al-Wasat*, 28 February 2003.

'*da'wa ila taqnin wazifat rijal al-hisba* [A Call for the Regulation of the Work of Religious Policemen].' *al-Majalla*, 30 April 2000.

'*hal kan ibn abi dawud mazluman?* [Was Ibn Abu Dawud Unjustly Treated?].' *al-Hayat*, 23 February 1999.

'*qissat bayan al-muthaqqafin al-sa'udiyyin* [The Story of the Statement of the Saudi Intellectuals].' *Elaph*, 13 November 2002.

'*al-qa'id khattab asad min usud al-islam* [Commander Khattab, One of the Lions of Islam].' www.qoqaz.com, 2002.

'Al-Qa'ida Leader Calls for Attacks on Americans in Iraq Rather than on the Saudi Government in Saudi Arabia.' *MEMRI Special Dispatch*, no. 635 (2003).

al-qadiyya al-filastiniyya bi-aqlam sa'udiyya [The Palestinian Cause in Saudi Authors' Words]. Mecca: Umm al-Qura University, 2002.

al-Qahtani, Majid. ''*isa bin sa'd bin muhammad al 'awshan: faris al-'ilam al-jihadi* [Isa bin Sa'd bin Muhammad Al Awshan: The Knight of Jihadi Media].' *Sawt al-Jihad*, no. 30 (2007): 16–21.

Al-Qaida's (Mis)adventures in the Horn of Africa, Harmony Project. West Point: Combating Terrorism Center, 2007.

al-Qatari, Hamad, and Majid al-Madani. *min qisas al-shuhada' al-'arab fi'l-busna wa'l-harsak* [From the Stories of the Arab Martyrs in Bosnia and Herzegovina]. 2nd edn. www.saaid.net, 2002.

al-Rasheed, Madawi. *Contesting the Saudi State: Islamic Voices from a New Generation*. Cambridge University Press, 2007.

A History of Saudi Arabia. Cambridge University Press, 2002.

'The Local and the Global in Saudi Salafism.' *ISIM Review* 21 (2008): 8–9.

'The Minaret and the Palace: Obedience at Home and Rebellion Abroad.' In *Kingdom Without Borders: Saudi Arabia's Political, Religious and Media Frontiers*, ed. Madawi al-Rasheed, 199–220. New York: Columbia University Press, 2008.

al-Rashid, Abdallah. '*al-'alim al-mujahid hamad bin 'abdallah al-humaydi* [The Mujahid Scholar Hamad bin Abdallah al-Humaydi].' *Sawt al-Jihad*, no. 29 (2005): 16–19.

intiqad al-i'tirad 'ala tafjirat al-riyadh [Criticism of the Objection to the Riyadh Bombings]. www.qa3edoon.com, 2003.

al-Rodhan, Khalid R. *The Impact of the Abqaiq Attack on Saudi Energy Security*. Washington, DC: Center for Strategic and International Studies, 2006.

al-Rushud, Abdallah. '*bayan hawla ahdath al-ifta'* [Statement on the Ifta' Events].' www.tawhed.ws, 2002.

'*talab munazara ma' al-shaykh nasir al-'umar* [Request for Debate with Sheikh Nasir al-Umar].' www.qa3edoon.com, 2004.

al-Salim, Muhammad. *39 wasila li-khidmat al-jihad wa'l-musharaka fihi* [39 Ways to Serve Jihad and Take Part in it]. Sawt al-Jihad, 2003.

'*la tadhhabu ila al-'iraq!* [Don't Go to Iraq!].' *Sawt al-Jihad*, no. 7 (2003): 23–4.

'*labayka ya 'iraq* [Woe to you, Iraq].' *Sawt al-Jihad*, no. 11 (2004): 15–16.

'*ya ahl kuwayt!* [People of Kuwait!].' *Sawt al-Jihad*, no. 13 (2004): 10–11.

'*yusuf al-'uyayri: shumukh fi zaman al-hawan* [Yusuf al-Uyayri: Standing Tall in an Age of Lowliness].' *Sawt al-Jihad*, no. 1 (2003): 15–18.

'*yusuf al-'uyayri: shumukh fi zaman al-hawan* [Yusuf al-Uyayri: Standing Tall in an Age of Lowliness].' *Sawt al-Jihad*, no. 2 (2003): 15–18.

al-Sharqawi, Muna bint Salih. '*ya nisa' dawrukun – fa-qad nam al-rijal* [Women, it's Your Turn, for the Men have Slept].' www.qa3edoon.com, 2004.

'*al-shaykh abu layth al-qasimi ahad qiyaday al-jama'a al-muqatila ba'd fararihi min sijn al-ruways* [Abu Layth al-Qasimi, One of the Leaders of the Fighting Group, after his Escape from Ruways Prison.' www.almuqatila.com (undated).

al-Shishani, Murad. *The Rise and Fall of Arab Fighters in Chechnya*. Washington, DC: Jamestown Foundation, 2006.

al-Shu'aybi, Hamud. '*al-bayan al-awal 'an ahwal ikhwanina al-muslimin fi filastin* [The First Statement on the Situation of our Muslim Brothers in Palestine].' www.aloqla.com, 2000.

'*al-bayan al-thani ila 'umum al-muslimin 'amma yadur fi filastin* [Second Statement to All Muslims regarding what is Going on in Palestine.' www.aloqla.com, 2000.

(al-Shu'aybi, Hamud, cont.)
'*al-jihad fi'l-filibin* [The Jihad in the Philippines].' www.aloqla.com, 2000.
'*al-musharaka fi ihtifalat al-alafiyya* [Taking Part in Millennium Celebrations].' www.aloqla.com, 1999.
'*al-nawadi al-nisa'iyya* [Women's Clubs].' www.aloqla.com, 2000.
'*al-qawl al-mukhtar fi hukm al-isti'ana bi'l-kuffar* [Selected Sayings on the Ruling of Seeking Help from the Infidels].' www.aloqla.com, 2001.
'*al-radd 'ala man afta bi-'adam jawaz muqata'a al-yahud wa'l-nasara* [Answer to those who Ruled against Boycotting Jews and Christians].' www.aloqla.com, 2001.
'*al-wala' wa'l-bara' wa wujub nusrat taliban wa hukm man zahar al-amrikan 'alayha* [Loyalty and Dissociation and the Obligation to Assist the Taliban and the Ruling on Whoever Helps the Americans against them].' www.aloqla.com, 2001.
'*bayan 'amma hasal min labs fi shurut al-ifta'* [Statement on the Confusion in the Conditions for Religious Rulings].' www.aloqla.com, 2001.
'*bayan 'amma jara fi amrika min ahadith* [Statement on the Events that Happened in America].' www.aloqla.com, 2001.
'*bayan fi hathth 'ala al-muqata'a al-iqtisadiyya didd a'da' al-muslimin* [Statement on Encouraging Economic Boycott of the Muslims' Enemies].' www.saaid.net, 2001.
'*bayan li-a'da' munazzamat al-mu'tamar al-islami bi-sha'n tahtim hukumat taliban al-islamiyya li'l-asnam* [Statement to the Members of the Organisation of the Islamic Conference Concerning the Destruction of the Idols by the Islamic Taliban Government].' www.saaid.net, 2001.
'*da'm al-imara al-islamiyya fi afghanistan wa ta'jil al-zakat laha* [Supporting the Islamic Emirate in Afghanistan and Directing Alms to it].' www.aloqla.com, 2001.
'*fatwa fi'l-katib turki al-hamad* [Fatwa on the Writer Turki al-Hamad].' www.aloqla.com, 1999.
'*fatwa fi kufr al-mughanni 'abdallah al-ruwayshid* [Fatwa on the Infidelity of the Singer Abdallah al-Ruwayshid].' www.saaid.net, 2001.
'*fatwa fi takfir al-hukkam wa'l-musharri'in li'l-qawanin al-wada'iyya* [Fatwa on Takfir of Rulers and Legislators of Man-Made Laws].' www.saaid.net, 2001.
'*hawla shar'iyyat hukumat taliban* [On the Legitimacy of the Taliban Government].' www.aloqla.com, 2000.
'*hukm al-jihad fi shishan wa wajib al-muslimin tijahhum* [Ruling on the Jihad in Chechnya and the Duty of Muslims towards them].' www.qoqaz.com, 1999.
'*hukm al-jihad wa isti'dhan al-walidayn fihi* [Ruling on Jihad and Parental Permission].' www.aloqla.com, 2001.
'*hukm bitaqat al-mar'a* [Ruling on Identity Cards for Women].' www.saaid.net, 2000.
'*hukm iqamat al-yahud wa'l-nasara fi'l-jazirat al-'arab wa tamallukhum al-'aqarat wa istithmarha* [Ruling on Jews and Christians Residing on the Arabian Peninsula and their Owning and Development of Property].' www.saaid.net, 2000.

(al-Shu‘aybi, Hamud, cont.)
‘*lu‘bat bukimun* [The Pokémon Toy].’ www.aloqla.com, 2001.
‘*ma‘na al-irhab wa haqiqathu* [The Meaning and Truth of Terrorism].’ www.aloqla.com, 2001.
‘*mashru‘iyyat al-‘amaliyyat al-istishhadiyya* [The Legitimacy of Martyrdom Operations].’ www.aloqla.com, 2001.
‘*muqaddamat radd ‘ala wazir al-shu’un al-islamiyya salih al al-shaykh* [Introduction to the Answer to the Islamic Affairs Minister Salih Al al-Shaykh].’ www.saaid.net, 2001.
‘*musharakat al-nisa’ fi’l-janadiriyya* [The Participation of Women in Janadiriyya].’ www.aloqla.com, 2000.
‘*nida’ ila hukkam al-‘arab wa’l-muslimin* [A Call to the Rulers of Arabs and Muslims].’ www.aloqla.com, 2001.
‘*nusrat taliban li-hadmihim al-awthan* [Supporting the Taliban in their Destruction of the Idols].’ www.aloqla.com, 2001.
‘*risala ila ahl al-hisba* [Letter to those who Carry out *Hisba*].’ www.aloqla.com, 2000.
‘*taqrib al-muharifin wa takrimihim* [Approaching and Honouring Deviants].’ www.aloqla.com, 2000.
al-Shu‘aybi, Hamud, Ali al-Khudayr and Sulayman al-Ulwan. ‘*khitab ila kafat ‘ulama bakistan* [Letter to All Religious Scholars in Pakistan].’ 2002.
‘*khitab li-amir al-mu‘minin muhammad ‘umar wa’l-mujahidin ma‘hu* [Letter to the Commander of the Faithful Muhammad Umar and the Mujahidin with him].’ 2001.
al-Subay‘i, Abdallah. ‘*musa‘id al-subay‘i: rajul fi zaman qalla fihi al-rija*l [Musa‘id al-Subay‘i: A Man in a Time when Men are Scarce].’ *Sawt al-Jihad*, no. 19 (2004): 39–41.
‘*al-sulta taftah bab al-damm: awwal shahid fi masirat al-islah* [The Authorities Open the Gates of Blood: The First Martyr on the Road to Reform].’ *Bayan (CDLR)*, no. 38 (1995).
al-Suri, Abu Mus‘ab. *da‘wat al-muqawama al-islamiyya al-‘alamiyya* [The Global Islamic Resistance Call]. www.tawhed.ws, 2004.
‘*al-taqrir al-ikhbari al-hadi ‘ashar bi-sha’n tafasil ‘amaliyyat sariyat al-quds* [News Report Eleven on the Details of the Quds Brigade Operation].’ www.qa3edoon.com, 2004.
‘*al-taqrir al-ikhbari al-hadi ‘ashar bi-sha’n tafasil ‘amaliyyat sariyat al-shaykh usama bin ladin* [Eleventh News Report on the Details of the Operation by the Sheikh Usama bin Ladin Squadron].’ www.qa3edoon.com, 2006.
al-Utaybi, Dhayyab. ‘‘*abd al-rahman bin ‘abdallah al-harbi* [Abd al-Rahman bin Abdallah al-Harbi].’ *Sawt al-Jihad*, no. 26 (2004): 59–60.
al-Utaybi, Sa‘ud. ‘*ibrahim al-rayis: thabat hatta al-mamat* [Ibrahim al-Rayis: Steadfastness to the Death].’ *Sawt al-Jihad*, no. 9 (2004): 27–9.
al-Uyayri, Yusuf. ‘*al-hamla al-‘alamiyya li-muqawamat al-‘udwan* [The Global Campaign of Resistance to Aggression].’ www.tawhed.ws, 2003.
‘*al-mizan li-harakat taliban* [The Taliban in the Balance].’ www.tawhed.ws, 2001.
‘*al-riyada al-badaniyya qabl al-jihad* [Physical Exercise before Jihad].’ www.qa3edoon.com, undated.

(al-Shu'aybi, Hamud, cont.)

'*hal intaharat hawa am ustushhidat?* [Did Khava (Baraeva) Commit Suicide or Martyr Herself?].' www.qoqaz.com, 2000.

'*hamsa fi udhn fadilat al-shaykh salman al-'awda* [A Whisper in Sheikh Salman al-Awda's Ear].' www.qa3edoon.com, undated.

'*haqiqat al-harb al-salibiyya al-jadida* [The Truth of the New Crusade].' www.alneda.com, 2001.

'*hidayat al-hayara fi jawaz qatl al-asara* [Guiding the Confused on the Permissibility of Killing Prisoners].' www.qoqaz.com, 2000.

'*la takun ma' al-'aduw diddna! risala 'amma 'an amn al-ma'lumat* [Don't Help the Enemy against Us: General Note on Information Security].' www.drasat.com, 2002.

'*mustaqbal al-'iraq wa'l-jazira al-'arabiyya ba'd suqut baghdad* [The Future of Iraq and the Arabian Peninsula after the Fall of Baghdad].' www.tawhed.ws, 2003.

'*risala ila ra'is qism da'irat al-riqaba 'ala al-sujun fi'l-mintaqa al-sharqiyya 'an awda' sijn al-dammam* [Letter to the Head of the Department of Supervision of Prisons in the Eastern Province on the Conditions in Dammam Prison].' www.qa3edoon.com, 2000.

'*silsilat al-harb al-salibiyya 'ala al-'iraq* [The Crusade on Iraq Series].' www.drasat.com, 2002.

'*tariqat talab al-'ilm* [The Way to Seek Knowledge].' www.qa3edoon.com, 1998.

'*thawabit 'ala darb al-jihad* [Guidelines for Jihad Training].' www.tawhed.ws, undated.

al-Wardani, Salih. *fuqaha' al-naft: rayat al-islam am rayat al sa'ud?* [Oil Scholars: The Banner of Islam or the Banner of the Al Saud?]. Cairo: al-Madbuli al-Saghir, undated.

al-Zahrani, Faris. '*bayan hawla al-da'awa al-kadhiba min safar al-hawali wa ashbahihi* [Statement Regarding the False Claims by Safar al-Hawali and his Ilk].' www.tawhid.ws, 2004.

'*talab munazara ma' safar al-hawali* [Request for Debate with Safar al-Hawali].' www.qa3edoon.com, 2004.

al-Zawahiri, Ayman. '*fursan taht rayat al-nabi* [Knights under the Prophet's Banner].' *al-Sharq al-Awsat*, 2–12 December 2001.

al-Zubaydi, Fathi. *al-jihad al-afghani fi'l-kitabat al-'arabiyya al-mu'asira* [The Afghan Jihad in Contemporary Arab Writings]. Damascus: Dar al-Ma'rifa, 1996.

al-Zulfawi, Abu Hajir. '*al-radd 'ala takahhunat jaridat al-watan* [Response to the Speculations of *al-Watan* Newspaper] (Statement 3).' (2006).

'*awwal bayan rasmi li-kata'ib sada tuwayq bi'l-zulfi* [First Official Statement by the Echo of Tuwayq Brigades in Zulfi].' 2005.

Al Awshan, Isa. '*khalid bin 'abdallah al-subayt: fida' wa tadhiyya* [Khalid bin Abdallah al-Subayt: Courage and Sacrifice].' *Sawt al-Jihad*, no. 15 (2004): 24–8.

'*risala maftuha ila shabab al-marakiz al-sayfiyya* [Open Letter to the Youth of the Summer Camps].' *Sawt al-Jihad*, no. 19 (2004): 22–5.

Alfaleh, Matrook. 'The Impact of the Processes of Modernization and Social Mobilization on the Social and Political Structures of the Arab Countries with Special Emphasis on Saudi Arabia.' Ph.D. dissertation, University of Kansas, 1987.

"*ali al-ma'badi al-harbi: batal badr al-riyadh* [Ali al-Ma'badi al-Harbi: The Hero of the Badr of Riyadh].' *Sawt al-Jihad*, no. 24 (2004): 22–6.

"*amir al-shihri: himma wa anafa … wa thabbat hatta al-shahada.* [Amir al-Shihri: Loftiness and Pride … and Trustworthiness until Martyrdom].' *Sawt al-Jihad*, no. 12 (2004): 26–9.

Anas, Abdallah. *wiladat al-afghan al-'arab* [The Birth of the Afghan Arabs]. London: Saqi, 2002.

Ancygier, Andrzej. *Al-Qa'ida in Saudi Arabia 2003 and 2004.* Berlin: Grin Verlag für akademische Texte, 2005.

Anonymous. *Through our Enemies' Eyes: Osama bin Laden, Radical Islam and the Future of America.* Washington: Brassey's, 2002.

Ansary, Abdullah F. 'Combating Extremism: A Brief Overview of Saudi Arabia's Approach.' *Middle East Policy* 15, no. 2 (2008): 111–42.

Ayoob, Mohammed, and Hasan Kosebalaban, eds. *Religion and Politics in Saudi Arabia: Wahhabism and the State.* Boulder, CO: Lynne Rienner, 2008.

''*aza' min al-mujahidin li'l-umma bi-ahad abtal al-jihad khattab* [Condolences from the Mujahidin to the Umma for (the passing of) Khattab, One of the Heroes of Jihad].' www.alneda.com, 2002.

Azzam, Abdallah. *al-difa' 'an aradi al-muslimin* [The Defence of Muslim Lands]. Amman: Maktabat al-Risala al-Haditha, 1987.

ayat al-rahman fi jihad al-afghan [Signs of the Merciful in the Afghan Jihad]. Amman: Maktabat al-Risala al-Haditha, 1986.

'*ayat wa basha'ir wa karamat fi'l-jihad al-afghani* [Signs and Tidings and Miracles in the Afghan Jihad].' *Al-Mujtama'*, no. 569 (1982).

Azzam, Maha. 'The Gulf Crisis: Perceptions in the Muslim World.' *International Affairs* 67, no. 3 (1991): 473–85.

'*badr al-riyadh* [Badr of Riyadh].' Al-Sahhab Foundation for Media Production, 2004.

Bahgat, Gawdat. 'Saudi Arabia and the War on Terrorism.' *Arab Studies Quarterly* 26, no. 1 (2004): 51–63.

Bakier, Abdul Hameed. 'Lessons from al-Qaeda's Attack on the Khobar Compound.' *Terrorism Monitor* 4, no. 16 (2006): 7–9.

Bakker, Edwin. 'Jihadi Terrorists in Europe.' In *Clingendael Security Paper no. 2.* The Hague: Netherlands Institute of International Relations, 2006.

Bakr, Ali. *tanzim al-qa'ida fi jazirat al-'arab* [Al-Qaida on the Arabian Peninsula]. http://islamyoon.islamonline.net, 30 August 2009.

'Battle of Tishin, North Bosnia, October 1992: 25 Mujahideen Defeat 200 Serb Special Forces.' www.azzam.com.

'*bayan bi-khusus al-asir al-amriki pul marshal junsun wa shurut itlaq sirahihi* [Statement on the American Prisoner Paul Marshall Johnson and the Conditions for his Release].' www.qa3edoon.com, 2004.

'*bayan bi-sha'n ghazwat sariyyat al-quds* [Statement on the Raid of the Quds Squadron].' www.qa3edoon.com, 2004.

'*bayan hawla al-taraju'at al-akhira* [Statement on the Recent Retractions].' *Sawt al-Jihad*, no. 5 (2003): 4.

'*bayan hawla 'amaliyyat al-dakhiliyya fi'l-riyadh* [Statement on the Interior Ministry Operation in Riyadh].' www.qa3edoon.com, 2004.

'*bayan hawla 'amaliyyat al-qunsuliyya al-amrikiyya fi jidda (ghazwat falluja)* [Statement on the American Consulate Operation in Jidda (The Falluja Raid)].' www.qa3edoon.com, 2004.

'*bayan hawla hawadith al-tafjirat* [Statement on the Bombing Incidents].' www.islamtoday.net, 16 May 2003.

'*bayan kata'ib al-haramain* [Statement of the Haramain Brigades].' www.hostinganime.com/kataeb, 2004.

'*bayan man nahnu wa madha nurid wa ma 'alaqatuna bi-tanzim al-qa'ida fi jazirat al-'arab* [Statement on Who We Are, What We Want and What is Our Relationship with al-Qaida on the Arabian Peninsula].' www.al-hesbah.org, 2006.

'*bayan min tanzim al-qa'ida fi jazirat al-'arab yubashshir bi-indhima' mu'assasat al-basha'ir li'l-intaj al-i'lami taht liwa'ihi* [Statement from the al-Qaida Organisation on the Arabian Peninsula Announcing the Inclusion of the Good Tidings Foundation for Media Production under its Banner].' www.al-boraq.com, 2006.

'Behind Closed Doors: Unfair Trials in Saudi Arabia.' Amnesty International, 1997.

Benthall, Jonathan. 'L'humanitarisme islamique.' *Cultures et Conflits*, no. 60 (2005): 103–22.

Bergen, Peter. *The Osama bin Laden I Know*. New York: Free Press, 2006.

Bergen, Peter, and Paul Cruickshank. 'The Unraveling.' *The New Republic* (11 June 2008).

Berntsen, Gary, and Ralph Pezzullo. *Jawbreaker*. New York: Crown, 2005.

Bin Abd al-Aziz, Abd al-Qadir. '*radd kalam al-hawali fi kitab al-difa'* [Response to al-Hawali's Talk on the Book "The Defence" (of Muslim Lands)].' www.tawhed.ws, 1990.

risalat al-'umda fi i'dad al-'udda [Treatise on the Pillar of Military Preparation]. www.tawhed.ws, *c.* 1988.

Bin Huzzam, Faris. '*amir al-lajna al-i'lamiyya* [Commander of the Media Committee].' *al-Riyadh*, 18 July 2006.

'*limadha 'adu ila afghanistan?* [Why Did They Return to Afghanistan?].' *al-Riyadh*, 10 October 2006.

'*shababuna ila afghanistan mujaddada* [Our Youth are Going to Afghanistan Again].' *al-Riyadh*, 3 October 2006.

Bin Jibrin, Abdallah. '*hal al-mujahidin wa-wajib al-muslimin nahwhum* [The State of the Mujahidin and the Duty of Muslims toward them] (Decree no. 1528).' www.qoqaz.com 1999.

'Bin Laden and the Balkans.' Brussels: International Crisis Group, 2001.

Bin Laden, Najwa, Omar bin Laden and Jean Sasson. *Growing Up bin Laden: Osama's Wife and Son Take Us Inside Their Secret World*. New York: St Martin's, 2009.

'*bin ladin fi risala khassa ila ahl al-jazira: ihmilu al-silah li'l-difa' 'an 'aradikum* [Bin Ladin in a Special Message to the "People of the Peninsula": Grab your Weapon and Defend your Honour].' *al-Quds al-Arabi*, 28 November 2002, 1.

Bin Ladin, Usama. '*ma'sat al-busna wa khida' khadim al-haramayn* [The Bosnia Tragedy and the Treason of the Custodian of the Two Holy Mosques].' Statement no. 18 from the Advice and Reform Committee, 1995.
Bin Sayeed, Khalid. *Western Dominance and Political Islam*. Albany: State University of New York Press, 1995.
Bin Uthaymin, Muhammad. '*Untitled Fatwa on Chechnya*.' www.qawqaz.com, 1999.
Blanche, Ed. 'The Egyptians around Bin Laden.' *Jane's Intelligence Review* 13, no. 12 (2001).
'Blowback Time Beckons as Saudi Jihadists are Squeezed in Iraq.' *Gulf States Newsletter* 29, no. 767 (2005).
Bodansky, Yossef. *Chechen Jihad: al Qaeda's Training Ground and the Next Wave of Terror*. New York: Harper, 2007.
Bonner, Michael. *Jihad in Islamic History: Doctrines and Practice*. Princeton University Press, 2006.
Boucek, Christopher. 'Extremist Reeducation and Rehabilitation in Saudi Arabia.' *Jamestown Terrorism Monitor* 5, no. 16 (2007): 1–4.
Saudi Arabia's 'Soft' Counterterrorism Strategy. Washington, DC: Carnegie Endowment for International Peace, 2008.
Bruce, James. 'Arab Veterans of the Afghan War.' *Jane's Intelligence Review* 7, no. 4 (1995).
Burr, J. Millard, and Robert O. Collins. *Alms for Jihad*. Cambridge University Press, 2006.
Byman, Daniel. *Deadly Connections: States that Sponsor Terrorism*. Cambridge University Press, 2005.
Calvert, John. *Sayyid Qutb and the Origins of Radical Islamism*. London: Hurst, forthcoming.
Cigar, Norman. *Al-Qaida's Doctrine for Insurgency: Abd al-Aziz al-Muqrin's 'A Practical Course for Guerrilla War.'* Washington, DC: Potomac Books, 2008.
Cline, Lawrence E. 'Changing Jihadist Behaviour: The Saudi Model.' *Small Wars Journal*, 10 April 2009.
Coll, Steve. *The Bin Ladens: An Arabian Family in the American Century*. New York: Penguin, 2008.
Ghost Wars: The Secret History of the CIA, Afghanistan and Bin Laden, from the Soviet Invasion to September 10, 2001. New York: Penguin, 2004.
Collins, Aukai. *My Jihad: The True Story of an American Mujahid's Amazing Journey*. Guilford, CT: Lyons Press, 2002.
Commins, David. *The Wahhabi Mission and Saudi Arabia*. London: I.B. Tauris, 2006.
Cook, David. *Understanding Jihad*. Berkeley: University of California Press, 2005.
Cordesman, Anthony. *Islamic Extremism in Saudi Arabia and the Attack on al-Khobar*. Washington DC: CSIS, 2001.
Cordesman, Anthony H., and Nawaf E. Obaid. *National Security in Saudi Arabia: Threats, Responses, and Challenges*. Westport, CT: Praeger Security International, 2005.
Saudi National Security: Military and Security Services – Challenges and Developments. Washington, DC: CSIS, 2004.

Cragin, R. Kim. 'Early History of al-Qa'ida.' *The Historical Journal* 51, no. 4 (2008): 1047–67.

Crile, George. *Charlie Wilson's War.* New York: Grove, 2003.

Cullison, Alan. 'Inside Al-Qaeda's Hard Drive.' *The Atlantic Monthly*, September 2004.

Curcio, Sharon. 'Generational Differences in Waging Jihad.' *Military Review* 85, no. 4 (2005): 84–8.

Cutts, Mark. 'The Humanitarian Operation in Bosnia, 1992–95: Dilemmas of Negotiating Humanitarian Access.' In *New Issues in Refugee Research.* Geneva: UNHCR, 1999.

Davis, Anthony. 'The Afghan Files: Al-Qaeda Documents from Kabul.' *Jane's Intelligence Review* 14, no. 2 (2002).

'Foreign Combatants in Afghanistan.' *Jane's Intelligence Review* 5, no. 7 (1993).

Della Porta, Donatella. *Social Movements, Political Violence and the State: A Comparative Analysis of Italy and Germany.* Cambridge University Press, 1995.

Denoeux, Guilain. *Urban Unrest in the Middle East: A Comparative Study of Informal Networks in Egypt, Iran and Lebanon.* Albany: State University of New York Press, 1993.

Di Justo, Patrick. 'How Al-Qaida Site was Hijacked.' *Wired.com*, 10 August 2002.

'*dima' lan tadi' – al-juz' al-awwal* [Blood Not Spilt in Vain – Part One].' Sawt al-Jihad Foundation for Media Production, 2006.

Edgar, Iain R. 'The Dream Will Tell: Militant Muslim Dreaming in the Context of Traditional and Contemporary Islamic Dream Theory and Practice.' *Dreaming* 14, no. 1 (2004): 21–9.

'The True Dream in Contemporary Islamic/Jihadist Dreamwork: A Case Study of the Dreams of Taliban Leader Mullah Omar.' *Contemporary South Asia* 15, no. 3 (2006): 263–72.

'Extending a Helping Hand to Those in Need Throughout the World.' *Saudi Arabia* 16, no. 3 (www.saudiembassy.net, 1999).

Fandy, Mamoun. *Saudi Arabia and the Politics of Dissent.* New York: Palgrave Macmillan, 2001.

Filkins, Dexter. *The Forever War.* New York: Alfred A. Knopf, 2008.

Gallab, Abdullahi A. *The First Islamist Republic: Development and Disintegration of Islamism in the Sudan.* Burlington: Ashgate, 2008.

Gambetta, Diego, and Steffen Hertog. 'Engineers of Jihad.' *University of Oxford: Sociology Working Papers*, no. 10 (2007).

Gause, F. Gregory. 'Saudi Arabia and the War on Terrorism.' In *A Practical Guide to Winning the War on Terrorism*, ed. Adam Garfinkel, 94–100. Stanford: Hoover Press, 2004.

Gerges, Fawaz. *The Far Enemy: Why Jihad Went Global.* Cambridge University Press, 2006.

Ghandour, Abdel-Rahman. *Jihad humanitaire: Enquête sur les ONG islamiques.* Paris: Flammarion, 2002.

'*ghazwat al-hadi 'ashar min rabi' al-awwal: 'amaliyyat sharq al-riyadh wa-harbuna ma' amrika wa 'umala'iha* [The 12 May Raid: The East Riyadh Operation and Our War with America and its Agents].' www.qa3edoon.com, 2003.

'*ghazwat al-qunsuliyya al-salibiyya al-amrikiyya* [Raid on the American Crusader Consulate].' Sawt al-Jihad Media Production, 2006.

Glass, E., and Y. Yehoshua. 'Saudi Arabia's Anti-Terror Campaign.' *MEMRI Inquiry and Analysis Series*, no. 425 (2008).

Gold, Dore. *Hatred's Kingdom: How Saudi Arabia Supports the New Global Terrorism*. Washington, DC: Regnery, 2004.

Goldberg, Jacob. 'Saudi Arabia and the Iranian Revolution: The Religious Dimension.' In *The Iranian Revolution and the Muslim World*, ed. David Menashri, 155–70. Boulder, CO: Westview Press, 1990.

Grossman, Dave. *On Killing: The Psychological Cost of Learning to Kill in War and Society*. Boston: Little, Brown, 1995.

Gunaratna, Rohan. 'The Terrorist Training Camps of al Qaida.' In *The Making of a Terrorist: Recruitment, Training and Root Causes*, ed. James J. F. Forest, 172–93. Westport, CT: Praeger, 2006.

Habib, John. *Ibn Saud's Warriors of Islam: The Ikhwan of Najd and Their Role in the Creation of the Sa'udi Kingdom, 1910–1930*. Leiden: Brill, 1978.

Hairgrove, Frank, and Douglas M. Mcleod. 'Circles Drawing Toward High-Risk Activism.' *Studies in Conflict and Terrorism* 31, no. 5 (2008): 399–411.

Hamza, Mawlana Amir. *qafilat dawat jihad*. Dar al-Andalus, 2004.

Hardy, Roger. 'Ambivalent Ally: Saudi Arabia and the "War on Terror".' In *Kingdom without Borders: Saudi Arabia's Political, Religious and Media Frontiers*, ed. Madawi Al-Rasheed, 99–112. New York: Columbia University Press, 2008.

Hastert, Paul. 'Operation Anaconda: Perception Meets Reality in the Hills of Afghanistan.' *Studies in Conflict and Terrorism* 28, no. 1 (2005): 11–20.

Heffelfinger, Chris. 'Statement to the Saudi Mujahideen Summons Iraq Returnees.' *Terrorism Focus* 3, no. 26 (2006): 3–4.

Hegghammer, Thomas. 'Deconstructing the Myth about al-Qa'ida and Khobar.' *The Sentinel* 1, no. 3 (2008): 20–2.

Dokumentasjon om al-Qaida: Intervjuer, kommunikéer og andre primærkilder, 1990–2002 [Documentation on al-Qaida: Interviews, Communiqués and Other Primary Sources, 1990–2002]. Kjeller: Norwegian Defence Research Establishment (FFI/Rapport), 2002.

'Jihad, Yes, but not Revolution: Explaining the Extroversion of Islamist Militancy in Saudi Arabia.' *British Journal of Middle Eastern Studies* 35, no. 3 (2009).

'Jihadi Salafis or Revolutionaries? On Theology and Politics in the Study of Militant Islamism.' In *Global Salafism*, ed. Roel Meijer, 244–66. London and New York: Hurst and Columbia University Press, 2009.

Saudi Militants in Iraq: Backgrounds and Recruitment Patterns. Kjeller: Norwegian Defence Research Establishment (FFI/Report), 2007.

'Violent Islamism in Saudi Arabia, 1979–2006: The Power and Perils of Pan-Islamic Nationalism.' Ph.D. thesis, Institut d'Etudes Politiques de Paris, 2007.

Hegghammer, Thomas, and Stéphane Lacroix. 'Rejectionist Islamism in Saudi Arabia: The Story of Juhayman al-Utaybi Revisited.' *International Journal of Middle East Studies* 39, no. 1 (2007): 103–22.

Henderson, Simon. 'Al-Qaeda Attack on Abqaiq: The Vulnerability of Saudi Oil.' In *Policy Watch*. Washington, DC: Washington Institute for Near East Policy, 2006.

After King Abdullah: Succession in Saudi Arabia. Washington, DC: Washington Institute for Near East Policy, 2009.

Henderson, Simon, and Matthew Levitt. 'US–Saudi Counterterrorism Cooperation in the Wake of the Riyadh Bombing.' In *Policy Watch*. Washington, DC: Washington Institute for Near East Policy, 2003.

Hertog, Steffen. 'Segmented Clientelism: The Politics of Economic Reform in Saudi Arabia.' D.Phil. thesis, Oxford University, 2006.

Holden, David, and Richard Johns. *The House of Saud*. London: Sidgwick & Jackson, 1981.

Hollingsworth, Mark, and Sandy Mitchell. *Saudi Babylon: Torture, Corruption and Cover-Up Inside the House of Saud*. Edinburgh: Mainstream, 2005.

'How We Can Coexist.' www.islamtoday.com, 2002.

Huband, Mark. *Warriors of the Prophet: The Struggle for Islam*. Boulder, CO: Westview, 1999.

'*i'tirafat al-mu'taqal al-awwal* [Confessions of the First Detainee].' http://alquma.net, undated.

'*i'tirafat al-mu'taqal al-thani* [Confessions of the Second Detainee].' http://alquma.net, undated.

Ibn al-Mawsul. '*istishhad ahad shabab al-jawf fi bilad al-rafidayn* [One of the Jawf Youth Martyred in Mesopotamia].' http://topforums.net, 2005.

Ibrahim, Fouad. *The Shi'is of Saudi Arabia*. London: Saqi, 2007.

Ibrahim, Saad Eddin. 'Anatomy of Egypt's Militant Islamic Groups: Methodological Notes and Preliminary Findings.' *International Journal of Middle East Studies* 12, no. 4 (1981): 423–53.

'Interview with Sheikh al-Mujahideen Abu Abdel Aziz.' *al-Sirat al-Mustaqeem*, no. 33 (1994).

'Intifada Stirs up Gulf Arab Resentment Against Israel and the USA.' *Jane's Intelligence Review* 13, no. 5 (2001).

'Israel and the Occupied Territories Shielded from Scrutiny: IDF Violations in Jenin and Nablus.' London: Amnesty International, 2002.

'*jam' min al-'ulama' al-sa'udiyyin yuwajjihun khatiban maftuhan li'l-sha'b al-'iraqi* [Group of Saudi Scholars Direct Open Letter to the Iraqi People].' www.islamtoday.com, 2004.

Jamus, Abd al-Rahim Mahmud. *al-lijan al-sha'biyya li-musa'adat mujahidiy filastin fi'l-mamlaka al-'arabiyya al-sa'udiyya* [The Popular Committees for the Support of Palestine's Mujahidin in the Kingdom of Saudi Arabia]. Riyadh: Darat al-Malik Abd al-Aziz, 2001.

Johnsen, Gregory. 'Tracking Yemen's 23 Escaped Jihadi Operatives – Part 1.' *Terrorism Monitor* 5, no. 18 (2007).

'Tracking Yemen's 23 Escaped Jihadi Operatives – Part 2.' *Terrorism Monitor* 5, no. 19 (2007).

Jones, Toby. 'Rebellion on the Saudi Periphery: Modernity, Marginalization, and the Shi'a Uprising of 1979.' *International Journal of Middle East Studies* 38, no. 2 (2006): 213–33.

Katz, Mark N. 'Arabian Tribes in the 21st Century.' *Middle East Times*, 2007.
'*kayfa mat al-hudhayf* [How Did al-Hudhayf Die?].' *Bayan (CDLR)*, no. 39 (1995).
Kepel, Gilles. *Jihad: The Trail of Political Islam*. Cambridge, MA: Belknap, 2002.
'Les stratégies islamistes de légitimation de la violence.' *Raisons Politiques*, no. 9 (2003): 81–95.
'Terrorisme islamiste: De l'anticommunisme au jihad anti-américain.' *Ramses* (2003): 43–58.
The War for Muslim Minds: Islam and the West. Cambridge, MA: Belknap, 2004.
Khalil, Mahmud. '*al-qa'ida tutliq silsilat tahdidat jadida wa miyah al-gharb muhaddada bi-tasmim* [Al-Qaida Issues a Series of New Threats and the West's Water is Threatened with Poisoning].' *al-Majalla*, 25–31 May 2003.
'*al-qa'ida: ajrayna taghyirat fi haykaliyyat al-tanzim wa natafawwaq 'ala al-amrikiyyin istratijiyya* [Al-Qaida: We Have Made Changes in the Organisational Structure and We Prevail over the Americans Strategically].' *al-Majalla*, 10–17 May 2003.
'*al-qa'ida: hadafna irbak amn al-khalij* ["Al-Qaida": Our Aim is to Undermine Security in the Gulf].' *al-Majalla*, 18–24 May 2003.
The Kingdom of Saudi Arabia's Economic and Social Development Aid to the Islamic World. Riyadh: Ministry of Finance and National Economy, 1991.
Knights, Michael. 'The Current State of al-Qa'ida in Saudi Arabia.' *Sentinel* 1, no. 10 (2008): 7–10.
'The East Riyadh Operation, May 2003.' JTIC Terrorism Case Study (Jane's Information Group), 2005.
'The Khobar Rampage, May 2004.' JTIC Terrorism Case Study (Jane's Information Group), 2005.
'A New Afghanistan? Exploring the Iraqi Jihadist Training Ground.' *Jane's Intelligence Review* 18, no. 7 (2006).
'Operation Conquest of Falluja: Assault on the US Consulate in Jeddah, December 2004.' In *JTIC Terrorism Case Study*. Coulsdon: Jane's Information Group, 2006.
'Saudi Terrorist Cells Await Return of Jihadists from Iraq.' *Jane's Intelligence Review* 17, no. 12 (2005): 12–15.
Kohlmann, Evan F. *Al-Qaida's Jihad in Europe: The Afghan–Bosnian Network*. London: Berg, 2004.
'The Role of Islamic Charities in International Terrorist Recruitment and Financing.' In *DIIS Working Paper*. Copenhagen: Danish Institute for International Studies, 2006.
Kostiner, Joseph. *The Making of Saudi Arabia: From Chieftaincy to Monarchical State*. Oxford University Press, 1993.
Kramer, Mark. 'The Perils of Counterinsurgency: Russia's War in Chechnya.' *International Security* 29, no. 3 (2004): 5–63.
Krueger, Alan B., and Jitka Malečková. 'Education, Poverty and Terrorism: Is there a Causal Connection?' *Journal of Economic Perspectives* 17, no. 4 (2003): 119–44.
Lacey, Robert. *Inside the Kingdom*. New York: Viking, 2009.
The Kingdom: Arabia and the House of Saud. New York: Avon, 1981.

Lacroix, Stéphane. 'Between Islamists and Liberals: Saudi Arabia's Islamo-Liberal Reformists.' *Middle East Journal* 58, no. 3 (2004): 345–65.

'Islamo-Liberal Politics in Saudi Arabia'. In *Saudi Arabia in the Balance*, ed. Paul Aarts and Gerd Nonneman. London: Hurst, 2006.

'Le champ politico-religieux en Arabie Saoudite après le 11 septembre.' Master's thesis (*mémoire de DEA*), Institut d'Etudes Politiques de Paris, 2003.

'Les champs de la discorde: Une sociologie politique de l'islamisme en Arabie Saoudite (1954–2005).' Ph.D. thesis, Institut d'Etudes Politiques de Paris, 2007.

'The Double-edged Role of Islamic Networks in Saudi Politics.' Paper presented at the Annual Meeting of the Middle East Studies Association, Montreal, 19 November 2007.

Landau, J. M. *The Politics of Pan-Islam: Ideology and Organization*. Oxford University Press, 1990.

Lanskoy, Miriam. 'Daghestan and Chechnya: The Wahhabi Challenge to the State.' *SAIS Review* 22, no. 2 (2002): 167–92.

Lawrence, Bruce, ed. *Messages to the World: The Statements of Osama Bin Laden*. London: Verso, 2005.

'Letter from Abu Hudhayfa to Abu Abdallah.' *HARMONY Database (AFGP-2002–003251)*, 20 June 2000.

Lewis, Bernard. 'License to Kill: Usama Bin Ladin's Declaration of Jihad.' *Foreign Affairs* 77, no. 6 (1998).

Lia, Brynjar. *Architect of Global Jihad: The Life of Al-Qaeda Strategist Abu Mus'ab Al-Suri*. London: Hurst, 2007.

Lia, Brynjar, and Thomas Hegghammer. 'Jihadi Strategic Studies: The Alleged Policy Study Preceding the Madrid Bombings.' *Studies in Conflict and Terrorism* 27, no. 5 (2004): 355–75.

'*liqa' khass ma' qa'id sariyat al-quds – fawwaz bin muhammad al-nashmi* [Special Interview with the Leader of the Quds Squadron Fawwaz bin Muhammad al-Nashmi].' *Sawt al-Jihad*, no. 18 (2004): 20–6.

'*liqa' ma' ahad al-matlubin al-tisa' 'ashar* (1) [Interview with One of the Nineteen Wanted Men].' *Sawt al-Jihad*, no. 1 (2003): 21–4.

'*liqa' ma' ahad al-matlubin al-tisa' 'ashar* (2) [Interview with One of the Nineteen Wanted Men].' *Sawt al-Jihad*, no. 2 (2003): 22–6.

'*liqa' ma' al-mujahid salih bin muhammad al-'awfi* [Interview with the Mujahid Salih bin Muhammad al-Awfi].' *Sawt al-Jihad*, no. 8 (2004): 23–8.

'*liqa' ma' al-shaykh al-mujahid sa'ud bin hamud al-'utaybi* [Interview with the Mujahid Sheikh Sa'ud bin Hamud al-Utaybi].' *Sawt al-Jihad* 2003, 18–22.

Looney, Robert. 'Combating Terrorism Through Reforms: Implications of the Bremer-Kasarda Model for Saudi Arabia.' *Strategic Insights* 3, no. 4 (2004).

McCarthy, John D., and Mayer N. Zald. 'Resource Mobilization and Social Movements: A Partial Theory.' *American Journal of Sociology* 82, no. 6 (1977): 1212–41.

McCleod, Scott. 'The Paladin of Jihad.' *TIME*, 6 May 1996.

'*majmu'at maqalat al-shahid muhammad bin 'abd al-rahman al-suwaylimi* [Collection of Articles of the Martyr Muhammad bin Abd al-Rahman al-Suwaylimi].' www.al-hesbah.org, 2006.

'*man huwa al-shaykh al-battar?* [Who is Sheikh Sabre?].' www.qa3edoon.com, 2003.

'The Martyrs of Afghanistan.' www.alfirdaws.org.

Meijer, Roel. 'The "Cycle of Contention" and the Limits of Terrorism in Saudi Arabia.' In *Saudi Arabia in the Balance*, ed. Paul Aarts and Gerd Nonneman, 271–306. London: Hurst, 2005.

'Yusuf al-Uyayri and the Making of a Revolutionary Salafi Praxis.' *Die Welt des Islams* 47, nos. 3–4 (2007): 422–59.

'Yusuf al-Uyairi and the Transnationalisation of Saudi Jihadism.' In *Kingdom without Borders: Saudi Political, Religious and Media Frontiers*, ed. Madawi al-Rasheed, 221–44. New York: Columbia University Press, 2008.

Moody, James. 'Fighting a Hydra: A Note on the Network Embeddedness of the War on Terror.' *Structure and Dynamics: eJournal of Anthropological and Related Sciences* 1, no. 2 (2006).

'*mu'assasat al-basha'ir li'l-intaj al-i'lami tuqaddim al-asdar al-awwal: kasr al-asr* [The Good Tidings Foundation for Media Production Presents First Publication: "Breaking Captivity"].' www.w-n-n.org, 2006.

Muhammad, Basil. *al-ansar al-'arab fi afghanistan* [The Arab Supporters in Afghanistan]. 2nd edn. Riyadh: Lajnat al-Birr al-Islamiyya, 1991.

Muhibb al-Jihad. '*shuhada' ard al-rafidayn* [Martyrs of Mesopotamia].' www.al-hikma.net, 2005.

Mujahid, Abu. *al-shahid 'abdallah 'azzam bayna al-milad wa'l-istishhad* [The Martyr Abdallah Azzam from Birth to Martyrdom]. Peshawar: Markaz al-Shahid Azzam al-Ilami, 1991.

Munro, Alan. *An Embassy at War: Politics and Diplomacy behind the Gulf War*. London: Brassey's, 1996.

'*muqabala ma' ahad al-matlubin, abu hammam al-qahtani* [Interview with One of the Wanted, Abu-Hammam al-Qahtani].' *Sada al-Malahim*, nos. 1 and 2 (2008).

Musharraf, Pervez. *In the Line of Fire: A Memoir*. London: Simon and Schuster, 2006.

Naji, Abu Bakr. '*idarat al-tawahhush* [The Management of Savagery].' www.tawhed.ws, 2004.

Naylor, Sean. *Not a Good Day to Die*. London: Penguin, 2005.

Niblock, Tim. *Saudi Arabia: Power, Legitimacy and Survival*. London: Routledge, 2006.

'The Nineteen Martyrs (video).' Transcript available on www.jihadunspun.com, 2002.

'*nubdha 'an al-shaykh* [Biographic Note on the Shaykh].' www.alkhoder.com, 2003.

'*nubdha 'an al-shaykh 'abd al-'aziz al-jarbu'* [Biographic Note on Shaykh Abd al-Aziz al-Jarbu'].' www.geocities.com/aljarbo, 2003.

Obaid, Nawaf. 'Remnants of al-Qaeda in Saudi Arabia: Current Assessment.' Presentation at the Council of Foreign Relations, New York, 2006.

Obaid, Nawaf, and Anthony Cordesman. *Al-Qaeda in Saudi Arabia: Asymmetric Threats and Islamic Extremists*. Washington, DC: Center for Strategic and International Studies, 2005.

Saudi Militants in Iraq: Assessment and Kingdom's Response. Washington, DC: Center for Strategic and International Studies, 2005.

Ochsenwald, William. 'Saudi Arabia and the Islamic Revival.' *International Journal of Middle East Studies* 13, no. 3 (1981): 271–86.

Okruhlik, Gwenn. 'Networks of Dissent: Islamism and Reform in Saudi Arabia.' *Current History* (2002): 22–8.

'Operation Enduring Freedom – Operations.' www.globalsecurity.org, 2007.

'Overview of the Enemy – Staff Statement Number 15.' www.9-11commission.gov, 2004.

Paz, Reuven. 'Global Jihad and WMD: Between Martyrdom and Mass Destruction.' *Current Trends in Islamist Ideology* 2 (2005): 74–86.

Pedahzur, Ami, Leonard Weinberg and Arie Perliger. 'Altruism and Fatalism: The Characteristics of Palestinian Suicide Terrorists.' *Deviant Behaviour* 24 (2003): 405–23.

Peterson, J. E. 'Saudi Arabia: Internal Security Incidents since 1979.' *Arabian Peninsula Background Note*, no. 3 (2005).

Piscatori, James. 'Imagining Pan-Islam.' In *Islam and Political Violence*, ed. Shahram Akbarzadeh and Fethi Mansouri, 27–38. London: I. B. Tauris, 2007.

'Religion and Realpolitik: Islamic Responses to the Gulf War.' In *Islamic Fundamentalisms and the Gulf Crisis*, ed. J. P. Piscatori, 1–27. University of Chicago Press, 1991.

Posner, Gerald. *Why America Slept: The Failure to Prevent 9/11*. New York: Ballantine Books, 2003.

Prokop, Michaela. 'Saudi Arabia: The Politics of Education.' *International Affairs* 79, no. 1 (2003): 77–89.

'*qabilat 'utayba tazuff ahad abna'iha shahida* [The Utayba Tribe Celebrates One of its Sons as a Martyr].' *Sawt al-Jihad*, no. 4 (2003): 26.

'*qararat wa tawsiyat ahamm al-mu'tamarat allati 'aqadatha rabitat al-'alam al-islami* [Resolutions and Recommendations of the Most Important Conferences Organised by the Muslim World League].' Mecca: MWL, 1991.

'*qissat al-asir al-amriki muhandis al-abatshi bul marshal* [The Story of the American Captive, the Apache Engineer Paul Marshall].' *Sawt al-Jihad*, no. 19 (2004): 18–19.

Quandt, William B. *Saudi Arabia in the 1980s: Foreign Policy, Security and Oil*. Washington, DC: Brookings, 1981.

Rana, Muhammad Amir, and Mubasher Bukhari. *Arabs in Afghan Jihad*. Lahore: Pak Institute for Peace Studies, 2007.

Randal, Jonathan. *Osama: The Making of a Terrorist*. New York: Vintage Books, 2004.

Rashid, Ahmed. *Descent into Chaos*. New York: Viking, 2008.

Reeve, Simon. *The New Jackals: Ramzi Yousef, Osama bin Laden and the Future of Terrorism*. London: André Deutsch, 1999.

'Report of the Joint Inquiry into the Terrorist Attacks of September 11, 2001.' Washington, DC: US House of Representatives and US Senate, 2002.

Riedel, Bruce. *The Search for Al Qaeda*. Washington, DC: Brookings Institution Press, 2008.

Riedel, Bruce, and Bilal Y. Saab. 'Al Qaeda's Third Front: Saudi Arabia.' *The Washington Quarterly* 31, no. 2 (2008): 33–46.

Rosen, Nir. *In the Belly of the Green Bird: The Triumph of the Martyrs in Iraq*. New York: Free Press, 2006.

Rougier, Bernard. *Everyday Jihad: The Rise of Militant Islam among Palestinians in Lebanon*. Cambridge, MA: Harvard University Press, 2007.

Roy, Olivier. *Islam and Resistance in Afghanistan*. 2nd edn. Cambridge University Press, 1990.

Rubin, Barnett R. 'Arab Islamists in Afghanistan.' In *Political Islam: Revolution, Radicalism, or Reform?*, ed. John Esposito, 179–206. Boulder, CO: Lynne Rienner, 1997.

The Fragmentation of Afghanistan: State Formation and Collapse in the International System. 2nd edn. New Haven, CT: Yale University Press, 2002.

Sada al-Da'wa. '*ma lakum la tuqatilun fi'l-'iraq wa jami' al-turuq maftuha?* [Why Are You Not Fighting in Iraq When All the Roads are Open?].' www.sadaaljihad.net, 2003.

Sageman, Marc. *Understanding Terror Networks*. Philadelphia: University of Pennsylvania Press, 2004.

'*sariyat al-quds* [The Quds Squadron].' Sahhab Foundation for Media Production, 2006.

'Saudi Arabia Remains a Fertile Ground for Torture with Impunity.' Amnesty International, 2002.

'Saudi Arabia: A Secret State of Suffering.' Amnesty International, 2000.

'Saudi Torturers Rape Mujahideen During Interrogation.' www.azzam.com.

Schbley, Ayla Hammond. 'Torn Between God, Family and Money: The Changing Profile of Lebanon's Religious Terrorists.' *Studies in Conflict and Terrorism* 23 (2000): 175–96.

Scheuer, Michael. *Imperial Hubris: Why the West is Losing the War on Terror*. Washington, DC: Brassey's, 2004.

Scheuer, Michael, Stephen Ulph and John C. K. Daly. *Saudi Arabian Oil Facilities: The Achilles Heel of the Western Economy*. Washington, DC: The Jamestown Foundation, 2006.

Schulze, Reinhard. *Islamischer Internationalismus im 20. Jahrhundert*. London: E. J. Brill, 1990.

Schwartz, Stephen. 'Wahhabism and al Qaeda in Bosnia Herzegovina.' *Terrorism Monitor* 2, no. 20 (2004): 5–7.

Selim, Mohammad El Sayed, ed. *The Organisation of the Islamic Conference in a Changing World*. Cairo: Center for Political Research and Studies, 1994.

Sheikh, Naveed S. *The New Politics of Islam*. London: RoutledgeCurzon, 2003.

'*shuhada' al-muwajahat* [Martyrs of the Confrontations].' Al-Sahhab Foundation for Media Production, 2003.

Silm, Bouchaib. 'Notes on al Qaeda in Saudi Arabia.' *Asian Journal of Social Science* 35, nos. 4/5 (2007): 528–53.

Sindi, Abdullah M. 'King Faisal and Pan-Islamism.' In *King Faisal and the Modernisation of Saudi Arabia*, ed. Willard Beling. London: Croom Helm, 1980.

Snow, David A., and Robert D. Benford. 'Ideology, Frame Resonance, and Participant Mobilization.' In *International Social Movement Research: From*

Structure to Action, ed. Bert Klandermans, Hans Peter Kriesi and Sidney Tarrow, 197–218. Greenwich: JAI Press, 1988.

Steinberg, Guido. *Religion und Staat in Saudi-Arabien*. Würzburg: Egon, 2002.

'Strategy for Eliminating the Threat from the Jihadist Networks of al Qida: Status and Prospects.' National Security Council Memo, 2000 (www.gwu.edu/~nsarchiv).

Suskind, Ron. *The One Percent Doctrine*. New York: Simon and Schuster, 2006.

'*tarjama* [Biography].' www.al-fhd.com, 2002.

'*tasa'ulat hawla al-jihad didd al-salibiyyin fi jazirat al-'arab* [Questions about the Jihad against the Crusaders on the Arabian Peninsula].' *Sawt al-Jihad*, no. 11 (2004): 28–30.

Teitelbaum, Joshua. *Holier Than Thou: Saudi Arabia's Islamic Opposition*. Vol. LII. Washington Institute for Near East Policy, 2000.

'Terrorist Challenges to Saudi Arabian Internal Security.' *Middle East Review of International Affairs* 9, no. 3 (2005).

Tenet, George. *At the Center of the Storm: My Years at the CIA*. New York: HarperCollins, 2007.

Testas, Abdelaziz. 'The Roots of Algeria's Ethnic and Religious Violence.' *Studies in Conflict and Terrorism* 25 (2002): 161–83.

Thomas, Dominique. *Les hommes d'Al-Qaïda: Discours et stratégie*. Paris: Michalon, 2005.

'Torture in the Saudi Prisons.' *Nida'ul Islam*, no. 21 (1997): 13–14.

Trofimov, Yaroslav. *The Siege of Mecca: The Forgotten Uprising in Islam's Holiest Shrine and the Birth of al Qaeda*. New York: Doubleday, 2007.

'*turki al-dandani: rahil al-abtal* [Turki al-Dandani: The Departed Hero].' *Sawt al-Jihad*, no. 8 (2004): 29–33.

'*turki bin fuhayd al-mutayri* [Turki bin Fuhayd al-Mutayri].' *Sawt al-Jihad*, no. 20 (2004): 32–5.

ukhuwwat al-islam: al-mamlaka al-'arabiyya al-sa'udiyya wa muslimu al-busna wa'l-harsak [Brotherhood of Islam: The Kingdom of Saudi Arabia and the Muslims of Bosnia-Herzegovina]. London: Al-Hani International Books, 1993.

Ulph, Stephen. 'Al-Qaeda's Diminishing Returns in the Peninsula.' *Terrorism Focus* 2, no. 1 (2005): 7 January.

'Another al-Qaeda Group Forms in Saudi Arabia.' *Terrorism Focus* 2, no. 19 (2005).

'Mujahideen Explain Away Failures of the Abqaiq Attack.' *Terrorism Focus* 3, no. 9 (2006).

'Shifting Sands: Al-Qaeda and Tribal Gun-Running along the Yemeni Frontier.' *Terrorism Monitor* 2, no. 7 (2004).

'Urgent Action 200/95.' London: Amnesty International, 1995.

Vassiliev, Alexei. *The History of Saudi Arabia*. London: Saqi Books, 2000.

Vego, Milan. 'The Army of Bosnia and Hercegovina.' *Jane's Intelligence Review* 5, no. 2 (1993).

Wagemakers, Joas. 'Framing the "Threat to Islam": al- wala' wa al-bara' in Salafi Discourse.' *Arab Studies Quarterly* 30, no. 4 (2008): 1–22.

Waldmann, Peter. 'Ethnic and Sociorevolutionary Terrorism: A Comparison of Structures.' In *Social Movements and Violence: Participation in Underground Organisations*, ed. Donatella Della Porta, 237–57. Greenwich: JAI, 1992.

'*wasaya al-abtal: shuhada' al-haramayn* [Wills of the Heroes: Martyrs of the Two Sanctuaries].' Saudi Arabia: al-Sahhab Foundation for Media Production, 2003.

'What We are Fighting for – A Letter from America.' Institute for American Values. www.americanvalues.org, 2002.

Wilhelmsen, Julie. *When Separatists Become Islamists: The Case of Chechnya*. Kjeller: Norwegian Defence Research Establishment (FFI/Rapport), 2004.

Woodward, Bob. *Bush at War*. New York: Simon and Schuster, 2002.

'World Exclusive Interview with Field Commander Shamil Basayev.' Azzam Publications, 2000.

'World Report 1997.' New York: Human Rights Watch, 1998.

Wright, Lawrence. *The Looming Tower: Al Qaeda and the Road to 9/11*. New York: Knopf, 2006.

'The Rebellion Within.' *New Yorker* (2 June 2008).

Yehoshua, Y. 'Are Saudi Summer Camps Encouraging Terrorism?' *MEMRI Inquiry and Analysis Series*, no. 241 (2005).

Yousaf, Mohammad, and Mark Adkin. *Afghanistan: The Bear Trap*. 2nd edn. Barnsley: Leo Cooper, 2001.

Zaidan, Ahmad Muaffaq. *The 'Afghan Arabs' Media at Jihad*. Islamabad: ABC Printers, 1999.

Zuhdi, Karam, ed. *tafjirat al-riyadh: al-ahkam wa'l-athar* [The Riyadh Bombings: Rulings and Effects]. Cairo: Maktabat al-Turath al-Islami, 2003.

Index

Page numbers in **bold** refer to appendices and tables

CAMBRIDGE MIDDLE EAST STUDIES 33

1. Parvin Paidar, *Women and the Political Process in Twentieth-Century Iran*
2. Israel Gershoni and James Jankowski, *Redefining the Egyptian Nation, 1930–1945*
3. Annelies Moors, *Women, Property and Islam: Palestinian Experiences, 1920–1945*
4. Paul Kingston, *Britain and the Politics of Modernization in the Middle East, 1945–1958*
5. Daniel Brown, *Rethinking Tradition in Modern Islamic Thought*
6. Nathan J. Brown, *The Rule of Law in the Arab World: Courts in Egypt and the Gulf*
7. Richard Tapper, *Frontier Nomads of Iran: The Political and Social History of the Shahsevan*
8. Khaled Fahmy, *All the Pasha's Men: Mehmed Ali, His Army and the Making of Modern Egypt*
9. Sheila Carapico, *Civil Society in Yemen: The Political Economy of Activism in Arabia*
10. Meir Litvak, *Shi'i Scholars of Nineteenth-Century Iraq: The Ulama of Najaf and Karbala*
11. Jacob Metzer, *The Divided Economy of Mandatory Palestine*
12. Eugene L. Rogan, *Frontiers of the State in the Late Ottoman Empire: Transjordan, 1850–1921*
13. Eliz Sanasarian, *Religious Minorities in Iran*
14. Nadje Al-Ali, *Secularism, Gender and the State in the Middle East: The Egyptian Women's Movement*
15. Eugene L. Rogan and Avi Shlaim, *The War for Palestine: Rewriting the History of 1948*
16. Gershon Shafir and Yoar Peled, *Being Israeli: The Dynamics of Multiple Citizenship*
17. A.J. Racy, *Making Music in the Arab World: The Culture and Artistry of* Tarab
18. Benny Morris, *The Birth of the Palestinian Refugee Crisis Revisited*
19. Yasir Suleiman, *A War of Words: Language and Conflict in the Middle East*
20. Peter Moore, *Doing Business in the Middle East: Politics and Economic Crisis in Jordan and Kuwait*
21. Idith Zertal, *Israel's Holocaust and the Politics of Nationhood*
22. David Romano, *The Kurdish Nationalist Movement: Opportunity, Mobilization and Identity*
23. Laurie A. Brand, *Citizens Abroad: Emigration and the State in the Middle East and North Africa*
24. James McDougall, *History and the Culture of Nationalism in Algeria*
25. Madawi al-Rasheed, *Contesting the Saudi State: Islamic Voices from a New Generation*
26. Arang Keshavarzian, *Bazaar and State in Iran: The Politics of the Tehran Marketplace*

27. Laleh Khalili, *Heroes and Martyrs of Palestine: The Politics of National Commemoration*
28. M. Hakan Yavuz, *Secularism and Muslim Democracy in Turkey*
29. Mehran Kamrava, *Iran's Intellectual Revolution*
30. Nelida Fuccaro, *Histories of City and State in the Persian Gulf: Manama since 1800*
31. Michaelle L. Browers, *Political Ideology in the Arab World: Accommodation and Transformation*
32. Miriam R. Lowi, *Oil Wealth and the Poverty of Politics: Algeria Compared*
33. Thomas Hegghammer, *Jihad in Saudi Arabia: Violence and Pan-Islamism since 1979*